A History of The Orkneys

introduced by

A Description

of the Islands and their inhabitants

by

George Low
(1747 – 1795)

Edited by Olaf D. Cuthbert

Orkney Heritage Society

1st edition published 2001
Reprinted 2001

Published by
The Orcadian Limited,
Hell's Half Acre,
Hatston,
Kirkwall,
Orkney,
Scotland.

Cover illustration
*Map of Orkney and Caithness engraved by
Petrus Kerius (Peter Keer) in 1627*

Acknowledgements

I am grateful to the staff of the Library of the University of Edinburgh for their help in providing me access to Low's manuscript and the typescript copy made by Dr. John Traill in 1920. It was from a photocopy of the latter, provided by the Library, that I used as my chief source for this book and I therefore owe a debt of gratitude to the late Dr. Traill for his meticulous reproduction of the work which made my own endeavour so much easier.

Thanks are due to The Bodleian Library, University of Oxford, for permission to use The Sketch of Kirkwall, page 93. (Shelfmark MS. Top. Orkney B. 1, fol. 2r).

I have to acknowledge with gratitude the encouragement I have had from the committee of the Orkney Heritage Society who have agreed to be responsible for the publication and especially from their Chairman, Mrs. Daphne Lorimer, who accepted my suggestion for the production of a limited edition with such enthusiasm.

To Roger Cullingham, of Thameslink Ltd., who has been of such assistance with his helpful advice and encouragement and his patience in accepting my confused and often contradictory requests, I owe a special debt of gratitude.

Finally I must thank my wife who, as always, has supported my efforts and been ready with help and advice when needed.

Preface

George Low, minister of the parishes of Birsay and Harray in Orkney from 1774 to 1795, was born in the County of Forfarshire in the year 1747, educated at Aberdeen and St. Andrews Universities and came to Orkney in 1767 as tutor to the family of Robert Graham of Stromness. In 1774 he was invited by the well known traveller and naturalist, Thomas Pennant, to undertake a tour of the islands of Orkney and Shetland and to make a record of his journey. This was intended to form an addition to Pennant's account of his *Scottish Journey* fiirst published in 1769. In the event publication of Low's tour under the title *'A Tour thro' Orkney and Shetland 1774'* only took place in 1879, many years after his death. Meanwhile Low was occupied in studying and writing about the natural history and antiquities of the islands and wrote the first full account of the former in his *Fauna Orcadensis* (published posthumously by the naturalist William Elford Leach in 1813) and a *Flora Orcadensis*, a section of which found its way into the Edinburgh University library but most of which was lost and has only recently been rediscovered.

His other principal work was a history of Orkney together with a description of the islands and their inhabitants. Although a description of Orkney in the late eighteenth century might logically be considered as a conclusion to a history of the isles, it is clear that Low envisaged it rather as an introduction to his historical account, I have, therefore, followed the authors intentions and placed the *Description* before the *History*. The *History* is clearly the result of much study and research, despite the remoteness of the isles which made it difficult for him to obtain books of reference. Happily, he was befriended by an Edinburgh bibliophile, George Paton, who supplied him, or got others to supply him, with most of the works he required. Among these was the work of the Danish historiographer, Thormodus Torfaeus, whose *'Orcades seu Rerum Orcadensium Historiae'* is a Latin history of the isles derived from Norwegian and Icelandic sources. Low's own translation of this work forms the basis of his *History*. In the course of this work he frequently refers to Torfaeus as 'our author'. Low was familiar with the classical writers who recorded the accounts of travellers venturing as far north as the isles during the Roman occupation of Britain and with the works of the Scottish historians such as Boece and Buchanan (with whom he was not always in agreement). On his occasional visits to Edinburgh, he was able to refer to the Scottish archives, Acts of Parliament and other official documents. In addition to the main History Low added a chronological summary which I have included as an appendix.

Readers familiar with the *Orkneyinga Saga* will recognise many of the events in the Viking period. Some of the names however may appear unfamiliar, for example Hakon, which Torfaeus renders as Haconus, is given by Low as Haco; John sometimes as John but more often as Ion;. where Torfaeus uses Olafus and the Norwegians Olav, Low prefers Olave. Low's prose is occasionaly obscure, this may be because he is writing as he translates from the latin, sometimes rather more literally than is comfortable for the modern reader. His punctuation is frequently erratic and he favours the use of capital letters for many of the more important nouns. I have endeavoured to alter some of the punctuation for the sake of clarity.

What happened to these works after Low's death is not clear although it is probable that they came into the possession of Paton and subsequently into that of the Edinburgh libraries. The manuscripts are now in the library of the University of Edinburgh.

Low's natural history notes are believed to have been in the possession of George Barry after their author's death and been used by him in his *History of the Orkney Islands* published in 1805. It is possible that Barry also made use of Low's History or his translation of Torfaeus in compiling his own work.

Several histories of the county have been written since Low's time, the most recent is that of William Thomson published in 1987 . To present day scholars there is little if any knowledge to be gained from reading Low's account which must contain many inaccuracies but it is, of itself, an historical document and contains a number of entertaining episodes not appearing in the *Orkneyinga Saga*. His account of eighteenth century contemporary Orkney is a valuable addition to our knowledge of those times. Though unlikely to be of interest to a wide audience, it may attract readers from Orkney itself especially those who collect books concerning their county and its history.

The original manuscript of the *History* in the University library is in nineteen sections each bound together with string. The final section comprises the various acts of parliament and official documents to which he refers toward the end of his account. All except one of these was written in medieval latin and I have omitted them from the published text, though marking their inclusion with an asterisk. Scholars who wish to consult these documents may refer either to the library manuscript or the originals in the relevant archives. The single reference in English refers to the Act of Parliament annexing the Earldom of Orkney to the crown. The majority of the manuscript is in Low's handwriting but a part of sections

3 to 7 and section 11 are in copper plate and were probably dictated and reflect the fact that the author's eyesight was deteriorating toward the end of his short life.

Where the *Description* is divided into fourteen chapters, the *History* is written as one continuous account. In a short 'Introduction' Low announces that he has divided his account into three periods, the contents of each of which he describes but, in the text, only provides headings for two of these 'periods . I have therefore omitted the headings he gives for these two 'periods' and made a division of the work into twenty-one chapters, in order to accommodate changes in scene or incident and to allow Low's marginal notes to be inserted at the end of each chapter. Lows 'Period 1' is contained in Chapter 1; his 'Period 2' in Chapters 2 to 20 and his 'Period 3' in Chapter 21. .

Both the the *Description of Orkney* and the *History of Orkney* were probably written after Low had left his employment as tutor to the family of Robert Graham and taken up the ministry in the parishes of Birsay and Harray and therefore date from the last quarter of the eighteenth century.

In addition to the History itself Low added *A Chronological Sketch of the History of the Orkneys from their first accounts of their becoming a fief of the Kingdom of Norway.* This I have added as an Appendix to the main History.

The *Description* shows that he had a poor opinion of the state of agriculture and trade in the islands of his adopted home. As far as the former is concerned, he could claim considerable knowledge having been raised on a farm in Forfarshire where his father was joint tenant with his uncle of the farm of Meikle Tullo. Here improvements in agriculture were already under way and the primitive methods in use in the islands aroused his dismay. Low was a keen fisherman and was surprised to find the Orcadians neglectful of the riches of the seas around them. He has a poor regard for the Orcadians as workers deeming them lazy and feckless but finds some excuse for them in the attitude of their landlords whose methods of rent renewals supply their tenants with little incentive for improving their holdings. However he confesses that "Orkney is not without numbers of natural geniuses" who produce "pieces of work finished with a good deal of nicety". Though often critical Low obviously developed a great affection for the islands and, though censuring the 'better sort' for their love of luxuries and the 'common people' for their indigence, he was eager to offer advice that was always well meant though, no doubt, less than welcome to many of those toward whom it was directed.

Comparison of the state of affairs in Orkney in the eighteenth century and with those pertaining today shows what great strides have been made both in the attitude of the inhabitants and the state of their agriculture. Farming has always experienced its ups and downs and, if today it is suffering from one of the latter, it is still way ahead of the conditions met with by Low two and half centuries ago. Nor could he criticise today the state of industry in the isles and would certainly be delighted with the number of fishing boats and greatly surprised and pleased at the many other industrial enterprises now established here. As an advocate of the mining of minerals it is likely that Low would have approved of Orkney's involvement in the oil industry but would doubtless have been among the protesters against the mining of uranium had such a move occurred in his time!

It would be interesting to know how he would regard the influx of luxuries which he so condemned in his time now that, what he considered luxuries, have become available to the vast majority of the inhabitants of the isles and not just to the wealthy few.

Finally it may distress some Orcadian readers to find that Low always refers to the islands as 'the Orkneys' and not simply as 'Orkney' as the purists might wish. It must be remembered that he was not Orcadian by birth and may therefore be excused the solecism.

It is often the outsider who is able to get the best view and, if Low's view of Orkney two hundred years ago was at times less than complimentary, then it is satisfying to realise that today the outsider can view Orkney and the Orcadians with little to criticise and much to admire.

Olaf Cuthbert
Evie, Autumn 2000

A Description of Orkney
Contents

Chapter 1
Of the name

It is very difficult at this period to assign the true reason why these islands were called Orkneys[1], Orcades , Orcadia[2] Arkuar, Arkive[3], Orkneyar[4], Orcanay or Orcanoy, contracted for Orcadnay[5], for by these names we find them mentioned by authors as quoted in Torfaeus but his reasons for their being called so do not seem sufficiently conclusive nor to be much depended upon. It is very probable these Islands received this appellation from some natural circumstance and that of such a kind as would forcibly strike the first discoverers. I shall submit the following conjecture concerning the name of these Islands, offering it however only as a conjecture, and that perhaps no better founded than most of the explications of this obsolete appellation. As I said before, it is probable their name has been bestowed on these Islands from some very remarkable natural circumstance which, upon their arrival, would forcibly strike the first discoverers. I have been told, in many ancient languages both northern and oriental, these Island are expressed by words signifying the Islands of whales or something relative to this, possibly then this name might have been given from the numbers of the Orcae or Grampuses found by the ancients in their voyages through these seas and which, in the months of May or June, are found in great numbers on our coasts, at which time of year the first voyagers would be most ready to venture themselves in these unknown seas. It is well known the ancient traders were accustomed to make long voyages and were as attentive to keep their route a profound secret which perhaps is one reason why so lame accounts of Commerce and Navigation in the first ages have been handed down to us. It is well known the first merchants were wont to fix the name of a country from its produce or some remarkable property of it, all which in my opinion render it that this or some similar circumstance has occasioned the name which may have undergone many alterations by the difference of people who have used it, each of whom may have retained the original sound but modelled it according to the genius of their different languages.

The latin Orca, from which I take Orcades to be derived, comes from signifying the same fish in all probability, as may be seen in

Pliny and might have been borrowed from the Greeks by some or other of the Mediterranean voyagers whether Phoenicians or others who ventured first so far into these seas, in latter times after these people had corresponded with the Grecian nations, or perhaps the Greeks according to their well known custom might have substituted a word of theirs of like signification with the original name imposed by the first discoverers on these Isles. Historians have derived this name from other particulars but perhaps with the foregoing there may be more fancy than justice, it is however certain, whatever may be the derivation, these Island have born this title from the earliest times; we find them mentioned by writers of credit in the former ages under this name and it is difficult to say with certainty whether they were ever known by any other. Writers of most nations who have occasion to mention these Islands, do it under a name much like or the same with one another, which may inform us this appellation is very ancient and given by some people who not only had a good deal of weight in their time but a general intercourse among the other nations and by this rendered their discovery and name so current among them, though now this particular is so completely buried by the rust of ages in oblivion.

Authors, both ancient and modern, have agreed (says Buchanan) in fixing the name of these Isles, but nobody has explained this name.

Notes: 1. English; 2. Latin; 3. Irish; 4. Norwegian; 5. Old English.

Chapter 2
On the Situation and Number of the Orkney Islands

With regard to their situation as to the rest of the world. The Orkneys lie almost N. from the N.E. point of Scotland called Dungsbyhead, being divided from it by the Pightland Firth, a strait of sea about six miles over, on the south; having the German Ocean on the East, the Atlantic or Deucaledonian, as it is called by Buchanan, (a part of the Atlantic) on the west and the narrow sea which separates them from Shetland on the North. They are in the Northern temperate Zone, the thirteenth Geographical climate, Latitude 34 degrees North, the length of the longest day being, in our Northern Isles, eighteen hours fourteen minutes, as the sun is seen to rise there at two hours fifty-three minutes and set at nine hours seven minutes, but through the whole night the twilight is so strong that I have with ease read any print in any east window at twelve o'clock at night and this light continues from May to July, so that well may the old Poet's words concerning Britain in general 'et minimus contenos nocte Britannos' be applied to the Orkneys and are here more particularly verified. Our winter days indeed are proportionably short and uncomfortable but here too the twilight sustains them and makes them appear longer than they really are.

The ancients seem to have been indifferently acquainted with the number of these Isles, some enumerating forty, others thirty, while others reckoned thirty-three, of which they say thirteen were inhabited, while the rest were left for pasturing of cattle. Even Torfaeus, the professed writer of the affairs of Orkney, is not very exact in this particular but he mostly copies Buchanan who had his description of these Isles from hearsay. According to Mr. MacKenzie's maps of Orkney, wherein small and great are laid down with great precision, they consist of sixty-seven isles, whereof twenty-eight (not all the larger) are inhabited, the rest which are commonly called holms, are reserved for pasturage but afford a great deal of Tang for kelp and others abound in a variety of wild fowl.

The names of the Orkney Islands are as follows, together with those given them by Torfaeus, Buchanan etc.

Pightland Skerries Greater, and less called Clet.
Swanna; Sunna[1]; Svincy[2]
Waes; Valis[1]; Kalfey[2]
Switha
Flotta; Flata[2]
Calf of Flotta
Fara; Fara[1]
Barrel of Butter, a holm so called
Cava
Rissa
Hoy; Hoja[1]; Haey[2]
Graemsa; Granisa[1]; Grimsey[2]
Outer and inner holms of Stromness
S. Ronaldsha; Ranalsa[1]; Rongvaldsey[2]
Burray; Burra[1]; Borga[2]
Hunda
Grimsholm
Lamb-holm
Copinsha; Cobesa[1]; Kolbeinsay[2]
Three holms of Copinsha
Mainland; Pomona[1]; Pomono[2]; Maein-land; S.Meginland
Burgh of Birsa
Thieves holm
Grimbuster holm
Damsa; Damisey[2]; S.Daminsey; (Urridafords)
Shapinsha; Siapinsa[1]
Grassholm
Gairsa; Gersa[1]; Gareksey[2]
Wire; Vera[1]; Faerae[2]
Inhallow or Enhallow; Eninhelga[2]
Auskerry
Greenholms greater and lesser
Stronsa; Stronsa[1]; Strionsey[2]
Papa Stronsa
Papa Groina
Holm of Huip
Lingholm
Little Lingholm
Three Holms of Spurness
Eda; Eida[2]

Calf of Eda
Fara be north; Fara[1]; Fridarey[2]
Holm of Fara
Sanda; Sandey[2]
Holms of Ire, greater and lesser
North Ronaldsha; Ronaldsey[2]
Rusk-holm
Wart-holm
Westra; Vestra[1]; Vesturey[2]
Papa Westra; Papa[1]; Papey[2]; Papuley
Holm of Papey Westra
Egilsha; Egilsa[1]; Eigilsey[2]
Holm of Egilsha
Killiholm
Rousa; Rusa[1]; Rolfsey[2]
Ellerholm
Redholm

Besides many other rocks scattered up and down the sounds which appear only at low water are not reckoned into the number of Isles.

The following are inhabited, Viz. S. Ronaldsha, Swanna, Hoy, Waes, Burra, Lambholm. Flotta, Fara, Cava, Graemsa, Mainland, Copinsha, Inner Holm of Stromness, Shapinsha, Damsey, Inhallo, Stronsa, Papa Stronsa, Sanda, North Ronaldsha, Eda, Rousa, Wire, Gairsa, Egelsha, North Fara, Westra, Papa Westra.

The nature and extent of these are very different, as some are twenty-four miles long, while others are not half a mile. The appearance is very different, some being high, others very low, this sandy, the other moorish etc. producing oats, bear and grasses indifferently according to the nature of the soil, but all without wood which gives the country in general but a very ordinary look in the eyes of strangers who have seen other parts of the world but, notwithstanding of this forbidding appearance, Orkney is far from being despicable and might serve many useful purposes to Government, Trade and Navigation in general, as no country is better furnished with everything that can render it desirable to people from long sea voyages, nowhere better harbours and nowhere can refreshments be more easily had, with many other conveniences as we shall see in course.

Notes: 1. Buchanan; 2. Torfaeus.

Chapter 3
Of the Climate, Weather and General State of the Atmosphere

From our northern situation it would naturally be expected the air would be proportionately cold, yet though this is in some measure true, we have no reason to complain in this particular for, though we seldom experience such long tracks of good weather as our more southern neighbours, so we seldom or ever feel these dreadful and long continued storms of snow (especially) which so often harass them. Generally speaking the weather is unconstant and variable, breaking sooner than on the main of Scotland. The heats of summer are neither so strong, nor the frosts of winter so intense, as they are found to be in larger Continents, which may be easily accounted for from the narrowness of our Islands and their being altogether surrounded by the sea, the vapours of which take off the influence of the frosts and render our winters warmer than otherwise could be expected. We seldom have much, if any, snow till Christmas and even then of no long continuance in ordinary years, perhaps a fortnight at a time, though there have been instances, specially in winter 1771-2 of their continuing much longer. But, though we seldom have long snows, our seasons are not much more comfortable on that account, for we are frequently amply repaid with rain which is even less agreeable than snow and, as it mostly falls in great quantities in the winter and harvest season, does incredible damage by wasting our corn in harvest and thus rendering our crops very precarious.

Tempestuous winds too are very frequent and hurtful, both in Spring and harvest. These are sometimes so violent as to involve every fruit of the earth in one common destruction. Of this we had the most melancholy instance as late as 1765 when, by a westerly storm, the sea was so raised that by the spray of it, every vegetable was destroyed, the whole crop suffered and the whole hopes of the year were blasted, the saltness was perceived on garden plants at a distance of five miles or more within land, the standing corn being caught in the bloom and were for that year rendered quite useless, a single day defeated the labours of a whole season. Though these tempests are happily seldom so universally destructive of make such a general havoc, yet few years pass without their being felt in some measure and, what makes the calamity the more terrible, is that it is wholly inevitable.

Thunder is frequent, especially in winter, and sometimes has a great effect. I have heard of its tearing up the earth, killing animals and demolishing houses, several instances of which are recorded and many remembered, as the burning of the Steeple of Kirkwall in 1670, and several others which have happened within these late years. The thunder storms are commonly accompanied with heavy rains or hail and these sometime very sudden and severe.

We are frequently startled with the appearance of Meteors of several kinds, such as those the country people call starshots which, every night (according to the weather), are seen sparkling through the sky and others of a more fiery and sulphureous nature, which appear much larger and like balls of fire, whirling large tails after them, these frequently dart through the gloom even when the sky to appearance is most serene.

These are frequent but, as yet, we are not so much familiarized to them as to those the Philosophers call the Autora Borealis or northern lights and, by out country sages on account of their motion, Merry Dancers, which are the constant attendants of our clearer evenings and much relieve the gloom of our long winter nights. They commonly appear at twilight near the horizon, of a dun colour approaching to yellow, sometimes continuing in this state for several hours without any sensible motion, after which they begin to break out into streams of stronger light, spreading into vast columns and altering slowly into ten thousand different shapes, their colours from all the different tints of yellow to the obscurest russet, at other times they cover the whole hemisphere and then make a dreadful appearance, their motions are at these times very quick and in all directions, altering their appearance in a surprising manner, now they break out very strong in new places where none could be perceived before, skimming briskly along the heavens and soon extinguishing, leaving behind them a dusty track, immediately they are renewed and with equal speed traverse their former track and die away in as short time as before. In particular nights we may observe them putting on the appearance of vast columns, having one side very dense and yellow and the other gradually fainter till they can be no longer distinguished from the rest of the sky. These columns often have a quick oblique tremulous motion proceeding from end to end of them for a long time together till the whole gradually vanishes. Sometimes they vary in their appearance from the foregoing and then they look like a vast bank in the north and thus continue for many hours without any appearance of change. In a word the variety of their motions is scarce to be described and the quickness of their motions hardly to be followed, the whole is hard to be accounted for and what makes it more so is that it is scarce a century since they were first observed even here but have been since gradually proceeding to the southwards. It is observable the Aurora borealis differs not only in the vast variety of the motions but likewise in colours, when this meteor proceeds very high into the atmosphere, it then puts on a bloody red colour and indeed a dreadful appearance, then with our country sages whether male or female it becomes prophetical and terrifies the amazed spectators with the dread of war, pestilence and poverty.

The air in general is moist and, when the east wind blows, very penetrating. The moisture is soon perceived by the rusting of iron which, in a few hours time, though laid by bright, is covered with a coat of rust, indeed it is scarce possible to keep metals, but specially iron, clean, owing I suppose to the sea breezes which melt the nitrous particles in the air and, making them adhere more firmly to anything of iron, more easily dissolves it, but this dissolution of the nitrous particles renders our air much warmer than we could otherwise expect it in winter and the sea breezes make it cooler in summer.

Chapter 4
Of the Face of the Country and its division into Land and Water

The first look of Orkney is rather forbidding to a stranger and apt to give him but a mean idea of the country in general, as it has few or none of those romantic beauties which recommend other countries more favourably situated. Orkney is generally hilly particularly the Mainland, having but few plains of large extent, some of the islands indeed are low and flat, consisting of one continued plain as Sanda and a few more, while others, as Hoy, are the highest lands in the country, a continued chain of hills running the whole length of it, Rousa, Eda, part of Westra etc. are likewise hilly, while the south isles are rather flat. There is little variety in most of the islands of Orkney, a little arable land near the shores, the rest moorish, boggy or moss reserved for pasturage is a general view of most of them, a few excepted, as the Mainland which is intermixed with hills and dales, in the skirts of which are many spots of valuable ground, both arable and pasture, with moss and heath for the convenience of fuel and pasturage of cattle in the summer season, but wholly destitute of shelter as we shall further see in course.

The narrow bounds of the largest of these Islands denies us rivers but we have numbers of lakes of fresh water, several of which the sea flows into. These are well furnished with fish of many kinds and covered with wild fowl, especially in the winter season when the duck tribe return from their summer's haunts. Few islands but have small burns if their size will admit, and all are furnished with wells at least, of fresh water.

The chief lakes on the Mainland are the following:-

The lochs of Stenness and Harra (for both are joined by a narrow communication at the bridge of Broygar) running into the sea by a small channel at the head of Kirston road, through which the tide flows into the Loch. This loch abounds with fish of several sorts, as trout, Flounders etc. as shall be mentioned more particularly elsewhere and in the Harra Loch abounds in small holms where several species of wild fowl as Swans, Ducks, Peewit, Gulls, Terns and Mergansers build in vast numbers and whence the proprietors fetch great quantities of eggs in the season. Some few of the trout that swarm in the loch are caught by the country people in trout houses so contrived that they can force their way in but neither get forward or return but, with industry, many more might be got and these in reason, for they never are got in these trout houses till Autumn, when they run up the burns to spawn and then they lose both taste and colour, besides destroying the breed by catching them at that season. Mr. Wallace, for I know not what reason, calls this "a large loch but unfruitful", if he meant that it had no fish, he is mistaken for no fresh water lake have I ever observed with more, a greater variety or finer of their kinds, as I have often had occasion to see, and I have caught as fine trout in it both for size and taste as ever I observed anywhere, besides several others not so usual in fresh water but come into this with the tide.

The Loch of Skeal, about a mile in length a fine piece of water and having that beautiful hill called Kurfu on one side, with corn grounds surrounding the others, forms a fine landscape, a view of the sea and the sea beat rock terminating the scene. The loch is no further useful but that it affords water to a mill, for it is wholly destitute of every species of fish except Eels, even though it has a communication with the sea at a short distance, but this is not very clear which may hinder them from getting up. This is the more surprising as the loch abounds in excellent food, both insects and weeds, and the passage though something difficult is not so much so as many leaps in the Sottish rivers over which I have observed both salmon and trout spring with incredible strength and agility, so that this seems not to be the only obstacle which hinders trout from resorting to and breeding in it, perhaps something in the water that is noxious to trout though not so to the stronger or the less delicate Eel which here find a retreat and, in its turn, furnishes a meal to its enemies. Vast quantities of the duck kind frequent this loch in winter but, as they have no convenience of holms or reeds, none build in it but all go off regularly with the coming in of the Spring.

The loch of Birsay is a beautiful piece of water situated in one of the most pleasant spots in the country, communicating with the sea by a pleasant winding burn which waters the finest arable land in Orkney, the loch is full of trout and, contrasted with the Burgh or headland and the roaring sea, adds much to the beauty of this so beautiful scene which, both on account of its fertility and pleasantness induced the Earls of Orkney here to fix one of their places of residence.

The Loch of Swaney, likewise in Birsay, of which Mr. Wallace tells us "it has in some places a thick scum of copper-colour upon it", but this is not peculiar to this alone for many others, and springs, have the same owing to the great quantities of bog iron ore found everywhere through the Mainland and Isles which tinges the water of this brown colour and leaves behind a very thick okery sediment which renders grass and everything it runs off the same colour.

The Walkmill Loch in the parish of Orphir abounds in trout and this draws numbers of otters to it, as to the rest where they find such a delicate living.

Besides these there are several others on the Mainland but of little use, some that have communications with the sea and others not, drying with summer and covering a large space of ground in winter, the consequences probably of bad husbandry. There are many other fine pieces of water through the different isles as we shall see in their description.

Several of the Parishes in the Mainland and Isles are tolerably well cultivated (after the country method, of which in its place) and, not withstanding of the rude state of agriculture, bears a good deal of ordinary grain.

What takes much from the natural beauty of Orkney is the total want of wood, none of which it seems can be made to grow in the open fields here, which not only gives the country a bare and dreary look but leaves both fields and dwellings exposed to the utmost rage of the seasons, whose fury would no doubt be less felt were they warded off by such plantations as are common elsewhere, not to speak of the great beauty and vast advantage that wood of our own growth must necessarily give us and which we purchase at present at such dear rates. We are told that notwithstanding several trials have been made to raise wood, it could not be made to grow to any height, owing, say they, to the sea breezes and the stormy winds which chill and stunt it when it rises above the enclosing fences, but I am apt to think these trials have not been sufficiently conclusive, many circumstances having been omitted to make the experiments succeed properly, such as choosing the proper woods, raising these rather from seeds than plants which would in a manner naturalize them, planting them in such a method as to make the young plants shelter one another as well as enclosing the grounds to screen them from the blasts till they acquired strength and were enabled to bear the blasts of the climate.

It is certain no judgement can be formed from a trial made of two or three, a dozen or even a hundred young plants set in a row as they can afford no shelter to one another and of consequence must either perish or grow crooked and deformed, as we see single trees often do in the most woody parts of Scotland, where shelter is not perhaps so essentially necessary as in this country where every place is open to every blast and the spray of the sea no doubt does harm to everything before it has arrived at a proper strength to resist it. Likewise a few trees planted in a garden can be no proper trial or a rule what might be expected where every necessary precaution in planting is attended to.

What led me into these thoughts, namely that wood might thrive in Orkney, provided the proper kinds were chosen, was the inspection of many of the mosses where the people, in cutting peats, often meet with large logs of wood and sometimes whole trees both roots and branches which when dug up look pretty fresh, likewise tradition places woods in many places where now little or no trace of them remain but they are turned either into mosses or marshy lochs with large stumps here and there still appearing, all which makes it pretty certain there has been wood in Orkney at some time of other period, though by what means or when it has been destroyed is not so easily ascertained, at this day there is a pretty shrubbery of Birch, Willow, Rowan, Hazel and Poplar which covers the Burn Banks of Hoy which together with the plenty of Ivy and Honeysuckle adds much to the beauty of these only romantic scenes in the Orcades. The same may be seen in other places, though by the browsing of cattle and other obstacles they do not rise to any height and yet they do not look more sickly than in similar places in the south of Scotland, so I should not think it the fault of the air alone which hinders wood from coming to greater perfection in these Islands.

Chapter 5
Of the Headlands, Bays, Harbours in Orkney

In general the south and west coasts of Orkney are much bolder than the east and north and have many headlands which serve as excellent landmarks for seamen, especially those going to or coming from America who commonly take their departure from Hoyhead or some other land of these Islands and wish this as a landfall in their return, and besides affords shelter for myriads of wild fowl which repair thither to build but remain only while the summer continues, when great quantities are got by those of the inhabitants who live near these heads and are desperate enough to venture their lives in this dreadful employment in which many are killed, but the hope of gain pushes others on whom even the fear of death staring them in the face cannot scare.

The most remarkable of these headlands are Hoyhead, an excellent landmark for shipping from the westward, and with the Black Craig over against it, forms the entrance to Hoy Sound which is the passage into the harbour of Stromness.

Marwickhead, Burgh of Birsa, Costa-head, Moul-head of Deerness, Houton head in the Mainland, Cantick-head and several other vast rocks in Waes, Hoxa-head, Halero-head and Green-head in S. Ronaldsha, Stanger-head in Flotta, besides Rousa head in the island of that name, Noup-head of Westra which is sometimes apt to be mistaken for Hoy-head by seamen and often misleads them, Calf of Eda is a very high rock where vast quantities of sea-fowl build and several species of the Hawk tribe which are also to be found in the fore-named highlands, as also many others of less note round the country.

The west coast of these Islands is much less dangerous to seafaring people than the east side which in general is very low and flat and, at a very short distance from land presents them with many false appearances of sounds and bays and thus leads them upon the shallows before they are aware and which are scarce seen in the most dangerous cases before they are too near to avoid them. Accordingly many more shipwrecks happen in the Islands of Sanda and N. Ronaldsha and several other of the low North Isles than in other places of Orkney, notwithstanding the great resort of shipping to the other places of Orkney from all quarters. Many and valuable ships have within these late years been lost on the rocks which run far out to sea from the North Isles and no doubt numbers of valuable lives and cargoes perish, which are never heard of, on the many flat and hidden rocks scattered round these deceitful shores. These deplorable accidents might in some measure I think be prevented by affixing proper marks on the lowest Isles which might be seen at some distance and a light house on North Ronaldsha where there is most danger, because of the rocks and a large reef which lies at a good distance from the land.

It would take up too much of this short description to point out every inlet, creek and harbour round these Islands with the passages to and from them. I shall only therefore describe those most frequented by seamen and, on that account, most useful.

The best and most frequented harbour in the Mainland is that of Stromness on the South West side of the Island, fenced against wind and weather by highland on the north and west sides and by two holms on the east. It is large enough to contain more than a hundred ships riding at anchor and deep enough to receive ships drawing about - - or - - feet of water[1]. The anchor ground is good but much plowed up owing to the continental and great concourse of shipping which put in here, both from the eastward and westward, this harbour lying in the common passage or thoroughfare by which ships entering through Hoy sound pass through Holm Sound, Watersound or Cantick to the east sea. The road called Kerston Bay or Road at the back of the Holms (where the larger ships or those which are bound to the westward rather choose to lie, because of the mouth of the harbour lying to the eastward and of itself narrow when the wind comes fair makes it difficult for them to work out) is safe, having a good stiff holding of clean ground and water enough for vessels of any burden.

The next is Deersound, a safe road with good anchor, capable of receiving a navy but, at present, little frequented except by the Iceland fishing ships which commonly stop there in their going out to procure hands to assist them in their summer fishing and for part of whom, they always depend on the Orkneys; in their return they stop to dismiss them.

Kirkwall road is rather open but has good anchorage, lies much out of the way of being often visited except by ships which have particular business there.

Storehouse bay is not very safe either for good ground nor is it covered from the winds, however ships may and often do lie here for short time in summer weather without much danger, as they may in many other places, to spend a tide or wait a wind to send them to a better shelter.

St. Margaret's Hope in South Ronalsha is a very safe harbour and good anchorage in three or three and a half fathom of water where many ships yearly touch in their way to and from the east sea. Widewall harbour on the west side of the same island, a safe and well sheltered harbour with about two and a half or three fathoms of water, besides several other creeks round the island.

Longhope of Waes, a very safe harbour where ships going to the West Indies often touch and wait a wind to convey them to the westward, as also in coming home, because here they are sure of refreshments after their long voyage. In the same island are likewise Lyrwa, Or-hope, Rirk-hope, Mill-bay and Pegill-Burn in all which ships on occasion may ride with great safety.

Panhope of Flotta is a secure harbour and clean ground, pretty much resorted to by shipping where they ride in about three fathom of water and, in a word, many other places about the south Isles where ships may ride very safe especially when catched short by the tide, particularly that of the Pightland Firth which would soon hurry them to sea again, in case they may be safe in the eddies of any smaller Isles according as the tides run.

Nor are the North Isles destitute of many excellent harbours, most of which may be entered either from the eastward or westward and, at present, too little occupied and, as the country is cut through with so many natural channels, might serve many useful purposes as these all lead to some one or other of the following viz:-

Elwick-road in Shapinsha, good and well sheltered having good ground and deep water, not much frequented except by country ships bound for the southward, also all round this island a vessel may stop a tide with great safety.

Small vessels or those which draw not above ten feet of water may find many excellent harbours in the North isles such as Otterswick, Kettletoft and bay of Stove in Sanday, Papa Sound, Linga-sound and Rowsholm bay in Stronsa, all are safe to stop a tide or more as is convenient, besides Pierowal a good harbour in Westra, Howa sound in Rousa and Wire-sound accessible from all quarters and yet sufficiently guarded from the weather, with very many others where ships may be accommodated for a time and, in cases of necessity saved from the violence of the waves.

These constitute the value of the Orkneys and render them convenient for all the purposes of trade, navigation and fisheries, as we shall see when we come to speak of the importance of these Isles in these and other respects, especially as they are now in the hands of such a trading nation as Great Britain which, at the present seems willing to encourage every scheme for its promotion and may be of vast use in future times when their own inhabitants as well as others begin to open their eyes to their true value and to see their natural advantages.

1. *These figures are omitted from the manuscript* - Ed.

Chapter 6
Of the Tides

Ancient authors who have taken notice of these isles have said a great deal concerning the dangerous tides which run round them; according to these writers there was hardly any passing through these seas on account of the Remoras which infested them, which stopped and threw their ships on the shallows. Claudian gives a most dismal account of them in the following verses:-

> Locus Arctoo qua se Germania tractu,
> Claudit, et in regidis Tyle ubi surgit aquis.
> Quam juxta infames scopuli et petrosa vorago
> Asperat undissonio saxa pudenda vadis.
> Orcadas has memorant dictas a nomini Graeco.

But this, like several other descriptions of this particular must be placed to the account of a very narrow acquaintance with the navigation of these seas and, no doubt, to the inclination travellers have to magnify every danger they are beset with, besides it is but of late that true observations have been made upon the state of the tides in these parts and ignorance always looks at danger through the magnifying end of the glass.

Being divided into a number of Islands, Orkney must necessarily have many sounds and tideways, through which the currents run with great rapidity and are dangerous when the wind and tide meet and occasion in particular spots a violent tumbling sea, here called a Roust[1], some times fatal to those who may be passing in boats if they are so unhappy as to be hurried into them because of the short and broken waves attack the boat on all sides and soon subdue her, however at a proper time, i.e. a little before high or low water or at (as they call it here) slack water, these sounds may be passed in safety with the smallest skiff. The stream setting from N.W. runs at the rate for about eight miles an hour in Spring tides and three at the time of the Neap tide in Hoy Sound, in some places more, in others less, according as the channel lies in respect to the Ocean and according the breadth of this channel. This however is no fixed rule for the numerous rocks, skerries and small islands which almost everywhere obstruct and divert the course of the stream, cause such irregularities, counter tides, eddies and whirlpools, as are both amazing and dangerous to those unacquainted with the causes and inexperienced how to make advantage of these very distractions, which are often their greatest safeguard, setting their ships clear of every obstruction if they are so happy as to follow their course, without any help of theirs, which would, in any case, be in vain.

In the harbour at Stromness at full and change of the moon it is high water at nine in the morning and three in the afternoon, in other places sooner or later according to the lead of the stream and their situation with respect to this, however there are many irregularities in the times and manner of the ebbings and flowings of the tides that must be accounted for from the interruptions the stream meets with from its encountering so many and so differently situated islands. Such are these which our fishermen call tide and half tide where it ebbs nine hours and flows but three, which is observed in several places. On the east side of North Ronaldsha the stream runs for the most part north, between Spurness in Sanda and the north end of Stronsa, the stream side towards the N.E. during the first four hours of flood, from that time till low water its motion is westward , but very slow. At the first hour of ebb it begins to run towards the N.W. and continues so for four hours, then runs eastward very gently or becomes almost quiescent again till flood begins. This last particular and the following are not so easily accounted for. On the west side of Sanda from Mirigar to the holms of Ire, the stream, within three fourths of a mile of the shore, runs always north, except for two days before and two or three days after the new and full moon when it runs south, with a very slow motion, during the first three hours of flood. Also in the Pightland Firth there are many irregularities both in the time and manner of its tides and so many and diverse motions as render it indeed frightful to those unacquainted with these but, to the Orkney and Caithness boatmen who are well acquainted with it, the Pightland Firth may be crossed with as little danger as other very rapid tideways, always taking care to avoid what is known to be dangerous, as a wrong tide, the rosts called the Swelchie of Stroma and the Merry Men of May and the Wells of Swanna, all which are dangerous to boats but especially the last which are able to swallow a small boat after whirling it about in a surprising manner but are not large enough to have any such effect on a larger vessel. These whirlpools are much in the form of a funnel growing narrower toward the bottom, the cavity of which is largest when first formed, diminishing as it is carried away by the stream till it be lost and another whirl succeeds it, several having in this manner been observed to succeed one another till towards the latter end of the tide when they disappear altogether and then may be passed without the smallest degree of danger. Indeed all our Pilots and boatmen seem to make light of them and know how to avoid them or, should it happen at any time that they are drawn too near them, they know that by throwing anything bulky overboard such as oar, cask, straw etc. dissipates them immediately and gives them time to pass over in safety. But they seldom come so near them as to be in any danger.

1. Account of the current of the Tides about the Orcades by Mr. Mat: Mackaile, communicated by him to Sir Robert Murray, President of the Royal Society and published in No. - (*the number is omitted - Ed.*) also published by Sir Robert Sibbald.

"In Fairay Sound betwixt the isles of Fairay and Etha in Orkney, the sea runneth N.E. for the S.W. in ebbing. This is the course of the tide only in the middle of the sound which is but one mile broad. The next isle to Fairay towards the S.W. is Westra which is an Isleland about five miles in length and three or four miles in breadth. Upon the S.E. side of this Island within a mile of the shore lyeth another little isle which is not half a mile in circumference. S. and S.W. from these two Islands is Westra firth, eight miles in breadth running betwixt them and the Isle called Pansa. Thro' this firth the English ships do ordinarily pass in the course to Iceland."

" While the sea runneth from west to east in flowing thro' this Westra Firth there are no greater surges than in any other place of the sea and, in a calm day it is smooth as any lake tho' there is constantly a great current in the Flux and reflux of the sea. Yet at the S.E. end of the aforementioned little island the sea no sooner begins to run westward in ebbing but there begineth a surge to appear which continually increaseth until the ebb be half spent, and afterwards it decreaseth until it be low water, at which time there appeareth no such thing. East and west from this great surge there are some few lesser surges seen which are gradually less towards the east and west after this manner." The gentleman adds, "I having occasion to pass that way in a little boat after we had passed over the eastermost surges and were beginning to ascend the biggest upon the 10th of April at one of the Clock in the afternoon, the surge before us was so high that it intercepted the sight of the sun and some degrees of the firmament above it. This surge is about a quarter of a mile in length. When there is any wind which occasioneth the breaking of the tops of the surges there is no passing that way. The current of the tide is so strong here that there is no need of sails of oars save only to direct the boat as doth the helm."

Chapter 7
Orkney divided into Islands

The largest island in Orkney is that called Pomona or the Mainland, about twenty four miles long, of unequal breadth, jutting out into many promontories and pierced with many bays and inlets of the sea which render its figure very irregular. On an isthmus near the middle of the island stands the only town in these Islands, called Kirkwall by the Danes, in whose power the Orkneys remained for a long time. Cracoviaca according to Buchanan, but Torfaeus says it was by them called Kirkiuvogus and from either of which words the modern name is easily derivable having been no doubt changed by time from the one to the other.

The Town consists of a single street of near a mile in length, narrow except at the market place, here there is a large opening with a public well in the middle of it. All the buildings of the town are stone, some of them have good gardens belonging to them, in which all kinds of garden stuff thrive well but, though they have some wall trees, fruit does not answer well and but very little is produced over this in any perfection. To the town belongs a neat building supported on pillars in front called the town house, here is a hall in which the Sheriff and other courts are held, in this is the assembly hall, under these, the common prison, and above, the Masons Lodge. Near the former is a low building for schools where Grammar, English, Writing and Arithmetic are taught, the Grammar School is supported by a fund for that purpose; the English etc. School, which has a distinct master, by subscription.

In this town the Custom house and Post Office are kept and here the store for the Superior of Orkney's rents, great part of which are paid in kind and from thence transported by the factor or tacksman merchant to the proper markets.

The mount, taken notice of by Wallace, is still in being though much in ruins. It has not been so regular as his draught of it would persuade us, being a sort of square, the corners something like bastions but these not well defined. A few of the cannon belonging to it are still there but dismounted and one in particular has a double Coat of

Arms on it, I suppose that of the commonwealth of England and has been brought thither in Oliver's time, but...

What in this town strikes the eye of a stranger and engages his attention is the Cathedral or Church of St. Magnus, a beautiful and magnificent pile founded by Rognvald, Count of Orkney, about the year eleven hundred and thirty eight but since enlarged by others, especially the bishops Stewart and Reid, the last of whom added much to the length of it on the west and beautified the front with carved work. It is a plain Gothic structure supported by pillars in the form of a Cross, containing two large churches, one to the eastward of the steeple which is supported on the four middlemost pillars and the other to the westward. In the former, divine service is performed by two ministers in their turns, the outer part is quite empty. The steeple is not very high in proportion to the church, it contains three bells which are tolled in a rather whimsical manner for warning to divine service. The larger of these bells was rent in 1670 when the steeple was burnt down and, being recast, seems to have been reduced from its ancient dimensions and scarce in proportion to the other two which are ancient and have inscriptions on them in Danish or Norwegian. Besides these there is a small bell called by the inhabitants the Skillet, which is only rung on extraordinary occasions as in the case of fire etc.

In an aisle of this church the Annual Provincial Synod meets for the regulation of the general affairs of the church through the country. Here also the Presbytery of Kirkwall hold their diets for the dispatch of their particular business within their own bounds.

The other public buildings which have in former times been remarkable are the castle, built by Henry, Lord Sinclair, the first nobleman of that name in Orkney, about the year One thousand three hundred and seventy nine, now quite in ruins; it stood on the west side of the Cathedral, but now scarce to be distinguished. On the south side stand the ruins of what they call the round tower or the old bishop's palace said to be built by Bishop Reid, together with some other buildings which he designed for a College in which the youth of the time were to be taught the branches of learning then in vogue, now turned into dwelling houses.

Near the round tower which forms one side of the court stands what remains of the Earl's palace, commonly called the Bishop's because, after the forfeiture and death of the Earl of Orkney (then Patrick Stewart) it was given to the Bishops as their dwelling house in Kirkwall. This building is not yet so much in ruins as the others and appears to have been erected by the foresaid Patrick Stewart the last of the name, Earls of Orkney, in the year 1606, the Arms date with P.S.E.O. being yet to be seen above the gate, which show the builder. It has been a fine building according to the taste of the times but now going fast to ruin as men and time can send it.

The town itself is ancient and early dignified with large privilege, even in the time of the Danes it was erected into a royal Burgh and since their charters have been confirmed by several of the Kings of Scotland, as in 1486 when King James the third gave them a Charter of Confirmation on their old erection, specifying their antiquity, empowering them to hold Burrow Courts within their own district, to imprison and arrest, to make laws for the government of the town and to choose their own Magistrates yearly. By this charter they had power of pit and gallows (as it is called in Scotland) but this has been long discontinued and all criminals are now carried to Inverness, the most northerly place of the circuit which the Justiciary Lords make, there to be tried before them. They had two weekly markets on Tuesday and Friday but these were discontinued and three fairs in the year - one at Palm Sunday, another at Lambmass and the third at Martinmas - but none of these are held except the Lambmass which is still kept in August and continues for four or five days instead of the three days each of the rest. There is no particular commodity sold at this fair, these consist mostly of family necessaries, with cattle sheep and lambs. Sometime ago this was a famous fair for young horses, great numbers of which were brought hither from the northern shires of Scotland and their sale drained the country a good deal of money but this trade has of late much failed, owing to the Orkney farmers having got over their prejudices of raising their own horses which till late was not the case (The Orkney people had a vast antipathy to mares, they would keep none, were afronted if they rode one and the names they gave them were those of contempt).

King James the fifth ratified the charter in 1536 by a new charter of Confirmation and in the year 1661 King Charles the second after his restoration ratified the former charters by his royal signatures dated Whitehall May 25th upon which the Scottish Parliament met at Edinburgh in August 1670, confirmed all by their act with this special provision "That what was granted them by that act , might not prejudice the interests of the Bishop of Orkney."

The town, as other Burghs in Scotland, is governed by a Provost, four Baillies, a Treasurer whose business it is to look after the town lands and profits arising from them etc. and a Dean of Guild to inspect weights, measures etc., assizes of provisions and a Council of Burgesses in number sixteen. On extraordinary occasions they muster and arm a bodyguard consisting of the tradespeople, for repressing of broils, especially in time of the market, to prevent riots among such a concourse of people as there assembled from all corners of Orkney and the northern shires of Scotland. In conjunction with several northern Burghs, Kirkwall chooses one member of Parliament.

The place of next note in Orkney is Stromness, a pretty thriving village, very irregularly built on the side of an excellent harbour, excellently situated for trade , either to America or the East countries, being a throughfare from the German to the Atlantic Oceans, now well known to most seafaring men and, on account of the goodness and easy access of its harbour, much resorted to.

The Mainland is decorated with several Gentlemen's Seats in the modern taste, which have but a naked appearance from want of wood which surrounds such houses in the south country. Also there are scattered up and down through it many ruinous buildings formerly belonging to families of note in Orkney but fallen like their masters. The first of these, after what has been said of Kirkwall, was the Palace of Birsay the seat of the Sinclairs, Earls of Orkney, but afterwards repaired and great additions made to it by Robert Stewart towards the end of the sixteenth century. It has been a large building, consists of a square court (with a well in the middle of it) built quite round, the front and the wings are the additions made by Earl Robert, but all in that suspicious but unhappily necessary taste which reigns through all the buildings of these times, every door and other passage has cannons pointing from it, the walls are full of ports for small arms and everywhere pierced with peep holes for viewing the motions of an enemy. It is said to have been painted with Scripture Stories with the texts they refer to but these are all defaced together with the Motto "Sic fuit est et erit" said to have been placed above the Arms and not so much as a bit of plaster on the walls, so that if it is true that it was built by oppression it stands a witness that the Goods of the wicked, the unjust or the oppressive seldom remain to the third generation. The stone containing the famous inscription "DOMINUS ROBERTUS STUARTUS FILIUS JACOBI quinti REX SCOTORUM hoc opus instruxit" is now gone and nothing but the hole above the gate where it was placed to be seen. This structure is now going fast to ruin and, like a multitude of others, shews

Non possidentem multa vocaveris
Recte beatum

and that the most famous monuments are not able to perpetuate the memory of men who have left no other cause of remembrance, but molder away to the dust like their lofty possessors.

There are several other ruins of Gentlemen's seats but this is the most remarkable. Others, called by the country people Picts' houses, the history of which is not so well known, shall be described among the other monuments of antiquities to be found scattered up and down the country in their proper place.

The Mainland is pretty well inhabited, the arable land being divided into small farms and maintaining a great number of but lazy people, yet the value of this large island is not so great as might be expected, the whole real rent of it not rising to three thousand pounds sterling, as that of he whole islands at the common conversion does nor exceed seven.

The other islands are divided according to their situation with respect to the Mainland into South Isles and North Isles. Of the South the best is S. Ronaldsha, very fertile in corn and grass, the soil sandy and producing the best and greatest quantity of potatoes of any of the Orkneys. It is the staple of the South Isles and upon it both Kirkwall and Stromness in good season depend for malt and meal, as it seldom misses having a good crop even when this fails in other parts of the country. It is about six miles long, well situated for fishing, especially lobsters of which many thousands are yearly caught by the country people and sold for a penny a piece to the English who send down yearly smacks proper for the purpose and pay down the price immediately, which means many poor people are subsisted and much money brought into the country.

Hoy and Waes though commonly reckoned two Islands are in fact but one, indeed that part called South Waes is parted from the other on occasion by the sea which at high tide flows over a small neck of land joining them together, but this is but seldom the case, though in time I imagine it will be cut through altogether and entirely disjoin them. The Island is about twelve miles in length, the most mountainous part of Orkney, that part properly called Hoy is but thinly inhabited only a small part of it being cultivated, the rest wholly mountainous and rocks, among the valleys of which there is a great deal of excellent pasture for young cattle in summer but no shelter against the storms of winter. The Wart Hill of Hoy looks higher than it really is, being a large clump by itself, the sides very steep and rugged, in some places rocky and others covered with heath and moss but marshy to the very top on which is a small loch which seldom dries out in the hottest summer. The sides and tops of these hills are covered with various Alpine plants as the salix herbacea, reticulata and glauca. The Senecio paludosus, a variety of which grows near the top of the hills among the moist hollows of the rocks, several saxifrages, the plant Rhodiola rosea and the Rumex digynus are very frequent and many other useful and curious plants, the inhabitants of the alpine countries. There are several minerals to be found in this island as through the rest of Orkney, Iron is nowhere more frequent, the ore of two kinds found in different parts of the Island, that dug up near the church is a Flematite and, I am told, but a poor ore, the other which may be had in vast quantities from the sea rocks of Hoy head is of a blacker colour than the former, to appearance it is much more solid and weightier, looks as if it had been in fusion at some or other period which however I dare say has not been the case, its first formation is from an infinite number of minute particles adhering together very firmly and growing still more solid as it imbibes more of the iron, till at length it becomes a flinty mass of the colour above described. A company of adventurers came down from London some yeas ago and dug up some tons of this last ore, which was, by them, thought to be Cobalt but with no foundation and it was given up as not capable of bearing the charge of working and transportation. They sent a quantity to London but how it turned out I could not learn. When Mr. Banks was in the Orkneys in his way homeward from Iceland, he visited this mine and smelted a bit of it. He told me it was an ore of iron and none of the richest and, as we lie at such a distance from any iron manufactory, our ore of this kind can be of little value to us and if we had spirit we have not fuel to work it in Orkney.

There are Lead mines in Hoy as well as other isles but, though these may be a source of wealth for future generations, as yet little of this has been drawn from them. It is very probable this mine might be very valuable if a vein was hit upon but as yet they who wrought it seemed rather to find it in disjointed clumps than in vein. What I have seen of the ore is heavy and seems to be rich but I never heard what metal was got from any quantity of it.

The Island of Hoy has the most natural beauties, the most romantic appearance of any of these isles. Its hills are interspersed with deep valleys through which run several burns full of trout, the banks of which are adorned with shrubs of various kinds which agreeably relieve the eye after long viewing the other woodless isles. There are many curious echoes amongst the hills of Hoy, the best of which I had an opportunity of observing as one day a-fowling. On the top of the hill, the air clear and a little wind blowing, I fired off my fowling piece and imagined the explosion was far from so loud as if on even ground but, to be sure, I made the same experiment again and with the same effect, for it was evidently not near so loud nor sharp and indeed the report seemed no greater than that of a child's pop gun. But, as I came down towards the valley, the case was much altered for there was not only the first report was augmented but rebounded from all the neighbouring hills. I was much pleased when I heard it re-echoed from the opposite hill but more so when, a few seconds after this was concluded, a second much louder resounded through the valleys, this was scarce concluded when Echo a third time called from her cave in a voice like distant thunder murmured through the remotest dales, dying away by degrees and at last losing herself in the song of the birds and the lowing of the cattle at that time scattered through the hills, for this echo succeeds best in a fine summer day when the earth is quite dry and ready to repulse the slightest impression made upon it even by a sound. It succeeds best when one stands on the North West shoulder of the Ward hill and has the greatest effect when the piece is fired directly at the opposite hill, when fired the contrary way it is not so strong and the third time could scarce be heard at all.

That part of the Island called Waes is much more cultivated and produces more grain than Hoy. All its hills furnish pasture for vast numbers of cattle and turf for firing which several of the neighbouring isles are destitute of and here supplied.

Burra is situated near and to then north of S. Ronaldsha, it is naturally fertile and has of late been much improved, especially in grass. Here lived the Stewarts of Burra, who once had a good estate in the Orkneys which the last Sir James was turned out of for being concerned in the rebellion, now in the hands of Sir Laurence Dundas superior of the Country and proprietor of a good part of it.

The other south Isles are Fara, Flotta, Swanna, Switha, Cava, Graemsa, Rissa, Lambholm, Copinsha and several holms all more or less fertile in corn and grass and excellently situated for fishing, either in the eddies of the Pightland Firth or, if they had proper boats, in the German Ocean. Vast numbers of Coothes (*Cuiths*) are caught through these small isles and these are most easy to be got, they seldom give themselves much trouble for any other. Of the north Isles the nearest the Mainland is Shapinsha parted from it by a narrow channel leading to Kirkwall harbour. Great part of this Island is cultivated and produces a good deal of grain. Lead ore is to be found in several places of it but is not sought after. It is about six miles long and is well known for its harbour.

The next is Stronsa of equal bulk but very irregular jutting out into a great many promontories and peninsulas, well cultivated and decorated with several Gentlemen's seats.

To the north of Stronsa lies Sanda, the largest of the north isles, being about twelve miles long but of unequal breadth, from one to five miles over, however these measures give no true notion of the quantity of ground in it, as it runs out into many points on both sides and is oddly hollowed by bays and lochs which render the figure of it very irregular and deceiving as to the contents but form bays and harbours for the convenience of shipping. This island and some others very considerable among the north isles have heretofore had but a very ordinary character and one they are far from deserving. Buchanan does not so much as name Sanda, Eda or North Ronaldsha in the enumerations he gives to the Orkneys, though these are much more considerable than many he has admitted into his catalogue. Sir James Sinclair, a natural son of the Earl of Orkney, begged these Islands of Sanda and Eda from King James the Fifth, representing them as no better than holms and fit only for pasturage but, when the truth came out, he paid dear for his deceit and for fear of the King's wrath threw himself into the sea. Sanda is the best cultivated of any of the north isles and produces the greatest quantity of grain and has in it vast numbers of rabbits, being wholly either arable or warren ground but wholly destitute of firing which they are obliged to bring at a great risk and expense from the neighbouring isle of Eda. Many of the poorer sort who cannot afford this expense are obliged to substitute instead of peat, sea weed and cow dung mixed with straw and dried in the heat of the sun, both which are unhealthy and smoky.

The whole island is very flat and level, falling lowest towards the north east end which is, unluckily, the more dangerous for vessels in their passage through the channel betwixt it and the Fair Isle which lies midway betwixt this and Shetland. In many paces it is so near the level of the water that at the distance of a league (if the waves are high) it appears disjoined and, as it were, separated into several islands.

Sometimes when the tides flow high the water spreads itself a great way over the plain and in several places makes a passage quite over. When this happens which is but rare, the cattle that were fattened upon the grass grounds at night will be found up to the belly in water in the morning. It is highly probable that a great deal of lands have been swallowed up and overrun by the ocean which is daily making encroachments and 'tis very likely through time may overflow the greater part of the Island. Tradition hath preserved the remembrance of one of the most remarkable of these inundations, which is in some measure confirmed by the appearance of things even at this distance of time. The tradition is this, that the Bay of Otterswick on the north side of the Island which is about two miles in length and nearly of the same breadth was formerly a wood and indeed this is the more probable as the stumps and the roots of trees are still to be seen along the sands pretty far into this Bay. In this and some other of the north isles are the finest and largest farms in the Orkneys, some of these rented at £40, £50 or £100 sterling per annum.

In Sanda there are a vast number of rabbits, of which one year with another about three thousand are shot and caught in nets, from the skins of which a good deal of profit is drawn but the most lucrative branch of trade in this island and indeed in the whole is the Kelp, vast quantities of which is made here and adds much to the value and rents of the Estates and the poorer sort of people, who would otherwise be idle, are employed. The profits arising from this commodity are in many places greater than the proprietors free rent, having nothing to pay to Superior or Clergy out of this most considerable part of their income. There are about three hundred tons yearly made on this island which at the lowest will sell for £900 Sterling but often gives much more, the expenses for making each ton of which is 10/- Sterling, which comes among the hands of the poor people and 10/- for freight, the rest or thirty shillings a ton when it sells for £3 (though it has been known to give five guineas), comes into the proprietor's pocket and may be reckoned the surest part of their income while the price of this commodity continues. The sea weed found growing on the higher rocks commonly called tang was the only kind formerly used in making Kelp but it has of late been found out that the larger weeds, which grow in deeper water and drive ashore, make better Kelp than the other kind, so that is probable greater quantities may be prepared.

The same seaweed is the Sanda farmers whole dependence for manuring his land as the soil is so sandy that it could not nourish any kind of grain were it not fattened with plenty of seaweed. They frequently sow their seed here without tillage and only harrow it into the sand which never hardens like common earth so that, if a storm or wind happens before the grain springs, a great part of the sand and seed with it is blown away and lost. By this means many fine fields have been rendered entirely useless, as also others rendered quite barren by their being overblown by the sea sand and that even within the memory of the present age. Some grounds are found so overspread with stones that one would think nothing could spring amongst them however, upon removing the stones, it is found that the crops are spoiled and by replacing them the crops are bettered.

There are several small lochs on this island where a variety of ducks bring forth their young and to these the swans resort in winter.

The Farmers keep vast numbers of horses in this island, few of which are reared in it but purchased at great expense which, and the expense of keeping them, is no doubt a great loss to the farmer and, in my opinion, might be supplied by oxen at a much easier rate. They pretend indeed that oxen cannot supply the place of horses for work, however I should imagine if they could work it anywhere it might be here where the ground is flat and level, besides the difference in expense and maintenance. Horses when past work are good for nothing whereas, in a country like this, oxen are valuable at any age and when past work may be fattened for slaughter as well as when younger and then answer as well or better for beef for export or the supply of strangers who are daily calling for such refreshments. A few cows, sheep and swine are sold from Sanda but in no great numbers.

The people live to a good age here as well as elsewhere in Orkney, are afflicted with the same diseases and given to the same superstitions as in the other isles, which shall be taken notice of when we come to speak of these particulars in general.

North Ronaldsha, the most northerly of all the Orkneys, is about two miles in length and from one to two miles in breadth, lies on the north side of Sanda and is separated from it by a narrow channel or firth. This island as well as the former is sandy, with a good deal of waste and unimproved ground, that part of which is under tillage yields good crops, indeed in this respect this and the former excels most of the Orkneys. They rarely need to buy any grain but in the most ordinary crops can export. Oats and barley are the only kinds of grain cultivated here as in the other islands.

This island is well inhabited and the inhabitants are much attached to it. They rarely got abroad or even remove to any other Island, therefore their notion of things is very narrow and contracted, yet they have a great deal of cunning and hidden artifice. They use a great many ambiguous expressions and there is always something more couched under their language than is expressed if they are to

affirm anything, they commonly do it by denying the contrary. They have an excess of complacence in answering any question. If they answer in the negative they attempt to soften the denial by saying "yea yea" before they give direct answer, by this they mean they are sorry to disagree with you in opinion or to contradict you, that they would not do this if there was not a necessity of your being informed of the truth. They have a great desire for money and, considering the smallness of their farms, the richest farmers in Orkney. They never lend their money to any person, nor own they have any, but hide and hoard it up when they can scrape a little together and this sometimes in the ground and holes of walls. It is probable the general principles of honesty were formerly a better security for property than now, the old people affirming that, notwithstanding their temptations to theft by the easiness by which it might be accomplished, yet this vice was very seldom heard of among them. In former times they made use of locks to secure their wealth but, as was said before, trusted it to the bosom of its first mother earth, however now they do not so much trust it to chance but secure it under iron locks.

These people in general are frugal and parsimonious and take every method to gain a penny. They seldom eat oatmeal but reserve it for sale as it gives the best price so that, although the scurvy is general among them, it cannot be attributed to the frequent use of this grain but is perhaps owing to the cold and sea damps for there is no sort of fuel here but seaweed, yet the people in other respects are very healthy, this they owe to their temperance and sobriety. They are all of a florid complexion and fully answer Tacitus' description of the norther, *Sanguine plenoreduntantur Septentrionales.*

The inhabitants live for the most part to an advanced age without many diseases, are rough in their manners and on this account slighted by the inhabitants of the neighbouring isles, though even these are not very high in the scale of good breeding.

North Ronaldsha like Sanda consists of very low land and its rocks run far out to sea, the greatest part of these covered at high water often prove fatal of shipping, of which there have been many instances even within our own times. In these last thirty years there have been no less than eight vessels left on this island, most of them ships of great burden, particularly in 1740 a Swedish East-indiaman, having a most valuable cargo on board and a number of gentlemen passengers, was lost here and most of the people and cargo perished, indeed the greatest part of these wrecks are Swedes and Danes who all choose rather the passage between this Island and the Fair Isle than those narrow sounds which lead through the Orkneys. However many ships trading to the Baltic belonging to the western parts of Scotland and England likewise take this passage and some of them perish in it which shows the need of a lighthouse on it, for the convenience of trade in these parts of our Islands.

The whole Island is the property of one gentleman and though small is valuable, the rents are paid as in other parts of Orkney in kind, as malt, meal, butter, oil, feathers etc., the tenants here too, as is too much the case through Orkney, have no leases but all removable at pleasure.

The houses are half underground and like most other farmhouses in Orkney most ordinary huts, where people and cattle all sleep under the same roof and sometimes the calf has a better apartment than the heir of a family that can boast of twenty four generations of uninterrupted lineal succession.

There are vast numbers of seals round this Island of which many are caught by the inhabitants in nets for their skins and oil, as also the younger for eating and indeed I see no reason why a young seal may not be eaten a well as a cod, their diet being much the same and their whole method of living in many respects similar.

(The greater part of these observations on the Islands of Sanda and North Ronaldsha I acknowledge myself indebted to the Rev. William Clouston, Minister of Sanda)

Eda is situated south west of Sanda, not much inhabited but very valuable on account of the vast quantities of peats with which it supplies the other Isles that are not so well provided with that article. The Island is about five miles long and one continued moss, except about the skirts or sea shores where there are a few farms. There is a pretty good harbour facing the north, fenced by a holm, called Calf of Eda. In this holm were formerly several salt pans but they have been discontinued working these many years.

Westra lies N.W. from Eda, is about nine miles and a half long but unequal breadth containing two parishes under one minister, tolerably well cultivated and fertile but in several places much subjected to sand blowing which has ruined several spots of excellent arable land and is not on the decrease. The West side of the Island is very high especially that part called Noup or Westra head, the east side is low and has a tolerable harbour. In the Island is the unfinished castle of Noutland, begun by Hepburn, Earl of Boswell, made Duke of Orkney previous to his marriage with Mary Queen of Scots. It as intended as a refuge in case of the storm he dreaded from the Nobility on account of the murder of King Henry and his marriage with the Queen but never inhabited for, when he was obliged to fly from Carberry Hill whether he had come to engage Morton, Mar and other Nobelmen who had joined forces against him, he betook himself to the Orkneys but when he came thither his castle was not habitable and, being denied entrance into the castle of Kirkwall by the Keeper, he was forced again to sea without being able to finish this building or long to enjoy his title as Duke of Orkney. Since this time this castle has been falling gradually to ruin.

Between Westra and the Mainland lies Rousa, a large hilly island and little cultivated except near the seashore where there are small spots of arable and pasture ground. The hills abound with wild fowl as Moorfowl, Plovers, Lapwings and several other waders which frequent hilly grounds for hatching, also in pasture for cattle in summer and numbers of sheep. The rocks are a summer habitation for vast numbers of seafowl, as Auks, Gulls, Tystes, Shags and other birds of these kinds which frequent the Orkneys.

Near Rousa to the Eastward lies Egilsha, a small but fertile island where St. Magnus, patron of Orkney, was killed about the year 1110, says Torfaeus, and buried says some but this is a matter of doubt, as his reliques would, no question, be deposited in the Church which a few years after was built and dedicated to his honour. It is certain that some years ago, as some workmen were at work on a pillar in the Cathedral of Kirkwall, they found it hollow and in a box placed in this space were the bones of a man tied up carefully in ribbons, probably those of St. Magnus or other great man of antiquity whose history like his name is obscured by the mist of ages.

The lesser isles to the northward are Papa Westra famous for the superstitious regard paid by the inhabitants to St. Tredwell's Chapel and loch. This is not the only chapel to which superstition has affixed an extraordinary veneration, the Chapel of the Burgh of Birsa and that on the Mull of Deerness, the extremities of the Mainland, the Chapel of Clet in Sanda and several others are much sought to by the inhabitants in former times especially when under any misfortune, disease or other difficulty. They then vowed an alms to these chapels and seldom failed to pay in money or corn and this, they imagined, would gain them the goodwill of the supreme power, by this collation they would be freed from their difficulties but, if the cure should not follow, they took care not to lose much for the most part of these offerings were very trifling, a small piece of money or a handful of corn, they imagined would suffice. These offerings were presented at particular chapels only probably those dedicated to the most reputable saints and whose mediation they thus imagined they could procure. However these superstitions are now much wearing out and are practiced by only a few of the oldest and most ignorant of the inhabitants some of whom are remarkably tenacious of their former customs.

Fara with only a single house on it, Gairsa, Inhallow, small but infertile islands and, in a small bay of the Mainland, called by Torfaeus Urridafirod, Damsey Island and holm where, they very gravely tell us, neither cat nor mouse will live though carried into them (in this island still remains the ruins of an old Chapel called by the country people, Hellie Boot.).

Besides there are several to be found in the catalogue which are only reckoned as holms and kept for pasturage, though some of these are larger than many of the inhabited isles and, in these, many of the duck tribe and other wild fowl find what they love, an undisturbed habitation to hatch in.

Chapter 8
Of the inhabitants in general, their manners, temper, disposition and pursuits

The generality of the inhabitants of Orkney are of the middle size and well enough proportioned, though in this respect I imagine they have degenerated from their ancestors the northerns who are, by all authors, said to be of the first size and of the most robust make. When at home they take but little pains, are inactive and their industry goes little further than a beggarly livelihood but their character is drawn by one of their own countrymen with trust and I shall add it in his own words. 'The Commonalty,' says he, 'are healthy, hardy, well shaped, subject to few diseases, capable of an abstemious and laborious life at the same time but, for want of profitable employment, slow at work and many of them inclined to idleness.' I cannot altogether agree with this gentleman that the want of sufficient return is the cause of the Orkney commons being addicted to idleness, for profit (as it is called) is a relative terms and there is scarce any country in which industry will not become profitable. I should therefore rather think it is the slavishness they have all along been kept in by their masters, their want of effort to make what they labour for turn out well, the want of example and method in carrying on their labours, for it is well known that no people drudge more while their work lasts, nor sooner sink into laziness when it is finished, the whole of their labours is done without design and altogether in a hurry. It is also well known no people become more faithful and industrious when they go through the world and see what work is and how it is conducted, so want of judgement rather than want of toil have given them the name of lazy, we shall see by their methods of Agriculture etc. what grounds there is for this assertion.

'In sagacity and natural understanding (adds he) they are inferior to few of the commons in Great Britain, sparing of their words, reserved in their sentiments, especially in what seems to have a connection with their interests, apt to aggravate or magnify their losses and studious to conceal or diminish their gains, tenacious of old customs though never so inconvenient, averse to new till recommended by some successful experiments among their own rank and acquaintances and then universally keen to imitate. Honest in their dealings with one another but not so scrupulous with respect to the master of the ground, often running deeply in arrears to him while they punctually clear credit with everyone else.'

This last particular may arise from a rooted notion they have of the injustice of the land masters rent in contradistinction to that claimed by the superior and this notion has its origin in the following particulars: All the Estates of Orkney are either feus from the King (Earl) or Bishop, except a few Feudal tenures of which afterwards. These feus were originally taken at the then full rent of the land, which was continued as a feu duty and payable to the Superior, whatever improvements can be made or rents raised are the Landmaster's emoluments, but the people, still averse to innovations especially where they are chargeable, never can be brought to think that the master of the ground has any right to impose new burdens or that they are liable to any other exactions than the superior's rent which they call the "just debt" and are very willing to pay. Besides these they have another bad custom which may contribute much to this, which is the landmaster allowing the tenants to run and continue in arrears always for the rents of the two last years, which is apt to make it sit easy upon their minds and make them regardless whether they be exact in their payments or not and has furnished them with a proverb to the purpose namely "that they need not be very anxious concerning their payments, for they found a year's rent owing after their fathers and there will be the same in arrears at the day of judgement."

These and some other equal singularities prevail here and are not easily rooted out and indeed but little pains taken to do so, as the spirit of true improvement, which must always begin among the better sort, has not yet made great progress in Orkney.

Buchanan gives the inhabitants of Orkney a tolerably harmless character though not a virtuous one, as though their frugality and its consequent health of body and mind were not the effect of choice but necessity or ignorance. *In convictu quotidiano* (says he) *multum e vetusta parsimonia vulgus adjuc retinet. Haque perpetua corporis et animi sanitate fere omnes fruntur - Eadem parsimonia et ad formae elegantiam et ad staturae proceritatem plurimum facit.* But adds he - *plus apeed cos deliciarum ignorantia quam apud alios medicorum ars et diligentia ad salutem tuendam prodest.* And again after describing their heartiness on a certain occasion, he draws the following consequences - *Undi facilis conjectura et illam quan dize parsimoniam not tam e ratione et studio quam penuria ortum ipse, cademque quae cam initio pepererat due apied posteros conservavit necessitas* . Suffice it to add to what Buchanan has said, that though this might have been the case in former times, that want of means of indulging in luxury might have prevented any large encroachments on their manners, now that is not the case, luxury begins to make large strides and descends very fast, as a number of our Anti-patriots seem to plume themselves on furnishing the means of indulging it in its utmost latitude and this is not like to be confined as of old to the richer few but to be spread among the multitude. One particular which must make luxury the more pernicious with us is that it is not the effect of an increase of industry or of wealth procured by that but imported like other ill fashions.

In their manner, their genius and the bent of their inclinations the Orkney people differ much from their next neighbours on the mainland of Scotland. Their dress, their language and every attachment is different, more resembling those of the Danes and Norwegians in whose power they were for a long time, than those of the Highlanders of Scotland, so that a very little acquaintance with both will soon let anyone see their origin has been different and to be looked for from another quarter.

The language of these Islands was a dialect of the Norwegian, the same as is used in Iceland to this day. It was called here Norn (contracted I suppose from Norwegian) but it is now so much worn out that I believe there is scarce a single man in the country who can express himself on the most ordinary occasion in this language. Even the songs, which are commonly longest retained of any part of a language, are now (except a few of the most trifling) altogether lost though this, little more than half a century ago, was the prevailing tongue of two parishes in the Mainland.

They now altogether speak English but with a great deal of the Norwegian accent and even with some words of that language intermixed, though it is probable in a few years longer by means of a greater communication with the rest of mankind and other advantages which they formerly did not enjoy, their old language will wear out entirely and will not in these parts be understood at all. The only fragments I have seen or could procure of this language are the Lord's Prayer as preserved by Wallace and copied by Dr. Percy in his preface to Mallet's Northern Antiquities and is as follows, but much corrupted

45

from its original no doubt by the concourse of strangers and the division of these isles from other countries where it was spoken in its greatest purity.

> Fvor i ir i Chimrie 1. Hellent ir i Nam thite 2.
> Gilla cosdum thite cumma 3. Veya thine
> mota var gort o Yurn sinna gort i Chimre 4.
> Gav vus da on da dalight Brow vara 5.
> Firgive vus sinna vora sin vec firgive Sindra
> mutha vus 6. Lyv vus ye i Tumtation 7.
> Min delivera vus fro Olt ilt. Amen

In this specimen it is easily seen that, though the genius of the northern language is retained, yet there are many words which seem derived from the English with little difference but what would arise from the false pronunciation of it when it was first introduced and to this day there are many sounds in the English language which the Orkney people cannot master but pronounced according to their old Norn dialect for example qu in queen, question, quarrel etc. etc. is usually pronounced as if it were written wh, hence to a man they say wheen, whestion, wharrel etc. th they pronounce without the aspiration as thing ting, three tree, thumb tumb, thousand tousand and in many other particulars this corruption of their English is observable at first hearing them talk to any stranger though not so much so to themselves.

The dress of the commons in Orkney has no resemblance to that used in the Highlands of Scotland their neighbours. They in general wear very course undyed cloth made in the country, though when they intend to be finer than ordinary they have a jacket made in the form of that used at sea made of coloured cloth, with very course linen, stockings the produce of the country, shoes made of leather of their own tanning and in some places as Sanda etc. they use a shoe made of rawhide laced to the foot with a thong of the same, this is called a ravlin and they tell us it is much easier for the foot than that usually worn but, though this may be true in some measure when worn in the flat sandy islands and those free from stones, yet where these or rocky ground prevail they can be of little service as they cannot defend the foot from any external injury.

The Gentry indeed, all except the poorest sort, do not content themselves with homespuns but love to go very fine and indeed here broad cloths, silks, velvets, cambrics, laces and other fineries are much more used than even in the richest shires of Scotland; in these articles our better sort of people affect to follow the fashions of our southern countrymen and often in these outdo them without having their funds to support them.

These islands have produced vast numbers of most excellent seamen and this is more particularly the bent of their inclinations. Their education and whole turn of mind seems to adapt them more for sea than land service, insomuch that for one soldier from Orkney we shall find a thousand sailors, few corners of the world are without them and hence it may be at once perceived what a valuable nursery for seamen Orkney be were there any method struck to keep our youth at home in their own country, till they were required for the necessary purposes of Government or otherwise. For example, were fishings, for which the country is most excellently situated, encouraged and carried on with vigour, was agriculture on a better footing, was there in a word incitements to thrive at home, there would be means of retaining great part of these swarms of youth which, not finding employment at home, are obliged as things are to go through the whole world to seek bread wherever they can find it and who, no doubt, would rather stay nearer home if it were possible for them to gain a livelihood amongst their friends.

This would be a never failing source in time of any exigency of Government where men could always be had on a short warning to man a fleet and these experienced to sea affairs and inured to fatigue. But want of spirit and industry seem at present to have put an entire stop to this profitable and useful branch of business, at least it is no further carried on to supply present necessity with fish of the most ordinary kinds, as we shall further see when we come to make a more particular view of the different branches of trade etc. as they are at present in the Orkneys.

Orkney is not without numbers of natural geniuses who have made surprising progress in several mechanical employments, such as smith several of whom are in great part self taught having but little opportunity for improvement and yet I have seen pieces of work in their way finished with a good deal of nicety. We have several joiners likewise self taught but the greatest part of our self taught workmen are those who perform on horn, bone, ivory and metals of which they make many neat trinkets as snuff boxes of the shape of eggs, hearts and otherwise, staff heads and many other things too tedious to mention. I have seen a Guitar made in Kirkwall which was acknowledged by judges to be equal to many made abroad. Everyone tans his own leather and does most of the joiner or other business about his farm and though this is performed sometimes but clumsily yet it saves to those who could not well afford to pay for the doing of it.

Orkney being blessed with tolerable air and the inhabitants in general being as yet used to a temperate method of living may be the reason why we see many instances of longevity and not a few remarkable for their strength or otherwise. Mr. Wallace in his description of Orkney takes notice of several about his time who arrived at a vast age, considering these times, particularly one, a man in the parish of Holm who lived upwards of four score year in a married state and that with one wife. He mentions another, a gentleman in Stronsa, who begot a son when he was a hundred years of age and lived till he saw his grandchildren by that son, which could not be less than eighteen or twenty years at least but these do not come up to the story Buchanan tells us of a Shetland man who when above a hundred married a wife, at a hundred and forty went to sea in his little boat afishing in the stormiest weather, dying a patriarch indeed, not by disease but for mere old age. I have observed many instances of great age even in our times when luxury prevails more than formerly though perhaps none of them equal to the last two examples, yet numbers here live to an advanced age. I have known several both men and women above a hundred, though most of these like Dean Swift had lost their memory and with it the particular number of their years and, with him, we were obliged to compute them by what they remembered.

Mr. Wallace records a man remarkable for stature who was called the Meikle or great man of Waes but I cannot say I have observed any very remarkable on this account, though there are many very stout men to be seen here.

Nor is longevity or strength the only particulars in which Orkney has been famous. In general they are remarkable for fecundity or how shall we account for the numbers which yearly leave the country and seldom if ever return. Every quarter of the world but particularly America swarming with men from these Islands, but to bring an example or two. There is yet alive, and of no great age, a Clergyman who has been but once married and by his wife, who is not yet (1773) 46 years of age, has had 23 children, many of whom are come to men and women's estate. A second who, though not native of Orkney, lived there a long while in service of the customs and by two wives had 28 children. I am informed of a hearty old cock who by several wives had 38 children and only complained he could have no more and, in a word, it is far from uncommon to see six, eight or ten children running about a man's house who perhaps can scarce afford rags to cover them and yet these or most of these come to be healthful, stout and hardy seamen and many of them to be commanders of ships, for these boys make docile, tractable and obedient servants and, by their obliging behaviour, often get preferment sooner than those who are higher bred and more indulged. We have many examples of children going from us whose fathers could scarce afford them a jacket or a pair of shoes and stockings at their departure and, in a few years, arriving at vast fortunes, which to me is a proof that it is want of example how to conduct their affairs and management to make them turn out well, as much as want of profit in their pursuits, that hinders them from doing much better at home.

We have a certificate in Mr. Wallace's book that a woman had a child very late in life but I cannot say I have heard of any particular example of this. I think most of our people begin rather too soon to breed which in time weakens the race much for, says Tacitus, *sera juvenum venius eoque inexhausta pubertas, nec virgines festinantur eadem juventa similar proceritas pares validique miscentur, ac robura parentum liberi referunt.* This was the manner among the Germans, probably our ancestors, but the case is much altered among us.

I lately received an anecdote from a very worthy friend, whose researches into natural history of our country in general have done us great honour, relative to a personage remarkable for other circumstances than the foregoing which I shall give nearly in his own words: "as I dare say you will give what account you can of the remarkable peronages in your country, I send you the following of a print with an inscription importing that 'Ann Macallame born in the Orkneys of Scotland in the year 1615 was presented to the King's majesty sight October 1662 and under the engraved Portrait which is in man's apparel with a very long beard are the following verses:-

> Tho' my portraiture seems to be
> A man, my sex denies me so,
> Nature has still variety
> To make the world her wisdom know."

My friend adds "The above engraving is in the collection of Mr. Bull, a gentleman of fortune in Upper Brook Street, London."

(Since writing the above, I received further information concerning the personage mentioned above, a picture of whom is preserved likewise in the hall of Whalley Abbey, Lancashire. It is full length in a female dress, red petticoat, white apron, long plaid fastened before with a broach, having a great beard. By her stand cock and a hen to mark the duplicity of sex.

I observe in Keysler's travels through Germany etc. an account of a woman having the same appearance as above and in the note below an attempt to account for this error of nature which whoever would see may consult the book page 116 & note Vol. 1st.)

Ignorance and its companion superstition prevail very much in many places of this country especially among the oldest people, who believe in a great many old wives tales of which it is scarce possible to convince them of the absurdity. For example they are at vast pains when a woman is delivered to hinder the child or mother from being carried away or changed by the fairies and, for this end, place a bible and knife in her hand and, burning a rag, wave the fire around her. This they imagine hinders them from attempting to carry her away to make a nurse of, for this is the notion. They tell us many stories of this and add that always a stupid log is left in the place of the person thus carried away. And, if one from the torments of a disease is seized with a languor through weakness as is sometimes the case, they immediately conclude that he or she is carried away and this is sometimes fatal to the patient, for none will have anything to do with one they imagine to be under the dominion of these demons and they are apt to desert the poor creature in this condition, nay sometimes they hurry him to his long home, which they think a meritorious action. I was lately informed of a most fatal example of this credulity , where a young stout county fellow falling into a lethargic distemper and being abedrid, he still kept his looks though he could not get up or apply himself to anything. Nothing however would persuade his friends but he was changed or, as they express it, 'in the hill', upon which they sent for a bloodletter and made so free with the fairy blood they imagined to be in him, that in a short time, by repeated attacks upon it, they sent him not to the hill but to the Churchyard. Many frightful stories of peoples being rid by the fairies (hagridden) for whole nights together, of being caught up and involuntarily being obliged to attend their meetings, with many such saws which are faithfully recorded by both sires and dames, thereby entailing their follies upon posterity.

If they forget anything upon beginning a journey and are obliged to return for it they will not proceed on their journey that day; they think it unlucky if they happen to row the boat round contrary to the course of the sun when they go a-fishing; they imagine some misfortune will happen to them if they set their foot on the tongs in the morning and, to avoid that, they take care to hang them over the fire at night. In North Ronaldsha they have a most slovenly and ridiculous custom which however there is scarce any such thing as getting them over, that is they never wash their churn of milk or pails and this from a notion that thereby the cows give less milk and that also less nourishing. Some imagine when they throw out the water from washing they throw out the profit from their cattle.

The belief of Witchcraft is almost universal among the lower rank of people, however this seems to be on the decline among the younger generation. The inhabitants of several of the isles formerly believed that shipwrecks were the effects of their incantations and they were foretold by these diviners, here as elsewhere they gave them the power of inflicting punishments by their art on those that offended them and therefore they took as much care as possible to avoid their displeasure.

They are afraid of hurt either in person or goods from an evil eye (this is no new superstition *Nescio quis teneros occulus miki fascinat agnos*) , and have particular ceremonies to avert the malignity of it but pretend to make a mighty secret of their rites. They also fear an evil tongue and there have been not a few instances of poor creatures falling ill through mere imagination upon being cursed by an enemy. Nobody must praise a child or any other thing they set a value on for, if anything afterwards befalls it, these poor ignorant creatures will be sure to attribute it to the tongue that spoke it and very probably quarrel for it. This they call forespeaking and pretend to cure persons so forespoken by washing them with water composed with great ceremony.

(This water is composed by several of our female sages who make the composition an impenetrable secret, however the effects cannot so well be kept which are these. When the person is washed the water is thrown out of doors and the first man or woman that enters takes the patient's disease and dies, while he immediately recovers. As usual many instances are brought to prove the efficacy of the water in thus transferring the disease and the names of many who have been thus cut off, brought to prove its effects the other way. I once indeed heard of one of these old wives who succeeded badly in her part of the operation. She had composed the bath and performed the operation of washing but, when she was about to throw away the water, the patient, who it seems was stronger than ordinary in these circumstances, whipped up the vessel and threw it about her, she knew her doom and immediately (says the story) set herself about submitting to it with good grace.)

They use great pains in recovering cattle struck with Elfshot of which as many stories are told and as firmly believed as Sir Robert Sibbald would pick up in Aberdeenshire (Vid. Sib. Sc. ill: p.49) or all of Scotland besides. I have often heard it advanced that they have been found in the steps of stairs in houses but oftener in stables and cowhouses, these northern Lamiae, it seems, being fonder of cows or horses flesh than that of mankind but perhaps they kill them more for diversion in their nightly frolics than otherwise or has Puck been affronted by the owners and thus takes his revenge.

(I cannot say I ever heard of any of them being found in a Boot top as Sibbald's author relates, though an honest gentleman showed me one which he said was darted after him on his stairs where he found it.)

However all this is, when any beast is so unlucky as to fall under the stroke of these pigmy sprites, an old woman skilled in these matters is called, who pretends to find the hole still open by which the arrow entered and which in this case is not to be found, for it is to be observed that it is only when it falls short that it is picked up. She then washes the part with mighty ceremony and expects a cure.

In a few words, if we may believe our country neighbours, these gentry serve them as many tricks as ever Shakespeare's Robin Goodfellow did, though without his obligingness.

> "Are you not he,
> "That fright the maidens of the villages
> "Skim milk and sometimes labour in the Zuern,
> "And bootless make the breathless huswife churn
> "And sometimes make the drink to bear no barm,
> "Mislead night wanderers laughing at their harm
> "Those that Hobgoblin call you and sweet Puck,
> "You do their work and they shall have good luck.

There are many other particulars of this kind of folly still remaining among the more ignorant vulgar, as charming diseases from one to another, foretelling events by dreams, deaths by death lights, drops, watches and ghosts or, as they are here called, Ganfers, and which they place more confidence in than in the most reasonable propositions that can be adduced to convince them of their absurdity.

The more modern superstitions are most continued from the times of Popery and consist in an attachment for particular churches, chapels and days, as those dedicated to the Virgin Mary and several of the Saints. They are wont to vow in any distress a pilgrimage to such or such a church or chapel or to carry a load of peats to the Johnsmass fire, which is regularly kept up on the 24th day of June. This last is the only public custom they seem to have great anxiety to keep up and is thus, they light a large fire on every most conspicuous place in the parish, commonly facing the south and this is augmented by every person who attends, none of whom come empty. Likewise every person whose horses have been diseased or who had any of these gelded, brings them loaded with fuel to the fire, every beast is led round the same, always taking care to follow the course of the sun in their several turns, else they imagine their thanks for the recovery of the beast is not properly returned. The people go round in the same manner and take the same number of turns as before described and this with a great deal of solemnity and are very ill pleased if anyone attempts to turn these things into ridicule or even to argue with them on the absurdity of the custom. Sometimes great part of the parish assemble at this time and dance round and through the fire till late in the evening, nay so anxious are they to get to it that I some time ago saw a fellow, who was employed in burning kelp, give another, who happened not to be scrupulous as himself, his days wages on condition to supply his place for about three hours of the evening which he wanted to make up his days work and which he could not get leave to absent himself. I shall have occasion to take notice in course of the most probable conjectures of the institution of this solemnity, of which the inhabitants can give no further account, but it was an old custom transmitted them by their fathers and which they incline to continue. I am informed however that even this is not kept up with that spirit as in former times, so that is probable, like other customs it will in time be forgotten.

Buchanan tells us the people of the Orkneys were seldom troubled with diseases and enjoyed long health of body and mind, being most cut off by old age. In these days this is not altogether the case, diseases of different kinds have made their appearance which were never before known and have added themselves to those that were more common. The diseases which were reckoned common were, the scurvy which I believe very few of the common people are free of, indeed there are few but are more or less tainted with this, which arises from the damp sea air and unhealthful colds of winter, which there is no such thing as guarding sufficiently against. Among the commons the labour they undergo hinders it from rising to any height or touching the nobler parts and so long as it gives them little trouble seldom apply any cure, except taking flower of brimstone or rubbing their skins with the same.

Agues, consumption and fevers are pretty frequent and make some havoc but nothing near so much as the new distempers which are sometimes imported to us by strangers and even by our own people, such are spotted fevers which sometimes make vast havoc among all ranks and ages. The Lues Venerea only of late made its appearance among us but seems to love the soil well. The smallpox raged with great violence formerly but much of its danger is taken off by the practice of inoculation which in general succeeds well and numbers of lives are saved by it in these isles where it was very fatal. Besides these the Epilepsy and other nervous complaints are pretty frequent and very severe, as the poor country people have few or no medicines to mitigate their severity and the help of a physician is not always to be had, even in cases where there is a probability of success. The King's Evil may be reckoned among our new diseases which though confined to a few is likely to spread and is a most miserable malady. Upon the whole the greatest part of our common diseases spring from the moistness and unhealthful cold of our winter, spring and autumn air and by guarding against it many of these may be prevented which, by being disregarded and let run on, become, from trifling complaints, serious and often fatal.

Though the country people of Orkney in general live but a lazy indolent life, yet they do not fill up part of the time which they spend so idly even with diversions. The only time when their spirits seem to be a little more exhilarated is about the Christmas holidays when they meet by hundreds and play at football and other sports, though I think the cheerfulness that seems too reign in every heart is much disgraced by a cruel custom of setting up cocks for money to be fired at with fowling pieces, a custom barbarous in itself and inconvenient as it takes off their attention from the more healthful, innocent and more cheerful exercises of the season. Weddings too are kept with great mirth and afford a holiday to the sons of labour. Formerly there were many more festivals in use, in which sports of all kinds were exercised as on the many saints days throughout the year but particularly on that saints day to which their church was dedicated. Now these are laid aside and only a faint remembrance of them kept up, by abstaining from particular kinds of work at these times, for example, on one of these they will not fish, on another they must not cut corn etc.

Funeral ceremonies are much the same as in Scotland. The corpse is laid out, after being stretched on a board, in a bed and thus continues till it is to be coffined in order to be buried. I know not for what reason they lock up all the cats of the house and cover all looking glasses as soon as any of the family dies, nor can they give any satisfactory account of it.

Late wakes are much in use, they invite all their friends and neighbours, male and female, to them and both at these and after burial set in to serious drinking, while the younger part of the company often go to hot cockles and other frolics and continue their sports at night as long as the corpse is unburied but diversions on these occasions are not so much in use as formerly and seem to be on the decline. At the funeral the male part of the company walk mostly by themselves before the corpse and the women follow it. It was said before, the Orkney men's genius leads them more to sea employment than land and indeed this is so visible that every notion the greatest part of them have is taken from or has some connection with sea affairs. This is nowhere more evident than in the epitaphs which are found engraven on several of the grave stones in the churchyards most of which have some or other of their sentiments taken from naval life. I shall add two of these, whether original or copies I cannot say, but to be found in the churchyard of Stromness. The circumstances of their deaths seem to have been much alike and, though this is expressed in but ordinary poetry, let it be remembered that this like other arts has an infancy and perhaps the friends of the persons thus rendered memorable were better sailors than penmen.

"Death steers his course to every point
"Of this terrestrial globe,
'And where he lands cuts quickly down
"All living in this orb.
" For I who underneath this stone
"Lie sleeping in this grave
"While here on earth, did stoutly scorn
"Proud Neptune's raging wave.
"Great swelling seas I overpast,
"When stormy winds did boast,
"Yet Death me seiz'd when I was near
"Unto my native coast.
"Kind reader then be thou advis'd
"Whether by land or sea,
"To learn to live well, then thou shall
"Prepared be to die."

"Kind reader if thou be inclin'd
"As thou art passing by,
"To read my epitaph, then mind
"All flesh is born to die.

"As for myself, when I had come
"From Lewis to Kerston Bay,
"And dropt my anchor near my home,
"Death made no more delay.

"My corpse was brought from sea to shore,
  "My wife and children wept,
"With them I merry was before,
  But then lay still and slept.

"Gainst raging waves, and ruffling winds,
  With success I have fought,
"But death that every mortal finds
  "Me to this grave hath brought.

"Dear Masters, Mates and Foremastmen,
  "Take this advice from me,
"The anchor of your souls to cast
  "In Christ before you die."

Chapter 9
Of the several Arts which are performed by the people of Orkney in a manner most peculiar to themselves or other northerns etc.

As was said before the natives of Orkney are by no means deficient of genius and perform many things in mechanics with much neatness. This is easily observed in their trinkets made of ivory, horn, bone or metals which some of them work in, and show what they could be brought to perform were they assisted by example and education. In general what belongs to agriculture is but clumsily performed, whether as to the construction of their instruments or the using of these, yet this is excusable in a set of people who never saw anything better than the manners of their own country and which they are most obstinately inclined to follow almost in spite of precept.

All or most of the country people tan their own leather, which they do either with bark brought from the northern shores of Scotland, Norway or elsewhere or, which is frequently the case in several of the lesser isles, with the roots of Tormentil here called Ketmoor bark (the same plant is used for the same purpose by the people of the Ferro islands, Vid Lin. Fl. Suec. No. 459 Tormentilla erecta), found in great plenty in all the uncultivated grounds of the country, but especially in Hoy from whence pretty large quantities are brought by people who take the pains to collect it, and sold for the same weight of oatmeal or 2 shillings sterling per Settin equal to two stone or 32 lb. This root answers the purpose of tanning very well and was much more used formerly than now, since bark was introduced it has been much disused because of the difficulty of procuring it in quantities. Roots of water flag answer the same purpose and were often mixed with the former as were the roots of the plant Roseroot, found in vast quantities among the rocks of Hoy etc. and all were formerly the only substitutes for oak or other tan barks.

Till of late the inhabitants of Orkney were not much acquainted with dying as a separate trade or of dye stuffs brought from afar. Every field, moorstone and meadow afforded them those without expence or any further trouble than that of collecting them and applying them to use. To this day I have observed them gathering the heads of corn, marygold, crowfoot flowers, water marygold, heath, water pepperwort and several others to dye yellow of different tints; Liverworts for a kind of tawny orange; blacks from different barks and woody plants, but one peculiar where they boil the cloth, wool or worsted in the water of the Meadowsweet and afterwards in a mineral water which is found in Hoy which impresses a sort of black colour on the cloth so prepared.

I imagine the reason for this water's having the forerecited effect is that it is highly saturated with iron, which acts upon the wool opened by the boiling in the meadowsweet in the same manner that any salt of iron would upon meeting with Oak Galls or any other vegetable styptick.

We have no maltmen in Orkney, everyone makes his own, and vast quantities of this is made as the greater part of the rents of the country is paid in this which necessitates them all to be acquainted with how to make it.

There are no better Kelp manufacturers anywhere than in these isles, from whence a great deal of this profitable article is yearly drawn and more might if demanded. The method of making Kelp is as follows, in the summer season they cut the sea tang from the rocks with hooks made for the purpose and immediately carry it up above the high water mark where it is dried as quickly as possible by often turning in the way of haymaking and without exposing it to rain, which would wash away the salt and diminish both the strength and quantity of the Kelp. When it is fully dry and ready for burning they make a small hollow in the beach and light a fire in it and one or two people continually feed it with tang taking care that it burns with as little flame as possible, which would carry off the finer and more volatile parts. After the Kiln as they call it is full and whilst the matter is still red hot they take two instruments called rakers and keep continually stirring it till it cools and forms itself into a uniform mass or half vitrified cake when it is what is called Kelp and ready to be put on board for the markets. The properties of good Kelp are that it be free of all impurities of sand or stones, that it be well burnt and that the tang has been properly dried without being washed by rains so as to lose its salt, which will soon be the case if not attended to and kept turning.

Sometime ago there was a project tried in Orkney to reduce the large tangle to ashes or kelp which was done in a sort of Kiln built with grated bars of iron on which it was burnt and fell down to the bottom in the form of course white ashes which then tasted very sharp and contained a great quantity of very strong salt but the ashes did not coagulate like common Kelp, I suppose because it was not raked. What these ashes were intended for was kept a mighty secret by the employer, a gentleman in Newcastle, and in a few years the scheme fell to the ground, but I am informed the same sea plant is now used with success in making common Kelp and great quantities are made from it and indeed it is reasonable to suppose all sea plants are capable of being manufactured into the same, as it is well known many of the land plants are, as thistles, thorns, hops and several sorts of trees, marsh plants, ferns etc. all the saline plants without exception.

Chapter 10
Of the tenures and divisions of the Lands of Orkney

The estates or gentlemen's livings in Orkney are in general but small when compared with those in the southern parts of the Kingdom but, with the ancient frugality, may serve all the necessities and conveniences though not many of the superfluities of life. In this respect indeed, things are much altered since the time of the great Buchanan for, though necessity in some measure with the poorest sort keeps up the ancient mode of life, with other it is not so, *sed vetire disciplena labefacta blandientibus quo delicus ipse sese diddere.*

Most lands in Orkney as elsewhere through the Kingdom are now held in feu. These feus are from different hands, as the Crown, the Earls of Orkney and the Bishops generally having the old rental continued as a feuduty or perhaps augmented at the time of feuing as Churchmen especially could not diminish this without wronging their successors. These feus are held by a written deed of conveyance from the Lord to the vassal and infefment thereon and these feus were transferable by the same means, yet there is a tenure in Orkney called Udal right where no such deeds appear, nor were they requisite to ascertain the possessor's property. Here it was sufficient to prove an unquestioned possession of these lands as heritable proprietor thereof and that they were transmitted to him by this usage, which stood in the place of all the solemnities requisite to the constitution of heritable right.

The institution of this tenure is very ancient and the nature of it not very well known, the different usages relevant to it have led people to think differently of it and to draw its original from the custom of nations which differed very much from one another, but a good deal of this I presume depends on that fondness which men commonly express for the honour of their own country and their prejudice for everything that concerns it. We shall examine the different notions concerning this matter and thence judge with what reason they are advanced.

Some there are who think that the tenure had its foundation in the Mosaic institution and they allege this from the following customs which are said to have taken place with regard to the alienation and succession of these lands. The first was "That none can sell his Udal land without making the first offer of it to his next heir and that, if he is not able to purchase it, he has a privilege to redeem it from the purchaser," Secondly "That the succession goes to all the sons or brothers with a praecipuum to the eldest, of the mansion house and pertinents" and indeed if the first of these prevailed it is very much similar to the custom of the Israelites as described in Scripture in their alienations but how the Jewish customs came to prevail in these parts especially in a time when these usages must have been instituted is, I confess, a mystery not so easily cleared up. As to the other it is probably Gothic more than Jewish as we shall have occasion to observe but, however they are, these customs are altogether disused and the succession for aught I can learn is determined in the same manner with regard to Udal lands as others, nor do people possessed of such lands ask questions of the next heirs but transfer them at pleasure so that if these customs ever existed, whether of equal or secondary authority to the tenure itself, they are now lost, as will, in a short time, the tenure itself which is wearing out every day.

Again the act of transmitting heritable property from hand to hand without any interposition of a Superior has given occasion to think these lands were held of, or acknowledged none, as a Superior, in effect that they are Allodial and, as they acknowledged no superior, so neither homage, rent of other ervice was due for lands so held. Whether they were so or not we shall be the better able to judge from the nature of Allodial and feudal property. "Allodial" (say the best lawyers) "is the property of things to which one has right without any recognizance or acknowledgement of another". This is carefully to be distinguished from the feudal holding which is what one has only right to under the recognizance of a Superior. Now if there was no redendo chargeable from these lands, whether of service or tribute, this would indeed encourage us to think that they were allodial or holding of no superior, but it is certain that these lands in former times paid to the Crown of Norway and still continue to pay a duty or quitrent call Skatsilver which never could have been imposed upon them had they not been considered as dependent on the Sovereign. Nor was this Skat what is commonly called a tribute or land tax but a real rent service, for it has been still continued under the same name and meaning even after these very lands were made liable to the cess or land tax with the others in Scotland. Upon the whole this constant payment to the Crown or others in its right of this Skatsilver whether it be called tribute or feuduty is a cerain demonstration that these lands are not Allodial but feudal especially if we consider the nature of Allodial lands among the Romans (where lands were generally so) and among whom it was never heard that a ground subsidy was required or paid for them. It must be allowed indeed that when the word feudal tenure, when applied to these lands held in Orkney by the Udal usage, must be taken in the most original and general sense of the word as will be seen.

If we consider the origin of the Feudal system we shall find it had its first rising, among the northern nations, among the Goths, in these very countries whence in all probability the first inhabitants of these islands came but who certainly held them under their sovereignty for a long time. The northerns it is well known overrun the greatest part of Europe and established their customs wherever they came and, among the rest, the feudal system which they took great care to propogate as upon it depended their plan of government and this was the best system for indulging their favourite inclination for war. We never hear of any Allodial lands among the northerns, among them almost everything was given in fee, in the earliest times even banquets, horses and arms came under this denomination and, in latter times, land. Among these nations land was held by a tenure of military service and an oath of Fidelity because as they had made their conquests by arms so they were to retain and defend them and by the same means attempt the gaining of more.

The most probable notion then of this tenure is that of a great Lawyer who inagines that it is the remain of the most ancient manner of feudes or holdings by military tenure, before Charters or writings of any kind were introduced and, after they became hereditary, they continued in the same manner to be good by possession alone for anciently fees were constituted without writing, the Lord only gave the vassal a verbal grant of the lands and seisin and possession of the same. Before, convassals and fees given in this way were revocable at pleasure, they afterwards became hereditary and in many places a short Charter was given on them by the Lord testifying that the grant of the feude was made and possession given of the lands to the vassal which was intended for the security of the vassal and his heirs, but it is probable these very ancient feudes had been made before any of these charters had been made.

That particular custom of sons or brothers succeeding agrees well with this system if the reddendo was military service, as none but males were capable of performing these services and this was no doubt meant to show them that, as they were all capable of succession, they were all called upon when the public service required them.

Such probably has been the origin of this obsoete tenure and though the history of its institution is much obscured through time, there is little doubt but lands held by it were the reward of valour as the other feudes and had been given by the chief to his followers and fellow soldiers in requital of their services and to bind them to the like in time to come but, in after times and in times of peace when their serices were not so necessary, these might have been changed into a yearly tribute for supporting their government or the dignity of the chief, as their personal service was the means of this in the time of war. This tenure by military service though now abolished is the most ancient feude among the northerns but, as in these Islands personal services could not, on account of their distance from their Mother Country Norway, be of much service to her. These it is probable might in time be converted into a tribute or rent service for the support of Government and thus the Udal and feudal customs are only a different latitude of the same thing.

This last position is rendered more apparent by the case with which the Udal tenure in the strictest sense can be converted into a proper feu for, on many occasions, charters have been granted by the crown of these lands to the possessors and are of course given upon adjudications and the heritors and adjudgers take infefments thereon, which must necessarily convert them to feudal holdings and, in such cases, the Skat becomes a feuduty in the most proper sense, but none of which could happen had not the crown a right of superiority over these lands.

And even where there are no infefments and the heritors have no other title than possession by the Udal right, they often transmit these lands by ordinary dispositions and base infefments whereby they become proper feudal rights in the persons of those they are deponed to and require infefments thereafter to the conveyance of them. All which seems to prove that the Udal tenure must have been originally the same with the feudal and that it is only accidental circumstances that have rendered them different.

To conclude the article this usage, by what we have seen of it, seems neither to have been Israelitish not Roman but, like other customs of the country, really Gothic and with others received from our ancestors.

Chapter 11
Of the Soil

Before we treat of the state of agriculture in these parts it will be proper to speak a few words concerning the nature of the soil that we may better judge whether it is the fault of this alone that makes the Orkney farming so contemptible in the eyes of many who visit us.

The soil of these islands is as variable as can be expected in such a narrow country. In most paces it is a light and hot sand, in some a fine black mould, towards the hills it is clayey and colder, it is seldom deep and has generally a rocky bottom. We have earths of many kinds and tinged with many colours, according as they are mixed with any foreign matter, such as iron which runs through the soil of a great part of the Mainland and some of the Isles, where it renders the earth of a yellowish brown colour and, wherever it abounds near the surface of the earth, puts an entire stop to vegetation but this is but very seldom and that in the most uncultivated spots where they have scraped off all the vegetable mould and left this bare. We have clays red, blue and yellow, moss, sand and spots of these jumbled together which however prevails most in the low grounds and by the sea shores, also in some of the flatter Islands; clays of different consistences are found high up, and moss, in the mountains and bottoms between them. Wherever this last prevails it is not only valuable for fuel but often covers a very thick stratum of marle which though of vast use to the farmer is here of but little used and with little judgement. In some places of the Mainland the bottoms are swampy and not fit for tillage but most of these are capable of being drained and turned into excellent meadows and, with proper management, may be brought to yield most excellent natural grass and that in very large quantities but, in this branch as well as others, the Orkney farmers are very deficient as we shall see in course.

Upon the whole the soil of Orkney is not so proper for grain as many places in the richer shires of Scotland, is much more so than the west coast and as fit for pasturage as most of the northern shires of it.

Chapter 12
Of the State of Agriculture

Agriculture in these Islands is as yet in its infancy. The Orkneymen make but rude farmers and have arrive at but a small degree of perfection in the management of their lands so as to make them bear well or even in the economy of their produce when come to maturity. Indeed improvement in agriculture lies under the most signal disadvantages in the Orkneys, more so than in most parts of Great Britain and these may be owing to several causes, as want of proper measures in the Landlords or want of the same in the farmer.

It is sufficiently known that a spirit of improvement in any branch can never take its rise among the poorer sort of mankind, this must be the part of those who are able to lay out time and money in the necessary experiments and this without incommoding or hurting their main stock but which can never be done by one whose all depends on the uncertainty of a season or the caprice of a Landlord.

The great stops to improvement on the part of the Landlord are want of proper leases to enable the farmer to improve his ground, high rents, and these paid in kind, his being liable to be turned out at every expiration of a three or five years lease unless he pay such a grassum as frequently rises to more than he has gained the whole time of his possession, various and undetermined services and these liable to be exacted when he can worst spare his time and labour, a total want of example from the master to the tenants or attention in the former to bring them to a true method of farming by methods adopted to the nature of the country, to which may be added great part of the country's being held by people of very small incomes who, notwithstanding, must by one means or other squeeze a livelihood out of them, which in this age of luxury is not so easily done, so as to make both ends meet and therefore they are obliged to fall upon various ways and means to eke out their scanty provision, now all this must fall on the heads of the poor farmers and keep them still in such a state of poverty, of slavish dependence, as must for ever if not remedied strike at the root of all improvement. A spirit of true patriotism has not yet begun to unfold itself in the Orkneys else these particulars might be in a great measure remedied, indeed the fault perhaps is not altogether in the Landlord, though the root of it is, for who can suppose a man having common sense that will take any pains to improve a farm which perhaps he must leave at the next three years end, in favour of some designing wretch who wants to reap the fruit of his labours. Who can suppose that a people naturally lazy will take much pains to amend, if they can make out a sort of beggarly livelihood with bodily ease and are at the same time sensible that the less they have they run the less hazard of being turned out. Which of the Orkney tenants can lay down any proper plan for his year's work when he is certain that all his schemes may and will be broke through by his services to his Landlord. There are indeed other impediments to agriculture which seem not so easily remedied, such as want of proper markets to bring the produce of their small farms to, I do not mean what grain they can spare but many other lesser articles, which in a trading country might be valuable and turn to account but, as things are here, rather prove a loss to the farmer. The Climate too is rather unsettled than in places farther south and often proves hurtful by the weather early breaking. However though providential occurrences are to be guarded against as well as circumstances will permit, an improvement in these things which are in our power, is much more the object in things relating to agriculture. He must be a choice spirit who will at last open his eyes to the true interest of his country and set an example to the gentlemen proprietors of the landed interest and lend a hand to the poor farmer in the first place by letting him have such a lease of his farm as would enable him to make what improvement the nature of it would allow, even though he were bound and obliged to such and such terms of improvement provided they were well adapted to the nature of the country and he were allowed a sufficient space to recompense himself for his pains and expence, this would be no hardship. Secondly by introducing a set of instruments more proper for the purposes of tillage than these at present used in the country seem to be and teaching them how to use these to the best advantage and lastly by setting the farmers an example of the method of managing their farms and making the produce of them turn out to the greatest purpose. The assisting the farmer in bringing his grain, cattle etc. to market (as this cannot be properly done here) must lie more upon the merchant who, by giving the farmer such a price as will be advantageous to both, would encourage him to be more careful of his grain, cattle, sheep and other articles fit for sale and be ready to bring these where he was sure of finding a ready and advantageous sale for what he could spare and, in this manner, the produce of the country would turn out to much better account and be much more advantageous both to the merchant and the farmer. At present things are on a very poor footing in the farming way, the farmers are in general very poor and cannot afford to weather a failing crop but, in this case, are ever ready to go to beggary; however with a little indulgence on the one part and more industry on the other this, as well as other branches of our economy, might be rectified, all improvement in our circumstances must descend, it can never ascend.

It is very surprising that people, who seem so bent upon making every advantage, should be so very blind to what alone can be real gain. If, instead of racking rents and large grassums, a spirit of improvement were once thoroughly lighted up amongst us, instead of a set of poor beggarly slaves drudging for little or nothing through the whole year, passing a life of continued poverty and obliging their landlords every term to dun them for rents and arrears, we should see a set of thriving farmers, who could pay their rents punctually, improve their grounds to advantage and, by this means, both Landlord and tenant would know what they were doing, whereas at present as the lands are all held at a high superior rent and the tenants often not able and sometimes not careful to clear this, the land is affected and oft-times run away with before a careless landlord knows what he is indebted for. All these inconveniences spring from and might be remedied by a little more attention to that very useful part of mankind who seem here too much to be considered merely as steelbow and little else than the property of their masters.

"In short" says the author of 'True causes of the poverty of Orkney', " the joint endeavours of master and tenant are wholly wanting, although these together with careful experience and observation would soon correct what may be amiss in the first essays and enable them to adapt many valuable improvements to the entire nature of their soil and climate."

I am perfectly sensible that a thorough reformation in this particular would be a very difficult undertaking and a work of time as most of the country farmers are really ignorant and most obstinately wedded to their old customs, yea unreasonably so, but even this with persevering attention might be amended when once they were brought to see the superior advantage of improvement.

The instruments used in agriculture are but trifling, have but little effect to render the earth mellow in order to produce good crops.

They consist of a plough with a single stilt or handle, a harrow with wooden teeth, a mallet for breaking clods and a spade in which in some places they delve all or most of their ground. All these instruments are original and singular in their construction and, for ought I know, none to be found like them in any part of Scotland. Of late years there has been introduced into several places of these Isles a small plough with two handles, called a Highland or Caithness plough by our country people, however I am far from thinking this last is properly fitted to supply the difficulties we labour under in the construction of our own. Though the Caithness plough is furnished with two handles, these are placed so much upright as render it very hard to manage, the workman having no command of it, which must render the work performed by it but ordinary, though not in the eyes of our farmers, who seem to imagine if their grounds are shifted in any manner it may answer the purpose of tillage. This construction being commonly made very weak cannot sustain the force necessary to cleave strong grounds but, in this respect, our own is in the same case. As it is constructed with mold-boards it has the advantage of the Orkney plough, which has only a few sticks placed in the room of these in a position not at all fitted to turn the furrow but shift it from its place often leaving the same side uppermost which is very hurtful as their wooden toothed harrow has not the weight to break it properly when ploughed in that manner. The structure of the Orkney plough requires to have the beam very long and a very long rope fixed to the muzzle of it, all which, throwing the horses at a great distance from it, renders the draught heavy and tiresome and indeed this, with the shape and method of placing the irons, makes this small one which a man may easily carry in one hand, as hard for the horses to work as the heaviest Scotch plough.

Lest these hints should not be sufficient to make these instruments understood I have added drawings[1] which at the same time that they show the simplicity they will point out their defects and the need of improvement in this as well as other articles of our country affairs.

Not only the instrument but the whole manual operations[2] in the farming way are clumsily carried on in the Orkneys, the only particular they seem to know to any purpose and to perform with any degree of care is the throwing of vast quantities of manure on their grounds but this too is often done without judgement and the intention of it, by bad management, entirely frustrated. It is not extraordinary thing to see an Orkney farmer spread his cattle dung on his land perhaps some weeks, nay some months, before he intends to till it down, the consequence is the whole substance is dried up and it is rendered useless. Another pretty extraordinary method they have is the fleecing the finest sward and throwing it on their corn lands without any previous preparation and which, in my opinion, can have no other effect on most soils but to chill them and render them still more unfit for vegetation than their clumsy ploughing left them.

In general near the seaside they use for manure the broad leaved Alga or, in short, any sea weed which they lay on as was said before in vast quantity. This, where they have access to it, is their favourite manure and is carried up immediately as the tide leaves it, or they have use for it, in creels through very narrow passages often cut through the rock. This is performed by men and women, horses being useless in these dangerous footways. I have often seen sixty or seventy of these poor people hard at work in this slavish employment from morning to night, scarce allowing themselves time for eating, one part employed in filling the creels, and these mostly men, while the patient females lent their shoulders to the burden. This was continued as long as any was to be had or they had use for it, without intermission, a most fatiguing work and fitter for asses than women, who indeed are here very much of burden as well as among our neighbours, however patience is a virtue. Where they have no access to the sea they use manure composed of

earth mixed with dung but if they can possibly have the other they neglect this. I have not heard of Limes being used as a manure though it is very plentiful in some of the Isles, often the sea rocks consist of little else, besides shell lime, and a congerie of sand and broken shells found frequent round the shores run into a sort of rough stone which will burn into lime and no doubt would make excellent manure.

Marle of different colours and excellent quality is to be had in many places and a very few is used as manure, but its use is not general nor with much judgement.

Add to the general ignorance of the true principles of farming a want of proper method in conducting the labour of the different seasons, which are all done carelessly, in vast hurry and with great slavery to man and beast while they last but, as soon as any particular task is done, they immediately descend to downright indolence.

As the Orkney plought cannot go deep or so as to turn up the new soil, the same few inches of earth are always in action which, if it were not for their plenty of manure must run out and be incapable of bearing. However though this is in some measure remedied by dung etc. it has this inconvenience (as they never fallow their land) that it renders the ground extremely foul and their corns always ready to be choked by weeds or, if it escape this, still the crop being mixed with such a great quantity of more succulent plants, is difficult to dry (a circumstance of the utmost consequence in a country where harvest weather is so precarious) the grain is rendered small, hungry and often unwholesome as the cutting of it green which is too often practised, in rain or, for want of care, letting it heat, nothing diminishes the evil.

It would be endless to enumerate the many instances of want of care and bad management in this branch in Orkney, suffice it to say it is an evil that calls aloud for help with but very little appearance of being soon heard.

The most common kinds of grain are only sown here, as a small rough kind of black oats and bear of the same standard which are raised alternately. The great black oat has been introduced and thrives so well that it has become pretty general among those gentlemen who have farms in their own hands but not so among the common farmers. The large white oat has been tried but found not to answer so well as it is very late before it ripens and very apt to be shaken, both highly inconvenient for this part of the world.

Peas and beans have been tried (but not in any great quantity) by many and answer tolerably well but neither are these come to general use and, contrary to what is practised elsewhere, are here mostly sown in the worst ground. I am indeed very much surprised that rye has been all along neglected in Orkney, as it is a grain which endures all the rigours of the northern climate and makes good bread either by itself or mixed with other grain.

Flax answers tolerably well and is cultivated in pretty large quantities in the parish of Holm etc. but has, I believe, in former times been mors universal than now as in several farms they still show what they call lint rigs and tell us they were formerly destined for the cultivation of this plant. The cultivation of Flax seems at present to be on the increase and bids fair to become more universally cultivated as the linen manufactory has been introduced and the people have got more into the method of spinning than formerly.

Wheat has been tried in such small quantities and the experiments have been so inconclusive owing to want of the necessary preparation of the ground etc. that there is no saying whether it will succeed or not, however there are many chances against it, as our winters are generally rainy which might rot the roots, our springs windy which might blight it and our harvests precarious which might hinder it to ripen.

Grazing as a branch of Agriculture is but little known in Orkney, cultivated grass answers tolerably well when raised with care and on a proper soil but has not yet descended to the common farmers, they use that from the meadows and in many places make a great deal of hay, notwithstanding of the numerous disadvantages they allow themselves to labour under by not having their meadow grounds properly enclosed and by not keeping them in spring grass, that all their cattle and sheep are suffered to pasture on their meadows till the end of May or beginning of June which keeps their meadows low for the season. For cutting their bog hay they have a scythe of a peculiar structure and for ought I know used nowhere else. It is very short and broad and they imagine answers much better with their uneven grounds than the long scythe would. However when in the hands of unskilful workmen they are apt to fleece the earth which, mixing with the hay, often rots it. I have added a drawing of the Orkney scythe on account of its singularity.[1]

The pasture grounds mostly lie run-rig like their lands, that is to say in undivided commons, and are commonly rendered quite bare by the undiscerningness of the farmers who yearly fleece them for their lands and this practice, destructive as it is, seems not to be much discouraged by the landlords. The hills abound everywhere with the most excellent pasture for black cattle and could maintain many more than at present are on them, however they have one objection to keeping more, that they cannot winter them and, as the country is altogether destitute of wood, there is no shelter for them in the hills. But this objection may in some measure be answered by observing they keep a useless number of horses which, when past work, serve no purpose whereas, if they could be persuaded to keep more oxen, their ends of tillage I think would be as fully answered and in a country like this where there is a continual resort of shipping, always calling for refreshment, oxen at any age would be valuable. Sheep are not so much an object at present as they seem to have been in former times, as we may see by looking into the old regulations of the country.

Potatoes thrive well in the sandy grounds of South Ronaldsha and elsewhere and are becoming pretty general, they contribute much to the saving of grain among our country people. They are sold for about 8d. or 10d. Ster. per setten or two stone.

In Orkney they make use of no sacks for preserving their grain but a sort of straw hampers by the inhabitants called cazies and make bigger or less according to the intention of them, whether for standing by way of chests in their barns or for carriage, either on horses or people's backs. In these all their grain is transported from place to place and in these they use no measures of capacity, it is weighed and the weight of the cazie subtracted which is, by the regulations of the country, to be eighteen mark.

For dressing their grain they use no vans, riddles, sieves, canvasses etc. as through the southern parts but take a cazie full of corn from the flail under their arms and go to the next dry hillock here, standing with their faces to the wind, they let the corn run out of the cazie through their fingers and, this repeated, is all the winnowing it receives (I speak in general though there may be some who perform this in a neater manner than described), the whole bad and light grain remaining amongst it, besides all the seeds and weeds etc. which must render the meal both illtasting and unwholesome, add to this that they seldom skill their bear or separate the dust from any of their grain at the mill's eye which makes the meal rough and illcoloured.

Mills are common through the Mainland and most of the Isles, though there are some places where they are obliged to use the Quern or handmill especially in grinding malt, in the use of which they are very dextrous and perform a great deal of work in a day, for it must be held continually going, which those accustomed to it do equally well with both hands, keeping it going with one and feeding it with the other, and this they continue for a long while together, notwithstanding of the severity of the labour.

In buying and selling they use no measures of capacity as in Scotland but all their grain, whether unground or made into meal, is weighed. For this end they are provided with balances of a peculiar structure which they first received from Norway then their mother country and which still retain their Norse, or Norn, names but very probably have undergone several alterations since their being introduced into the Orkneys.

These balances are both on the same principles but differ in their shape and use. That for weighing greater quantities is called a Poundler and consists of a large beam suspended near one of its ends by an apparatus something like a common balance, which divides it into two very unequal arms. Into the end of the shorter they drive a hook to support the object to be weighed. The longer arm is divided into several parts proportionally to the number of settings which may be weighed upon it. On the longer they, by a ring and chain, hang a large stone and slide it backwards or forwards according to the weight of the object. The principles are on the whole the same as the steelyard, though the divisions are different. Upon this is weighed any quantity above a setten and it takes in about 10 settens. There is a difference in that called the bear poundler from the malt one. The stone of the malt poundler ought to be a setten or twenty mark weight, while that of the bear of only sixteen mark. This, as they can only weigh pretty large quantities on it, is supported on the shoulders of a couple of assistant people by a beam run through the ring of the supporting apparatus while a third runs the ring of the weight till it stands in equilibrium and determines the quantity. The Orkney balance for smaller quantities is called a Bismore and is held and supported in one hand, while the other regulates the weight. It consists of a beam divided proportionally into marks as the poundler is into settens. One end has a large knol which serves as a counter-weight and in the other is a hook to support the object. When it is to be used, they sustain it by a bit of twine which is shifted to and again till the heavy end is in equilibrium with the object, they then count how many divisions the cord cuts and, according to the number of these, so is the number of marks, only it is to be observed that with a small space of the end every division points out two marks for, if every mark was specified, it would confuse the instrument too much but the inspection of them will supply the place of the most elaborate description. I have therefore added sketches of them both with the manner of using them[1].

The denominations in the table of Orkney weight are marks, settens or liespounds and miels for the division of which see the following table:-

Table

24 Marks make 1 setten or Liespound

6 settens or Liespounds make 1 miel.

The mark is said to contain 18 ounces but, by the custom of the country, will weigh a full pound and a half.

These weights do indifferently well for a guess and come tolerably near the weight of anything to be weighed but are not at all nice, nor are the country people nice in the use of them. When one receives a mark of meal e.g. from another, he does not think it just weight except the cord which supports the Bismore be half past the division which points out a mark, by which means he receives a mark and a half, which half is for the bag but, in all greater quantities they use the same freedom which upon the whole renders these weights but an ordinary guess. I suppose the large weight now claimed has begun from a goodwill to one another and a generous disposition amongst neighbours but is now insisted upon as a right and this vague way makes the use of these instruments dangerous to those not well acquainted with them, and precarious to all.

The only lucrative articles worth speaking of, that our Orkney farmers can make anything by, are a little grain in very good crops, a few cattle for beef, butter, stuffs, geese and feathers, which taken altogether is pretty considerable but under the disadvantages this country labours under is not of very great account to the first sellers for, as there is no established market, all these things must be sold to these merchants who have most of the trade in their hands and who, by importing the necessary indispensibly required by the needy inhabitants, are the gainers, as they take care to part with their commodities only at the highest price and, in exchange for these, take the produce of the country at the lowest, and thus the country people are obliged to deal as there is no public sale of their goods and, as they are in general in arrears to the merchants, they are often obliged to let them have what they can spare the cheaper on this account and this too is a considerable drawback on the profits of the poor sort of the inhabitants and a discouragement to industry.

I have indeed often wondered how our country people on their very small farms, considering how many particulars they have at a very dear rate to procure such as wood, iron, flax, hemp, wool, soap etc. etc., horses till of late, all which one would think should run away not only with profit but stock of their farms. I say I have often wondered how they could sustain themselves, their wives and numerous children, indeed in general living is cheap and, except what is imported, everything is easily had, their wants too excepting the above articles are but few and their living but very mean, else never could afford the prices charged on imports and, as things are, become a heavy article against them.

Among the lower rank luxury has not yet made a very rapid progress, though it seems to be upon the increase. Their diet is mean, consisting of the most simple viands and their drink milk or perhaps the pure stream however, as Buchanan observes, this is perhaps not so much their inclination as want of ability to afford more costly cheer. At particular times of the year such as Christmas, Weddings etc. they are fond of feasting and every house has something better than ordinary. At Christmas it was usual for the tenant to invite the Landlord with his family when they were treated with the best he could afford and a cheerful cup of ale to digest it, then gin, rum and brandy were but little known and better it had been they had never been so much known as they are at the present. These Boumacks are now much discontinued and there are instances where what was designed the offering of goodwill is charged as a right and these are insisted upon as an additional rent and converted into a stated charge. I have assisted at a Boumack within these few years and it was really pleasing to consider with what cheerfulness these sons of labour welcomed their master, how happy they were at the honour of his presence, with what goodwill and heartiness every heart and eye seemed to thank him for his visit, with what pleasure and satisfaction they enjoyed this little relaxation from their toil.

Now these things are much discontinued, the present generation removing themselves much farther from their tenants than their ancestors did who considered themselves as allied with and sprung from them, but indeed the better sort of people have much changed the simple manners of their ancestors and have fallen into a luxury and extravagance which their forefathers knew nothing of, who enjoyed the fruits of their labours in peace. This behaviour in the better sort has had a very bad effect upon the morals of the commons who, by this, are become envious, artful and pay their superiors but forced submission, a deal of fawning flattery without much sincerity.

1. *The drawings or sketches, if made, are not to be found in the surviving manuscript. (Ed.)*

2. These operations in husbandry are very pointedly described by an unknown writer "Of the husbandrae used by the Orchadians".

They tiell not (says he) while the spring of the yeir and as they tiell, so they saw the aittes, their pleuch is drawin by four beastis going side for side, the Caller gangis before the beastis backwart with a whipe, the halder of the pleuch lyes on with his side on the pleuch, the Culter and the Socke be not twa pound in weight.

The Ozen be zoked with cheattis and heamis and bracimis quilk they call wasiss alneit they have horns; they saw in a Criel made of the stra called ane Cassie and of ane handful they make four casts Their cornes are very guid to with Beare and Aittes all handled by men. The women neither (shake) the stra nor zit windowes the corne, they guid ther land with sea ware and lightlies midden mucke.

Chapter 13
Of the state of Trade in Orkney, of Manufactures and Fishing

We have already seen in what a miserable condition agriculture is in these islands, if we take a view of their trade, manufacturers and fishings we shall see them very little more attended to or managed with more skill or industry. The trade of this country is mostly employed in bringing us a great number of articles which we have little use for, which make us no returns and are only calculated to feed luxury or hurt the morals of the people. The spinning of linen yarn is the only kind of manufactory that has yet been introduced here and, while it continued, brought in a great deal of money but it seems to have been introduced on a wrong plan or little pains taken to make it take thoroughly and therefore seems on the decline between the merchants and the people, indeed they have got into a method of sowing lintseed which may help to keep it up in some measure. Fishing as a branch of commerce is altogether at a stand and serves no other purpose but to supply present necessity and that with fish of the most ordinary kinds, "it is only prosecuted as far as the poverty and want of the inhabitants force them from day to day to seek in the sea an addition to that scanty subsistence which the land affords them."

But let us enquire more nearly:-

The narrow bounds of this country does not, as things stand with us at present, admit of a very extensive exchange of commodities with the rest of the world, our demands being mostly for family necessities, indeed these may be made as extravagant as turn the balance against us, which we see is already the case. Our real wants are but few, consisting of several articles not the growth of our Country nor to be had in it, such as a little wood and iron, soap, salt and several other smaller articles indispensably necessary. But the wants of luxury are innumerable and swallow up all we can scrape up. A large sum is expended here yearly for articles really destructive of the health, the wealth and the morals of the public and are really of no use but to enrich a few who seem to give themselves no concern about the public good, if they can line their own coffers. Of this kind are all kinds of spirits, tobacco, tea, coffee and sugar, besides flour, biscuits, silks, velvets and fine broad cloths, which run away with the greatest part of our exports and this without any return, except we call the debauching the mind, enervating the frame, rendering the whole body of the people who are readiest to run into extremes indolent, vicious and short lived, I say except we call all this a proper return for all the toils of a year.

Our exports which balance all these articles are, in a good year, a little grain but this is precarious, a little beef, butter, oil, tallow, cowhides, calf and rabbit skins (of the last but few of late years), feathers, pens, stuffs the manufacture of the country which altogether produce a good sum, but the staple commodity of the country is kelp which is burnt in great quantities round all the shore of Orkney and not only employs a great number of hands in preparing it and thus brings in a large sum which must circulate but brings in a large profit to the proprietors. This is the most lucrative commodity our country produces and is sold to great advantage at several markets as Newcastle, Liverpool, Whitby and London, to be used in the Glass, Soap and Alum works. The price of the tun varies according to the demand but generally runs between 3 and 5 £ sterling and the whole Kelp burnt in the Country may bring about   £ sterling yearly[1]. Of old there was a salt work in the Calf of Eda which was not only a saving in this article but the produce of it was among the articles exported, but this is given over. About a century ago there was a very considerable fishery in this country which no doubt was much in Orkney's favour but this is likewise gone or at such a stand that we are like people starving in the midst of plenty. We are obliged to our neighbours of Shetland for ling though we have plenty in our own seas, to the West Highlands for herring, though at particular times of the year they swarm with us, we seldom or ever see a mackrel though they are here innumerable. In a word indolence and a slavish timidity had taken such an entire possession of both rich and poor that except there be a certainty of becoming rich at once without the least risk and with little trouble they cannot think of venturing any part of their stock, even in the most laudable scheme where they imagine the profit will be more diffusive. In short we have such a narrow mindedness that except the whole be ingrossed in the hands of a few they will take every method to render every scheme abortive but what in some or other way promotes their interest; party broils are the ruin of the country.

The nature of our country as things are at present with us forbids large importation and if we meddle in a foreign trade it must only be forced, that is to say we must only pretend to exchange the commodities of different countries with one another, without consuming any part of what they produce for, as our fisheries are employed, we have little demand for the wood of Russia, the iron of Sweden, the hemp and flax of Prussia and Dansick, we can consume but a very small quantity of the rum and sugar, the rice or other produce of the western world and, what is worse, we have no commodity to exchange for them so that, if we will have them, we must be always paying money, soon eat ourselves out and, except we either become factors or carriers for the rest of the world, we cannot pretend to do anything extensive in the way of trade. Were however a time to come in which our Countrymen, aroused from their present lethargy, would properly attend to the natural riches of these isles, then we might think to make some figure in the way of commerce. Were our fisheries of cod and ling, herrings and mackrel - not to speak of skate, coal and dogfish as well as many other kinds - all which are valuable when brought to a proper market; were these advantages followed with that spirit which here might easily be exerted, no country being better situated for the prosecution of such a probable scheme; then and not till then may we hope to see real wealth flow in upon us from all quarters; then may we hope to see our numerous bays and harbours crowded with busses, stoop and wherries of our own; our youth instead of being scattered through the world kept and employed at home, serving their native country with their present labours and ready at a call to defend her; then might we see these numerous bays and harbours, which nature never designed to be useless, crowded with thriving traders, taking and giving, there we could change commodity for commodity and thus throw the balance on our side, which is far from being so at present. If we must feed luxury then we might have the means of doing so from industry. The number of people being increased, the country would be better cultivated; both the Heritors and farmers would have their profits increased, as there would be a greater demand and surer market for what provisions they could spare; manufactures of all kinds would be improved and flourish, in a word everything would be changed for the better. Instead of the sad and lifeless appearance of both town and country we should soon see them filled with industry, upon such a scheme as this of fishing depends our country's welfare, everything else being on such a plan as scarce to be recovered without something of this kind to revive them. Husbandry is at a stand and makes no progress on account of racked rents and short leases, which keep the farmers always low and they never can weather a bad season or live without being reduced to beggary. Manufactures seem to have been introduced on a wrong plan for the poverty of this country for, instead of affording materials for the poor people to employ themselves upon and paying them for their trouble as elsewhere, the merchants, in whose hands the whole trade was, forced these poor creatures to purchase their lint and accept of what price they inclined to give for their work, which of itself was a vast drawback on this branch, for it often happens that a man or woman might be brought to work who cannot afford materials. But this is not all, this trade was knocked on the head by the payments which were made for work of this kind, these consisted of commodities only fit to add to the natural sloth and diseases of the country such as spirits, tobacco and what else of this kind the merchants could have large present profits on but were not at all calculated to render this trade either beneficial or lasting and the event has shown it has been carried on on no proper foundation. Alas things are in such a case at present through the divisions and incurable prejudices of the inhabitants, few of whom can be got to unite in any public spirited scheme that, if they do not soon mend, I can see nothing for it but the inhabitants of these isles with the others of their (now) countrymen must leave house and home and go in quest of some more hospitable clime were exerted industry will find a due reward, where example and encouragement will not be wanting to rouse them from their wonted indolence and prosperity crown their endeavours. The averting of this, and in consequence the ruining of the country by depopulation, depends altogether on a bold push from the richer few, who are only able by their influence and example to save the country from ruin.

It is far from unreasonable to think a fishery would succeed here, in the end of the last century there was a very considerable trade in this way, partly carried on by the inhabitants themselves and partly by strangers and why may we not expect the same success now if we will be at the same trouble? If this fishery was carried of old, why not now? There is no natural reason to hinder it from being pursued with the same success. They tell us indeed that the smoke of the kelp which is burnt round all the country has frightened the fish from the coast but this I dare say is only a wretched palliation of their own want of industry to which I must still attribute that scarcity in this particular article so much felt through the Orkneys. But further, it is but reasonable for us to expect success if we are as industrious as our neighbours, even at this day. We lie in the midst of a sea swarming with fish of all kinds, much nearer us, than it is to those who are daily pursuing this very branch even on our own coasts. Our good neighbours the Dutch do not seem blind to the advantages which may be made here. Yearly fleets of their fishermen cover all the fishing grounds of these seas, from the Moray Firth to the coasts of Shetland and fish with great success even under our noses. While they are supplying us at one hand with the articles of luxury they, with the other, are filching away the wealth which ought to procure these if they are so indispensably necessary to us, and they are surely right if we are so blind to our own interest as not to put in for a share.

In this trade there are many branches which, though when viewed alone seem but trifling, would with others much increase our gains. To speak of one which within these several years has brought in more real wealth to this country than all the rest put together, this is the fishing of lobsters. These swarm about the coasts, vast numbers are caught and many more might were there greater demand. The only merchants who purchase them are in London, who send or come down in vessels proper for the purpose, in a few days make their cargo and return immediately. These vessels carry from four to ten thousand at a trip and can come and go several times in a season, so that I presume one year with another there have been sent up to sixty thousand marketable lobsters which, at a penny a piece the price paid for them here, brings in no considerable sum. This branch is almost wholly confined to South Ronaldsha and other south isles but lobsters may be had everywhere through all the Orkneys.

With the same advantage and with the same case might other branches of fishery be carried on without allowing a single member of society to be idle for, while one part were employed at sea, the others might be busy in drying, salting, curing different ways as would fit particular markets, in transporting to the proper markets, whether these were the Mediterranean, the Continent or other places where they could sell to advantage.

A fishery on our own coast has this great convenience that everything about it can be carried on by our own hands and at a great deal less expence than if it were at a greater distance, besides the difference of a long run at seas in which, by accidents of weather or otherwise, vessels are often so hindered and so long in getting to the ground that everything must be conducted on a hurry and without all the caution necessary to make the voyage succeed well, not to speak of the length of the voyage which often runs away with most of the cargo. In our case all these things are obviated, while fishing on our own coasts our people can find themselves at a great deal less expence as all their necessaries come from their friends on shore. In case of bad weather or other accident they have but a very short run till they fall in with some or other of their own isles. Their friends and those especially of them who are not otherwise much employed may procure them bait, lines, hooks and other articles which elsewhere must be purchased at the dearest rate, also much time may be saved by thus fishing near our coasts which may enable us to procure still a greater quantity of sale. Our people may always be employed as well as our ships in carrying the produce of our labours to all parts of the world which, as it is done altogether on our charge and risk, must the more advance our gain.

When trade of any kind takes thoroughly it necessarily draws a vast concourse of different manufactures to supply it with implements, but though all these at first perhaps must be purchased with us, in time we might see them all thriving in this corner. In fishing a very great variety of necessaries is required as hooks, lines, nets, ropes, ships etc. etc. all which are the work of different mechanics and might in time be the work of our own people or others whom the hope of gain would draw hither to settle and, becoming naturalised, would be still a valuable acquisition as by their means the number of people would be increased and all ranks would find the benefit of their settling among us.

Were our fishing to succeed we would no doubt have demands upon the rest of the world as our country cannot supply us with all things requisite for such a scheme, but we could then afford it, while we have saleable commodities and these of such a kind as could not fail meeting a good market, there is little fear of our not being able to answer all demands upon us, besides saving a good deal for our pains and which we would then deserve. Though our Islands produce no fir, hemp or iron, yet we could purchase those things out of the profits of our trade and no people in the world are more capable of being taught to construct these into ships, sails, busses, boats, masts and cordage or more fitted to endure the fatigue attending such a scheme, the profits of which would soon reconcile them to the pains of it.

It is to no purpose the Government has provided for the security of this branch, by giving us an exclusive right to the fishings of these seas, if our countrymen in general and we in particular take no care to avail ourselves of this privilege and to insist on the exertion of these laws for excluding others who daily take it out of our hands, but it seems to be a general disease of the Britons that they despise everything that is easily come at, which may be at their own doors, and think nothing valuable but what is brought from the farthest corners of the globe. French fropperies are yearly imported at a vast expence, though it is certain we have a very thriving growth of these amongst ourselves. Flanders lace and other trumpery are brought in at all risk while our own country manufactures are neglected. The seas of Newfoundland and Iceland are ransacked for cod, while our own are a desert. Herrings are brought from Sweden to supply our West India market, which surely could be done out of these swarms which annually visit our country. In a word though things have need of improvement in general yet no where have they greater reason to wish for another scene than among our Orkney isles, where all that was said above of fishing is but merely ideal and must be the work of time, patience and perseverance as well as good sense and spirit.

1. *Low has omitted to include the actual sum in pounds sterling. (Ed.)*

Chapter 14
Of the other advantages of Orkney

Till of late years these islands have been little known or frequented, by many they were thought barbarous and a very insignificant part of the kingdom. This was not the case of old, these islands were then of great importance to their masters the Kings of Norway. The Danes and Norwegians were sensible of what advantage they were to them in their incursions into Britain. They found succour from them in their expeditions thither and to them they fled in case of defeat. The Romans, if we can believe Cutrapius, Beda and Orosius and other writers, did not think them below their notice but enumerated them amongst the kingdoms they at that time possessed and we afterwards find them reckoned in the division of the Empire among the children of Constantine the Great and with other kingdoms which fell to the lot of his son Constantinople. They are now much fallen from their ancient reputation and have never as yet been thought of so much importance to Great Briatain but, if their natural advantages were duly attended to and applied to use, they might still be of as great service to us as ever to the Norwegians.

We have seen before that they abound in the most excellent harbours, for the convenience of trades and, of consequence, there has been for some years past a vast resort of shipping to all parts of the country who put in on their voyages from all parts of the world, No part therefore can be a more proper place for a general rendez-vous for the trade between America and the northern parts of Europe, especially in time of war, because these islands lie much out of the way of privateers and then the trade is much safer than coming through the Channel.

In no place can they find refreshments more readily or cheaper which is a vast advantage to sailors in long voyages. Here might be constructed warehouses for all kinds of goods fit for the northern markets, here all the northern fishermen might find people to navigate their ships in times of strait or might have storehouses for materials ready for them in case of accidents or, if they found it inconvenient to run to their own ports, here they might lay up their ships for winter, as well as make their oil and transport it in smaller vessels to the proper market. Here they can be provided with carpenters to refit their ships and numbers of stout hands ready to engage at a days warning, as is yearly experienced by the Iceland fishermen who always depend upon Orkney for part of their crews and the Hudson Bay Company, ever since their institution, have manned their forts almost all with Orkney men, besides vast numbers who go through the whole world in quest of bread but would much rather stay nearer home had they a prospect of succeeding here.

In time of war there is no place better fitted for stationing Guardships for the protection of the northern parts of the Kingdom or the trade which in time of war comes mostly this way, against privateers or a threatened invasion, the access to the eastward and westward being easy and every passage well known. Here the old Norwegians and the Danes, the once haughty masters of Great Britain, taken with these very advantages, fixed their general rendez-vous in their attempts upon the northern and western parts of Britain and Ireland and, their having these isles so near, often contributed most to the success of their designs as from thence they could always be certain of help in time of need and here they were sure of an asylum in case they were worsted as was often the case, when their chiefs always fled hither with the remains of their fleets or armies and here wither procured reinforcements or awaited for these from their Kingdoms.

There can be no place better situated for all the purposes of trade, but especially fishing on the British coasts, no place lies more central for all the most noted fishings on the east and west coasts of Scotland, its own and those of Shetland. Here therefore might be a convenient store or place of necessaries for the use of the British fishery as this is the most commodious place for the shipping employed in it to resort to. These islands have for this purpose many advantages over the other northern isles, as they are better situated for importing fishing materials and exportation of the fish. Storehouses placed here would serve the purpose of those placed in many different parts, because all vessels from one side of Scotland to the other or from the Shetland Isles must necessarily run through or very near the Orkneys. They are situated within a day or two's sail from all the fishings on the coasts and from them a more ready intercourse with the rest of Britain can be had than any of the other isles are capable of, besides the easy access of their produce whether from sea or land.

Any one who inclines to try any new project here will have this encouragement that neither work nor provisions are dear and men are to be got in great plenty, as many here want employment in any way; they could be set to work in the mines, if those of lead and iron were found valuable enough to defray the charges of working or, in a word, in any branch as, with a little pains, they would soon become handy enough, all which renders any design of this kind both easy and practicable.

It is hard to say whether our mines would take or not, no conclusive trials have been made of them, those adventurers who have wrought in them, seldom continue so long as to make any progress or indeed to begin a scheme of that kind. Whether there are regular veins of the more valuable metals or not here is doubtful, none such as yet having been discovered, but in many places large beds of metal are found and to appearance rich, as may be seen from some specimens which have been dug up from the lead mines of Hoy and Stromness. It is probable in future times these may add to the wealth of Orkney when industry prevails more and timidity less, but at present, if they are valuable, their wealth is buried without much appearance of our attempting to disinter it. The iron mines of Hoy proceed in regular and large veins but our distance from the foundries renders it almost useless, as it can scarce clear the charge of work and freight.

We have seen already the soil is good and proper for grain, which is the more observable when we consider the number of people that are maintained upon their small farms, the least of which are occupied by at least five or six young and old, besides their horses which are not the least extensive, for such farms as these they perhaps pay no more than a miel (Orkney boll) of Malt or Meal, a goose or two and a few pence in money, upon which however in good years they could maintain their families and keep both ends together besides paying their rents. There are perhaps about ten thousand people on the Mainland (besides the inhabitants of Kirkwall and Stromness), the yearly rent of the whole island is not above three thousand pounds sterling. Now, if we can suppose ten thousand people maintained upon the produce of this island in the way that agriculture is carried on in this country, this may easily show us that it is not the fault of the soil and that, by improvement, much more grain could be raised and many more people maintained and which all makes for us a case for trade reviving in any future period.

All the rocks round the country are clothed with sea ware, from which is made vast quantities of Kelp, which indeed is the only commodity we have had these many years worth speaking of and has held our heads above water, else it is hard to say what we might have been driven to, I suppose to seek our fortunes with our unhappy brethren, hundreds of whom we see yearly forced to fly their country from the terrors of oppression.

A History of Orkney

The History of Orkney

Contents

Appendix

View of Kirkwall, the capital of the Orkney Islands

A History of Orkney

Introduction

After thus giving a short description of the Isles of Orkney, as divided into land and water, islands greater and less; having also noticed the inhabitants - their genius and disposition - the present state of art and manufactures among them etc., it will be necessary in pursuance of our plan of a general history to enquire concerning the first and most ancient inhabitants as far as probability in history can lead us, and also of the more modern possessors as we may be directed by history. This part may be divided into three periods.

First from the peopling of the islands to their being subjected to the Kingdom of Norway which may be called the uncertain or fabulous period.

Second from their coming into the hands of the Norwegians, to their being pled to our King James the Third by Christian, King of Norway, which period is far less involved in darkness as being connected with the history of the countries and the relations made in general by eyewitnesses of the transactions they relate.

As to the third period, it is authenticated by Charters, Contracts and other public Records.

In every one of these periods mention will be made of the monuments that still remain of the most ancient times and the whole, as far as possible, reduced to an uniform series of events.

Chapter 1

Historians are very much at a loss whence to bring the first inhabitants of Orkney. None that I know have given any good account of this, indeed the time when it happened is now so obscured by the rust of ages, that it cannot be traced with any degree of certainty. Our Scottish historian Buchanan is entirely at a loss about this and, only with others, imagines they came from Germany but which of the numerous German tribes is not easily investigated. Even they who more professedly set themselves to write the history of the Orkneys, give us but very confused notion of these times, differing very much in several circumstances, specially what we find transmitted to posterity concerning these isles by writers of different nations, each of whom had very probably different purposes in their relations.

The first period in which we find the history of Orkney connected with that of Scotland is in the time of Ewen, second King of Scots, about the year B.C. 29, though it is certain they must have been inhabited long before this time, as is evident from the figure they then made in the world, being governed by a King and making war upon the neighbouring people which is never the business of a colony in its infancy if not acting on the defensive.

The Roman historians take notice of Orkney but many of them in such a manner as leaves us room to suspect the truth of their accounts, especially as they contradict one another in the plainest terms. Europius writes that the Romans in the time of Claudius added the Orkneys to the empire but how shall we reconcile this with what Tacitus relates, that these were altogether unknown to the Romans till the time of Agricola who first sent a fleet round Britain, which probably discovered and overran these islands. Juvenal in his second Satire takes notice of their being conquered by the Romans under Domitian about the year of Christ 81.

Littora Juvernae promovimus et modo captas Orcades

Now he lived under the Emperor Adrian or about the year of Christ 118. It is then scarce probable that these islands were altogether uninhabited and overrun with rushes and other weeds in the time of Solinus who possibly lived but a few years before him. We shall have another opportunity to enquire how these differing accounts may be reconciled and in the meantime go on to consider the accounts other writers have left us of this matter.

Thormodus Torfaeus, the Norwegian writer of the affairs of Orkney (Ch.2) places the discovery of these islands at a great distance from any of the periods we have before taken notice of. According to the quotations he makes use of, the discovery of Orkney happened in the year of the world 3563, or as others 3588, anti Christ 375, which is about 55 years after the period in which our greatest sticklers for the antiquity of the Scots nation place the commencement of its monarchy, a time in which, I am much afraid, ignorance and barbarity too much prevails to transmit to posterity annals that can much be depended upon; to omit the arguments of those who explode the history of Gurguncius (in whose time this discovery happened), and very many other names both Scottish and British and cut off many years from their antiquity. We hear nothing of Orkney from this till the year before Christ 260, when we are informed that an Orkney king made war upon the Sicambri or Franks, probably the old inhabitants of Guelderland which, if we can depend upon what has been said before of their discovery, shows that they had been peopled soon after their discovery by Biscayers or Gurguncius.

Here again is another large space of time in which historians are silent in relation to the transactions of these parts, nor do we hear them again mentioned till the time of Ewen, the second King of Scotland who, according to chronology, died 29 years before the birth of Christ after a reign of 17 years. In one or other of these, for historians are silent as to the particular year, the Orcadians under their king Belus, made an attempt upon Scotland, but he was met by Ewen so unexpectedly that he was soon put to flight and, after being long tossed about, his men being mostly killed, he laid violent hands upon himself lest he should fall into the hands of the conqueror. Mr. Wallace from the Scottish history takes notice of this Belus and pretends that in his time there was a stone to be seen in the kirk of Birsa having his name Belus engraved on it in ancient characters; but in this he is in some part mistaken, but though I cannot controvert the being of such a person as Belus after the testimony of so many writers[1] which record his existence, I think there is no danger in saying that the characters engraving on that stone are no memorial of him for, as it still remains, a single look will convince anyone that the characters are not above a century or two old, besides it is not *Belus* but *Bellus* and seems to be a fragment of some more modern gravestone. The stone is not built into the church wall of Birsa[2], but for the satisfaction of the curious who may not have an opportunity to examine it, I have given an exact copy of what it contained on it

About this time or somewhat later Caractacus reigned in Scotland, who was carried prisoner to Rome by Claudius Caesar; and in his reign authors will have it that the Romans conquered Orkney and carried their king Ganus to Rome where he was led in triumph with other noble Britons; whence Wallace grounds this story I have not had an opportunity to enquire[3], or if it is confounded with the story of Caractacus of whom the same particulars are narrated by Tacitus the historian of these times, to whom most credit is to be given. Buchanan's opinion is that we are not rashly to credit what writers have said concerning the conquering of the Orkneys by Claudius, because Tacitus affirms that before the time of Agricola these islands were so far from being conquered that they were unknown to the Romans. The only way we can reconcile these contradictions is to suppose that Claudius might have discovered them or made some trifling inroads in them, but that these were so very insignificant that they were immediately abandoned and the very memory of them lost before the time of Agricola and this is the more probable as the time that Claudius stayed in Britain, which was but six months, could not allow his conquests to be very extensive amongst these people that were then without the pale of the empire, nor could he use the proper means to secure these. Upon the whole then we may venture to affirm that Agricola's fleet in prosecuting the discovery of Britain were the first Roman ships which had attempted a seduction of the Orkneys. Whether the Romans continued long here or not history, as far as I can find, does not inform us but I should rather think not, as what his fleet did in its passage in several places were rather descents than regular invasions; nor can I hear of any traces of Roman monuments that can with certainty be called such to be found in Orkney; indeed Wallace takes notice of a place in Shapinsa called Agricola very probably from the loss of some of his fleet there, but this might have happened even though there had been no intention of an invasion in the course of their route round Briatain. Never could I learn with any certainty that any works, urns etc. had been found in Orkney and, though we find it among other great kingdoms in the division of the empire, no historian informs us whether the Romans ever drew anything by way of tax or otherwise from it or that they ever placed any officer in it. So that upon the whole, we may reasonably suppose, though Agricola's ships may have made some stay here and given time to his men to overrun all or part of the country, yet that it was soon left with the other northern conquests made by that famous general.

The concurring testimony of so many writers and visitors of these islands prove that they were inhabited very early, it therefore remains to enquire by the feeble lights we have who were the first inhabitants and here we are so much stopt by uncertainty as before and indeed the matter does not admit of any degree of proof, especially as former writers are so much at a loss about it; none of them agreeing who may have been the first inhabitants of these isles and indeed in circumstances which happened at such a distant period when the northern world was so much wrapped up in ignorance how to transmit the history of their actions to posterity and so little known to the politer nations by whom they were altogether reckoned savage and barbarous; I say, these things considered, it is no wonder at this time this of the first peopling of Orkney is so much wrapped in obscurity. Let us examine what the historians have said. All or most allow that the Orkneys were first peopled from Germany, but cannot agree which of the many nations which then possessed it furnished the colony. Cambden supposes it was the Pechts who first sat down here, and indeed Orkney is frequently called by our historians "The ancient kingdom of the Pights" which seems to confirm this opinion. Our Orkney traditional accounts too agree that this country was inhabited by the same people. However tradition here is not much to be depended on, if there were no other countenance for third opinion; but the many monuments both of a public, as temples, and of a private nature, as these buildings, called by our inhabitants Pights houses (of which in course), which are found scattered up and down the country and similar to those found on the continent confessedly the work of the first inhabitants of the north, are a great reason for thinking the inhabitants of these isles drew their origin from them as they did their manners and customs.

Here it will not be amiss to make a short enquiry who these Pechts or Pights were, seeing they are so much talked of by our historians, and who seem altogether to have confounded them with the ancient inhabitants of Britain Picti from the custom they had of painting their naked bodies and continuing to do after they were by them driven northward. Buchanan takes a good deal of pains in tracing their origin but he too seems too much carried away by the similarity of names and that circumstances of painting or scarifying their bodies, which I imagine can be at most an uncertain proof of the origin of any people but rather common to all nations in their savage state; as we find the Americans were used to paint themselves both to render them terrible in war and others to render themselves in time of peace agreeable to their friends and mistresses. Likewise we read of the inhabitants of the Cape of Good Hope that they are every moment anointing themselves with soot, grease or such like beautifying unguents; ornamental in their opinion, however this may be controverted by the rest of the world. In a word all nations in their savage or barbarous state have mostly the same notion of finery but none can judge from thence the origin of any one with the least degree of certainty. The Pechts were said to mark their bodies with figures wrought in the skin by the help of iron instruments but neither is this to be taken as a characteristic custom of any particular people, but late discoveries have shown that there are nations in the South Sea which have the very same custom, but from this it would be very hard to deduce the genealogy of these people from any European nation, because they agree in this single particular, which one would think not at all conclusive for proving the origin of a nation.

Buchanan's opinion that they were sprung from the Gauls who had their habitation about the Baltic Sea or on the Danube is likewise, I think, liable to great objection, for though we are informed by history that the Gauls made settlements in the provinces bordering on this sea, yet the best ancient historians precisely mark the great difference there was between their manners and the other nations which inhabited in their neighbourhood. It is evident by history that the Gauls and Germans were very distinct people, differing in all their constitutions though they might agree on such trivial customs as were common to all the nations of the world in their barbarous circumstances. The Gauls were descended from the Celts from whence were sprung the Irish, Welsh and Scots Highlanders and several others; to this day, notwithstanding the various changes they have undergone by war and otherwise, visibly different from other nations of Europa descended from the Teutons, and which may be seen by comparing what we yet observe of the manners of the people aforesaid with the Germans, Danes, Swedes, Norwegians or, to come nearer home, those of the Highland and Lowland Scots, between the last of whom the difference is so visible as at once to show they have drawn their origin from different sources. If however we compare the manners and customs of the nations sprung from each of these different races with one another, we shall find a manifest similarity, for example if we compare the Welsh with the Scotch Highlanders or with the inhabitants of Brittany or any other nation of Celtic origin we shall find but accidental differences and these, everything considered, but trifling, their language is intelligible to one another, their persons are much like and their ancient customs the same. But if we go a little farther and make a comparison of the Welsh with the English, the Highlander with the Lowland Scots; with the Germans, Holsteiners or other Danes, we shall find not the least resemblance, their every inclination and pursuit differs and all their attachments further than what may be common to all nations dissimilar.

If we trace the first inhabitants by their language we shall find here too new proofs that these were not according to Buchanan's position Celts or Gauls, as nothing of the old language of Orkney is similar to or deducible from the Celtick; even Buchanan himself tells us they spoke the Gothick tongue, (I suppose he means a dialect of it) which, if we consider the structure of the specimen given us by Wallace and compare it with others of Gothick derivation we shall observe the difference to be rather the effect of time, separation from the countries whence they drew their language or such like, than any radical disagreement and easily restorable to the northern language whence it was taken; but if we compare it to any specimen of Celtick whether ancient or modern to attempt to find a Mother Language amongst these, we shall soon see such an attempt to be fruitless, nothing can reconcile them. But here it may be objected that the language used by the inhabitants of Orkney some time ago, and called by them the Norn, was not the language of the first colonies, nor can be proved to be that of the Pechts, even though it were admitted they were the first settlers here. To this it may be answered that though the language may have suffered several changes and corruptions by the chances of war or the accession of new settlers, yet it is probably the bulk of it has till of late been preserved; for though Orkney might have been conquered by divers people, yet this might not affect the language, as we have several instances in history of the conqueror sitting down with the conquered and conforming to their customs and admitting their language. Indeed this seems to have been generally the case where the conquered were not wholly extirpated or forced to change their habitations; thus we see in the history of the revolutions in England when the Saxons, Angles and Jutes came over and settled in Britain, they totally exterminated the former inhabitants and forced them altogether to the more mountainous parts of the island where they still continue and, having but very little intercourse with them, allowing few or none of them to remain among them, they adopted few of their customs, laws or language, hardly retaining so much as the names of the places. But how different was from this was the case when the Normans conquered England, they sat down in the midst of the conquered and, though they attempted at first to introduce their language, laws and customs yet by degrees these were laid aside and, together with the revival of their customs and language, the English recovered the superiority and saw their language and manners adopted by their conquerors and their descendents. It would be useless to bring more examples of this behaviour of the conquerors to the conquered, suffice it to say that strangers wheresoever they came, if they allow the natives to remain with them, generally embrace their method of life. But to the other part of the objection whether the language of Oekney was that of the Pechts or whether introduced in later times, Venerable Bede affirms the language of the Picts was different from that of the Britons, Scots and other nations then the possessors of Britain; which Buchanan, to cover his favourite system, would make us believe consisted only in a difference of dialect, but his arguments in support of this does not seem sufficiently conclusive, for he affirms this of Bede to be similar expression with those made use of by the Greeks when speaking of different dialects and by Caesar in the beginning of his commentaries; that the Greeks made use of a phrase similar to this when speaking of their different dialects I shall not dispute but shall endeavour to show that the passage of Caesar has been misunderstood when led as a proof that the three nations of Gaul were the same people and used the same language only varying in dialect and that this way of speaking is to be considered as similar to that of Bede. The passage in Caesar is as follows: "*Gallia est omnis divisa in partes tres quarum unum incolunt Belgae, aliam Aquitani, tertiam qui ipsorum lingua Celtae, nostra Galli appellantur. Hi omnes lingua, Institutines, legibus inter se differunt etc.*" in which I should imagine we are not to understand Caesar as saying the Belgae or the Aquitani were Celts or Gauls but that they inhabited part of the country called, in general, Gaul and from whence they had probably before forced the inhabitants to remove; so far is he from saying that the Belgae were Celts that he tells us in another place expressly that they were from Germany who, having long ago passed the Rhine, had fixed their seats there, pleased with the fertility of the country after they had expelled the Gauls, the former inhabitants of these parts. As for the Aquitani whose language is said by Strabo to differ from that of the other Gauls but a little; this may be accounted for from a greater and longer intercourse with the common inhabitants of Gaul which might have brought their language to a greater conformity and nearer resemblance when Strabo, than it had when Caesar, resided in Gaul; thus is Buchanan's evidence which he brings to corroborate his opinion weakened and may be more so from many other parts of Caesar's Commentaries, where it is evident that the Germans from whom the Belgae sprung were then considered as a very different people. This of dialects seems to be the only refuge for those who set up for the Celtick system (may I call it). Accordingly a modern author[3] pretends the language of Gaul differed only in dialect from that of Germany, but the absurdity of this can in no way be more easily proved than the inspection of any of the modern languages descended from these very ancient tongues[4]. But to return to our Pechts. A modern writer[5] of the history of Scotland in the Life of Kenneth the second tells us "that a few of the Scots who spoke the Pictish language had the address to carry off Alpine's head from the capital of the Picts" etc. This too, which I suppose is from Fordun, proves the difference of their language, for only a few it seems could speak that of the Pights and even these had need of all their address with this advantage to compass their design; now if it had differed only in dialect it is probable that all or most of the Scots could express themselves in that language, as we see to be the case with the Welsh, Irish and Highlanders etc. who understand one another on ordinary occasions but the difference here seems to have been greater and the Pictish language must have been acquired by only a few and that by time and pain. But I expect it will be asked what has now become of the Pictish language, now that it is nowhere to be found; to this the answer would be very easy if we could believe with some that the whole race was extirpated by Kenneth the second, namely that it was lost with the nation but such a resolution, as it would have been a disgrace upon human nature, so it would have been unworthy and contrary to the character of a man so truly grave as Kenneth was. It is therefore more probable that this politic prince only put to death such of them as he dreaded might attempt new disturbances, but spared the gross of the people and, when we consider the genius , language and inclination of the peoples who to this day possess the counties of Angus, Mearns and, in a word, the whole east side of Scotland with the Orkneys, which are allowed to have been Pictish territories, it will not, I should imagine, be contrary to probability to suppose that these people are the descendants of the original Pights and that theirs is the original of what we call the broad Scotch which, though it has no doubt undergone a greater change, is resolved into the northern languages as well as the Norn or Old Language of the Orkneys, probably their language mixed with more words of Norwegian than the former. It now remains that we enquire what was the reason of the name which these people took to themselves and from which of the Teutonic nations they in all probability came. The name was probably significative of something very remarkable and observable in the temper, disposition or inclination of these people, accordingly when we look into the history of the northern nation, in the earliest periods, we shall find nothing more remarkable than a passion for war that was not to be satisfied, their whole life from their very infancy was passed amidst the din of arms; they were often born in a camp and spent their whole lives there; all their exercises were designed to harden their bodies either for war or peace, they were mostly of another kind, and designed either to incite them to perform great action or to record these by songs; it is then more probable that they gave a name from their favourite profession and in this we are countenanced by Verstegan[6] who informs us they called themselves Phightians that is the Fighters or warlike nation, an appellation justly due to all the northerns, but probably taken by them in their voyage in quest of seats by way of distinction or to give them the greater weight among the nations they expected to fall in with. The resemblance then of this, their assumed name, seems to have drawn away the writers of the history of Britain both Roman and British and led them into the error of their having derived their name from their painted bodies, a custom which, if these people had, they probably learned from the inhabitants of Britain. All authors who speak of the Pights represent them as a most beautiful and yet robust race of men. Verstegan says they were tall and strong bodied and of a very fair complexion and Boethius "quod erant corporibus robustissimus candidisque", all of which agrees in great measure with the Orkney people but entirely with the northern nations to this day. From what part of Germany these Pechtae came is still a question which is difficult to resolve, as the history of their emigration is so much lost that scarce a trace of it remains. The names of places and men still to be found in this country make it probable that they sat down here first, as the name they have left to the firth dividing Orkney from Scotland gives us reason to think it was by this passage they first entered Scotland. The verses of Claudian seem to mean that the Pights were then possessors of Orkney together with the Saxons, likewise Germans, and indeed some imagine that these people came from the Saxons and spoke the old Saxon language, a proposition far from improbable and not contradicted by the mutilated state we find the language in among them and the many words from the Norwegian and Icelandic introduced into it; for we must attend to the long time these islands were under the dominion of the Norwegians and how much its history is connected with that of Norway. In all the disturbances of government in Norway the discontented commonality fled to Orkney and Iceland and these islands were the ordinary stations of their pirates, so that it no wonder that in such a constant intercourse of these people the ancient language would undergo a change, though the ancient structure of it was not destroyed, nay some traces of the Saxon are discernible in these short specimens still preserved to us. Besides we cannot depend upon the genuineness of these specimens now to be got, as it is only to be found among the oldest and most illiterate of the common people none of whom can express themselves in it on the most ordinary occasion and cannot be supposed to give us it in its true orthography or idiom, but must mix it with many new words, especially as it has been these many years gradually wearing out; all which leaves it possible that if we had specimens of it before it began to be mixed with Norwegian, Icelandic etc. we should still have found a greater similitude between it and the old languages of Germany and of consequence been better able to trace its origin. From the above enquiry we may, without great danger of error, conclude that the inhabitants of the Orkneys, if Pights, were not Gauls according to Buchanan, but of German origin, probably a branch of these people who then inhabited the northern parts of Germany now called Upper Saxony who, having nothing to detain them in any place, betook themselves to their fortunes and, leaving a few of their number to people these islands, or after they came too narrow for them, sent those they had to spare into Scotland. As they had their all to hazard in the chance of war and their fortunes to acquire by the sword, they, without doubt, gave themselves a name expressive of this circumstance and applied to them by other nations without meaning but with one perhaps best adapted to their opinion of them and perhaps led by the sound though they lost the sense, as seems to have been the case with the Romans and others who wrote in Latin, they gave them a name not corresponding with their views and therefore confounded them with others whom their Roman name would suit better.

Besides what has been advanced above, the Orkney old language must have suffered a vast change from these islands continuing under the Norwegians for more than 600 years; even as we see that language has now almost worn out in a period about half the length of the former.

In this period we may probably place the building of these towers called Pights' houses or castles; ruins of which are so frequent round the shores, on the hills, in the lochs and other chosen situations in Orkney and Shetland as well as on the Main of Scotland where the Pictish dominion reached. These must have been the forts as well as the watchtowers of that era as they are all within sight of one another, some of them situated on the tops of mountains, others on the summits of stupendous rocks overhanging the ocean but all within sight of one another so that the alarm of an enemy might be the sooner spread round the country.

The Barrows or Burial Hillocks so frequent in this country may be placed about this era or rather a little later, especially some of those found in Westra which shall be described in their proper place, These are generally vast heaps of earth surrounding a stone coffin, in which is enclosed the body. Sometimes the coffin is roughly built round with coarse stone and afterwards covered with earth; oft times more than one coffin is enclosed in the same barrow. The bodies are all naked, though in some I have seen opened, coarse bags full of bones have been found. Beads of coal and stone, swords of iron and bond, helmets and in one a glass cup, are usually found in these cemeteries. Some of the tumuli are surrounded with stones set in the earth, others without. One in Birsa parish has two stones set upright on its top. They are of many sizes but all of them have been originally round. All of them are on dry places, many of them on sandy downs or hard brakes but none on wet ground.

It is to this period we must attribute these monuments of the rude though vast strength of our ancestors; these circles of stones which are here and there to be found through the country, most of them now in a state of decay, though this must have been the work of ages, as some of them yet remaining seem to be still able to defy the efforts of time for hundreds of years to come.

The most remarkable and entire of these monuments are to be seen on the main or largest island at the bridge which joins the Lochs of Harray and Stenness. To the westward of that bridge stands a circle of stones of moderate height, none of them exceeding twelve or fourteen feet, many much less, several broken and fallen down, while of others the stump or hole where they have been place is only discernible. Around and on the outside there is a pretty broad and deep ditch which probably has been formerly deeper but the growth of the moss has filled it up. The diameter of the circle is about 60 fathoms which may soon let us see that it has not been a camp as some pretend, as it must be small army indeed that could be included in such narrow bounds. Between the circle and the loch to the east side are two small hillocks or tumuli with as many at some distance to the westward side said to be composed of ashes, however this is a mistake for they are of the very same kind as the earth of the ditch being fragments of a shelvy brittle rock and probably have been formed of gravel etc. out of the ditch when it was made and thrown there to be out of the way, though there is nothing more probable than that they have served other purposes also, as we shall have occasion to enquire. At the east end of the bridge stands a semicircle of much more remarkable stones; as most of these are eighteen or twenty feet above ground and very massy in their dimensions; the largest five foot and a half broad and eighteen inches thick. But if we consider that these may be as much under the ground as above or at least a third of the whole length, we shall find their bulk and weight immense and, with astonishment, behold the works of our ancestors which we, assisted by all the powers of art, would scarce undertake to imitate. The diameter of this semicircle is ninety-six feet and the stones, though placed in a circular manner, are at so unequal distances as give room to think there have been more of them than is now to be seen. The drawing[9] shows these stones in their present state which is four entire and one broken. It is not ditched about like the former but surrounded with an artificial mound partly raised on the live earth as the other was cut from it. Here the circle has never been completed, both the position of the stones and the surrounding work show that the design has been semicircle; neither are there any mounds so near this as the former, the nearest being a quarter of a mile or more distant. Near the circle are several stones set on end without any regular order or several of them, being so much broken, hinder us to see the design of them; also at a little distance from the semicircle stands a pretty broad stone probably broke from its original height, with a round hole cut through it not in the middle but to one side of it, very much worn as if by constant friction in tying any thing by this hole and at the end of the bridge is a very large one equal to any of the semicircle. The drawing will give a tolerable idea of the above which are the most remarkable of their kind in Orkney; however we find in many places else relicks of such like constructions but more demolished. In several places we find circles enclosed with a ditch but without the range of stones; at a place about a quarter of a mile distance from the circle I have just described, where we find a small area surrouded with a ditch and a single tumulus a few paces distant but without the least appearance of stones. Also among the corn grounds of a town called Ireland I observe a circle exactly similar to the last, without stones, and indeed the like is to be found in several other parts of the country but whether these have ever been enclosed as the first with a row of stones I am uncertain, as not the least remains of them are to be found.

Many very large single stones are likewise scattered up and down the Mainland and isles, as in Birsay and Cairston, that near Turmiston in the parish of Stenness, others in the moors of Harra and many in the different isles, the history of all which is quite lost, teaching us that the most famous monuments of the rude ages are but ill fitted to preserve the memory of the most glorious action without the help of the finest arts and can, at most, when their traditions are gone, present us with only the effects of that great bodily strength which could erect such enormous masses.

If a modern Mechanick was to raise such vast columns he would require a preparation of numerous machines of masts, ropes, pulleys, levers and other instruments; but if enqire for these among the northern nations in former times we shall find ourselves very much disappointed, they were too much led by their passion for warlike matters to attend to the more studious pains which the sciences require, their lives were either passed in the rugged scenes of the camp or the utmost stretch of laziness; all their actions behooved to be performed by efforts of strength and not by a studied process of industry. The question then will be by what machinery these simple workmen erected these most unwieldy masses? To answer this in terms of art, probably nothing more than the lever and the wedge, tipping by its own weight and directed by their efforts assisted with a few rollers to transport them from the quarry.

After with vast pains they had raised these stones from the quarry which probably has not been far distant, they no doubt pulled them along with such ropes as they had, possibly thongs of hide, (clapping pieces of wood under them to make them slide easily) till they came to the place they were to stand. Here was a new task and the most difficult of the whole, where main force could not avail, as not so many hands could find room to act as were necessary to move such large pieces; then it was requisite that art should supply what was wanting in mere force to perform. Having pitched upon the situation and figure they were to be placed in, the workmen probably dug out the hole for each stone and built at each mound of earth in form of an inclined plane to the top of which they rolled the stone, then cut away so much of the front of the inclined plane till the stone dipping by its own weight and directed by their efforts sunk into the den prepared for it.

After this guess at the manner of their erection it comes next to be enquired into the purpose of these monuments of antiquity. Here as in most cases relative to our antiquities we have nothing in the tradition or accounts of these islands that can be depended upon to assist us, this must be sought from the history of kindred nations. Tradition in Orkney gives us to understand they were designed for religious purposes and to this day affixes a sort of reverence to these places but fails when it is asked by whom or in honour of what deity they were constructed.

Wallace from Boethius tells us such circles as these were called by the people the temples of the Gods and were first ordained in Scotland by King Mainus. But if we look into the history of the northern nations we shall find such circles as these adapted to other purposes than the service of the Gods. The excellent author of the Northern Antiquities[7] tells us, in such like places the Ancient Danes elected their kings and held their courts on extraordinary occasions. Speaking of the elections he says: "they still show the places where these were made; and as Danemark was for a long time divided into three kingdoms we find accordingly three principal monuments of this custom; the one near Lunden in Scanis, the other at Lujra or Lethra in Zealand and the third near Viburg in Jutland. These monuments whose rude bulk has preserved them from the ravages of time are only vast unhewen stones, commonly twelve in number set upright and placed in form of a circle. In the middle is erected a stone much larger than the rest, on which they made a seat for their King. The other stones served as a barrier to keep off the populace and marked the place of those whom the people had appointed to make the election. They treated also in the same place of the most important affairs. But, if the king chanced to die in war or at a distance from home, they formed upon the spot a place after the same model by bringing together the largest stones they could find. The principal chiefs got upon these stones and with a loud voice delivered their opinions."

The last paricular may account for several of these lesser enclosures we observe in several places, which seem to have been erected more in a hurry than the others, not near so regular nor ditched about as they are.

In the temples of the north we find the altar placed on a little hill, either natural or artificial, formed of several stones supporting the table or flat stone which made the upper part of it. This was surrounded by the circle of stones, within which stood the altar on which sacrifice was offered. In these we find in Orkney there is no trace of an altar within the circle or pale, near it, or on the stones mentioned before, at a small distance from the circle. The holed stone seems plainly to have been for securing the sacrifice. Some have imagined the circle should have been nearer, one to the other, to have been places of religious worship, nay some travellers who have visited the Orkney islands have imagined the circle was rather a place of justice than a temple. But, with submission, I should think the apparatus within and round the ditch would soon let us understand the purpose of their erection. For first the ditch and upright stones were assuredly for the purpose of marking the sacred ground, the neighbouring hillocks nearly corresponding with the four points, might be for the purpose of sacrificing at different times of the day or night, as the neighbouring stones might support a table, though this is now gone, for preparing the sacrifice; all particulars necessary in a heathen temple. Probably their shape may have been of use in pointing out the intention and tell us that in the circle the worship in honour of the Sun - confessedly an idol of the Germans - was performed; while the semicircle was dedicated to the Moon; both excellently situated in the openest, plainest spot in the Mainland, where the fullest view of these bodies could be had from their rising to their setting.

These are "the Circle of Loda and the mossy stones of power" but alas the echoing woods "being along the coast" have now vanished, leaving us no trace of them behind.

Near the circle is a series of tumuli of a much less size than the four above mentioned, being entirely sepulchral, many of them have been searched into and possibly it has been here Wallace's fibulae were found.

There is some reason to think the Saxons likewise had a footing in Orkney and Caithness, and this from Claudian lines before quoted, as well as several names in Caithness and Orkney evidentlally belonging to these people. Thus Thirsa is said by Mr. Pope to be derived from a corruption of Horsa the Saxon. The names of most places and many men in Orkney are of Teutonic derivation, as Wallace rightly observes, though he is wrong in his explication of the word Seater, which is not derived from Seater, a German idol, but these places for pasturage so frequent in Orkney called Saeters.

Before or about the time of the Emperor Claudius we find Herrandus, Earl of Orkney, who, after a two days struggle with Belius, one of the petty kings of Norway, in Papa, was deprived of his life and fortune together. Belius offered his new conquest, with the title of Earl, to one of his followers called Thorstein; which, out of affection to his prince and the attachment he bore to his person, he refused and Argantyr, another of that monarch's favourites, was created Earl and had a grant of the Isles 'jure clientelari' with the burden of an annual pension to be paid to the King.

The mode of payment and the name given to this annual tax occasioned sometime after a dispute between Argantyr and Fredthioff, a messenger sent from Helgi and Halsdane, Belius' sons and successors, to collect this part of their revenue from Orkney. The Earl did not object to the payment, only insisted it was not to be paid as a fixed tribute but as a voluntary contribution to which the ambassador might give any name he inclined; however he promised to satisfy his demand.

Argantyr is celebrated for his prudence and generosity both with regard to the affairs of the islanders and the safety of strangers. It was his constant practice in stormy weather to place a sentinel on the battlements of his castle, both to give notice in case of danger or to inform of ships that might want assistance which was immediately sent them. The sentinel was served with a large horn of spirituous liquor which always stood at his elbow to refresh him, this was often replenished. The sentinel was obliged to describe every occurence that happened 'in extempore rhime', but this was no hardship in a country where the art of poetry was so much cultivated.

Saxo Grammaticus takes notice of one Odde Ourvarod or, according to others, Multivag and Hailmar, two Danish pirates, who overran the Orkneys and remained there a winter.

This is most of what can be gathered of the Orkney history till the time of Kenneth the second of Scotland, when happened the downfall of the Pightish kingdom in Scotland which, with all its pertinents there and particuarly the Orkneys, came into the hands of the King of Scotland. This period is dark in itself and rendered still more so by the total inattention of the Scottish historians to the revolutions of the islands.

The same difficulty occurs in the seond period but in this we are assisted by the Norwegians under whose conduct we shall proceed.

1. Holinshed, Boethius, Buchanan.

(2. In fact the stone is now built once more into the wall of the Birsay Kirk - Ed.)

3. Since writing the above I have had the opportunity of consulting the Edition of Wallace printed in 1700: Lond. where he tells us the story of Ganus being carried to Rome is from Boethius.

4. Pelloutier "Histoire des Celts".

5. Whoever wishes to be more informed concerning this radical disagreement of the Language sprung from the Gothick and Celtick may consult the excellent preface to Mr. Mallet's "Northern Antiquities" by Dr. Piercy where this subject is handled to great purpose and at length.

6. Guthrie: Life of Kenneth MacAlpin.

7. Verstegan as quoted by Wallace p.124.

8. See the Pights Castles and the Barrows fully described in the Tour through Orkney and Shetland1774 & 1778

(9. No drawing is included in the MS.)

10. Probably at Lyking about a mile's distance where are yet to be seen stones of a similar kind in the quarry.

Chapter 2

The ambitious Harald, surnamed from the colour of his hair Harfagre, about the year 870, completed the conquest over the petty princes of his country; but, though he subdued their territories, he did not subdue their minds; they were far from submitting to the absolute authority he proposed to govern them by. Finding it impossible to live in their own country, the greatest part of the Norwegian nobility determined to leave a country where they had now lost their influence and go in search of new homes where they might take this up again. Many of the stripped chiefs retired to Iceland, the Faroe Isles, Schetland and Orkney and from these places, particularly the latter, retaliated on their oppressor.

According to the Norwegin chronicles Orkney was, about this time, a nest of pirates from that country who infested the seas till about 875 when Harald, now fixed in his kingdom, began to turn his thoughts to root them out. By this I suppose we are to understand that though Orkney was then well inhabited yet it was to a race of men well inclined to the Norwegian refugees and they, finding these isles convenient for laying up their ships while they were unemployed, chose them for that purpose.

Nor was it the least disgrace to the islanders to harbout or abet them in their piracy whatever modern usages may make us think; for then this was reckoned so far from disgraceful that they accounted it magnanimous and a proper method of training up their youth for war.

In these days it was no uncommon thing for a young chief to request a few ships from his father to try his fortune in piracy, which was seldom denied; the father applauding the early dawnings of courage in his son. Thus then these isles, though well inhabited might have served for a recess to these people in their acts of piracy until the great revolution in the Norwegian affairs brought about by Harald.

We shall not here enter into the dispute concerning what is affirmed by the Norwegian histories of these times, namely that Kenneth the second, a contemporary prince with Harold, held the kingdom of Scotland of him by a title of vassalage, as it does not much concern our purpose but proceed to the great revolution hinted at which changed the face of affairs very much in all the northern isles.

Before the time of Harald Harfagre, the first who governed all Norway, that kingdom was divided among a great many potent chiefs, who all ruled their territories as they thought proper and often with the greatest rigour. This prince, considering how much the kingdom was weakened by the jarring of so many different and often opposite interests, formed a design to unite them under one government and set himself to exercise such an absolute authority over these his new subjects as they could not think of submitting to, nay for which they had not a name. It is no wonder then that these haughty chiefs, when they found they could not resist his attempts, determined to abandon their country in which they were obliged to live depressed, impoverished and in obscurity; without that freedom to indulge themselves in all their actions to which they had been accustomed and which they could ill bear to be abridged of. Many of these chiefs therefore, rather than submit to the new government, voluntarily withdrew with their followers into exile, some retiring to people Iceland, others to Faro and Shetland, while others came to the Orkneys where they followed their wonted trade of piracy and, covering the seas between these isles and Norway with their numerous ships, for a long time imfested the coasts of the latter, spreading desolution wherever they came. Harald, as soon as he had completed the conquest of Norway, was determined to teach his subjects a new method of life and to procure his subjetcs who lived near the sea shore a life of more security than they either formerly enjoyed or allowed their neighbours; he therefore prohibited all pirates of Norway, under the severest penalties, from exercising any hostilities against their own country. And, when these exiled chiefs continued from Orkney islands to vex him, he determined to follow them thither and, by reducing them to obedience, to secure his kingdom and people from their insults. Having got togther then a competent force, the Norwegians tell us, he passed the seas and came first to Schetland and, surprising what of these freebooters he found there who dreaded no such visitor, he put them every one to death. Having finished his business in Schetland he next went to Orkney and, having reduced it to obedience, he likewise freed it from these pirates who made it their haunt; they add that, elated with this success, he improved upon his original plan which was to clear the seas from pirates, and carried his arms against the AEbudae of Western Isles likewise resorted to by pirates but freed from them by his victories and the death of their chiefs; that, not content with all this, he made attempts upon Scotland where, having made great slaughter, but with what advantage is not said, he retired to the Isle of Man which he found quite empty, the inhabitants having deserted it for fear and fled to Scotland. Here then there was no room for victory and as little spoil, because the people of Man had left nothing behind them. Harald therefore did not so much conquer the Isle of Man as seize it thus deserted by its inhabitants[8]. But though in this expedition of Harald's it is said he cleared the sea of pirates, yet we shall see in course that the inhabitants of Orkney did not give over this course of life but usually passed their whole summers in adventures of this kind, returning before winter laden with the fruits of their ravages; but of this afterwards.

Harald, at his return from his western expedition, gave the islands of Orkney and Schetland to one of his nobles by name Rognvald, famous for his valour and prudence and much loved by the king on account of his fidelity and good service he had performed in the reduction of Norway. This Rognvald had lost his eldest son Ivar in the course of the western expedition and these isles were given him to console him for his loss and no doubt as a reward for his former services. He and his heirs were to hold them of the kings of Norway by a fiduciary right as it was afterwards understood both by Harald and the following kings of Norway.

Rognvald it seems chose rather to be near the king by whom he was so much beloved and therefore gave this magnificent present he had just received at the hands of his sovereign to his brother but without any title or investiture. He however was afterwards created Count or Earl of Orkney by Harald at the instance and by the interest of his brother Rognvald who is represented to have been so rich that he could give away these islands without the least hurt to his private fortune. After Sigurd was settled in Orkney, which our author informs he held 'jure clientelari' by a tenure of vassalage, the King left these parts and Sigurd entered upon his administration. Our author here gives a long list of the forefathers of Rognvald, deriving his pedigree from the noblest familes of Norway, as also of his actions, but as these have little concern with the history of the Orknies we shall omit them.

Our Scottish historians, as far as I know, take no notice of this conquest nor do we hear by them of the Danes or Norwegians having got a foot in Orkney till the death of Malcolm Canmore when they were given up to them by Donald Bane on condition of assistance in his usurping the crown of Scotland several centuries after the times we now speak of. They are, by most, considered to have been under the dominion of the crown of Scotland till the forementioned event, from the time of their being conquered by Kenneth McAlpine and indeed, the way in which Torfaeus relates the King of Norway settled Sigurd in them, shews that they were not much thought of in the eyes of Harald, for though he was to be a vassal of the Crown of Norway yet he was to pay no tribute; or else the suppression of the northern rovers, having completed the king's project, he thought them no further worthy of his regard but gave them to his follower to be rid of the care of securing such a distant conquest. However this may have been, they seem not to have been taken much notice of by the Kings of Norway till the time of Magnus Nudipes or Barefoot which we shall see falls in about the time Scottish authors say they were given up to the Norwegians. But to return to Sigurd.

Having, by the liberality of his sovereign, been advanced to such dignity, riches and power, he contracted a friendship with one Thorstein Rufus or the Red, after which, says our author, he extended the limits of his government (regni) beyond the narrow compass of the islands and added to it a great part of Scotland[9] but as this event would be sure to have taken notice of by others than the Iceland writers, and all are silent about it, I imagine rather it has been only a summer inroad in quest of plunder, a thing common enough in these day when the Rovers, having got their booty, retired to their homes with precipitation. Sigurd it seems however paid dear for his conquests whatever they were for, when a certain Scottish Earl (our author calls him Melbrigdius) met him, and they had agreed to meet at a certain place to settle matters properly and attended with no more than forty followers. Sigurd, for fear of treachery in the Scottish earl, seems to have been determined to put the same in practice against him for, instead of forty followers he brought eighty, two and two on horseback, that the other, deceived by seeing only the agreed number of horses, might come up boldly. But, as soon as the Scottish earl saw them advancing, he immediately percieved the number of his adversaries' men to be double his by observing two men's legs hanging from each side of their horses. However, encouraging his men to sell their lives as dear as they could and not allow themselves to perish tamely like sheep but to avenge their deaths with all their might, he waited the event. When Sigurd saw this he ordered half of his men to leap from the horses and he, together with the others on horseback, attacked the Scots after he had given charge to the others to follow on foot. In the scuffle that ensued the Scots seem to have forgotten the instructions of their leader for, says our author, they did not stand the first attack of the horsemen but, worsted at the first onset, they afforded their enemies an easy vitory and were killed to the last man. If Sigurd got his victory by treachery he behaved himself with no less insolence after it for the heads of the slain were cut off and carried in triumph hung to the saddles of their conquerors, thus insulting even over their dead enemies. However his insolence did not pass unpunished for, whilst he spurred up his horse briskly for joy, no doubt of his success, he struck his foot upon a tooth which stood out of the Scottish earl's head which, wounding him, the part swelled, putrified and was the cause of his death; thus through the just judgement of God a speedy punishment and infamoue end following as the reward of his treachery and pride. He was buried at a place our author calls Eckialdzbaca, God, the revenger of broken faith, not even suffering his body to be carried home to handsel the sepulchral monument of his successors in his country. Nor did his issue long survive him, his only son Guttorm dying within a year of his father without leaving any to succeed him so that Orkney was again laid open to the northern pirates, a multitude of whom from Denmark and Norway soon flowed in upon it, now without a master.

To follow our leader Torfaeus we should now give a very long genealogy of Thorstein Rufus, the ally and friend of Sigurd, who was the son of Olaus the white, the King of Dublin; and, through a series of noble ancestors, drew his origin, as most of the great men of these times boasted, from Odin; nor was he less noble by his mother's side; but, as a long catalogue of strange names could serve no end but tire, I shall leave his genealogy in the original and proceed to account some of the memorable actions of Thorstein and his relations from whom sprung many noble families in Iceland, Faro and the Orkneys.

Harald having returned to Norway from his expedition among the Western Isles, Man and the Orkneys, the Scottish and Irish pirates were not long before they seized the Western Isles no doubt encouraged by his absence: but Harald, having got notice of this, sent Ketill surnamed Flatnose, the grandfather of Thorstein by the mother's side, to drive out the invaders and recover his power over the isles. He, though unwilling, durst not refuse the commands of his king and therefore having got a fleet and army sufficient for the enterprise, he removed all his family (except his son which he left in Orkney to take care of his possessions there) into AEbudae, as the king had made him Governor of the isles upon paying him an annual tribute for them. Ketill was fortunate and, after many engagements, victory still declaring for him, he again reduced the Isles and added them to his other possessions. And, that he might secure them against future insults, and himself in them, he not only formed alliances with the neighbouring chiefs but strengthened these by the marriages of his daughters which he gave to them and thus confirmed himself in the possession of his conquest. After these transactions, trusting in the friendship of these chiefs he had now so nearly connected to him, he sent home the king's fleet and army to Norway and openly set up for himself, throwing off his engagement with Harold and behaving himself as prince of the AEbudae he, for the future, refused other tribute or any kind of homage for them. When the troops upon their return home had given an account of the success of their expedition, at the same time informed the king of Ketill's behaviour, he immediately confiscated everything that belonged to him in Norway and made great enquiry for his son which, alone of his family, was left behind him that, by his death, he might revenge his father's treachery but his search was in vain. Even his more distant relations would have felt the effect of the king's wrath if they had not shunned it by a timely retreat.

Ketill had married his daughter Audur to Olaus White, the then king of Dublin; probably this happened before his expedition to the Western Isles and was one of the reasons why Harald pitched upon him for this project, as one allied to the chiefs of these parts where the scene of his actions was to lie, he would have more probability of engaging them to assist him in his attempts; though his unwillingness to enter upon the task seemed to suggest another reason for his being chosen, namely that Harald had an eye to his Norwegian estates. However this may be, Thorstein was the fruit of his daughter's marriage with Olaus, not less noble by his birth than by the relationship he contracted by his marriage; nor less famous for his valour than his friendship with Sigurd, Earl of Orkney, with whom he performed many famous exploits in Scotland but altogether unnoticed by her historians. He was at length taken off by the treachery and joint force of the Scots after he had made himself master of the half of their kingdom. Thus the Norwegians speak of these times. The posterity of Thorstein were numerous and our author gives us a long digression concerning their marriages and settlements in Orkney, Iceland etc. but which, as they do not at present much concern us, we shall pass to Orkney which we left to be dealt with at the pleasure of the Danish and Norwegian Rovers being deprived of its governor by the death of Guttorm the son of Sigurd the first Earl and who died soon after his father. As Guttorm left no children the right to Orkney returned to his uncle Rognvald who first received it from Harald. He still would not leave Norway but gave Orkney to his son Hallad and sent him to the King to be invested with the title of Earl; and , giving himself altogether to laziness and sloth, he led a retired life in the Mainland (Rosseya) hiding hmself, as it were, from the complaints of the rest of the Isles and leaving the inhabitants of them to be plundered, slain and, in a word, exposed to every injury which the ungoverned rage of these pirates thought proper to inflict on them and all this he suffered them to commit with impunity as if it had been no concern of his to prevent it. At length, being wearied out with the complaints which were daily made to him concerning the pilage these freebooters were making as if with his consent and, at the same time sensible that he could not put a stop to them, he was so far from protecting his people that, forgetting his rank and dignity, he abdicated his government and, with great shame and disgrace, returned to his country where he soon fell into contempt, degraded from the degree of Earl to a rank only something better than a Yeoman, called by our author 'status Hauloicus', being one who succeeds to a feehold estate whether by father or motherside, which sets him above the common husbandman who possesses only moveables but no estate by descent.

1. "Hornklofius." Poems on the subject.
2. Codex Flateyensis Liber originum Islandia.

Chapter 3

After the departure of Hallad, two Danish robbers finding the country again deserted of its lord, took the opportunity to seize on it then obnoxious to any injury. But as soon as Rognvald heard this, as well as the sloth of Hallad, having cursed his degenerate disposition and pronounced him a blot on the family, he ordered his other sons to be called upon and declare aloud which of them dared to recover the royal present and the honour of his house both, in his opinion, lost or hurt by the shameful indolence of their brother. Of six sons which were born to Rognvald, three were legitimate and as many natural, the eldest of the former, Ivar, we have already seen was slain in Harold's expedition to the Western Isles. The second, Rolfus or Rollo, afterwards better known as the first Duke of Normandy, which he gained by conquest in the days of Charles the Simple, King of France, and, after he was persuaded to embrace Christianity, called Robert the first. The third, Thorer Tacitus, deputed over his father's affairs as his successor and married to Olafa Arbota, daughter of Harold Harfagre. His natural sons were Hallad, the disgraced Earl of Orkney, Hrollang and Einar, whose mother was a slave. This last, on account of the condition of his mother, was undervalued and even hated by his father for, in these days of liberty, to be a slave was reckoned the highest disgrace and, though they sometimes made slaves of the prisoners taken in war yet, wherever there was a choice, the vanquished party always preferred death to life clogged with this ignominy.

When all Rognvald's sons had appeared, Thorer Tacitus first offered himself to redeem the family honour and begged his father would allow him; however he was denied as his father probably judged him not altogether fit for the business or that he could be of more service to him at home. Next Rollo, boiling with rage, demanded the government of the Isles; but his father, though he was sensible he wanted not courage to accomplish the recovery of the isles, thought the keeping of them in time coming would not so much depend on valour as a proper method of government which, probably, he thought Rollo at that time not so capable of, as he had been more excercised in pirating parties than the arts of peace, he therefore would not grant them to him. Hrollag, on account of the mildness of his disposition, was judged by his father likewise improper and now there remained none but Einar the least esteemed of his father's sons who, advancing, petitioned his father to send him were it for no other reason but to be out of his sight and to enable him to better his fortune in another country since he had so little expectations in his own. "Give me," adds he, "troops by the help of which I may recover these isles from the hands of these rovers and I will repay you by what I know will be agreeable to you, I will never return to your sight but pass my life there in continual exile." The father took him at his word and, for the reason he gave, namely that he should be freed from the reproach of his appearance. "Though," answers he, "thou are the least fit to be set over these isles of all my sons and promises the least to advance the honour of my family; as what can be expected of one sprung from a slave as thou art; yet go and the sooner thou riddest me of thy presence the better as I never expect thy return."

Sometime after being invested with the title and dignity of Earl by Harald, his father dismissed him with only a single vessel of twenty oars with which he was to make his way among the Islanders as he could.

Notwithstanding all these discouagements Einar crossed the sea without any remarkable adventures and, arriving in Schetland, soon got together forces enough for his enterprise, the islanders flocking about him as one who was to deliver them from the insolence of their tyrants which they no doubt felt as well as the Orcadians. He then came to Orkney and in a bloody battle routed the pirates who had two ships; again restoring tranquility to the Orkneys.[1]

The calm however did not long continue for the natural disposition of the northerns, always impatient of peace and who if they had not opportunity of foreign wars were always picking quarrels with one another, soon put an end to it. Harold was now some forty years of age and had several sons come to man's estate; these finding themselves slighted in the grants that were made of several parts of the kingdom and which were bestowed on Earls their inferiors by birth, though perhaps their father's favourite, while they, the king' sons, valiant men and worthy of government, were passed by. This could not fail to raise the highest indignation in men brought up as they were not to bear the least afront with impunity; and whose notions of honour, then strictly inculcated among all the nations, seldom took much pains to distinguish every alleviating circumstance which might have hindered them from running rashly into quarrels the issue of which they could not possibly foresee. Led away by this favourite passion they were seldom free from disputes either at home or abroad and, to put up with what they thought an affront, was just the plain road to infamy. No wonder then the sons of Harald, thinking themselves so much aggrieved at having the Earls put over their heads, should betake themselves to their arms for revenge; accordingly two of them, Halfdane, surnamed Atipes, and Gudrod Liom, having got together a number of followers, in the begining of the year, attacked Rognvald, Earl of Moria and father of the last two earls of Orkney, who was far from expecting such a thing; They burned his house and consumed himself and sixty of his satellites in the flames. Immediately on his murder, Gudrod took possession of the provinces Rognvald held, without any scruple, as if they had been acquired by war or his own right which he had thus recovered. His brother Halfdane, no doubt fearing his father's anger, seized upon three ships and, retiring to the westward, infested the sea with his piracies.

As soon as the death of his friend was told Harald, he marched against Gudrod, the only one concerned in the slaughter then in his power to revenge it; but he, distrusting his fortune when opposed to the King, yielded himself and was sent to a place our author calls Agdia; and Thorer Tacitus was made to succeed his father by Harald who also honoured him with the hand of his daughter Olafa Arbota in marriage; thus recompensing his loss by the punishment of the murderer, the affinity of the royal family and the restitution of all that pertained to his father.

Halfdane, as said before, fled to from Norway to the Western Ocean and betook himself to piracy when, coming unexpectedly to Orkney, he fell upon Einar and forced him to fly for safety to Caithness; he himself landing took possession of the isles as lawful heir to the crown of Norway and governed them under the title of King which he also usurped, many of the inhabitants adhering to him, either through cowardice or for fear of his power or cruelty; and thus things continued till autumn, from the spring when they began their projects by the murder of Rognvald.

Einar again taking courage returned about autumn to Orkney where, finding Halfdane surrounded by a numerous body of men and, as he thought, secured by the number of his adherents, he attacked him and routed all his forces and forced Halfdane to fly with all speed for his life. Now the scale was turned and Einar, now the conqueror full of hopes and boldness, orders his cheerful soldiers to keep a strict watch lest his enemy, deserted by all and only secured by the darkness of night and the byways and hiding places he had fled to, should escape. Next morning by break of day all the rebels that could be traced out were put to death and the Earl, setting himself to search everywhere for his enemy, at length observed something in North Ronaldsa but, by its quick motion, could not distinguish whether it was a man or a bird; he however sent out his spies, who found it was Halfdane, seized and brought him to the conqueror. The punishment Einar inflicted on him was remarkable but not uncommon in these days when the prisoners in war were often either all or in part dedicated to Odin and offered on the chief's return from war at his altar. Einar, driving his sword into his captive's back at the shoulders and tearing out his lungs, offered them to Odin to confirm his victory; at the same time singing an extempore ode to perpetuatethe memory of the transaction. The substance of the song was that "he had revenged the death of Rognvald and Halfdane had fallen by the justice of the fates. A royal slaughter" (says he) " has fallen to my snare²; cover therefore the corpse of Altipes with stones seeing we have the victory, though the homage I render him is but disagreeable"; alluding to the heap of stones he caused to be thrown upon him according to the then method of burial.

This Earl was a Scald or Poet and composed many pieces in the old language of Norway, indeed this accomplishment was then so far from contemptible as might have been expected among a people who breathed nothing but war, that it was held in the greatest esteem, as they were sensible their fame in a great measure depended on the character the Scalds might send down to posterity. The Scalds were admitted into the courts of princes and there received with the greatest honours, especially they were caressed by these princes who inclined to make a figure in the world and to be distinguished by their glorious performances. Harald Harfagre placed them above all the officers of his court at the feast and, in the History of the North, we find them charged with commissions of the greatest importance, both in peace and war. In all expeditions they attended the chiefs and sung the actions of past and present times; this last particular gave them great weight and was a great incitement to bravery for, as the Scalds were above flattery they delivered the history of famous and infamous actions with alike impartiality and, not to have the praise of the Scald, was, in a word, at least to have a doubtful if not an infamous character.

Kings and Princes were not ashamed to profess the art of Poetry, Regner Lodbrog was both a poet and a hero and many of his poems are still to be found. Rognvald surnamed Kalius, one of the most famous Earls of Orkney, boasted that he knew how to make verses on all subjects. In a word the Person and Characters of the Scalds and Bards of the Teutonic and Celtic nations were held as sacred and we often find Princes of the worst character and who defiled themselves with every crime yet afraid to meddle with this set of men.

Einar, the night in which he was victorious over Halfdane, composed another song in which he in a sort of concealed railery boasts "that the spear here was not darted at the enemy by the arm of Krollang or Rollo and, while he was engaged in this sea fight to revenge his father's death, Earl Thorer was silent[2] in his palace of Moria." He meant probably to insinuate that he - the least esteemed of his father's sons - had now accomplished the revenging his death, while his other favourite sons only, as it were, beheld his actions at a distance or indolently forbore to imitate them.

This period, according to our author, falls in the year after the birth of Christ 893.

The news of Halfdane's death being carried to Norway, his brothers were bent on immediate revenge but their father by various shifts and delays kept them in till he could make the necessary preparations for coming himself to Orkney. At length he came with a pretty large fleet and army and Einar withdrew into Caithness. It was however afterwards agreed between them that a place of meeting should be chosen where the King and Einar should make up matters. At the time appointed Einar came and, referring everything to the King's pleasure, promised he would submit to his judgement; and Harald, either because the inhabitants had assisted his vassal the Earl against his superior or that he thought them all more or less guilty of the death of his son, imposed a fine of sixty marks of gold on the whole people.

A peace purchased at such a dear rate seeming to be a vast hardship on the people, the Earl proposed to raise the whole sum and pay it in their name, on condition that all gave him immediate possession of their estates in pledge for his being repaid. This proposal, inconvenient as it at first sight appeared, was agreed to though with some backwardness and Einar paid the sum in question on receipt of which Harald, after some skirmishes in Scotland, returned to Norway.

The Norwegian Chronicles relate this transaction something differently from the above; according to them, the Orkney people were in the Earl's absence fined of their estates and forced by oath to transfer their rights to the King; that afterwards peace was made on condition that the Earl should hold Orkney in feu of the Crown of Norway but without any tribute, that being allowed him to enable him to defend the islands against foreign attacks which in these days were very frequent. That he should immediately pay down sixty marks of gold but this appears to have been done for the whole community, since it is certain he held their lands, for this very money, in pledge and in this condition they remained till the time of Sigurd the Fat.

After all this wrangling Einar governed the islands for a long time in peace and died at an advanced age, by his excellent behaviour wiping off the stain he received from his birth and the defects of his own appearance. He had (says our author) a noble soul in an ordinary body, his looks were as forbidding as his mind was engaging; he was blind in one eye but (adds Torfaeus) saw as acutely with the other as many do with both. His name de Cespite or Turf Einar he, it seems, received from the circumstance of his teaching the ordinary Orkney people to supply the want of wood, which then, as now, was not to be had in these isles, with turf from Torfness in Scotland; however this last particular is not easily reconcilable with that plenty of fuel of the same kind to be found in the Orkneys and which probably was to be got even then, so that there was little occasion to bring it from such a distance as from the nearest part of Scotland.

1. This victory is celebrated in a distich alluding to the names of the conquered, one of which was called Thorer Treskegg or Timberbeard and the other, Kalf Scurfa or theScabby:

> Ficosum and Lignobarbum dedrunt ad Orcum
>
> Einar cui Cespes nominis author erat.

2. Neo quadranti in the original. He had three brothers and reckoned himself the fourth; Hallad probably was dead or, because of his disgrace, was not reckoned.

3. He alludes to his name which was Tacitus, a proof that the noble art of punning as not entirely unknown to the Northern Scalders.

Chapter 4

Einar de Cespite, or Turf Einar as he is often called, was succeeded by his three sons Arnkel, Erland and Thorfin surnamed Head-cleaver, who seem to have divided the isles among themselves without any interposition or investiture from the King of Norway that we hear of, as was the case with the former Earls who all received them together with their titles immediately from Harald Harfagre.

Sometime after the death of Einar (the precise time of which is not known), happened also that of Harald Harfagre, upon which the disputes which arose between his sons Eric Blodox and Haco concerning the succession ran so high that they set all Norway in a flame and so divided the minds of people that there was nothing to be seen but uproar and faction. Eric's pretensions to reign were stongest as being founded on his father's will by which the kingdom "acquired by war and confirmed by a long possession"[1] was thereby become a part of his patrimony and was disponed to him. Haco, destitute of any such plausible pretext, had recourse to other means to render his design effectual; he took care to engage the assisitance of his foster father Athelstane, King of England, and to gain the minds of the people by his popularity; this he effected by fawning, flattery and a great show of generosity; to ingratiate himself the more he made a general offer of lands in freehold and, to those who already possessed them in this manner, he promised the complete property; all by which it followed that even they whom his father had conquered, forgetting the obligations they were under, upon the foregoing terms sold Haco the kingdom to which neither he nor they could pretend any title. There were many thing which, no doubt, very much forwarded this bargain, one was Eric's own disposition which it seems was not so pliable as that of his brother and which, by degrees, alienated his subjects minds, especially this was the easier done as he had such an able workman as Haco counteracting him with those who could ill bear the roughness of his disposition, heightened by the persuasion of his wife, and only looking out for an opportunity to shake themselves loose from him. Add to this that many of the nobles of Eric's faction, displeased at him for misgovernment, changed sides and drew over to Haco a vast number of followers; all of which reduced Eric to such straits that he was obliged to retire from Norway and betake himself to his fortune. The first place the banished king came to with such of his friends as chose to follow him was the Orkneys when, having raised an army, he went to England, with a view no doubt to revenge himself on Athelstane for the assistance he had given his brother in their contest for the kingdom. Athelstane however considered the great friendship that had subsisted between him and Eric's father, to make up matters, offered him a share of his kingdom on condition that he should become his vassal and embrace Christianity with all his family. Eric accepted the conditions and, having received Northumberland, was baptized with his wife, his children, his domestics and his army; which being performed, he fixed his residence at York. This happened about the year of Christ 935 and five years before the death of Athelstane which fell out in the year of the same era 940.

Edmund the brother of Athelstane succeeded him, a prince who was no favourer of the Danes and Norwegians that had settled in England and particularly bore no good will to Eric; hence it was publicly talked that Edmund was to displace him from his government of Northumberland and to give it to another. This was soon brought to Eric then absent in Orkney on an intended expedition against the Western Isles, in which he had engaged Arnkel and Erland, the Earls of Orkney, with their men to attend him. From Orkney he went with his fleet to the Isles where he added a number of pirates to his train, a set of people seldom blind where their advantage was concerned and now only drawn to follow him through the hopes of what plunder they would catch, which had a greater effect to persuade them than any regard they could have either to his person or his cause. After he had thus increased his forces among the AEbudae he proceeded to Ireland and thence to a part of England our author calls Bretland or Cornavia[2] both which he overran and plundered. His success emboldened him to advance to the southern parts of England and to fill every place he came to with bloodshed. The terror his name spread among the English did a great deal to his conquests and, the people all flying before him, now confident in the valour of his troops and of success, he proposed to plunder the very heart of England. Olaus who, under Edmund, acted as king of these parts where Eric's fury had mostly fallen, gathering a large army to put a stop to his outrages, engaged him in the height of his exultation. The battle continued the most part of the day and was fought with great obstinacy on both sides, victory inclining at first to Eric, Olaus having lost many of his men, but, these being soon supplied by others who came from all quarters to drive out the Normans, the latter part of the day proved fatal to them now quite worn out with toil and unable to resist the continued attacks of so many fresh men as were continually arriving to renew the encounter. Evening put an end to the contest and the life of Eric who, with five other Kings and two Earls of Orkney, Arnkel and Erland, were among the slain together with the greatest part of their army which was totally routed, the scattered remains of it being the messengers who carried the news of their defeat to Gunhilda, the wife of Eric in Northumberland.

There was now little hope of safety for any of Eric's family in England, accordingly Gunhilda with her sons and what followers they could get together that were willing to share their fortune, immediately went aboard a fleet which Eric had left and, taking with them everything valuable, came to Orkney. Here they passed the winter and, seizing these islands together with Schetland, from Thorfin Hausakliuf, now Earl of Orkney by the deaths of Arnkel and Erland, subjected them to tribute; and from thence vexed both Scotland and Ireland with continual acts of piracy and rapine[3]. The death of Eric happened in the year 941 in the beginning of Edmund's reign.

Orkney being thus in the power of Eric's sons (for Thorfinn took no pains to prevent their attempts on it) they ordered everything there at their pleasure, forcing the people to war and to maintain their soldiers and, in a word, imposing on the Orcadians what burdens they inclined.

While this was passing here, things in Denmark and Norway put on a warlike appearance and a breach was apprehended between Haco, the Norwegian, and Harald Bluetooth, the Danish King; and several irruptions were made by Haco into the territories of Denmark. Gunhilda, thinking this a proper occasion to get into favour with the King, determined to leave the Orkneys and go to Denmark. Accordingly she went thither with her sons, where they were wll received of the King but before her departure restored the management of affairs in Orkney to Thorfin and gave Rognhild her daughter in marriage to the Earl's son Arnfin or Arnvid.

Orkney being thus freed from foreigners, Thorfin again resumed government and continued in it till his death, which happened by disease, and he was buried in South Ronaldsha at a place our author calls Haugagerd. The character given him is that he was of a noble disposition, an industrious warrior and a valiant man; from these last particulars without doubt he received the surname of Hausakliuf or Headcleaver; although this does not well tally with his tamely allowing the sons of Gunhilda to seize on Orkney and manage it at their pleasure, as was before related, however he probably thought as they were Eric's sons they were his sovereigns and therefore he would not resist them.

Thorfin left five sons, Havard Arsoel; Hlodver or Ludovick born of Grelode, the granddaughter of Thorstein Rufus of whom before; Liot; Skuli and Arnfin or Arnvid married to Rognhild, daughter of Eric. His wife, who seems to have been a very wicked woman, murdered him at a place called Myrkol[4] in Caithness and soon married his brother Havard Arsoel. He, succeeding to the Earldom, for some time governed the Orknies with great happiness, enjoying plenty of provisions and every thing else as long as he lived, whence his surname. Like his brother Arnfin he too was murdered by the treacherous contrivances of his wife, though by the hands of another, the story of which is thus related. Havard has a sister's son called Einar Kliningus a man of great power and always surrounded by a number of followers whom he kept about him to accompany him in the piratical parties which he engaged in every summer. This Einar, as a relation of the Earls, was often invited to their entertainments which great men in these days frequently made to their men and followers, where he was observed to whisper a great deal and to affect a deal of secrecy in his talk wth the Earl's wife. She, who was now weary of her husband and wanted to get rid of him attempted, by all blandishments in her power, to stir him up to make away with his uncle. She represented to him that Havard was unfit for the management of public affairs, which he could do much better; and insinuated to him that he was a match for any woman, thereby working upon his love and ambition. He however had a better opinion of his uncle and affirmed that he was the best of the Orcadians, that his place could not be supplied by a fitter person and on this occasion ran out into many encomiums on him but which he deserved. His aunt however was determined not to give over the enterprise she had now so far begun and, that she might use another method to spirit up the nephew to act the mischievious design she intended against his uncle, she told him plainly that her marriage with the Earl would be of no long continuance; that there were other men in Orkney who would not stick to complete the point she so much laboured, if he wanted the spirit and resolution to better his own fortune. This last threat, as it shewed she was determined on her husband's murder, so at the same time it staggered all Einar's resolves and his mind being now hampered by avarice and ambition he was easily persuaded to attempt his uncle's destruction. Having therefore bargained about his marriage with Rognhild and the succession to the Earldom, he went a few days after to put the finishing hand to his villainy accompanied with an armed force. According to the prevailing notions of the times, it was reported that a soothsayers persuaded him to let alone the murder for that day and defer it to the next, otherwise parricides would happen frequently in his house.He however lent a deaf ear to this admonition and persisted in his design. Having met his uncle in Stenness in the Mainland accompanied by a few followers, he attcked him and, after a sharp scuffle which did not continue long, Havard was slain at a place afterwards called Havardzteigur or the place of Havard's battle. All who heard of this murder execrated and condemned the wicked perpetrator and even Rognhild herself destested him and falsely accused him of drawing her into a participation of his crime. She therefore sent to another Einar, surnamed Hardkioft of Hardmouth, a son of Havard's sister and, reproaching him with the stupidity of the rest of the family, exclaimed much that none of them attempted to revenge the death of such a worthy man. She told him that she would bestow all she was worth to bring the murderer to condign punishment; and let him know at the same time that the avenger would not only deserve the praise of all good men but would be entitled to the succession to the Earldom. To all this Hardkioft answered, "There are many who do not stick to say that your words are not at all times from your heart, for you must certainly reflect that the Earldom is the reward of this exploit to be done at your solicitation but you must also consider that another demand will be made of you and that not less valued than the other". By this he meant she should understand that he aimed at an alliance with her in marriage; of which, assuring himself in his own conceit, he immediately went to his kinsman Einar Klining who feared no harm from him, and slew him. Rognhild, having thus far succeeded in her designs, made herself happy that thus by procuring it to be revenged, she had removed all suspicion of the murder from herself and, as she had no design to reward Einar Haedkioft as he believed, she sent messengers to Liot, the third son of Thorfin and brother to her two former husbands, with proposals of marriage which were agreed to.

Einar Hardkioft was vexed to the heart to see himself thus deluded and to fail in the expected reward after being made a fool of in the murder of his relation, he therefore resolved to rest the Earldom by force from his uncle but also missed of this by reason of his not being able to obtain the goodwill of the Orkneymen who were more inclined to the sons of Thorfin. His designs, being known, he was a little time after slain by the command of Liot and thus (adds or author after the relation of all these murderous scenes) this wicked woman, actuated by the devil himself, outdid even her infamous mother in treachery, as she did in her cunning and every mischievous contrivance that was possible to be hatched in a deceitful mind.

Whilst these things were going on in Orkney, Skuli, the fourth son of Thorfin Hausakluif, going to Scotland obtained from its King the title and dignity of Earl of Orkney, the King (says our author) easily granting what was not his to bestow; we shall have occasion afterwards to enquire into the different pretensions of Scotland and Norway to these islands.

Sculi having obtained his suit from the King of Scotland came to Caithness and raised an army to dispute the title with his brother and, having sailed to Orkney, he declared war against Liot who had got together everyone he could that was able to fight. When no terms of accomodation could be received between the brothers, they engaged and, after stiffly disputing it for some time, victory inclined to Liot and Sculi fled to Caithness. Liot pursued him thither, stayed so long there till Sculi raised a larger army than his former and further strengthened it with auxiliaries he received from the King of Scotland and a Scottish Earl called Magbragd. Thinking himself now much superior to his brother, he returned from Scotland and again fought him in a place called Dale in Caithness. At the begining of the battle the Scots fought with great fury and bore hard upon Liot, who ordered his men to keep close together and repel their attacks as well as they could till their first fury should abate and, as soon as they found the opposite party begin to act more remissly, they should in their turn renew the attack with all their might. This method which showed the wisdom of Liot as a general, as his actions did his valour, succeeded and the Scots were at length put to flight, notwithstanding the bravery of Sculi who, though he was hotly engaged, yet not only fought with the greatest valour but did everything in his power to hinder his party from flying; he begged, he chid, he beseeched and prevailed so far as to bring back part of his men with whom he renewed the battle and sustained it by his bravery till he was slain fighting among the thickest of his foes[5].

Liot after the battle seized upon Caithness as the fruits of victory and by force retained it, which was the cause of the continuation of the war between him and the Scots. In a little time another fight happened between Liot and the foresaid Scottish Earl Magbragd in the marshes of Scibo, a part of Caithness where, notwithstanding of the superior numbers of the Scottish army, they were again routed by the bravery of Liot and his troops and many killed and wounded left in the field. Liot himself however did not long triumph in his victory for being being grievously wounded he died a few days later.

Hlodver or Ludvick succeeded Liot in the Earldom of Orkney who, according to our author, was reckoned a brave and praiseworthy prince although none of his actions have come down to us. His wife was Audna, the daughter of Kiarval the Irish King, and his son, Sigurd the Gross, Earl of Orkney. Whether Hlodver died by disease or in a war is not said but he was buried in Caithness at a place called Hofn where probably he had a castle. All these, the sons of Thorfin, governed the Orkneys but the precise years or the duration of their managing affairs here is unknown, though it was about the time of Haco and the son of Gunhilda in Norway.

About this time the Kings of Norway seem to have but little to say in Orkney, the Earls succeeded without investiture from them, they paid them no tribute and as little homage and what the Norwegians got from these isles seemed to be no more through strength of hand than any good will so that, granting the Norwegians had a right to them by the conquest of Harold Harfagre, yet this seems not to have been insisted on from the time of the succession of the sons of Einar de Cespite till now, nay we may justly suppose the Kings of Scotland had a claim to the sovereignty of them derived probably from the conquest of Kenneth the 2nd and that they asserted this claim by conferring the title and dignity of Earl of Orkney on Skuli the son of Thorfin as is said before. However this may be Haco, who was much engaged in home and foreign wars, either coud not find leisure or neglected to bring back the Orkneys to obedience and they were again molested by the sons of Gunhilda, which happened thus.

Norway had been for a long time torn to pieces by the factions which were formed by Gunhild and her sons to recover the Kingdom; till at length one of them being slain by the contrivance of a Danish

Earl and the consent of Harold Blatand or Bluetooth, King of Denmark; she with the other two, Rognfrod and Gudriod, was obliged to fly. These were the only survivors of eight sons and with them she came to Orkney, to which she laid claim from her former visit. After passing the winter there Rognfrod with a troop of chosen warriors and a strong fleet went back to Norway to try to recover the Kingdom. He landed in Norway and plundered several places there and forced many of the inhabitants to surrender and join him. Haco, by means of sending a spear (called Budstikke) then the sign of war, through the provinces, soon gathered together an army which he put aboard his fleet and went to meet Rognfrod whom he found and attacked in a sea fight, but with loss; for, though he had more men than Rognfrod yet the littleness of his ships was of vast disadvantage to him and gave the darts of the opposite party a fairer aim from the more elevated stations, Rognfrod's men had in his larger ships. For the manner was then to fight hand to hand from the prows of their ships and, so much did they stand on the point of honour with one another, that oftimes when one party met another at sea with a greater number of ships, the chief would order as many of his to withdraw as would set him on an equal footing with his enemy.

Both their fleets being put ashore by the tides Haco, as he saw he fought at a disadvantage by sea, thought this was a good opportunity to revenge himself by land and, having chosen a fit place to draw up his ships lest they should fall into the hands of his enemy, he did all he could to provoke Rognfrod to an engagement on shore, but in vain, Rognfrod being afraid of that part of his army deserting him who were natives of the country and the battle was continued, not without slaughter on both sides, for the greater part of the day, with darts and arrows or such weapons as they could use at a distance. After this battle they went into winter quarters and each governed a part of the Kingdom, Rognfrod placing his troops in the provinces he had conquered and which were mostly on the seaside.

The next spring which was part of the year 977, both parties prepared to renew the war with the greatest eagerness and each raised all the men he could in his quarter as, on their next encounter, depended their future fortune. They came at length to an engagement at a place called Thingness where, in a fierce fight and long sustained on both sides, victory at length declared in favour of Haco who had the greatest number of combatants, and Rognfrod, having now lost all hope of recovering Norway, together with three hundred of his men fled to his ships and departed the Kingdom, thus ridding Orkney from all apprehension of him.

1. This sentence when applied to the northerns is excellently expressed in the original "quod bello quantumvis injusto partum, longa tamen subditorum patientia in versa ipse sibi patrimoniale fecerat."

2. The Ancient Cornavia comprehended Warwickshire, Worcestershire, Staffordshire, Shropshire and Cheshire and probably part of Derbyshire, Cambden Horsley.

3. Now Earl of Orkney by the death of Arnhill and Erland.

4. Glumus Gerinus has two poems, the subject of this expedition.

5. Now Murkil, a seat belonging to the Earl of Caithness.

6, This battle was fought at Toftingale in Halkirk Parish. Liot was buried at Sten-hou near the Kirk of Watten. Mr. Pope in Mr. Pennant's editions to the Stuart's edition of his Tour, p.141, App.

7. Called Budstikke

Chapter 5

Sigurd, second of the name, Count of Orkney, succeeded his father Hlodver. In the disposition of his mind, his skill in warlike affairs and his wisdom in civil administration, he much resembled the first Norwegian Earl of Orkney whose name he likewise bore. He was a magnanimous and fortunate Prince, desirous of glory and particularly anxious to enlarge his bounds by adding what he could seize to his government; for besides Caithness, which several of the Orkney Earls had held before, and he kept, according to our author, against the inclination of the King of Scotland, he is likewise reported to have possessed the norther shires of Scotland as Ross, Murray, Sutherland etc. and every year to send out his fleets and armies to plunder the coasts of Scotland, Ireland and the AEbudae, which last he reduced so far as to subject them to the payment of an annual tribute which we find afterwards strictly demanded of them. It was then a common thing for the chiefs to challenge one another to a trial of arms and this sometimes when war was not declared between them; we find Sigurd thus challenged by a Scottish Earl called Finleic who appointed him a place and day to fight him but this was probably to revenge some of Sigurd's ravages in Scotland. Before Sigurd went he consulted his mother who, according to the prevailing notions of the times, was possessed of a natural knowledge, and complained that the enemy had the better even though he excelled them in number of men. She answered him, "I should have kept thee all along in the cradle if it had been possible to be always victorious; the fates (adds she), not the measure of danger, have the power of men's life which is much more glorious when ended by an honourable though early death, than when dragged about a long time with disgrace." She afterwards gave him a standard on which she told him she had exhausted all her cunning, at the same time informing him of its virtue, that it brought certain victory to him before whom it was carried, but as certain death to the bearer. The standard itself was the figure of a Raven which, when moved by the wind, seemed as if flying. This present, togther with his mother's stimulating admonition, was received by the Count with some vexation.

He next proceeded to get togther an army but found he could not force the people to go to war out of their own country at his pleasure; to encourage them therefore to follow him, he restored their estates which we have seen before were pledged to Einar de Cespite and had been detained in this manner till now. Having raised an army he marched to the place appointed where, meeting Finleic, they soon engaged and, in the heat of the battle Sigurd's standard bearer was soon slain, another however was soon put in his place and he too fell, nay his mother's words were fulfilled by the death of a third bearer of this fatal ensign before the end of the battle, in which victory declared for the Earl of Orkney.

What were the consequences of this victory were not said and were probably nothing farther than securing what part of Scotland the Earls of Orkney pretended a right to for the present and affording them a peace, which however was of no long continuance for we find them in a very short time after again by the ears about these Scottish provinces.

Our author here gives an account of the officers of the Earl's court, particularly from the Icelandic history of four Icelanders who held the most honourable places there. These were Kari Solmund, whose grandfather Thorbiorn Iarlakap a Norwegian, had first come from thence to Orkney and afterwards gone to Iceland. This Kari, who was the first that had been promoted to the honour of attendant on the Earl, was afterwards likewise made the Earl's treasurer or received of the tribute which had been imposed upon the Western Isles. His family arms was a Lion on a gilded shield. Two of his relations, Grime and Helgi, the sons of Nial, were likewise created satellites. Helgi had for an armorial bearing, a Stag on a shield painted purple. These were entertained by Thorstein, the son of the chief of Sida, from whom sprung afterwards two Earls of Orkney, Magnus and Rognvald. The last of the four was Flosius, too an Icelander, and whose actions make some figure in the course of the history; he was a famous man and married to a sister of the just mentioned Thorstein.

The actions of these men serve to throw a good deal of light on the history and manners of the times, therefore it would be a pity to pass them over.

The first particular we find of their deeds which concerns us, is an adventure of Helgius and Grimus the sons of Nial (which last, according to our author's quotation, was a good man and a strict lover of justice). These sailing to Norway, were by contrary winds put into one of the Scottish bays, where they were soon found out by the sons of Moddan, Earl of Dungalsbey, Snaekol and Griotgard, who came suddenly on them with two vessels full of armed men. As it seems they were no friends to the Norwegians, they gave them an alternative either to deliver up their vessel and all that she contained or fight them. The latter was accepted and the battle begun. It is very probable that the Scots should have got the better of it, as in the heat of battle one of the Norwegian steersmen was killed, which was no doubt a great disadvantage to them, but happily for the Norwegians Karius, coming that way with ten ships, placed himself on the weakest side, without knowing whom he was assisting, and renewed the battle. This however was soon finished by the slaughter of both the assailants, one of whom fell by the hand of Helgi and the other by that of Grime. After this victory Kari carried the sons of Nial with him into Orkney and strenuously recommended them to Sigurd for courage and bravery, of which he had so lately been a witness. Being well received by the Count they stayed all the winter in Orkney. In the beginning of spring Helgi, seeming unusually melancholy and being desired to account for such a change in his manner, he asked whether the Earl did not possess several provinces in Scotland and, upon being informed he did, he told him the Scots had risen and killed all his Deputies and, lest the matter should be known, had laid an embargo on all the harbours and shipping that none should escape to him with the news. The Earl, being much moved at this recital and scarce knowing how to trust it, promised him great rewards for his information if it proved true but, if false, threatened to strike off his head. He was however persuaded to give credit to it by Kari who affirmed Helgi to be a sober and good man, one who would not impose on him; he likewise informed the Earl that Helgi's father was a prophet, meaning possibly that his son was the same and that therefore his intelligence was not to be slighted. Sigurd, being staggered by all these reasons, sent orders to Arnliot, his Officer and Deputy in Stroma, to make a strict enquiry what was doing in the transmarine provinces. Arnliot soon found by sending out scouts that all was in confusion in Scotland, that two Scottish Earls, Hundi and Melsnati, had slain Halvard of Trasvick, Sigurd's relation and, by him, charged with the management of affairs in Scotland; and of this he sent word to the Earl with all possible speed. Sigurd, having ordered an army to be levied, with all haste made preparations to attack the Scots and, having passed the Pightland firth, he heard the two Earls were not far off with a pretty numerous body of men.

Having therefore increased his army with such supplies as he could raise in Scotland, he advanced to attack the Scottish Earls, which he did near Dungads Rock, a place so called. Sigurd's army was pretty much hurt by a body of men which the Scottish Earls had placed in ambuscade and who made a fierce attack on, and with great loss to, the Orkneymen; the battle however was stoutly maintained by Grime and Helgi the sons of Nial who fought bravely by the Earl's standard and were a great means of getting the victory and which a feat performed by Kari at once determined in favour of his friends; which action, though it appears incredible, is as follows. Kari, being posted in the battle opposite Melsnati, the latter threw his spear at him which, notwithstanding its rapidity, Kari catched in its flight and, returning the weapon, with it pierced the breast of its master. Melsnati's death struck a sudden terror into his party and Hundi, with the remains of their troop soon consulted his safety by flight. Sigurd pursued and many fell in the chase but he was diverted from the pursuit upon being told that Melkolf or Malcolm, afterwards King of Scotland, was at Dungaldsbey[1] with fresh troops and there waited for his coming. Calling therefore his chiefs together they resolved to retire homewards with what plunder they had got. They therefore returned to Orkney and, when they came to Stroma divided the pillage according to custom; which, being done, the Earl went to the Mainland where he invited all his friends to the feast and, being willing to honour those who had behaved themselves well in the expedition, he presented Grime with a sword and a gilded Buckler and Helgi with a ring of gold and a robe of honour and placed them among the number of his satellites.

Nor did Kari go without his share of the Earl's countenance as his valour deserved, he received a sword and a gilded spear and all three remained in the Earl's court for two years, exercising themselves in the summer season in piratical adventures and thereby acquiring both wealth and fame. Grime and Helgi afterwards went to Norway and were ill-used there by a Norwegian Earl who at that time managed affairs there for Harold Blatand, King of Denmark; of which afterwards. Kari stayed in Orkney and was employed in receiving the tribute of the Western Isles, which seems at this time to have been exacted both by the Norwegians and Earls of Orkney or else these last had demanded it alternately with them but by what right seems not so clear, probably by the tenure that was much in use at these times, namely the longest sword which commonly was made a pretext for any imposition, yea and what was called tribute was sometimes rather forced from the vanquished than given from goodwill or as a right.

Besides these four who were Icelanders, we have an account[2] of another satellite who was called Thorkel surnamed Krafl, a relation of the Earl, the son of Thorgrim Curio of Karnsa, but born a slave.

In consequence of the meanness of his birth, as his father thought him a disgrace on him and at the instance of his wife, Thorkel he was exposed when an infant; however in this particular the northerns were not very scrupulous but did the same with such of their lawful children as they did not incline to bring up[3]. Thorkel was found by his father's uncle Thorstein, Governor of Vatradoel, half dead and scarce breathing, on a wreath of melting snow, who took him up and gave him to be brought up by his brother, which brother had long laboured under an incurable disease. Thorstein made a vow to that God who made the sun[4] that he would bring up the child upon the restoration of his brother's health which happened from the day he received the boy, that he felt not the least remains of his disorder.

Thorkel, being thus rescued from destruction by the divine interposition in his favour, grew up under the tutelage of his friends till he was about twelve years of age when, in election for the place of Governor, his father and another were candidates; and, the other appearing to have the best chance of succeeding, Thorkel slew him, thus opening a way to the magistrate's chair for his father. After which, going to Orkney, he was entertained by Sigurd for a whole winter, upon giving a slight account of his family and connections, and which was not given much heed to by the Earl. The difference however in his behaviour from the others in the Earl's court and his assiduity to recommend himself to him, soon drew on him the envy of the courtiers and the attention of the Earl who, in the spring being almost alone with Thorkel, publicly commended his behaviour to those few that were about them and asked more particularly about his family, which he now gave him a very particular account of; and gave the Earl to understand that he was allied to him by blood but much more by friendship. From this day forward Thorkel was much regarded by the Earl and followed him in his expeditions into Scotland, in which he held an honourable position in the army. In one of these adventures, when the army after some skirmish had returned to their ships,

Thorkel alone was missing and, upon a search being made, he was found being engaged with two and four, lying near, which he had slain. Upon the Earl's asking what had detained him, he answered that he had often heard from him "that when an army made a sally it ought to be in the face of their enemies from their ships to the land and not from thence to their ships". "Right," says the Earl, "and therefore let it be henceforth a rule that none who flies to the ships and deserts his standard will be entitled to any part of the plunder".

Upon being asked more particularly the cause of his stay, he told the Earl he had, in his walks, gone to see an old castle belonging to the Scots in the wall of which, happening to move a stone, he had discovered a pretty considerable quantity of silver that, upon this discovery and his attempting to remove it, those belonging to the castle came out and attacked him but he had slain or worsted them all. The treasure weighed twenty marks of silver and, after a friendly contest about the property of it, t'was equally divided between the Earl and Thorkel. These and such like actions set him still higher in his master's favour and brought him many valuable presents from him, but he seems not to have been loved by any of the Earl's followers, possibly on account of his pride and his valuing himself too much on his relationship to him for, when he was missing and the Earl ordered the rest of his men to seek him, they grumbled not a little and proceeded so far as to tell him "that such a sour fellow could be spared without damage to the rest of his army". The Earl's kindness did not stop at what he did for Thorkel himself but he likewise extended it to his mother, whom he presented with a rich garment and as much money as purchased her liberty from Thorkel's father. Thorkel himself, after staying two winters with Sigurd, departed and, coming to Norway, was made Curio of Vatxdal and afterwards became a Christian, being converted, says our author, by a miracle and convinced that it did not essentially differ from the religion professed by his ancestors, they being used to worship "him who made the sun".

In these times lived an inhabitant of Sanda called Ulf surnamed the Bad, a man whose manners did not in the least belie that appellation. This Ulf, taking a fancy to his neighbour's land asked the proprietor (who was called Harold and dwelt in North Ronaldsha) to sell it and, upon his refusal, threatened to make him repent it. In a few days he was as good as his word and came upon Harold unawares who, being taken, was bereft of life and land together. This fact, which was blamed by all good men, was soon brought to the Earl's ears and greatly displeased him; however Ulf found means to excuse himself having only taken off a man who was not undeserving of death and, being ordered to satisfy the heirs of the deceased, promised he would do it. Harold had a son called Helgi, a deserving young man, who was absent on a piratical expedition in the Scottish Seas at the time of his father's murder. This youth, though a heathen and following the customs of the times in regard to piracy, was yet less severe upon the merchants and others who fell into his hands than many others that led that way of life. On his return from Scotland, Helgi soon heard of his father's death and the manner of it and, meeting with Rard, a relation of Ulf but unlike him in manners being an honest man and who hated his kinsman's behaviour so much that he had no correspondence with him and had withdrawn himself till matters should be made up between his kinsman and Helgi, he killed him in vain pleading his innocence and fighting bravely though with inferior force. This revenge which it was then common to take on all the family, being known, Helgi was severely reprimanded by the Earl for thus taking upon him to right himself while the cause between him and Ulf was depending and likely to be made up. When Helgi would have excused himself by observing that as yet he had received no satisfaction for such a great loss and would have intimated that he was still willing to adhere to and submit himself to his sentence, the Earl replied that nothing could give him more satisfaction than to see peace among his people. Helgi afterwards returned home but, finding himself not safe from Ulf who, upon the slaughter of his kinsman Bard, had got together a number of armed followers while he remained in the isles, he sold his estate and departing from his own, went to the house of his enemy who, happening to be absent, Helgi plundered it of everything and carried away his only daughter Helga, saying that his father's death could in no way be better repaid than his enemy's daughter in exchange for it. The lady, it seems, was not backward to follow him and afterwards. Being obliged to flee from Ulf, they withdrew themselves to the main of Scotland and hid themselves in a peasant's house who knew Helgi and did him all the service in his power in return for the civilities he and others of his rank had experienced from him when in his piratical expeditions. In this poor cottage they passed the winter and here Helgi married his companion whence in two years they returned to Orkney and he succeeded to his father's and, in right of his wife, to all the lands that belonged to his father-in-law who was now dead and, by his death, obviated his return from this voluntary banishment. Helgi's son Bard was afterwards converted to Christianity and became an Irish Bishop.

About this time the Icelandic and Norwegian authors tell us the Christian religion was introduced into Orkney and spread among the people; though we have seen before that it must have been known some time before in Norway and that there were some converts to it from the Orknies. The account these authors give of its first rise here is as follows:

The famous Olave Trygueson in one of his expeditions about the year 995 happening to come to Orkney, landed in S. Ronaldsha and, in a bay or harbour, there found Sigurd the Orkney Earl with three ships, ready for entering upon an expedition as usual in these times. Having ordered Sigurd to be called, the King of Norway thus addressed him: "It is well known to you that Harald Harfagre after having brought all Norway to obey him, likewise subdued the Orkneys, Shetland and other places and added them to the territories of Norway. That he afterwards gave these islands together with Shetland in a present to his friend Rognvald, surnamed the Powerful, to console him for the loss of his son who fell in the expedition to the AEbudae. That the Earl Rognvald gave them to his brother Sigurd, with provision however that the right of investiture and conferring the dignity of Count, should be in Harald. That sometime after Harald, on account of the death of his son, had passed the sea from Norway to attack Einar de Cespite but that, by the interposition of friends, the affair was made up on condition that all the Orkney and Shetland isles should remain Harald's property and pay moreover sixty marks of gold for the slaughter of his son. That not long after, Harald's son Eric Blodox, when flying from Norway, accounted Einar's sons no more than vassals; and, for proof of this, that he carried two of them along with him to England where they were both slain with him and after them Thorfin Headcleaver, their brother, governed the isles. That the sons of Eric, when forced to fly from England, had possessed them in their own right and, upon their departure, had given them to your ancestor Thorfin. That Harvard succeeded him in the Earldom, who was followed by Liot, this last being the immediate predecessor of your father Hlodver. You are sensible," adds he, "that this part of my patrimony (for I reckon as such all that belonged to Harold Harfagre) is now in your possession since the death of the greatest part of the sons of Eric Blodox. For though his daughter Rognhild is still alive, she is accused, and with great appearance of truth, of so many and horrid crimes committed on these islands, as not only to render her unfit for the government of them but, in the judgement of good men, worthy of a capital punishment. But leaving these things, since you are now in my power, I offer you the choice of two things; either profess yourself a Christian, be baptized with your people and pay homage to me for these islands and hold them from me in a fiduciary right though with the same immunities you or your ancestors have hitherto enjoyed, thus making you my future friend and, with me, becoming a partaker of that heavenly kingdom which is to be bestowed by God on those who obey his precepts. Or, if you refuse this, your death not only immediately follows but I will likewise lay waste these islands with fire and sword, unless the people embrace this true liberty, which is only to be found in the possession of Christianity; so that you ought to consider that you not only, by refusal of my offer, subject yourself and people to present and imminent danger, but render yourself obnoxious to what is more dreadful, namely to eternal punishment."

To all this the Earl boldly replied: "It will be in vain for you, O King, to attempt to make me forgo the religion transmitted to me by my ancestors or to deny that worship I have been so long accustomed to pay the Gods. I indeed reckon not myself more clear sighted than my fathers, nor can I perceive in what the worship of that Deity you command is to be preferred to that inculcated from our childhood." Notwithstanding this obstinacy of the Earl, the King determined not to give up his point, only to change the method of proceeding. He therefore caused seize Hundi the Earl's son and, standing over him with his drawn sword[5] as if immediately to kill him, he told Sigurd that now he would be convinced from experience that he would spare none who refused to worship the God of heaven and behave according to the precepts of that Gospel which he had proposed to them: "And," adds he, "you, the father, shall not only behold your son perish by this sword but you, together with your people, shall be involved in a common destruction, solely occasioned by your obstinacy; unless you save yourself by immediately entering with all your people into the service of that great God, of whom I also profess myself a worshipper. Nor will I depart these isles till I see all this performed and you, with this son which I hold, initiated into these mysteries by baptism." Sigurd, in spite of his love to the idolatrous rites he had been brought up in, was obliged to submit himself to necessity and, together with his son, whose name was changed into Hlodver or Ludovick, was baptized. After likewise coming into the King's terms as to the Earldom for which he did yearly homage, he gave up his son as a hostage in pledge for his performance of what had been agreed between them and the King carried him away to Norway, having first taken care that all the people should be entered as Christians, and left many clergymen and other learned men to instruct the multitude in their new religion.

After the King's departure, the Earl of Orkney's son lived but a very short time with him and, as soon as his father knew he was dead, he threw off his allegiance to Norway and contracted new connections with Malcolm, King of Scotland, whose daughter he married and by her, had Thorfin afterwards Earl of Orkney; he however strictly continued in the practice of that religion he had embraced together with his people.

The time when this transaction happened is disputed, some placing it in the second year of Olave Tryggueson's reign and in his return from England whence he had brought a great number of Ecclesiastics of all ranks to plant the Christian religion in his own country. Others that it was on his return from an expedition into Ireland, however the first account seems to be the truth, as he is said to have left several divines in Orkney it is probable they were of those he had brought from England.

We come now to the last adventure Sigurd was engaged in which proved fatal to him. He had been allured by promises to take part with Sigtrig Silkeskeg or Silkbeard in a quarrel between him and his father-in-law Brian, both Kings of part of Ireland; and, after leaving his affairs at home and his youngest son Thorfin to the care of his grandfather the King of Scotland, he took with him his elder sons by his first wife, Brus, Summerlid and Einar, surnamed Wrymouth. This war was said to take its rise from the following circumstances. Kormlod, Brian's wife, a woman of bad character, had behaved so ill to her husband that he was obliged to turn her away. This she took very much amiss and with great impatience and stirred up her son Sigtrigg by a former husband, Olaus Kuran, the King of Dublin etc., to revenge the afront. He, in name of his mother engaged (as was said) Sigurd on their side promising him, if they got the better, her hand in marriage and Brian's Kingdom for his pains. Sigurd was highly pleased with these terms and accepted them, notwithstanding the dissuasion of his friends who all of them were against his having anything to do with such a shameless prostitute; however all was in vain, he ran cheerfully to his ruin and promised to be in Ireland by Palm Sunday with all his army.

Nor was Sigurd alone engaged on Kormlod's party. She sent her son, upon his return from Orkney, to endeavour to gain Broder and Uspac, two famous pirates who then haunted the western side of the Isle of Man and commanded a fleet of thirty ships, themselves brave men and till then unconquered. He laboured his point by promising them mountains of treasure and adding, what before had been promised to Sigurd, the hopes of Broder marrying his mother and her husband's kingdom, which effectually secured him; but this agreement was to be kept a dead secret, especially from the Earl of Orkney.

This Broder, it seems, was a Christian and belonged to the church but is represented as a bad man who despised his religion and, without scruple, joined with the heathens in their idolatrous sacrifices to their idols; he is said to have dealt much in magic the practice of which prevailed then much among the northerns.

Upon Broder's joining himself to that side, he did all he could to induce his companion, Uspac, to take the same part but the latter, though a heathen, would not fight against so good a King as Brian whose virtue he revered, and indeed he is said to have been possessed of every Kingly virtue, his clemency and lenity in punishing offenders being so remarkable in particular that he seldom exacted the forfeit of their crimes till he found they were irreclaimable, by persevering and caught in them more than three times.

There were on the King's side his brother Ulf Hreda, a good commander and a stout companion; besides one Kiarthialfad, a nursling of the King's, a son of a neighbouring prince between whom and Brian there had been continual wars, the issue of which was that the former, whose name was Kilfi, had lost his crown and after embraced the life of a hermit. Brian, meeting this unfortunate prince while he was making a journey to Rome, was reconciled to him and educated his son, regarding him even more than his own children as he found him a forward and sprightly youth. When this quarrel happened Kiarthiafad was grown to man's estate and the King had three sons by former wives (or at least none of them by Kormlod) Dunglad, Margad (called by Sir James Ware, Murchard) and Thani or Tdde.

Upsac, the pirate, as he would not join his comrade Broder against the King, with reason began to fear what the treacherous disposition of the former might practice against him and therefore withdrew himself from Broder with his part of the fleet, which consisted of ten ships, and afterwards joined with the King.

When the fleets were parted they lay not far from on another but that of Broder was continually vexed with prodigies to which in these times much credit was given and they were reckoned a sort of divination from which much of futurity was expected to be drawn. One night it rained boiling blood which Broder and his men catched in their shields and other pieces of armour and, in the morning, a man was found dead in every ship. The next night all of their swords drew of their own accord and mixed with one another in a fierce fight, while the battleaxes, spears and such like missile weapons were seen flying through the air and often fell upon the men with such violence that they were obliged to save themselves with their shields and even this did not hinder many of them from being wounded, few escaping safe. A night passed in this manner left them little inclination for sleep, this they were obliged to indulge themselves with in the day time but what must have been their surprise when they found as the night before, in each ship, a man wanting. Nor was the third passed more quietly, for now they seemed to be attacked and torn by Ravens with iron bills and claws, which set upon them while darkness remained and they were obliged to secure themselves from these ravenous enemies the best way they could with their armour till daylight which delivered them from their fears and, what was most wonderful, the next morning they found, as the two nights before, a man missing from every ship. Struck with all these omens the meaning of which they could not fathom, Broder ordered his boat to be got ready and, going to Upsac, told him what had happened and desired his explanation. The latter, having first bargained for peace between them, being still afraid of Broder's treachery, deferred giving him his thoughts till it was near night when he told him the shower of blood foreshewed a bloody battle and cruel slaughter both of his as well as his enemy's troops; that the noise and clamour betokened sudden death; their swords drawn of their own accord shewed the battle to be nye at hand; that the attack made upon his men by those monstrous ravens armed with beaks and claws of iron meant that the demons which they worshipped would suddenly drag them in their talons to hell after their fall in battle. Grief upon this occasion had much moved Broder before but, upon this interpretation, rage and fear together took so far possession of him as to render him speechless and, returning in a hurry to his ships, he so far forgot the promise he had made to Upsac that he prepared to destroy him immediately; and would have done it if he, foreseeing what might happen, had not slyly got ashore and cut Broder's cables, vowing at the same time, if he got out of his hands, to become professor of Christianity; and, adds our author, the Deity lent a propitius ear to his pious vows and delivered him from the malicious hatred of this distracted man.

Upsac then went to Brian and laid open all his enemies' designs when, performing his vow and professing himself a Christian, he was received by the King into the number of his followers. Brian immediately set about raising men to defend himself and gave orders to his chiefs to levy troops through all his dominions with which they were to repair to Dublin by Palmtide ready for battle; his commands being quickly obeyed all things were soon ready on their side.

Sigurd came about the day appointed and many of note in their countries followed him, among these were Thorstein, the son of Hall, possessor of a place called Side; Waldor, the son of Gudmund surnamed the rich; and Hrafn surnamed the red; besides fifteen other Icelanders which Flosi spared him from his fleet, himself being on his way to Rome to pay a vow there and therefore could not, though he was willing, attend the Earl in this fatal expedition. He had, likewise, Erling a chief of the western isles in his train and many Orkneymen and would have had more but he refused to allow Harec, the first in dignity of the Orkney gentlemen, to accompany him, telling him it would be more convenient for him that he should stay at home and that he would speedily let him know how things went.

When the Earl came to Dublin he found Broder there who attempted by magical incantations to lay open the event of the war; by which he understood that if the battle was referred to the day of our Saviour's passion that the victory would indeed fall to the King's side but that it would be gained at the expense of his life; that if they engaged before that time, a universal destruction of the King's forces would ensue. The same day a certain man mounted on a grey horse and having a leader's staff in his hand, came to Broder and Kormlod with whom he had a long secret conversation; and on Good Friday both parties drew out their forces for the engagement. On Kormlod's side both Broder and Sigtrig were stationed in the wings and Sigurd in the centre; and to the first of these on King Brian's party was opposed Ulf Hreda; to Sigtrig, Upsac and Brian's sons; while

Kiarthiafad fought against Sigurd in the centre. King Brian, as he would not engage that day, remained at some distance in the midst of his guards as secure as if he had been in a garrison.

The battle began with the greatest rage on both sides. Broder fought with the utmost bravery and threw the opposite ranks into confusion, his soul being invincible, he had rendered his body, by the help of magic, impenetrable to the stroke of any weapon. However his opponent, Ulf Hread, though he could not wound him, yet struck him three times to the ground and, upon his getting up with some difficulty the third time, he was so terrified that he immediately fled from the battle and hid himself in the next wood, his men likewise following his example. The division commanded by the Earl of Orkney fared much worse, for Kiarthiafad made such a fierce attack that, all the vanguard being slain or by fear rendered useless and the standard bearer himself killed, the whole division began to waver but another, taking up the standard, the battle was renewed. But notwithstanding the intrepidity and valour of the Earl, which was nowhere more apparent than in this fight, for he often rallied his shattered forces and not only sustained but beat back the enemy in their fiercest assaults, encouraging his men by his example in fighting and earnest exhortations to bear up manfully; yet his adversary still prevailed and slew his new standard bearer in his next attack. The Earl, observing this, ordered Thorstein the son of Hall to carry the standard but luckily by Amund White he was forbidden, Amund warning him that it would be fatal to everyone who bore it. It was some time after offered to Hrafn the Red but he refused it and desired the Earl to be the bearer of his own Devil (this he called because composed by Witchcraft), who replied it was but reasonable the scrip should be hung to the elder and, taking the figure from the spear which supported it, he carried it wrapped up in his garment. Amund White soon after fell and was followed by the Earl who was run through with a dart; and thus his mother's charms with which she had prepared that fatal ensign, after the death of many others, at last brought about likewise her son's destruction; the flattering presents of these wicked Genii (adds our author) always having a bitter conclusion.

Upsac, after he had broken through and through that part of the army commanded by Sigtrig, put him to flight much wounded and with the loss of two sons and, after him, all the army fled in the greatest confusion except Thorstein the son of Hall who, while the rest were flying with all speed, sat down and fastened his shoestrings. Being found in this posture by Kiarthialfad he asked him what hindered him from saving himself with the rest. "Because," answered he, "I cannot reach home this night, I am an Icelander." Upon hearing this his life was spared. There follows in the original, a fabulous story concerning Hrafn Rufus who, in his flight was said to be stopped in a river by the Devils and there had a vision of hell and the torments of the damned, likewise he saw several of the evil spirits about to convey him thither; but upon his application to Saint Peter, the merit of two pilgrimages he had already performed and the promise of a third if he gave him his assistance to escape, he was freed from these troublesome companions and got over the river. Such was the influence of the Pope and his Monks even in the halls of Pluto, adds our author; and indeed the Monks seem in the earliest periods to have made the best use of their time in enslaving men's minds by superstition rather than by teaching them the true principles of Christianity into the practice of which religion these people had so newly entered.

Whilst the King's party were thus employed in a hot pursuit and many of those who had stayed by the King as his Guard, likewise joined the pursuers so that but a few remained with him; this was observed by Broder who lay concealed in a neighbouring wood and thence, rushing with his party, set upon the few that remained with Brian and, after a cruel slaughter and route of these, he beheaded the King himself. The writers of these times who were mostly monks, and never failed to interlard their stories with something of the miraculous, add that a young man named Thate, throwing his arm in the way of Broder's sword to ward off the blow from the King's neck, had his hand cut of at the same time with his head but that, upon its being stained with Brian's blood, the hand was joined to the arm and remained whole as before.

Broder was now pluming himself upon this slaughter and promising himself perpetual fame for the action when messengers came with news of it to the chiefs of Brian's party who were still engaged in the pursuit but soon left it off on receiving these mournful tidings and turned all their fury on the Pirate. They surrounded the wood or copse where he was again concealed and which seems to have been but of small extent, for they cut down the trees till they came to the place where he lay hid and, having seized him put him to a cruel death by opening his belly and fixing one end of his intestines to a post which they forced him to run round till, by thus tearing out his own entrails he breathed his last in torment. His soldiers were likewise all put to death, a practice not at all disagreeing with the manners of the times.

Besides the fifteen men which Sigurd, Earl of Orkney, received from Hosi and who all fell in this battle, others of his followers likewise ended their days there, as Haldor the son of Gudmund an Icelander and Erling of Stroma in Orkney. Hrafn Rufus escaped and related these transactions in Orkney.

Here the original entertains us with the history of several prodigies which were said to have happened on this occasion and these in several countries, some of which strongly mark the belief of that and the former ages, particularly the following reported to have happened in Caithness. A certain man called Darad observing a number of people riding towards a neighbouring hill and appearing to him as if they entered into it, went that way to examine whether his senses had not deceived him and saw twelve women[6] employed in weaving a web[7] in which they used human heads for weights; instead of warp, intestines; arrows supplied the place of woof and, to keep their work steady, they had a sword. Whilst they were at work on this strange piece they sung the following song which has been preserved by Bartholinus in the Danish Antiquities etc. copied by our author. Follows the Song in the original:-

> "Vitt er orpit
> fyrir valfalli
> rifs reidi Sky rignir blod
> nu er fyrer geirum
> guarr upkominn
> vefr verthiodar
> thoer (rectius than) er vinir fylla
> raudum vepte
> randves bana.
>
> Sia er orphinn vefr
> yta thaurmunn
> oc hardkliadr
> hofthum manna
> ero dryrrekin
> daur at skoptum
> jarnvardr yllir
> en aurum hryloadr

skolum sla sverdum
sigrvef thenna

Gengr Hildr vefa
oc Hiorthrimul
Sangridr Sirpul
sverdum rognum
Skapt mun bresta
mun hilamgagarr
i hlif koma

Vindum vimdum
vef Darradar
sa er ungr Konungr
Atti fyri
fram skollum ganga
oc i folk vada
thar er vinir varir
vaptum skipta

Vindum vindum
vef Darradar
oc siklingi
sidan fylgiom
thar sa bara
Gudr oc Gondul
er grami hlifdu.

Vindum vindum
vef Darradar
thar er ve vada
vigra manna
latun ei gi
lif hans faraz
eigu Valkyrior
vigs um kosti

Their muno lyder
londum rada
or utskaga
adr um bygdu
gued ec rikum gram

radinn dauda
nu er fyrir oddum
jarlmadr kniginn

Oc muno Irar
angr um bitha
that er alldri mun
ytum Jyrnaz
nu er vefr ofinn
en vollr rothinn
munu um londfara
loespioll gota

Nu er ogorligt
um at litaz
at dreyrugt sky
dregr mod kimme
mun lopt litad
lyda blode
athr spar varar
springa allar.

Vel gvedu ver
um Konung ungan
sigrhlioda fiold
syngium heilar
enn hinn nerni
er keyrer a
geirliotha fiold
oc gumum sigi

Ridum hestum
allz ut borum
brugdnum sverdum
a brott hedan.

    Instead of presenting the reader with the Latin translation of this famous song which, notwithstanding the encomium passed on it by our author, seems to possess but little of the Spirit of the Northern Poetry, I shall give it according to the beautiful version of our own countryman written entirely in the terribly beautiful manner of the Northern Scalds:-

    Now the storm begins to lour,

Haste, the loom of hell prepare,
Iron fleet of arrowy shower,
  Hurtles in the darkened air
Glitt'ring lances are the loom,
  Where the dusky warp we strain
Weaving many a soldier's doom,
  Orkney's woe and Randver's vane.

See the grisly texture grow,
  ("Tis of human entrails made)
And the weights that play below,
  Each a warrior's gasping head.
Shafts for shuttles, dipped in gore,
  Shoot the trembling chords along;
Sword that once a monarch bore,
  Keep the tissue close and strong.

Mista black, terrific maid,
  Sangrida and Hilda see,
Join the wayward work to aid,
  "Tis the woof of victory.
Ere the ruddy sun be set,
  Pikes must shiver, jav'lins sing,
Blade with clatt'ring buckler meet,
  Hauberk clash and helmet ring.

(Weave the crimson web of war)
  Let us go and let us fly,
Where our friends the conflict share,
  Where they triumph, where they die.
As the paths of fate we tread,
  Wading through th'ensanguin'd field,
Gondula and Geira spread
  O'er the youthful king[8] your shield.

We the reins to slaughter give,
  Ours to kill and ours to spare,
Spite of danger he shall live
  (Weave the crimson web of war.)
They whom once the desert beach,
  Pent within its bleak domain,
Soon their ample sway shall stretch

O'er the plenty of the plain.

Low the dauntless Earl[9] is laid,
   Gor'd with many a gaping wound;
Fate demands a nobler head,
   Soon the King[10] shall bit the ground.
Long his loss shall Eirin weep,
   Ne'er again his likeness see;
Long her strains in sorrow steep,
   Strains of immortality.

Horror covers all the heath,
   Clouds of carnage blot the sun,
Sisters weave the web of death,
   Sisters cease, the work is done.
Hail the task and hail the hands,
   Songs of joy and triumph sing,
Joy to the victorious bands,
   Triumph to the younger King [11],

Mortal those that hear'st the tale,
   Learn the tenor of our song,
Scotland through each winding vale,
   Far and wide the notes prolong.
Sisters hence with spurs of speed,
   Each her thund'ring faulchion wield;
Each bestride her sable steed
   Hurry, hurry to the field.

After the song was ended everyone tore a piece of the web which she kept and all of them, mounting their horses, half directed their course to the north, the rest southward. The same is reported to have appeared in the Faro Isles; besides several monkish wonders said to have happened in Iceland and which our author attributed to the juggling legerdemain of the actors, who were seldom wanting when any remarkable occasion could be laid hold of to amuse and enthral people's minds by admiring these empty fopperies.

I shall add the history of one more prodigy said to have happened on that occasion which, though like the rest fabulous, is admitted here to show the belief of the people of these dark ages with regard to the communication between departed spirits and mortals, a doctrine which neither length of time, a more progressive philosophy nor a more universal knowledge of the purer precepts of Christianity was able to root out of men's minds.

We have seen before that Sigurd at his departure would not allow Harec to accompany him in his expedition but promised to give him the earliest intelligence upon his return how matters went. He therefore appeared as if returned with a number of followers and, when he seemed at a small distance Harec went out on horseback to meet and salute him. He was observed by several people at a distance to come quite up to the Earl and, after mutual salutation, both of them, without lighting from their horses seemed to enter and disappear in a certain tumulus but henceforth neither the Earl not Harec or any remain of them could ever be found in Orkney.

The history of these times add that Gilli, Earl of the AEbudae, dreamed he saw a man who called himself Herfin and told him he came from Ireland. Upon his asking him "What news", the other answered in verse, which was customary in these times.

> Funistas refere caedes, bellique procellas,
> Et genus omne mali, quo jam glacialis Iverni
> Concupitur; metas mensi pervenit ad oevi
> Sigurdus, Comitum decus immortale vir ingens
> Sanguine defectos cecidit collapsos in artu
> Horresco referens, superato victor ab hoste
> Sternitur ipse Brian, Regum quo justior alter,
> Nec pietate fuit, nec belle major et armis.

This famous battle in which Brian and Sigurd fell and, in the event, made a great change in the Irish affairs, is reckoned to have been fought on the twenty third of April 1014, which calculation, though it disagreed with the Norwegian writers, yet is supported by the best writer of the Irish antiquities who relates the whole affair with not many differing circumstances from the foregoing.

1. Now Duncansbay, a large bay and headland opposite to Orkney,

2. Vatzdoela saga, or from the book of the history of Vatzdale.

3. I have rendered the word 'Curio' thus though perhaps wrongly for want of a more proper word.

4. This particular shows us what the opinion of the more thinking Northern was concerning their country's Mythology and indeed it would have argued the utmost stupidity in a national being to have adopted all the fables which had been obtruded on mankind by artful and designing men in this matter. No wonder then we find the wisest men of all the Heathen nations looking beyond the religion of their country though common prudence hindered

them from making too open attacks on it; this however was not the case among the northerns, they sometimes expressed their sentiments in the most public manners concerning their Gods, being born free, they could bar no fetters.

Vid: Piercy's translation of the North; antiq; p.151 et sec.

5. These isles are not the only country where Christianity has been planted with the sword; others have been dragooned into it who afterwards made very good Christians.

6. These women were the fates or Valkyrae of the Northerns and the web they were employed on, the scheme of the battle. They were the choosers of the slain and the bestowers of victory.

7. To understand this method of weaving we must have recourse to the times of the ancient Norwegians where their looms were not constructed with such art as now. Then they wove their course cloth called vamiel in what many called "opsta-gang" which was with stone weights at the end of the warp to keep it tight much in the manner of tapestry weaving. Instead of a shuttle made of reed, they used an instrument resembling a sabre of bone or iron which they thought preferable.

8. Sygrtig.

9. Sigurd.

10. Brian.

11. Sygtrig.

Chapter 6

The history here is connected with that of Iceland and goes a little back to explain the reason of Flosi and Kari's coming to Orkney, both of whom we have already seen were much esteemed and honoured by Earl Sigurd; and, as that digression takes in several events which strongly mark the manner of the times, we shall admit it.

It has been observed that Grime and Helgi the sons of Nial, upon their departure from Orkney for Norway, met with but sorry treatment there, being punished for another's fault, and narrowly escaped from the confinement they had been thrown into by Haco a Norwegian chief, through the interest and assistance of Kari. The story was this, one Thrain a noble Icelander, a favourite of Haco, was about to return to his own country after having deservedly gained Haco's friendship and felt the fruits of it in the honours and presents he had bestowed on him. While he was detained by contrary winds he was addressed for a passage with him by one Hrapp, a fellow guilty of the greatest crimes but unhappily his countryman; and, being moved with the imminent danger he saw him in, as he was strictly sought for punishment, he admitted him into his ship and concealed him till the wind came fair when he carried him off with himself. This Hrapp had been freely entertained for a whole winter by a nobleman called Gudbrand and, in return for his friendship, he abused his daughter, killed an old man who had been appointed her tutor by her father and impudently came into the hall for dinner carrying the bloody instrument with which he had committed the murder in his hand and himself all daubed with gore. He slew those who were sent to apprehend him and wounded the son of his benefactor and, not content with all this mischief, he set fire to a very splendid church which belonged to Gudbrand and Haco, stripping the images of their garments and carrying them off. Escaping afterwards by his speed from the pursuit of the Earl who followed him with armed men, he first met with the sons of Nial who were going to Iceland but refused either to receive of allow him to accompany them thither, but for both which he prevailed on Thrain who received him into his ship and carried him off from Haco's rage who, having no other object to wreak it on but Nial's sons, them he made to feel its utmost effects for no other reason than their being countrymen to the delinquent. He slew their seamen and what soldiers they had with them and threw themselves into prison, from whence, as is said, they were freed by the friendship of Kari.

On their arrival at Iceland together with Kari and his elder brother Skarphede, they demanded satisfaction of Thrain for so great an affront and, upon his returning a jeering answer, they slew him and Thrapp. This affair, by the mediation of friends, was made up with the deceased Thrain's relations and Nial, who is represented as a wise and prudent man, to ward off any ill will which might remain among Thrain's powerful friends, took home his son, then a child by name Hoskuld, and bred him up, giving him the best education the times afforded and took every method to reconcile him to his sons who had slain his father. When he grew up Nial got him appointed Governor of the district and procured for him in marriage a lady of great beauty and riches called Hildigune, Flosi's niece, whom he could not have obtained had he not been advanced to that post of honour; and by these and such like good offices he and all his family were altogether devoted to those of Nial.

In their neighbourhood lived one Maurd Valgard, powerful by birth, fortune and relationship; this man, upon the passing of the new laws which Nial and Hoskuld had contrived with great pain and attention and therefore changed the state of affairs as to judicial matters, had led the Curionate. Maurd depended upon his great interest and, by his father's advice, attempted every method to regain the dignity of Governor for which he too it seems had been a candidate, and not only this but wanted to render himself absolute in the quarter to which he belonged. This he thought impossible to accomplish as long as both Hoskuld, Nial and his sons were alive and in friendship; he therefore left no stone unturned by spreading what slanders he could invent, by sowing dissensions and divisions to set them by the ears, hoping by this means the slaughter of one or two more of them would ensue, all of which would make for him in his ambitious designs. The first step he took to make his mischievous project effectual was to make himself agreeable to both parties and, by an insidious liberality, force them to accept of many presents and entertainments, all this to give him the greater weight with them and make them place the greater confidence in him. This he had no sooner accomplished but he began his treacherous manoeuvres by calumniating each party to the other, by employing all his art in poisoning every good thought they might have for each other and raising and feeding rancour; all which he cunningly pretended was merely out of goodwill to the party he immediately attempted and that he had no design but to have them guard against the treachery of the other.

Hoskuld was so far from giving credit to his scandalous insinuations, that he told him openly it would be vain for him to make him doubt his friends, that he could observe nothing in their behaviour more suspicious now than at other times or differing from the benevolent behaviour he had always experienced from them towards him; he concluded with a reprimand for his thus attempting to cast him out with his friends and an assurance that he would rather be slain by their devices than think so meanly of them.

Though Maurd's designs were thus frustrated with Hoskuld, they succeeded better with the sons of Nial whom the former, either by contempt or forgetfulness, had neglected to inform of the mischief that was going forward; they gave ear to the wicked designer but concealed what they heard from their father, being persuaded however that unless they prevented their enemy, they should all fall by his treachery. That they might make trial of the certainty of what Maurd had informed them, they proposed to him to take part with them in the crime and danger of cutting off their adversary and which he, lest he should render himself suspected and spoil his own project, did not in the least refuse. The plot being thus laid Kari, with four associates early in the spring, attacked Hoskuld who had gone out to take a morning walk wrapped up in a gown he had got from his wife's uncle Flosi and killed him by a stab from each of them. All he said was 'God pity me and pardon you." His wife Hildigune preserved the bloody garment till the arrival of her uncle Flosi and, when he came, she placed him with great politeness on the highest seat or that reserved for Kings or Earls, notwithstanding his remonstrances against receiving this honour which did not belong to him. She then clothed him with the bloody vestment and, in the boldest terms, challenged him to revenge the cruel death of his relation, except he had a mind, by his refusal, to be reckoned by all posterity as infamous. Although Flosi saw the great danger he ran in obeying his neice's commands, yet he likewise was sensible he could not refuse them since, according to the notions of that age, this would have been attended with great disgrace; he was therefore, notwithstanding his great repugnance, forced to reply.

Nor was Nial less grieved for the death of his nursling than his nearest relations; for he owed him so much that he could never speak of him without shedding tears and professed openly that he would rather have lost two of his own sons than Hoskuld. He prophesied that this slaughter would be attended with a bloody revenge that he, together with his wife and all his male descendants except his son-in-law Kari, would by it come to destruction; as for the latter he foresaw he would escape and get the better of his enemies. Nor, adds our author, did his augury deceive him for, on the twenty-first of August in the autumn following Hoskuld' death, about nine at night Flosi, with a number of armed men (some say , seventy and others, as Arngrim, a hundred) beset Nial's house in which were twenty-five defenders. Notwithstanding the superiority of the number of the assailants they durst not advance very near, till the defenders were all of them retired into the house; and which Nial, fatally for them all, proposed, alleging that they could more easily defend themselves from within than from without the walls. The event was however contrary and they were no sooner in than Flosi, ordering the house to be surrounded by men, set it on fire; but that he might not seem to act altogether from cruelty without honour, he gave leave to the old man Nial, his wife and all the other women without exception to depart beforehand. Nial refused the favour, affirming that as he was so old he could not hope to revenge the death of his sons, he would rather die than live a little longer with shame. All the other women and children went away safe, according to permission, except Thord son of Kari and Nila's grandson who, though but a boy, declared he would rather suffer this cruel death with his grandfather and his grandmother than part with them; a story that carries several ways a good deal of improbability with it but, if true, shows how early the northerns took care to instil into their children's minds such high notions of filial affection and how early they were inspired with a contempt of death, though clothed in the most dreadful appearance. Finding him obstinate, Nial and his wife wrapped him and themselves up in a raw oxhide, thinking this would resist the fire and their bodies were found entire except a finger of the boy, all the rest being burnt to ashes. Halgi and Kari seem to have been the only two who attempted to escape from this cruel death; the former thought to get among the women but notwithstanding of his disguise in a woman's dress he was known by Flosi who observed he was too thick about the shoulders for a woman. When he saw himself thus discovered he immediately drew a sword he had concealed under his gown and slew one of his opposers as he himself was immediately by Flosi. Kari alone had the good fortune to escape though with great difficulty with his garments all burnt and his armour spoiled by the fire; however he threatened to harden his sword again in the blood of his enemies. By keeping himself hid in the smoke and following its course till at some distance, he got off and afterwards was the avenger of this cruel fact.

The year following, this affair was examined in the public assembly of the Island and tried with such heat and earnestness on both sides that the whole community took part in it, almost all joining with either party. Maurd Valgard, the spring of all the mischief and actor in part of it, as he had his share of the murder of Hoskuld, yet was free from all blame and even from any suspicion of any concern in it. Nay, so far was he from being suspected of having any hand in these troubles that he was chosen manager of the process after the death of Hoskuld, by his party and afterwards by Nial's. On the other side was Eyolf Bolverki, a man well skilled in the laws of his country, descended from a good family but drawn by the hope of pecuniary gratification to defend the cause of his constituents against Nial's faction whose solicitor Maurd, though inferior to few either in eloquence or knowledge of the law, was not equal to Eyolf. Maurd's party therefore got Thorhall, Helgi's wife's brother who had been brought up with Nial and had acquired a sufficient degree of skill in these matters to be his assistant. He was so much pained by an ulcer in his foot that he could not be present at the trial but lay in a sort of tent at some distance, however his advice was so useful to his partner that he baffled all the arguments his opposite Eyolf could bring against him. At length Maurd, insisting with the greatest heat that it was impossible that things could be made up, Thorhall grew so violent that, striking his foot with a spear, the boil immediately broke and in the instant jumping up without the least lameness, he ran one of the opposite party through the body. This immediately changed the face of things and, each party flying to arms, ended this civil dispute with their swords, a circumstance not at all unusual among the northerns who, upon the whole, were better at conducting a dispute by manual operation than by quirk and chicane. In the scuffle several were slain on both sides and among the rest, Eyolf, but his death was little lamented but was rather thought a punishment on him for allowing himself to be drawn aside by the love of money to defend so bad a cause.

The fray was at length made up for that time by the interposition of Snorro the magistrate of the district and a party of armed men;

however the cause was by no means decided because Kari and Thorgeir surnamed Skorargeir, another son-in-law of Nial (a brave and active man) would accept of no amends but what they afterwards took by dint of strength, by which they paid their enemies home in their own coin. The rest of Nial's faction were so far appeased that, besides satisfaction for the murder of their friends, they agreed to make it up if Flosi and all who were concerned with him in burning the house were banished for three years.

Kari and Skorargeir however, who had no such terms to keep with their enemies, never failed to indulge in their thirst for revenge whenever they had the opportunity and killed or wounded them wherever they found them, without regard to numbers. Kari and his friend had once found fifteen of their enemies asleep and, though alone, would not attack them till they had first wakened and allowed them to take their arms; yet in spite of their great superiority in number killed five and put the rest to flight[1]. At another time Kari and but a weakly second, but favoured by the situation of the ground, killed or forced eight to take to their heels. These and some other scuffles happened among them in their own country but they were not content with this, they even pursued them elsewhere wither they had retired on their banishment.

Flosi, according to agreement with the more moderate part of Nial's faction, withdrew from Iceland in the year 1013 but, meeting with bad weather, was shipwrecked in Orkney. The circumstance was a great inconvenience to him, he had everything to fear from Earl Sigurd for the slaughter of Nial's sons, his satellites, and there was no way to escape; he chose the only alternative that was most feasible for his safety, which was to trust to the Earl's generosity, he therefore waited on him and, on his enquiry about his name and country, ingenuously confessed both. The Earl had long been acquainted with his part of the action as it happened near two years before and knew that Flosi and his companions had a hand in it, he therefore earnestly enquired whether Helgi, the son of Nial, was alive or how he did, to which Flosi answered, "He lived till I killed him". The Earl who was much displeased for the death of his satellite and enraged at this barefaced declaration of his murder, ordered the perpetrator and all his companions instantly to be seized and slain. But Hosi, at the instance of Thorstein the son of Hall, then resident in Orkney and much esteemed by Sigurd and other of his friends, was pardoned; and, according to the custom of these times when any of a prince's servants or soldiers was slain, if the slayer could obtain his remission and was capable to supply his place, he was immediately installed in it with the same privileges and to perform the same duties as the defunct had done. In this manner Flosi was received into Sigurd's court in Helgi's place where he continued several years and, as first mark of the Earl's esteem, had a pardon granted for all his comrades.

While all this was going on in Orkney, Kari (always upon the hunt without doubt) in his way from Iceland, fell in with the Fair Isle between Orkney and Shetland where he lodged with one David surnamed the White; and, as he stayed there a good while, heard how everything had fallen out so luckily with Flosi. Wherefore at the yearly feast of Yule, at which time then as now, all were dissolved in mirth, especially in the Earl's hall which, to use our author's expression, rang again with festive jollity (probably they were merrier then ordinary by reason of the presence of King Sigtrig who, as said before, had come from Ireland to solicit the Earl's assistance against Brian; and the Earl's brother-in-law Gilli, Earl of the AEbudae who had come upon invitation to share in the festivity of the season). I say while the King, the two Earls and all their followers were on this occasion feasting in Sigurd's hall, the two stranger chiefs had a mind to hear more fully the story of the burning of Nial's house; and for that reason had pitched on one Gunnar Lambin to recount it and ordered him to be seated just opposite to them for hearing his tale more conveniently. This Gunnar was always an inveterate enemy of Nial's family, having first taken part with Thrain in his quarrel with them, and afterwards with Flosi. In the course of his relation, Sigtrig asked him with what strength of mind Skaphed bore the flames; to which the other returned, "for some time with a good deal of resolution, but at length wept like a woman". In the instant of his giving this answer, Kari (who with his landlord David White and one Kolbein had come to the Mainland) unexpectedly entered the hall; he could not bear this reflection on his brother and, disregarding time and place, nimbly stepped up to the defamer with his drawn sword and as quickly killed him at the same time holding up in extempore verse the short and empty triumphs of calumny. This rash action, as it was not only bad in itself but an afront upon the festival, the strangers and the Earl, could not be passed over; therefore, though Sigurd had a vast regard for Kari, he was obliged to order him to be seized and slain but so much was he esteemed by all who knew him that none would obey the Earl's orders to lay hands on him. He then told the Earl that so far from being punished for what he had done, he thought he had deserved thanks from him particularly for having thus revenged the death of his satellite.

Upon this, leaving the hall with the same speed he had entered, he hastened to his ship and, sailing with a prosperous gale to Caithness, he stayed there a long time with a gentleman called Skeggi at Traswick[2]. After Kari's departure the King, who was struck with the bold though rash action as well as the address he had shown in performing it, observed that he must be a brave man; Sigurd told him he was unmatched. Even Flosi, though his enemy, added in excuse for him that, as no reconciliation had ever taken place between Kari and himself, he had in this acted nothing but what was proper, since it was never against the laws of honour to kill an enemy when and wherever it happened, without the least regard to time, places or persons. Flosi afterwards faithfully related the story of Nial, without any of the ignominious circumstances the other had mixed with it.

We have seen before that, in the time of Brian's struggle, Flosi could not accompany Earl Sigurd to Ireland as he was on his way to Rome; he however stayed in the AEbudae till after the battle and, even at the time the before mentioned vision is said to have appeared to Gilli who related it to him, he had not left them. From the AEbudae he went to a place our author mentions several times under the name of Bretland or Carnavia; of which route Kari got word by his spies and followed him thither in a ship of Skeggi's, where he killed one of those concerned in Nial's murder called Kol Thorstein, a man whose loose tongue had aggravated his former crime; and then directing his course northwards, passed a year in a town of Scotland our author calls Whitburg with Earl Melcolf or Malcolm (probably afterwards King of Scotland). Flosi, after he had performed Kol's funeral rites, which he did with great solemnity, passing the ocean came to Rome where, at a vast expense, he obtained his Holiness' pardon for all his crimes, after which returning by Norway, he went home. Kari, in his turn, went to Rome and, having purchased a similar remission, came back before winter to Thraswick in Caithness and, while he passed the winter there, his wife Helga (Nial's daughter) died in Iceland. Next year in his return home, his ship was driven on the rocks of the province where Flosi was chief and he lost everything on board, only he and his sailors being saved. This was no place for him as things stood, nor could he get away without applying to Flosi, the only shift he had was to throw himself on his generosity, of which he might conceive great hopes from his character, he tried the experiment and went to his house where, instead of being received as an enemy, he was caressed as an intimate friend and, all animosities being composed between them, the peace was sealed by his marrying Hildigune, Hoskuld's widow.

The northern writers join in giving Kari an excellent character, Arngrim (in Crymogea) says of him, "he was among the first of men for address, his soul invincible, who, to great integrity, joined greater constancy and real greatness of mind." It is now time to return to the history of Orkney.

1. This was exactly in conformity to the northern point of honour, which scorned to take any base or unmanly advantage even of their most mortal enemies.

Chapter 7

After the death of Sigurd which, according to calculation and supported by the authority of the Irish writers[1], happened in spring 1014; his three eldest sons Sumarlid, Brus and Einar succeeded him, divided Orkney and Shetland among themselves in three equal portions and left Caithness and Sutherland to their youngest brother Thorfin, born of Malcolm King of Scotland's daughter, whose grandfather confirmed him in the possession of these provinces and invested him with the title of Earl. As no mention is made of Ross, Murray and other shires of Scotland said to be possessed by the Earls of Orkney, in this division of Sigurd's patrimony, it is probable, says our author, he had before his death either lost possession of them or that the writers of the times had attributed to him what belonged to the former of that name. If he lost them it must have been when he was obliged to retire homewards from the Scottish army commanded by Earl Malcolm in Caithness but, as I observed before, though the Earls of Orkney or other islanders might in their summers' inroads run over and plunder the Scottish shires, it seems scarce probable that they could maintain a constant and regular possession especially if contrary to the inclination of the Kings of Scotland; because they lay at a great distance from them and, though they might have men and ships enough to go upon plundering parties, it can scarce be thought they could leave a force sufficient to defend their conquests had they been as extensive as is pretended.

A great difference of temper soon appeared among the brothers. Thorfin the youngest as he grew up shewed a disposition inclined to avarice, he was bold, had a great deal of spirit and was much given to war. It seems he was in his nonage when his father died and tutors were appointed him. Einar was a man formed for great enterprises at which he was always grasping; but neither his person nor manners were engaging, his countenance was fierce and rough, his speech surly and his mind untractable, add to this that he was much more inclined to war than was consistent with the advantage or convenience of his people whom he continually harassed by his yearly expeditions into Scotland etc. As shall be seen.

Brus was the very reverse of Einar, he was more studious and excelled in the arts of peace than fond of war, he also differed from his brother in that his disposition was as pliable and courteous as his tongue was eloquent, in a word he was much better fitted than his brother for civil administration and, under him, the people had an opportunity to thrive while they were perpetually torn to pieces by the other. Summerlid resembled Brus in every thing; he was the eldest brother and died of a disease without leaving any child to succeed him in his third of the isles which therefore returned to his brothers, Thorfin claimed a part of his brother's third not only as being his due upon the death of his father, but then had been doubtful, but was now his without the least doubt as his brother's inheritance ought equally to be divided among the surviving brothers. Einar objected to this, alleging Caithness and Sutherland to be better than the third part of the Orkneys and therefore would quit none to Thorfin; but Brus parted with a third of what was possessed by Summerlid, refusing to detain from Thorfin what was really his due. Einar considered this cession in effect a desertion, immediately seized upon Summerlid's third and kept it by force, thus making himself master of two thirds of all his father possessed in the Islands but, though this addition to his fortune rendered him both rich and powerful, yet he was not contented with the produce of what he possessed in the Orkneys but every year went out pirating which was very hard upon his share of the people who were continually dragged off from their ordinary employment to serve in these expeditions and, not only drained them of their substance immediately but also he had not it always in his power to reimburse them by the profits of his enterprises which were not on every occasion successful. Though the inhabitants were much hurt by his severity in exacting their means and forcing out their youth to war, many of whom never returned, yet he lent a deaf ear to their complaints and, according to ancient custom, demanded the service of their youth when he saw fit; and thus, their labours being lost to their native country, a dearth of everything and, at length, a famine was the consequence in that part of the country which was under Einar while Brus' people enjoyed abundance of everything owing to the superior wisdom of their chief.

Thus things stood in Orkney under Einar till at length the people quite wearied out with his oppression began to look about for some way to be delivered from it; for this reason they determined to apply to Amund a man who (next the Earls) held the first place for riches, dignity and prudence among the gentlemen of Orkney. He possessed the estate of Sandwick[2] in the Mainland and lived at a place there our author calls Hlaupandisness or Lopandsness, together with his son Thorkel, a young man who for true virtue surpassed all those of his age in the islands. When the people saw no end of Einar's rigour in forcing away their sons and servants to his piratical projects, they addressed Amund as the spring (the time for fitting out for these expeditions) drew near, earnestly beseeching his help to lay their deplorable circumstances before the Earl; they begged that he would not refuse to represent to him in the most expressive terms the lamentable case his subjects now laboured under through a total scarcity of every convenience of life and to assure him at the same time that nothing but the utmost necessity could have forced them to lay these remonstrances before him. To this Amund calmly replied that though at present he was on good terms with Einar yet they were all sensible he was not easily to be diverted from his designs nor had he at any time been ready to give a favourable ear to the people's complaint however well grounded they might be. He gave them to understand it would be dangerous for him to meddle between them and the Earl and concluded by letting them know that, as he could not hope to soften him, he would not importune him with their complaints which he was certain would not be well heard. When the inhabitants saw they had nothing to hope from the father, they next attempted the son and, after much reluctance, got him to comply with their requests and, though his condescension did not altogether please his father, yet as he saw he now could not with credit get off, he judged him to go through with it if it should even expose him to the Earl's anger. When therefore the Earl called the next assembly Thorkel set forth there the people's grievances and at the same time their humble supplications for relief; he told the Earl: "that the famine made vast havoc among the commons; that they, who by their labours in agriculture, in fishing or hunting, could help to relieve them, under the common calamity were torn from their homes; that the country by continual wars was drained of the most useful of its inhabitants, few of whom returned home but to be a burden upon it, being either returned cripples or by too much liberty taught to disdain an industrious life, so that they either could not or would not be of any future service to their fellow citizens." The Earl gave a more then ordinarily favourable hearing to Thorkel's speech and told him he would thus far grant him that, as he intended the ensuing summer to have fitted out six ships, he would content himself with three, however he cautioned him that he should not again interest himself in the people's murmurs. Thorkel returned the Earl thanks for this favourable answer and he himself received the same from the people for his intercession on their behalf and the Earl proceeded on his intended expedition. When he returned in autumn he was far from being pleased with having lost his summer's profit for want of men, therefore threatened to make up this deficiency by a severe levy for the next voyage. He was as good as his word and next spring when he was exercising the utmost rigour in forcing the commons to man his ships Thorkel again, notwithstanding his former caution, ventured to put in a word for them. Einar, though he had given him a favourable answer formerly, yet showed by his caution he was not altogether pleased with his interposition but, when he now saw him persist in it, he fell into such a rage as left no room for further application. He told him so far from lightening the causes of complaint to the commons, he determined to increase them, nay giving himself up at length altogether to his passion he threatened publicly that at the next assembly one of them should have reason to repent that day's work and immediately broke up the meeting. Amund, hearing what had passed in the assembly, grew very concerned for his son and, that he might be out of the Earl's way, sent him to Caithness to Thorfin where he took care of the young Earl's education and thence got the surname of Foster. The greater part of the more substantial inhabitants quite tired of Einar's tyranny fled from the Orkneys, some to Norway and other places, while others went to Caithness to Thorfin. This last, when he came to man's estate, again sent messengers to his brother to demand his third of Summerlid's possessions in Orkney, this Einar, as before, denied, upon which Thorfin sent a fleet to take it by force, nor was Einar behind hand in raising men to defend himself. Brus, though the most pacific of all the brothers, soon saw that their disputes would destroy the public peace in the isles, therefore got together his men though he had little thought of fighting and rather, by this measure, designed to give himself some weight as a mediator between the brethren. The peace was made up upon the following terms, that a third of the islands should be given up to Thorfin and this without regard to his other possessions in Scotland and, between Brus and Einar, it was agreed that both their parts should be joined into one possession, that the administration and care of defending it should be committed to Einar, with this particular stipulation that the longest liver should be the sole possessor of both parts; an unjust agreement on Brus' side as it entirely cut out his son from the succession to his father's inheritance in case he died before Einar who had no son to succeed him. From these particulars, adds the author, it may be drawn that Orkney was of that kind of Fee which only passed to males and excluded females.

When now all disputes were over Thorfin, having committed the charge of his third of the isles to a deputy, returned to Caithness where he chiefly resided; and Einar returned to his old trade of piracy. Every summer he infested the coasts of Scotland, Ireland and Bretland but not always with the same success for, in one of his voyages engaging with an Irish king called Konufogur (thought to be Conochor O'Melaghlin, King of Midia now Meath) at a place called Ulfreksfiord, he not only lost a great quantity of rich goods which he had probably got in other places, but such a number of men that he was obliged to leave all but one ship in which he narrowly escaped by flight. This slaughter was in great measure imputed to a body of Norwegians on the King's party. The Norwegian leader was one Eyvind Urahorn a nobleman who, for his great merit and glorious action, had rendered himself very dear to his King, St. Olave of Norway. This Eyvind, returning from Ireland the summer after Einar's defeat, was forced in his passage to Norway by stress of weather to take shelter in that famous harbour of S. Ronaldsha called Asmundarvog, where Olave Tryggueson had formerly met with Sigurd the gross and which meeting and consequences of it has already been described. As the storm still continued, Eyvind could not get away but was forced to remain there till Einar, fitting out some of his ships, came upon him and, having taken him and his men, slew the chief but dismissed the greater part of his followers who, in autumn, brought the news of his death to Norway; at which the King, though greatly enraged yet, according to his usual custom when anything moved him, said little or nothing, at least never broke out into no angry words against the actor.

After Thorfin's departure to Caithness he appointed Thorkel to go to Orkney to collect his revenues there who, while he was thus employed, heard that Einar (who still kept up the old grudge with him) blamed him for advising Thorfin to claim the third of the isles and that he was so much offended on that account, that he earnestly sought an opportunity to kill him. He therefore dispatched his business with what haste he could and, on his return, told Thorfin what he heard, he added besides that if he stayed within Einar's reach either in the parts that belonged to him or even in the neighbouring provinces, one or other of them must fall, that it was his opinion the best way would be to fly from the danger and pass his life in some secure retreat at a greater distance from his enemy's power. Thorfin approved what he proposed and advised him to go to Norway to Olave as the best place he could think of to make himself agreeable and to procure him valuable friends. Thorkel took this advice and went the same autumn into Norway where he was received with great cordiality and entertained for a whole winter by Olave and, in a short time, got so much in his favour, that he was admitted to share his most secret thoughts and this he had the better title to as he was well skilled in the affairs and methods of government then in use. In many conversations he had with the King concerning the Orkney Earls, it was very apparent by his mode of speech that he was more inclined to the interests of Thorfin, the King therefore, in the spring, sent a vessel to Caithness with a friendly invitation to him and to bring him to Norway. This Thorfin accepted and, upon his arrival, was welcomed with the highest honour. He continued in Norway the great part of the summer and, at his departure, the King presented him with a vessel most excellently equipped to carry him home in as he, after the King's example, made a present of the ship he had come in to Thorkel who accompanied him homeward. Einar who seems never to have lost sight of his resentment manned his fleet and waited their arrival in the Orkneys, but Brus always ready to make up their differences, with some pains reconciled his brothers and prevailed so far upon Einar that Thorkel was taken again into favour and, to confirm this pacification, both parties were to feast one another at their respective dwellings, this to take away every scruple that might remain of the sincerity of their professions and encourage them to live with the greater confidence in one another for the future. This reconciliating feast was first to be held in Sandwick by Thorkel and thence he was to attend the Earl at home. Everything was prepared by the former with the greatest attention and given with the same cheerfulness, in a word nothing omitted that could divert or do honour to the Earl, who on his part continued the whole time absorbed in melancholy without the least sign of satisfaction or without in the least partaking in the general jollity.

When the entertainment was ended in Sandwick, Thorkel, who was to follow the Earl home but presaged the worst from his pensive behaviour, designedly contrived the means of delaying their departure and sent out spies to see how all was on the road. They on their return told him they had observed armed men lurking in three several places, without doubt intended for his destruction. Upon this information Thorkel, by all the shifts he could fall on, detained Einar till his friends and dependants (all of whom he had ordered to be called) were come up, but at length the Earl grew impatient to be gone, no doubt ill-pleased to have thus slipped his time and perhaps angry to be put off with so many trifling excuses. At length when all was ready and the Earl and Thorkel being in the hall which had two opposite doors according to the custom of the times placed in the shortest of cross-walls of the house, the highest seat which was designed for Kings or Earls was placed on the south wall and there Einar sat till Thorkel should get ready for this journey; the fire was placed on the floor opposite to the place of honour at some little distance from it. Thorkel as if busy in preparing sometimes came into the hall by one door and sometimes through the other, crossing between the Earl's seat and the fire several times and going out at the other till he had got a body of armed men stationed at the opposite door to that where the Earl's guards were placed in waiting and altogether unknown to them; these were to defend him in the design he had in hand and which we shall presently see. When all was ready he again came into the hall and Haldor an Icelander who accompanied him shut the door at which the Earl's guards watched; on this Einar asked him whether he was now ready for the journey; he answered in the affirmative and immediately advancing with his drawn sword struck the Earl such a blow on the head that he immediately tumbled headlong from his seat into the fire, out of which Haldor dragged him and threw him on one of the benches. Leaving the Earl in this condition they went out at the other door to their friends without the least disturbance from the guards who suspected no such thing and imagined every animosity had been made up, till they found their master dead and, even then, were struck with so much confusion that they lost all thoughts of revenge and indeed, had they attempted it, it would have been attended with difficulty as Thorkel was surrounded with his friends that would not flinch from him or his fortune. He then went quietly on board his a ship and proceeded to Norway where he was well received by St. Olave, the better that he had, by returning the death that was designed for himself upon the head of the Earl, thus revenged the slaughter of the King's friend Eyvind Urahorn. He remained the whole winter in Norway.

1. Sir James W are etc.
2. Now a parish of that name, but no estate to be found.

Chapter 8

It might have been thought that the death of Einar would have established peace in Orkney and that the aforementioned contract would have taken away every shadow of dispute between the surviving brothers Brus and Thorfin, however this was not the case; Thorfin's disposition which was rather avaricious could not see his brother in possession of the two thirds of the Islands, without putting in his claim, notwithstanding the famous contract to which he was privy and which had been made chiefly on his account; therefore on his brother's death when Brus possessed himself of both thirds of the Orkneys by virtue of the contract, Thorfin insisted that this bargain (so contrary to law) could never cut him off from his right; since it was neither lawful for them nor even in their power to exclude him from his heritage; he, for that reason, demanded the half of the islands from Brus, but this was denied and he kept possession of them for that whole winter at least, others say he kept them two. An Assembly of the Heritors (Proceres) being called to decide the dispute which however proved a vain attempt, both the brothers insisting so earnestly in their different pleas, Thorfin for his right of heritage and Brus for his contract. Had there been no contract Thorfin might with a better face required at least a part of his brother's inheritance but as it is probable he consented to the aforementioned partition and it is also evident that Brus, in order to accommodate matters before and preserve peace, had entered into that disadvantageous bargain which possibly might have cut him off from even his own third as well as the hopes of succeeding his brother, it was therefore both reasonable and equitable that now he should be indemnified. After much talk, when nothing could be done, the assembly was broke up and Brus, as he found himself too weak to resist his brother should he take by force what he could not otherwise obtain, resolved to go for Norway. Thither he went and took with him his son, Rognvald, and on his arrival was well received by St. Olave. When he acquainted the King with the points in dispute between him and his brother and craved his assistance in defending his right and promising at the same time his duty and observance, he had the following reply. "That the King's predecessor Harold Harfagre had by right of conquest acquired the property of all the estates (allodia) of Orkney which he had afterwards conferred on the Earls to be held by a tenure of vassalage, not in their own right but by his favour." He added "that his title was rendered indisputable by the circumstance of Eric Blodox and his sons when they were driven from the kingdom of Norway had come to Orkney and carried the Earls off with them in their expeditions as other vassals. But to come nearer the point, when my kinsman Olaf Tryggueson touched Orkney, he exacted and obtained an oath of fidelity from your father Sigurd, on this I particularly build, as I now enjoy everything that was his. I therefore require you to hold these islands from me in fee as my immediate vassal and pay me yearly homage for them as has been the custom, so enjoying them in time to come; or, if you despise my offer, be assured that I have determined to recover all the possessions my ancestors enjoyed in the islands. At the same time" concluded he, "I would have you consider whether my assistance and friendship can be more valuable to you already superior to your brother, than that of the King of Scotland can be to him."

The Earl was much struck by these unlooked for demands, he easily saw the King was determined to persist in them; he weighed everything which hopes or fears could suggest, and brought the whole to this point, in which he considerately guessed if he submitted, his freedom in government would indeed be lessened but, if he refused, it was plainly lost; and, as he knew the King's humour to be such that he would not quit his project till he had brought it to bear, he at length, though he well knew the inconvenience on both sides of the question, chose to comply with the King's proposal and submit himself with all the heritage that belonged to him and to bind this renunciation by oath, thus again, after such subjection had been cast off, reducing the Orkneys into a feud from Norway.

As soon as Thorfin heard of his brother's voyage to Norway he immediately suspected what might be the reason for it; that he therefore might not lose his pretensions, he likewise resolved to go thither. He was encouraged to hope for success from reflecting how he had been formerly treated by the King, as also on the friendship of his officers whom, he thought, these wanted nothing but his presence to prevail on to patronise his cause. To the king therefore he went with the utmost speed not knowing what had already been transacted between the King and his brother, for he never imagined Brus had become a vassal to Norway or had thrown himself upon the King's protection. St. Olave was overjoyed at his arrival as thinking he had now the best opportunity in the world to claim his right to the isles and re-establish his authority in them; he therefore told Thorfin what had been done between him and Brus, took great pains to explain his right of sovereignty in them, as before to his brother and, in the end, required of him the same homage for his third and the same oath of fidelity. Thorfin who wanted to shun this, laboured with all his cunning to give the King such answers as might not altogether displease him and at the same time keep himself out of the snare and, after some talk, told him he was not at liberty to enter in any such engagement with Norway seeing he was already a vassal to the King of Scotland. The King easily perceiving his scheme told him plainly if he refused to submit he would immediately set one under himself over the isles, whom he would oblige him to secure in his place by taking an oath never to disturb him; he added, that if he refused this as well as his former proposition, he had everything to fear from the treacherous designs this refusal made evident he was hatching and therefore he could not be blamed if he took the best method he could for his own safety. All these things were very much against Thorfin's inclinations, he therefore cast about how to get off without complying, he however could think of nothing but protracting time by petitioning a sufficient space to deliberate and confer with his council about so weighty a matter, seeing his own youth did not allow him to be sufficiently acquainted with everything he wished to know as to his behaviour in this case. This being granted, he next demanded this liberty might be conferred on him for a year, himself in the meantime to return home to take his measures; the reason he gave for the latter particular was that the greater part of those he wanted to consult were beyond sea and there he could, with greater freedom, canvas every point of dispute. The King knew much better than to agree to his return into Scotland; his having him in his power was the only security he had to bring his project to bear; accordingly he told him he must both consult and deliberate where he was without removing elsewhere. His old friend and dependant Thorkel (now belonging to the King's household) likewise secretly informed him that there would be no possibility for his returning home before he had gone into the King's designs and taken away every shadow of dispute by complying with his demands, he advised him to remember where he was and behave accordingly. Notwithstanding the sensible bitterness the Earl felt in thus being obliged by his own act to transfer his inheritance to another and confirm him in the quiet possession of it by oath, yet by necessity there was no resisting,. Thorkel's advice which he found too well corresponded with what he had heard from the King, besides some private reasons of his own determining him, he at length followed his brother's example and surrendered himself with his third of the Islands into the King's hands and thus became his vassal, by oath confirming his deed. The difference of disposition between the brothers was nowhere more observable than in their manner of managing this transaction and was particularly remarked by St. Olave. Thorfin was far from so discreet as his brother, trusting to his own designs he rendered every part of his conduct suspect by the easiness which, after his surrender, he entered into every one of the King's proposals none of which he refused. His too great readiness gave reason for suspicion that he would be no less ready in breaking than he had been in making this agreement; nor were such suspicions in the least alleviated by his connections with the King of Scotland; as there could be nothing more probable that he only entered into engagements to get away, and hoped, by means of the Scots, to recover his heritage which had been thus extorted from him by forcible means. Brus, on the other hand, was not one of those who are continually grasping after great things, content with his own, he allowed every one quit possession of their right but could not bear to be deprived of what belonged to him. Unlike his brother he came slowly and with more circumspection into the King's terms, whence the latter concluded there was less danger of his receding from them; as it is mostly seen that he who is slow in making a bargain, is the same to break it.

When all was now settled the King in full assembly of his people to which also the Earls of Orkney had been called and attended, thus addressed himself: "I have called you all together that you may be informed what has been concluded betwixt me and the Earls of Orkney. Know then they have acknowledged Orkney and Shetland as provinces belonging to me and themselves my vassals, binding themselves by oath to remain so for the future. I therefore have granted them what each of them formerly possessed, that is, each his third of these islands in feu; but the remaining third, the possession of Einar, I seize as my right in name of a fine for the murder of my dearly beloved Satellite Eyvind Urahorn who was slain by him and, over my third, I shall set a governor." Then addressing himself to the Earls, he added, "I incline also from my own motion to reconcile you with your countryman Thorkel if this shall be agreeable to you." To this last as in all other proposals of the King's the Earls also agreed without hesitation and Thorkel, promising to conform himself to the King's sentence, the court broke up. Einar (according to the custom of the times which seldom inflicted capital punishment even for murder but rather converted them into fines which were calculated according to the rank of the person slain) was, by the King, reckoned equal to three Barons and he laid a fine accordingly; However he forgave a third of it because Thorkel had killed the Earl at a time when he was determinedly resolved to slay him, and that even by unfair means, the rest was given to the Earls by way of satisfaction for their brother's death.

All things being now settled, Thorfin, having got the King's leave of departure, made haste to prepare for his voyage, no doubt much disgusted at the success of it which was far from what he promised himself considering his interest at the court of Norway. One day, being aboard his ship just ready to sail, drinking with his friends, he was much surprised by the appearance of Thorkel who, coming suddenly upon him threw himself into the humblest posture before him and professed that he put himself altogether in his power. Upon the Earl's asking him the meaning of this behaviour since the affair had been made up by the King and all disputes between them taken away, he answered, upon being desired to rise, that the King's judgement would secure him from Brus' resentment and therefore he trusted to it: "But for you" adds he, "do with me as you please, for I am sensible as long as I am at enmity with you, I can never be safe in my country and, though I might build a great deal on the composition procured for me by the King, yet if it against your inclination I am willing to swear never to return to Orkney," The Earl, after a short silence, told him since he preferred his protection and would rather stand to his sentence than the King's, he would take him with him into Caithness where he should remain with him during pleasure whence he was not to go without leave but to continue a faithful dependant on the Earl, always ready to defend him or to be employed in whatever else he should charge him with. To all this without exception Thorkel assented and, having sworn to the performance of his promises, accompanied the Earl home. After this time there was no further communication between the King and Earl Thorfin who, notwithstanding his obligations to Norway, seems all the reign of St. Olave to have concerned himself but little to fulfil them, nor did his behaviour on certain occasions (as we shall see) shew that he considered himself much bound by them.

Brus likewise prepared to be gone but this with his usual deliberation, he took care not to be too much in a hurry lest he should hurt his own interest by too much precipitation. Before he went, the King called for him and gave him the third of Orkney in dispute between him and his brother, that he might be more on a footing in power and strength to cope with Thorfin should he make any disturbance, and defend the interest of Norway in the islands. This last circumstance highly pleased him and he was well satisfied to leave his son Rognvald a pledge for his fidelity; after which, returning home on the strength of this donation, he took possession of two thirds of the isles. Thorfin for the present sat down contented in Caithness on his share of the isles over which he set one to take care of his interest there, leaving the care and expense of defending the whole from the descents of the Danish and Norwegian pirates (who in their voyages to and from the western isles were used to land and drive off the cattle and sheep to victual their ships) to Brus, without concerning himself in the matter, although he took care to collect the revenue duly and without making any abatement on that account. When Brus complained heavily of this injustice that he was burdened with the whole expense and exposed to all the danger of defending the isles, he was answered that it was but just he should defend the whole since he had the largest share, that if he would quit the disputed third, Thorfin promised to defend the whole without the least expense of trouble to his brother which however was not then agreed to.

Much about this time happened the death of St. Olave, King of Norway, and Malcolm II of Scotland; St. Olave was slain in 1030 and, according to the Scottish history, Malcolm in 1033 as he went to Glamis, or as others in 1034, but however this may be is not very material here, the disagreement between the Scottish and Norwegian authors concerning his successor is more so. Malcolm left, it seems, no male children and only two daughters, Beatrix who was married, says Fordun, to the abthane or chief thane of Dul (probably a corruption of Thule) and Doada married to the thane of Glamis. Beatrix' son Duncan is given by all or most of the Scottish historians as Malcolm's successor and said to have mounted his grandfather's throne in the year 1034, which probably was soon after his death in winter 1033. They take no notice of Thorfin's mother, nor does our author say whether she was either of the forenamed and, after the death of her first husband, married to Sigurd, or a younger daughter. Certain it is the old chronicles which were consulted by the Bishop and council in the year 1408 upon their writing the famous letter to the King of Norway relative to the succession of the Counts of Orkney[1], agree that Thorfin's mother was Malcolm's daughter, but neither is she there named, which leaves it possible she might have been either of the aforementioned. Instead of Duncan, the Norwegians affirm, Malcolm was succeeded by one Karl or Charles the son of Hundi, but who this Hundi was or by what right his son Charles got the Kingdom of Scotland, is not certain. Our author takes great pains to prove this Karl (who was engaged in long wars with Thorfin) to have been King not (according to the opinion of several) a Scottish leader, he owns his opinion runs against the stream of Scottish history but alleges to support it the authority of Arnor, the Earl's Poet Laureate (Iarlaskalld) who was present in these wars and could scarce be mistaken in taking a Duke or Leader for a King. It is certain the credit of the Bards or Scalds, as was said in another place, was great. In their hands at a particular era was the history of the times which was to be sought for in their songs, and it is not very probable as these songs were often rehearsed in memory of the actions they recorded or as incentives to similar. I say it is not probable Arnor would take upon him, as our author observes, to rehearse a song the falsity of which would so easily by found out, except they had been to such a pass that the Earl and all his followers would digest the grossest flattery the favourite poet could offer, in magnifying a Scottish commander into a King, that he might have the more room to celebrate his master's victories over him or his title to it had been so bad that he is not admitted into the catalogue but which, in this instance, is the more remarkable as nobody that looks into Scottish history can fail to observe the great luxuriancy of the royal tree and the many branches which serve rather to add to its appearance, than contribute to support it. Or shall we close with another conjecture of our author's, namely that there were then more than one King of Scotland at one time, which at that period is at least improbable.

The history of the wars between Karl and Thorfin follow.

Karl in consequence of his Kingly powers had levied tribute out of many provinces of the Kingdom and among the rest of Caithness which Thorfin no doubt considered as his own and independent, though Karl, upon Malcolm's death, might challenge the populous and rich provinces Thorfin had held during his grandfather's lifetime. Thorfin, it would seem, was not so ready to give these up, as he neither inclined to part with any part of his right nor to have this loaded with burdens by which he himself was not to be bettered, nor was he fond to come into any terms with the new king as there was seemingly little cordiality between them. This then was the ground of quarrel. Among other provocations, Karl or Charles, had made his nephew Moddan an Earl and given him Caithness as his appendage and in despite of Thorfin, Moddan hurried over to Sutherland at that time possibly under the Scottish government and raised as large a force as he could, no doubt to force Earl Thorfin to comply with Charles' intentions in his favour. Thorfin however soon got notice of his manoeuvres and speedily got together a pretty large body of the choice of Caithness. Thorkel likewise came over with a number of Orkneymen, so that they imagined themselves strong enough for Moddan. The Scots, when they saw Thorfin's preparations, began to distrust their own and retired backwards to increase their army before they should come to action, nor was Thorfin idle. He overran many of the northern shire of Scotland, subdued Ross and Cromarty and, returning to Caithness with the greatest part of his troops and five ships, he himself stayed at Dungalsbay (Duncansbay) and sent home Thorkel with the rest to Orkney.

Moddan, being unable to avenge the mischief Thorkel had committed, returned to Charles with such accounts of the dismembered provinces and other losses as to put him in a rage so that he lost no time till he proceeded northward.

Moddan was immediately sent with a large army by land for Caithness where the king himself with a fleet of eleven ships with his best troops on board was to meet him by a certain day, their project being to enclose Thorfin between both their armies and so destroy him at once. The Earl however who was never off his guard, having got notice of their design, soon shipped his troops and slipped over the Pightland firth into Orkney, whether likewise Charles, now trusting to his numbers both of ships and men, with the greatest expedition, followed. Thorfin was not so rash as to run himself into evident danger, he therefore steered into a place on the east side of the country near Deerness our author calls Sandwick (Sandside I suppose) and immediately sent orders to Thorkel with the greatest speed to get together as many Orkney men from his part of it as he could. Brus in the meanwhile, living at his ease in the northern isles, never troubling himself with the quarrels of his neighbours.

Arriving late in the evening, the Earl lay all night at Deerness in the greatest uncertainty how far behind he had left his antagonist Karl.

This however did long continue for, early in the morning, Karl came all at once with his eleven ships on the Earl who, as yet, was no match for him and easily saw he could have no assistance from his dependant Thokel. There was no time therefore for hesitation, Thorfin behoved either to lose his fleet and provisions and what else was on board it and trust himself by land or fight the king's seven with his five ships. He chose the latter, as shame of losing his fleet and his courage soon got the better of any apprehension the inequality of numbers might have occasioned. Wherefore in a short and lively speech having exhorted his followers to behave well, he immediately ordered the ships to be let loose and to fall upon the enemy with the utmost fury. Every thing (says our author) happened according to his wishes for, the King's fleet being greatly disordered and his men startled, it was some time before he could bring them to action. Nor was the Earl slack to make his advantage of their confusion but fell on briskly and, according to the custom of the times, having made fast the ships to one another by ropes, the opponents fought hand to hand from their forecastles. Those of the King's ships, being greatly distressed and many of them killed, began to desert their quarters and were drove from their stations to the further part of the ship, most of them greatly fatigued and wounded, whither likewise Thorfin followed, jumping from the poop of his ship, now almost destitute of defenders. His example was stoutly followed and the King, seeing the immediate danger of receiving such troublesome guests on board, ordered the ships to be cut loose and make the best of their way. Thorfin took care to prevent this and, seeing this the proper time for a bold push, ordered grapples to be flung on board and immediately rushed at the head of his men through the middle of the few that were left alive with the King, which bold action so terrified the latter, that he instantly with the few remains of his crew threw himself on board the next ship and forthwith fled off to the sea. The Earl pursued for some time but, finding he gained nothing on them, returned to Orkney. Here he met his trusty friend Thorkel with a numerous body of men which no doubt determined him to follow Karl who had put into a Scottish bay called Breidafiord (probably Murray firth) and was gathering a new force for another battle. Thorfin, according to custom, laid waste the coasts of Scotland wherever he touched but had not proceeded far till he heard that Earl Moddan lay at Thursa (now Thursa east) in Caithness with a number of men and that he expected auxiliaries from

Ireland. Thither the Earl detached Thorkel with a part of the army who, whilst he (the Earl) remained in his camp employing his men in plundering the country, by secret and forced marches soon reached Caithness; for (says our author) the whole country was so friendly that none gave the least information to Moddan of his arrival in these parts. Reaching Thursa then in the night time, Thorkel set fire to the house where Moddan lodged who, terrified at such a sudden alarm, flung himself from the upper part of his house, but was soon slain by Thorkel; nor did his men meet with much better usage, the greater part being either slain or escaping narrowly, except a few that surrendered and thus became lieges to Earl Thorfin.

Moddan being thus surprised and slain, Thorkel did not delay but, taking up as many troops as he could in Caithness, Sutherland and Ross, hastened away to Breidafiord to join the Earl in Murray where they halted sometime no doubt to refresh their men. Neither was Charles idle. He made up an army of the auxiliaries Moddan had expected from Ireland, together with what troops he could procure from the three quarters of the kingdom he was in possession of and, at the head of these, he marched against Thorfin. Both parties met at a place out author calls Thorsness, near Breidafiord, and a battle ensued. Although the Scots were superior in numbers, they were well received by Thorfin, his own example inspiring his men with the utmost courage, distinguished by his gilded helmet, his sword and lance, he fought with great fury, particularly against the Irish who, in the beginning of the action were so much broken and disordered that they could never again be brought to action. Charles himself fought bravely amongst the thickest of the enemy, he was everywhere at hand encouraging and supporting his men and, by his own valour, rendered the issue of the contest a long time doubtful, till the Earl of Orkney making at length a desperate attack, the Scots began slowly to give way and, their ranks being soon after broken, the rout became general. The King seeing the general confusion fled with the rest, though others say he was killed. Nor is this improbable as Thorfin pursued (it seems) his victory as far as it would go, making great havoc among the scattered Scots, whom he pursued a vast way over-running the country wherever he came. It is therefore possible that Charles fell in the pursuit among the straggling remains of his flying followers and this is the more possible as, notwithstanding (according to our author), Thorfin made a plundering progress through Scotland as far as Fife, which he is said to have entered, yet we hear of no opposition made by Charles, nor is his name any more mentioned in history.

While the Earl pursued his success in one part of Scotland, he sent Thorkel to another quarter on the same errand. The Scots, even those of them who had surrendered to Thorfin, thinking this a fine opportunity to be revenged for their late disgraces, made preparations to attack the Earl at this time, dreading nothing less. He however had time to recall the party he had sent out with Thorkel and immediately advanced to punish those who had been thus guilty of perjury. To understand this, we must observe that in these times nothing more was requisite to constitute one, another man (as it is called in Scotland), than an oath which, being often unwillingly given, was very readily broken. No wonder then that the inhabitants of some of the Scottish provinces, being forced to swear allegiance to the conqueror Thorfin, whenever they saw a favourable opportunity, should be very ready to throw this compelled allegiance and, through their national impatience, attempt in their turn to get the upper hand. This however at this time they failed in for Thorfin, coming suddenly on them, struck them with such a panic they fled through the deserts, woods and encountered every danger to screen themselves from the fury of the enraged Earl. He pursued them for some time, says our author, and, lest his easiness in this case should provoke others to the same mode of behaviour, he overran and destroyed with fire and sword these provinces whose inhabitants had rendered themselves obnoxious to his anger, he burnt their villages, slew what men he found and drove the women and men whom age had rendered incapable of bearing arms, in flocks to the deserts. After this massacre he returned to the north where he left his fleet and, reducing the provinces through which he passed to obedience, he passed to Caithness where he usually wintered, as he spent his summers in acts of piracy according to the custom of the times.

The truth of the above depends entirely on the credit due to the Icelandic Scalds and the manuscripts consulted by Torfaeus, some of which were very ancient. As to the first, the Scalds of ancient times were certainly worthy of great credit and their songs were to be considered not so much as the overflowing of a luxuriant fancy as real history. With regard to the Scald here referred to, he was a man of the first rank present at the transactions he celebrates and relates there so circumstantially that there is little room to doubt but they must have happened. As to the latter, viz. the authority of northern manuscripts, credit is likewise due to these, particularly of Iceland. Abstracted from the world for a great part of the year, they amused themselves in recording the actions of their ancestors and their contemporaries, not with the rapid enthusiasm of the poet but with the cool candour of the historian. Though most of their compositions were in verse yet it was easy to distinguish the sport of fancy from the historic ballad. The one abounded in all the wild allegories which were peculiar to their clime, while the other contained a narrative of actions as they happened, modelled indeed into poetry but this was that they might be more easily retained and strike deeper into the mind, as incentives to glory.

As to the silence of the Scottish historians, it is not much to be wondered at, anyone who has dipped into these may soon see they were careless, inattentive and biased.

We shall dismiss the subject by observing that there is at least a great probability that there is more credit due to the Icelandic than the Scottish historians in many particulars which happened in these ages, as we shall prove in the sequel.

1. Preserved by Wallace pages 121-138. The original said to have been in the possession of the family of Sinclair but probably lost with the rest of their writings in the fire at Dysart.

Chapter 9

To return to Thorfin. Having by his various adventures got together great riches, he began to grow famous for his magnificence, excelling in this particular not only his predecessors but all the neighbouring princes and kings. For they, (says our author) only feasted their courtiers and nobles in time of Yule (Christmas) at their own charge but Thorfin kept open table for all his friends and followers for the whole winter, supplying all with victuals and ale so plentifully that there were no occasion for any of them to frequent the tavern.

The era in which Thorfin lived was while Knut or Canute, the Great, reigned over England, Danemark and Norway. About this likewise died Brus the only remaining competitor with Thorfin in the Orkney isles which he now seized in entire without the least resistance.

He however did not long enjoy his good fortune without a rival. This was Rognvald, the son of Brus, who, as we have seen before, was left by his father in the hands of St. Olave as a pledge of the fidelity to the Kings of Norway. Rognvald had been bred at the court of Norway under the eye of St. Olave who took care his noble hostage should be instructed in every art then necessary for a gentleman to know. He afterwards followed the fortunes of his master and was present at the battle of Stiklastad, in which St. Olave was slain, where he gained great honour not only for his courage but for his gratitude to the King which he never failed in towards his children even in their most distressful circumstances. After the battle in which Rognvald was wounded, he made his escape first into Sweden and afterwards into Russia to Jarislaus who then reigned there and by whom he was soon advanced in his armies and made Warden of the marches.

In the meantime the Norwegians sent messengers to Jarislaus' court to invite Magnus the son of Olave home which, after some preliminaries was agreed to and he was proclaimed King of Norway Anno 1035. Rognvald accompanied Magnus into his Country where, getting notice of his father's death as also that his uncle Thorfin had seized all the Orkney isles, he petitioned the King for leave to visit the Orkneys. Magnus not only willingly granted this but immediately gave him investiture as Earl as also, besides his paternal part, he gave him in feu the third of the isles which had been seized on by St. Olave and possessed by his father. For his passage he gave him three large ships furnished with seamen, provisions and everything necessary for the voyage, with orders to visit him when and as often as he thought proper and, upon every emergency, to apply to him for assistance, which he promised should always be at his service and, with the utmost civility, dismissed him. The Earl went straight for Orkney and, having visited his patrimonial estate, he sent messengers to Thorfin demanding the surrender of the King of Norway's third, now granted him as Magnus' vassal. It did not at that time suit Thorfin to refuse his nephew's demands as he was engaged in several quarrels in which he thought he would need help, he therefore answered that, as for the third possessed by his father, he should freely have it, as for the other part he must be sensible that it was forced from the brothers by St. Olave when they were in his power but, rather than break with his nephew and if this should be a means of establishing a lasting friend ship between them and also if he would become his companion in his adventures, he would not stand with him in what he desired. Rognvald, when he saw his uncle's easiness, complied with his terms promising him what assistance he required and his friendship for war. As soon as the spring came in Thorfin let his nephew know that he expected him with his men to join him in his summer expedition. This was quickly complied with and, after they had joined fleets, the uncle and nephew set out through Ireland, the Western Isles and the Scottish bays, fighting and plundering as they went and, after a successful battle in a place our author calls Vatzfiord, they returned to winter in Orkney, though for the most part Thorfin stayed in Caithness at a place our author called Goddgedle but, whether this was a town or castle, our author knows not.

Thus passed the time for several years in great harmony although this was often attempted to be broken by designing persons for their own ends wishing to stir up strife between the relations.

Thorfin however could never be idle. One summer, while he was on a plundering party in Scotland and the AEbudae and provisions beginning to grow scarce with him as the Irish had drove their cattle far up the country, at least further than he dare pursue them, he sent a few of his men into the nearest part of England to get what they could. The English, falling upon them on a sudden not only deprived them of their prey but killed the bravest, allowing a few of the weakest to return to tell their master Thorfin how they had sped, at the same time insulting their impudence and rashness in the grossest terms.

Their return put him in a rage but, as he could not revenge the death of his men nor the English insults, he laid up his anger for a fitter opportunity and, in the autumn, returned to Orkney. No sooner did the spring arrive than Thorfin collected a large body of men from Ireland, Caithness, the AEbudae, Orkney and from several of the Scottish shires, that there might be no time lost in taking revenge on the English. Rognvald joined him with as many men and ships as he could raise and both steered directly for the English coast, wasting and destroying everything wherever they came. Hardicanute was then in Danemark, however his officers were not long in giving Thorfin a meeting but, after a most fierce battle, they were worsted and obliged to leave the country to the mercy of the enraged conqueror who was far from slack in making use of the opportunity. No sooner was the battle over then he carried fire and sword far and wide through England and the summer only put an end to the deprivation. Before he left off he is said to have engaged in three skirmishes and two pitched battles whence, coming off victorious, he returned home for the winter.

Much about this time one Kalfus Arninus[1], who had been appointed guardian to Magnus son of St. Olave, began much to be suspected by that King to have had a hand in his father's death at the battle of Stiklastad. Kalf was conscious that he deserved such a suspicion, for he had not only been the first in the rebellion but had even given the King a mortal wound in the battle. He therefore voluntarily left the kingdom and withdrew to his kinsman Thorfin upon which, his guilt being in a manner confessed, his whole estate was confiscated. Kalf brought with him a great number of followers which however were maintained at the Earl's charge, no doubt because he imagined they would be useful to him in his designs on his neighbours.

This however he began to find expensive but there were not wanting flatterers about him who insinuated to him that he ought to recall the disputed truce of the Isles which they said Rognvald had long possessed but that this was rather by his Uncle's connivance than from any right he could pretend to them by a surrender. Thorfin was never deaf to any that made for his advantage. He therefore, in the year 1046, sent messengers into Orkney to intimate this demand to Rognvald. Notwithstanding Rognvald's surprise at such a requisition, he ordered the messengers to remove till he concerted with his friends what was proper to be done and, after consulting, sent back the following answer. "Tell my uncle (says he) that neither he can demand nor can I part with this my right without being guilty of the highest wickedness. It is an addition to the crime if he who makes the demand is equally guilty. The right I have to the disputed third of the Orkneys depends on the will of another. It is a deed of trust and entirely unalienable." He desired him the oath that he had sworn, to hold it for Magnus of Norway which he could not possibly break and, in fine, refused by any means to surrender this his third in terms of his brother's demand. When Thorfin heard his nephew's determination, he flew into a great rage, upbraided him for making such a bad use of his indulgences in attempting to detain under the silly notion of right what he had possessed so many years entirely from his good will. As to St. Olave's claim, he treated it with contempt, as this had been acquired by force and could not be binding upon the brothers or their offspring. However as he saw he could not get possession by fair means he had recourse to force and, having collected what forces he could through Scotland and the AEbudae, he advanced to wrest from Rognvald what he called his possessions. The latter no sooner understood his intentions than he called together his friends and told them what his uncle threatened, he gave them to understand that he would not tamely give up either his patrimony or feu and therefore asked their advice in the matter. They greatly differed in their sentiments some, that favoured Thorfin, advancing one thing and others another but all in such a style that he soon saw they were not hearty in his interests. He therefore plainly told them that rather than give up any part of his estate willingly he would desert the whole for a time and depend on the assistance of his adopted brother Magnus to recover it.

He immediately darted for Norway and laid before the King a state of his affairs, who was overjoyed at his arrival and offered him everything that was necessary to recover them though, from the love he bore him, he would rather he would have continued in Norway and made him large offers and, begging a sufficient number of troops and a fleet to recover his native territories, the king soon dismissed him to his satisfaction, not only giving him troops but sending a message to Kalf Arnin that, if he would desert Thorfin and take part with Rognvald, everything should be forgiven and his estate restored. In his way to Orkney the Earl touched at Shetland where he took in an addition to his forces and then sailed for Orkney where he took care to let Kalf Arnin know the King's proposals and soon found he was ready to close with them, in hopes of recovering the King's favour.

Thorfin in the mean time raised a large army in Scotland and elsewhere with which he embarked for Orkney. In passing the Pictland firth he met Rognvald sailing for Caithness to seek him. Rognvald had thirty large ships and Thorfin sixty (our author calls Randabiorg, probably from their red colour). The whole of both fleets immediately came to an engagement. Kalf Arnin was present with six ships equal in bulk to Rognvald's, but took no part in the matter.

The battle continued fierce for a long time for, though Thorfin excelled in number, yet his ships being small had greatly the disadvantage. Every weapon flung or stroke from Rognvald's took effect, while Thorfin's men could not reach their adversaries. It was not therefore surprising that the carnage and destruction of ships should be vast. In the issue of the fight the admiral's ship was so mauled and Thorfim himself in such imminent danger that, at length, he was obliged to give over and make with all speed for the shore, with loss of seventy men in his own ship, besides the wounded, which was a great number[2]. The matter however did not rest there, Thorfin instantly manned his own ship with his bravest men and, having stirred up Kalf Arnin with the bitterest reproaches to take his part, representing to him that by his former behaviour he could engage neither party, he at length gained him over and both, turning their prows against Rognvald, renewed the fight. If Thorfin had before the disadvantage because of the smallness of his ships, the scale was now turned for Kalf, engaging the least of Rognvald's fleet, poured down into them such a shower of missile weapons as neither casque, shield or other defensive armour could resist. The consequence of this was that Rognvald's fleet in their turn fled in a most shattered condition to Norway, very few remaining behind with the Admiral. The fight thus manifestly inclining to Thorfin both he and Kalf Arnin attacked the ship which carried Rognvald and, after a stiff engagement between the wounded and worn out people that remained there and the numerous assailants on board his antagonists, Rognvald soon saw that nothing could be done and therefore, ordering the chains to be cut, by favour of the night he escaped to Norway where he was as usual received in a friendly manner by Magnus who renewed his offers of an asylum.

On the day after the battle, Thorfin went through the different islands apprehending those of the islanders who had saved themselves by flight, of whom some he pardoned but put the greatest part to death and compelled all those who had been subject to Rognvald to swear allegiance to himself. After all was settled he himself accompanied with a number of his favourite followers (Satellites), having procured what provisions they could in Orkney, went to winter quarter as usual having sent Kalf Arnin to take care of his affairs in the AEbudae

Notwithstanding his defeat and flight, Rognvald was not discouraged. He soon after told Magnus that he intended to renew his designs on Orkney only he intended to change his plan of acting. Upon the King's remonstrating that the conquest of the islands was above his power, especially at this season of the year and advising to stay till spring when navigation would be more easy and he could be assisted with a fleet and army, Rognvald told him this was not at all his plan. As he had before experienced Thorfin's strength, seeing he was furnished with men from Scotland, the ABudae and elsewhere, as well as the help of his friend Kalf Arnin, he was determined not to risk the King's fleet and army again but to try his fortune with one ship well furnished with warriors and such a sailer that she might outstrip anyone who might give intelligence of his design. In this manner he intended to pass over to the isles in the beginning of winter to try his fortune, imagining he might either catch his uncle tardy or, if his designs were blown, he could escape by sea.

Magnus approved of the project, gave him a fine ship and some of his men, some of the first rank of the court attending him, and lovingly dismissed him at the same time assuring him that if he did not succeed he should be as welcome as ever at the court of Norway. After taking leave the Earl touched first at Shetland where he got intelligence that Thorfin lived at his ease attended but by a small number of guards having dismissed the greatest part of his followers (Satellites) to their own coasts as he imagined himself entirely secure on the mainland of Orkney. Rognvald lost not a moment of time but landed before anyone knew anything of the matter, surrounded the house in which his uncle resided and instantly set it on fire. As this happened in the night time most of the people were fast asleep but Thorfin, who was up drinking when he heard the noise of armed men, sent to know who was their commander and, upon being answered Rognvald, every man flew to his arms and attempted to get out, but in vain. However he allowed the women and the slaves to escape from the flames to be made prisoners by his men who seized them as they came out, a favour denied to the Courtiers as they were a species of animals whose life or death gave Rognvald no manner of trouble. The house was now wholly on fire and Thorfin, seeing no other method of escape, broke through the shingles and, taking his wife in his arms, under favour of a dark night and clouds of smoke while everyone was busy, got off to the sea side where, quickly finding a boat, he rowed to a certain headland out of danger.

After this conflagration Rognvald soon reduced the Islands and, sending messengers into Caithness and the AEbudae, without the least resistance, made himself master of everything Thorfin formerly possessed, none of his friends having the least notion of his being alive. Rognvald, having thus settled matters , sat down in Kirkwall attended by a numerous body of armed men as guards whilst Thorfin lived in the strictest concealment in Caithness among a few of his most trusted followers. It was now approaching the feast of Yule when the Earl with a large retinue went to Papa Little (probably Papa Stronsa) to prepare malt for his Christmas etc.[3] and, while this was collecting, he lodged. In the evening, calling for a larger fire, the servant told him "the firewood was almost out". The Earl replied when it is finished "we shall be old" instead of "we shall be warm" but, immediately discovering his mistake, he guessed something extraordinary would befall him as he was so little subject to such reveries that this was the first time he had ever blundered so. He likewise called to mind that St. Olave, upon a like occasion at Stiklastad, had prophesied concerning him that, upon such an accident happening, his life was near a close. He immediately suspected his uncle might be alive and was soon convinced he was so when he perceived the house surrounded by an armed force. These with Thorfin at their head secured all the doors so that none could depart the house without their permission which however was granted to all excepting the Earl and his Courtiers and the house set on fire. Among many that were allowed to depart there was a man clad in linen appeared at the gate, him Thorfin ordered to be rescued, imagining he belonged to the church. This person no sooner heard this order than, leaning on the wood which had been piled up to burn the doors, he sprung over these with ease and through the crowds like an arrow from a bow and was out of sight in a moment. Though the darkness of the night soon hid him from Thorfin he instantly knew him to be his nephew by his strength and nimbleness. He therefore gave orders to pursue and, dividing his men into parties, examined every creek and cranny of the isle. Thorfin's party went under the sea banks and were directed to Earl Rognvald by the barking of a little dog which he carried about with him. Thorkel ordered his men to kill him and even offered a reward to him that would do it. However, upon their refusing to obey him, he himself (says Torfaeus) performed this cruel office for which Thorfin who was now come up to him, was far from being angry with him.

Our Author here observes that Thorkel would have done better to have preserved Rognvald alive because, upon giving up his right to the islands, Thorfin might have dismissed him upon his confirming this by oath, for then he had nothing to fear , as no man was more observant of an oath than Rognvald or, if this seemed too dangerous, he might have made him a perpetual prisoner. However this might have been, the day after the slaughter of Rognvald, Thorfin set out for Kirkwall and, by a stratagem deceiving his nephew's guards and several Norwegians who had stayed with him since his last visit to King Magnus, he put them all to death save one whom, in scorn, he sent to Norway to carry the news to his master. The latter particular is a plain sign how much Thorfin valued the Kings of Norway, though now and then he was obliged to succumb to their superior power, but this was only for the moment for, no sooner was he out of their clutches, than this was all laid aside and even his success in making up his peace at different times with different kings plainly tells us he was not a little formidable to the Kings of Norway nor did they choose to come to an open rupture with him.

Rognvald's body was carried to Papa major (probably Papa Westra) and buried there amid the lamentations of the inhabitants by whom he was greatly beloved. He excelled all the former Earls of Orkney both in the beauty of his person and the endowments of his mind. His stature was large with thick yellow hair, he was strong, bold and agile, wise and penetrating, steady and sagacious, in a word he possessed every princely quality and would have been happy had he enjoyed the smiles of fortune.

Upon the death of Rognvald, Thorfin once more possessed himself of the Orkneys etc. without disturbance for, though Magnus of Norway was greatly enraged when he heard of the slaughter of one he loved so well and who had been educated with him from their early years, and threatened deep revenge, yet diverted from executing it by many circumstances till Thorfin, by his sudden appearance in Norway, found means to make up matters.

At this period Harald the brother of St. Olave made his appearance in Norway. Ever since his brother's misfortune he had been at Constantinople where he had become very famous for his great actions which, at length on his return, got him the appellation of the northern thunder. Magnus shared his kingdom with Harald and they, being about to pass to Denmark on an expedition when they were detained with contrary winds, beheld a couple of barks entering the same harbour and coming close up to the King's ship. From one a man having on a white garment went on board the royal Galley when the King was at dinner and, after saluting him with great humility, began to partake. Magnus returned the salute and, as he had helped himself to bread, reached him his cup and desired to know his name. The guest answered 'Thorfin'. "What", says Magnus, "Earl Thorfin..." "So I am called in my own country," said the other, "and am come with these two ships well manned and furnished according to my ability as is my duty to follow you in your wars." The whole bystanders had flocked close to hear what was passing and were equally surprised at this address. The King at length told him that his presence had altered his resolution concerning him, desired him to follow him wither he was going and to wait till another time for a full remission of his faults. The Earl then went aboard his own ship and while they lay in that bay became so familiar with the King that he trusted him with his bosom secrets, so well was he pleased with his behaviour for the time he had been with him. Thorfin however soon forfeited the King's favour, the occasion of which was this. One day being as usual invited to sit with the King on deck, while they were drinking together in high glee, a stout likely man clad in red came up to them and, after saluting the King in a handsome manner, turning to Thorfin demanded satisfaction for the death of his brother who had been slain at Kirkwall. The Earl answered in a taunting manner notwithstanding this person was one of Magnus' courtiers and that of the first rank and even in the presence of the King: "And hast thou never heard say that I never give satisfaction to the relations of those I put to death, and this because I seldom kill any without a good reason." "It is nothing to me," replied the other, "How thou dealest with others, it only belongs to me to prosecute the cause of him with whom I was so nearly connected, nor is it any concern of mine that the King should think it consistent with his honour to waive his power and allow his servants to be dragged like beasts to slaughter, these things shall give me no pain if I am made amends for my brother's murder and my own loss." "I am sensible," says the Earl, "I am here only safe by not being in your power but are you the man I spared in Kirkwall?" "I am the man," answered the other, "that thou durst not kill with the rest," The Earl concluded that he was an example of the proverb, many things happen otherwise than people expect, that he never thought it would have proved a loss to him to have spared a fox, but adds he: "It was even a fault to have spared you for had I put you to death with the rest of your companions you had not been here to complain of me to the Kings of Norway." Upon this insolent reply the King, turning to Thorfin with the utmost rage in his countenance, asked him if thought he had not yet murdered enough of his subjects without answering for them, on which Thorfin, seeing things not likely to mend on his side, left the King's ship hastily, went aboard his own and for this evening nothing more was said of the matter. Early next morning the wind coming fair, the whole fleet sailed and, about noon, Thorfin leading the van into the Jutland seas suddenly changed his course westward and made straight for Orkney, leaving Magnus and Harold to perform their summer expedition as they thought proper.

Thus Thorfin delivered himself from his scrape yet he did not think himself at all safe till the death of Magnus, which happened in the autumn of the same year and entirely freed him from all his fears from that quarter.

Upon the death of Magnus, Harald succeeded him in the other half of Norway, which Thorfin no sooner heard than he sent messengers thither to pave the way for him to follow. The King received them kindly and let Thorfin know he would be welcome. He immediately set out for Norway with two ships of twenty oars, manned with a hundred men and, on his meeting with the King, was received with great honour and, at his departure, received several princely presents. From Norway he went to Denmark where he was honourably entertained by Swain and there he began to think of taking a journey to Rome in conformity to the Superstition of the times to obtain remission of his crimes at the Pope's hands, the best medicine, (says our author) at that time known for averting the Vengeance of Heaven.

From Denmark he proceeded to Saxony where, among other honours, he received from the Emperor Henry (surnamed the Black), several horses for his journey. Thence arriving at Rome and, having obtained a full remittance for all his sins, he speedily returned.

After a fortnight journey he returned quite another man than formerly. He entirely left off his piratical expeditions, applied his mind to civil government and the arts of peace, composed a System of Laws for his people and, to crown all, built a magnificent church in the province of Byrgisherad where he had fixed his principal seat, dedicated it to Our Saviour, which was the first Bishop's See in Orkney.

Though we now-a-days know but little of the private history of the Counts of Orkney except when they went to loggerheads among themselves or their neighbours yet it will not be amiss to venture a conjecture here at the site of this ancient Cathedral.

In no place is there a name in Orkney that in the least agrees with that from Torfaeus except Byrsa or Birsa, situate on the Northwest corner of the Mainland. The particular beauty of this quarter would naturally invite the Earl to reside here in times of peace (for we never hear it mentioned in time of war), as its fertility would assure him of provisions for his numerous retinue.

Accordingly we find the Earls in all ages have made this one of their places of residence in Orkney and built castles in the taste of the several ages in which they lived. Of the buildings erected in the ages of Thorfin and Rognvald we can form very little judgement. The foundations may yet be traced near the modern buildings and heaps of ruins now swarded over with green turf.

Part of the Sinclair's Castle still remains to which the Stewart earls made great additions but these, like the former, will soon end in total ruin.

Of the Ecclesiastic buildings there are still such traces left as shew us they have been strong, handsome and spacious. The old church lately pulled down was a neat cross with arches and, if it was not the same Rognvald built[4], it was far from modern. The foundations of vast buildings are yet to be traced under the Ministers' and other gardens, strongly built of stone and run lime with the numerous cut free stones proper for gates etc. yet seen, evidence that these buildings were not intended for ordinary purposes. Add to this the reigning tradition of this being the Bishop's palace, all these, I say, put together where there is no written evidence, will amount almost to a proof that Birsa was the seat of Thorfin's Bishopric and which continued in the same place till another period, as we shall see.

Thorfin seems to have passed the rest of his time in a profound peace till death, the time of which is disputed, however our author places this event from the Danish chronicle in the year 1064, that is two years before the slaughter of Harald the Imperius of Norway and in the seventh year of Malcolm the third of Scotland.

By his wife Ingibiorge he had two sons, Paul and Erland, afterwards Earls of Orkney.

Thorfin was certainly an enterprising genius according to the accounts we have of him. He possessed nine counties in Scotland, part of Ireland, the whole AEbudae besides at length the whole of Orkney and Shetland Isles, so that it was no wonder that he was formidable wherever he came.

At five years old he was created an Earl by his grandfather Malcolm the second of Scotland. At fourteen he began his piratical expeditions, even at that tender age infesting his neighbours' territories. He enjoyed the title of Count for fifty years. His body was buried in the church he himself erected at Byrgisherad, accompanied with the tears and lamentations of the inhabitants of his patrimonial provinces, whilst those he had subdued were glad of this opportunity to withdraw their allegiance heartily tired of his severe method of government, thus laying the foundation for future quarrels in Orkney.

Thorfin was a man of a great soul, his stature tall, his countenance thin and homely, his hair black, with large eyebrows, entirely inclined to a military life for which he was body and soul adapted, steady in his undertakings, fond of riches and honour, fortunate in war, skilful in contriving and active in the execution of his designs[5].

1. Thorfin was Kalf's near relation as he had married Ingibiorge the daughter of Fin Kalf's brother, afterwards the mother of two Orkney Earls, Paulus and Erlandus by Thorfin.

2. Here we have to observe the attention the northerns took to transmit to posterity the fame of their actions. Thorfin in the time of this battle had stationed his poet Arnor "ut obque periculi metu quae ab utraque parte gererentur observare memoriaeque metrica arte consecrase posset p.60.

3. The original has it "profectus magno comitatu in Papeyam minorem ad multam polentam domum venendam, cerevisiae conficienda". Where we may observe what a serious business it was among them the preparing of the materials and brewing the ale, in so much that the Earl himself must be present at the various operations necessary in preparing their favourite beverage.

4. The author must mean Thorfin rather than Rognvald, unless he is referring to St. Olaf's Church in Kirkwall originally built by Rognvald Brusison - Ed.

5. For all we know concerning Thorfin we are indebted to Arnor, the Earl's poet, who in all his expeditions constantly attended him. Many of Arnor's songs are still extant in the Libraries of the North.

Chapter 10

Here as elsewhere we have a mighty disagreement between the Scottish and Norwegian or Icelandic authors. According to the former Malcolm Canmore married Margaret, Edgar Atheling's sister, by whom he had six sons and two daughters, none of whom immediately succeeded him. His immediate successors, say they, first alienated the western isles from the crown of Scotland. We shall have occasion to examine this opinion afterwards. At present the question is, who the Duncan was that succeeded Donald Bane. Fordun, after him Boece and Buchanan, affirm he was a bastard son of Malcolm Canmore, but do not name his mother. This particular indeed could not exclude him from the succession, but even this is reprobated by the Norwegians who, from their own chronicles that Malcolm was first married to Ingibiorge, widow of Earl Thorfin, by whom he had Duncan, long before he married Margaret of England. By the Scottish account Malcolm began to reign A.D. 1057 according to Fordun's account. We have seen before that Thorfin, Earl of Orkney, died A.D.1064, seven years before he married Queen Margaret. It is therefore no mighty wonder that Malcolm could marry a widow and bury her in seven years time, nor is it any outrage on the penetration of the Scottish historians to suppose them either careless or ignorant of the matter, especially as they are evidently so in things of more moment. Indeed in the age before us there is some excuse for their ignorance as it is a period involved in darkness and fable owing to many reasons but especially an almost total destruction of the ancient records which could throw light on any period of history. It would be happy for their memory if the same excuse could be given for the false light in which they have placed many points of more modern history, the grounds of which were under their own eyes to examine if they inclined. After all it would be very unfair to reject any new light thrown on our history from this simple circumstance, that it was on the authority of a foreigner, and our own historians had taken no notice of it, for we know the most authentic parts of Scottish history are from the records of other nations. I should not have said so much on this subject had not Abercrombie in his 'Martial Achievments' imagined he had found a notable subject for ridicule in our author and which he indulges to the utmost. Whereas his character from unprejudiced people is that he was a man of great integrity and diligence, extremely well conversant with the antiquities of the North though, like most others, something credulous where truth is not easily distinguished from fiction. We shall see in course many other particulars relating to the Scottish history entirely passed over by our writers, most circumstantially related by our author and with all the appearance of truth.

To return to Ingibiorge and her sons Paul and Erland with the families sprung from them which occur in course.

The two brothers succeeded their father without the least disturbance either at home or abroad and were in good habits with one another, dividing the profits of the Earldom equally, only Paul as the elder brother had the civil authority.

About this time happened an event which made a great alteration in the affairs of Norway. Upon the accession of Harald of the Godwin family to the throne of England, his brother, Tosti Earl of Northumberland, envying his good fortune, made several attempts to stir up the neighbouring princes to assist him in dethroning him. He succeeded with Harald the Valiant, King of Norway, who sailed from home with a fleet of three hundred ships and, touching first at Shetland and afterwards at Orkney, left his Queen and two daughters there. Here he collected what men he could and carried with him Paul and Erland to accompany him on the adventure which was the last of his life. Sailing from Norway he landed at Scarborough in the month of September. Proceeding to a place our author calls Hellerness, he had a skirmish with the English and came off victorious. About the 21st of the month, advancing to York, he fell in with Valthiog and Morear, two earls of the King's party, and in an engagement which followed Morear was slain. Immediately after this bloody battle York surrendered to the King and Tosti, who had now joined him. Next day Harold, leaving his son Olave, the Earls of Orkney and his kinsman Orrius aboard the fleet, went to take possession and settle matters in the City of York, in his way met Harold King of England with a large army and, though according to Torfaeus, Harald of Norway was quite unprepared to fight his namesake, yet to it they went and Norway fell and, though the battle was renewed by Orrius and the Earls of Orkney with fresh troops, Harold gained a complete victory, cutting to pieces Orrius with the greater part of their army. After this great victory Harald allowed Prince Olave, the Earls of

Orkney with what remained of their fleet and army to depart, which wintered in Orkney.

This bloody business happened in the year 1066, a little before the Norman invasion.

At this time the affairs of Orkney were in a most flourishing condition, chiefly by the favour of the Kings of Norway to the Counts of the Country and by the excellent harmony that subsisted between the Earls themselves. However this at length was interrupted by the humours of their children.

Paul had one son, Haco, a youth of most boisterous disposition as will appear, and four daughters, Thora, Ingiride, Herbiorge and Rognhilda, of whom sprung many noble families in Orkney and elsewhere.

Erland had two sons, Erling and Magnus, afterwards canonised, and two daughters, Gunhilda and Cecilia, beside an illegitimate daughter named Iarvor.

Early in the spring, Prince Olave with his brother Magnus, returned to Norway and was proclaimed King, nor do we find anything remarkable in the history of Orkney or Norway through the greatest part of this prince's reign which seems to have been spent in peace. But, when the Earl's sons grew up, this pleasant day was soon clouded. Haco, proud of his illustrious descent being sprung by the mother's side from the Kings of Norway, despised his cousins like for like, Magnus was the best tempered of the three. The bickering between the elder cousins soon broke out into an open rupture, in such a manner that the Earls at length were obliged to enquire into the cause and attempt a reconciliation but, as each favoured his own most, this came to nothing. As their feuds were equally vexatious to themselves and the whole islands, many methods were tried to reconcile them, but all unsuccessful. At last it was agreed that Haco should leave the country for some time till these animosities should be forgotten. He was not very difficult to persuade as his banishment was put upon the footing of travelling for improvement. He immediately furnished himself with necessaries and went to Norway where he stayed some short time with his relation Olave in the latter end of his reign and thence travelled to Sweden where he was kindly received by Ingi on account of his grandfather, Haco the son of Ivar who, upon his banishment by Harold the Valiant, had retired to Sweden and received great honour and advantage from King Ingi and had been much beloved by the people.

At this period the Christian religion had been but newly received in Sweden and, though the King himself was a zealous promoter of Christianity, a most sincere Christian and very severe upon those of his subjects as still adhered to their ancient heathenism, yet there were many in the Kingdom that pretended to magic and the foreknowledge of events by magic. Haco had a mighty desire to consult one of these soothsayers and after some pains found him. The wizard upon hearing his name and family, after some taunts upon his consulting him rather than the King's priests, desired him to return in three days when he would satisfy him. At the appointed time Haco returned to the soothsayer's solitary habitation where he found him in a great agony and, wiping the sweat from his face as in great pain, complaining that he had suffered greatly in tracing the various mazes of his fortune. He told Haco: "That the fates had promised him a long life, that after many events he should be sole master of his country but that his desire to become so would cost him dear. That not only he but his posterity should enjoy this after him. That his home-going would afford great scope for poetical abilities. There (says he) you shall so gorge yourself with iniquity that it shall hardly be expiated. Though I cannot see the end of your travels yet you shall die in your native country. These (concludes he) are what I see concerning you and you may depend on it they will be fulfilled." Haco, after expressing his hopes that things would turn out better with him than the wizard had foretold, departed to King Ingi from whom, a short time after, he obtained leave to be gone and returned to Norway to his relation Magnus surnamed Barefoot, the son of Olave the Peaceable.

Magnus Barefoot succeeded his father A.D.1093, the same year in which Malcolm Canmore died. On the death of Canmore, say the Scottish historians, his brother, well known by the name of Donald Bane, assisted by Magnus of Norway, mounted the throne. For this business Magnus was rewarded with the possession of the northern and western isles which, say the same historians, had belonged to Scotland. Fordun indeed says he conquered them, but adds, from the most ancient times they were reckoned as part of the Scottish dominions. In this manner were we to give implicit credit to the Scots, the isles came into the hands of the Norwegians where they remained till the year 1468, that Orkney and Shetland were pawned to Scotland in lieu of part of Margaret of Denmark's marriage portion. The Hebrides, according to the same, were annexed to Scotland by Alexander the third after the famous battle of Air A.D.1263.

Here the Norwegian story differs widely from the Scottish, and I think with reason, as the accounts given by the former are countenanced by the history of other nations, which in general agree with what our author collects from the Icelandic historians and Scandinavian Bards, whereas the other is entirely unsupported by any authentic history and seems only to have been calculated to save our Scottish pride from submission to a conqueror.

We have already seen that Harald Harfagre upon his settling affairs in Norway turned his thoughts to root out those of his piratical countrymen who had taken refuge in the isles. In his course after these, he made an entire conquest of the northern and western isles, which from that time forward continued subject to the Norwegians for many ages. Even Scotland and Ireland felt the force of the Norman arms about this period without being able to resist them, how much less a few scattered isles. This we are informed by the Scottish writers themselves, and Sir James Ware tells they had laid waste great part of Ireland more than a century before the time of Harald. The ninth century is famous for their attempts upon Ireland in which they at last prevailed so far as to set up an Easterly King in Dublin from whence the Irish were never able to dislodge them. One great attempt to do this was about the beginning of the eleventh century when Brian Bore made vast preparations against Sigtryg Silkbeard, King of Dublin, and fought the bloody battle of Clontarf so fatal to the Irish and no less so to Sigtryg though he himself escaped. Here however we are to observe that Sygtrig's receiving supplies from the Danes and Norwegians that possessed Man and AEbudae as also (according to Torfaeus) from Siward (Sigurd) the Gross, Earl of Orkney (though the latter is not mentioned by Ware who gives a different account of the origin of the quarrel from Torfaeus, as may be seen in the life of Sigurd above), is a manifest proof that the Norwegians were in possession of both the northern and western isles long before the pretended cession by Donald Bane.

It is certain Magnus Barefoot at this time made an expedition to the west but, to trace the motives of this, we must return to Haco.

Upon his return from Norway to Sweden he understood that Erland's sons governed everything at their pleasure in Orkeny, that all ranks were pleased at his absence lest this should disturb the happiness they enjoyed under his cousins, and that even his father was perfectly acquiescent to their peaceful sway. This raised his envy against his cousins' popular government and his suspicion lest they should exclude him for which he thought it necessary to prevent them. To effect this he determined to draw Magnus into a foreign expedition. This he thought the more easy as that time Norway enjoyed a profound peace and that the King's genius, naturally inclined to action, would easily be brought to join in any enterprise he would propose. He was also sensible the King was not at all scrupulous in enquiring for pretexts to enlarge his own dominions or fall upon his neighbours. Building upon this, when he saw his opportunity, he began cunningly to set forth what a noble enterprise it would be for Magnus to pass the ocean and recover the isles which Harold Harfagre had before conquered as also, after the manner of his ancestors, renew their attempts upon Scotland and Ireland. He represented this as an affair of no difficulty, because every place he conquered would afford assistance to pursue his victories, so at length he might avenge on England the death of his grandfather Harold the Valiant.. Magnus without much hesitation, pricked on by avarice and a thirst for great actions, easily suffered himself to be persuaded to undertake such a project.

He immediately set about preparing a fleet, raising troops from all quarters of the kingdom, getting together stores of provisions and everything else necessary for the expedition which he now openly avowed to be designed for the west. Magnus soon got together an army which he embarked in sixty ships (the Chronicle of Man says) and, taking with him his son Sigurd, a promising youth eight years of age, he appointed his subaltern officers and sailed for Orkney. There the first thing he did was to make prisoners of Paul and Erland, Earls of Orkney, and send them to Norway, ordering their sons Haco, Erling and Magnus to follow him in his western expedition. He placed his son Sigurd over the Orkneys and assigned him a council to assist him in governing them. Thence he flew to the AEbudae and spread waste and destruction wherever he came. His first landing was at the Lewis, where he burnt the villages, slew the inhabitants and desolated the country. Those that escaped were obliged to fly one way, some another, some to the opposite shores of Scotland and many as far as the Mull of Cantyre, only a few he admitted to surrender. Next he fell upon Sky (Scidia) which he laid under contribution and plundered, driving off the cattle for use of his army. Uist and Tirey next felt the outrageous fury of the conqueror, however out of respect for St. Columba, he spared the isle of Iona, neither molesting the inhabitants nor disturbing the monastery. From thence he went to Mull which he reduced together with all that division of the AEbudae called Nordureys. Nor did the Sudereys or southern division fare a whit better, Magnus fell first on Ila which felt all the horrors of war which an enraged tyrant could inflict on a country. Here he seemed to take pleasure in glutting his fury and, for a long time, pursued the miserable inhabitants with rapine, fire and sword. From Ila he sailed to Cantyre and, in his passage through the sounds, made excursions into Ireland, Scotland and the islands lying in his way, but always leaving the destructive marks behind him till he arrived at Man, which he treated no better than the AEbudae. Here, says our author, Lagman the son of Godred, despairing to be able to defend the northern division of the isles from the fury of Magnus, was taken on his passage to Ireland and bound with fetters of iron. However there is some difficulty among the antiquarians whether Lagman was alive when Magnus conquered the Western Isles, the Manx chronicle placing his expedition A.D. 1098 eleven years after the death of Lagman. Magnus now flushed with victory did not stop at Man but carried his victorious arms into South Britain. Here he made the coast of Bretland or Cornavia[1] (now Cheshire) and pushed his fleet into the narrow and dangerous straits of Anglesey where, in spite of resistance, he landed and made himself master of the Island notwithstanding the united efforts of two brave Earls who encountered him with a large army. The battle that ensued was fiercely fought on both sides, with long and short weapons. One of the Earls whom our author distinguishes by the epithet Valiant (for they were both named Hugh, the other, Hugh the Gross) armed cap-a-pie performed wonders, encouraging his men to fight bravely both by example and exhortation, till at length Magnus (who that day fought with a bow) together with another of his archers letting fly at him struck him on the visor of his helmet and, one of the arrows glancing, the other striking him in the eye lodged in his brains and brought him to earth. The slaughter of the Earl immediately flung the victory into the King's hands, the other party fled and Magnus took possession of Anglesey, which indeed had formerly been in the hands of Harold Harfagre but no Norwegian Prince since his time had been so far south as this island. The battle of Anglesey cost the King's party a great deal of blood. Many of the first rank were killed, of the common men most that were left alive were wounded. Among the chiefs, Kali and Sigurd, both intimates with the King, were mortally wounded.

The former lingered for some time but at length died greatly lamented as an able leader and a wise counsellor. Erling, the son of Erland Earl of Orkney, likewise fell but authors differ whether here or, according to Snorro Sturleson, in Ireland.

Upon the occasion of this battle we have the first opening of that disposition to religion or rather superstition which afterwards so strongly marked the character of Magnus the other son of Erland. Whilst everyone on board the Norwegian fleet was arming himself for battle, Magnus was found totally inactive. Upon the King's asking him why he did not arm, he replied "These people never did me any harm, I have no quarrel with them, why then should I arm for their destruction?" Upon hearing this the King ordered him immediately to withdraw and hide himself lest he should be trampled to death by the combatants, adding that it was his cowardice and not his religion that hindered him to fight. Magnus, in the time of the battle, employed himself in perusing the Psalms of David without giving himself any trouble about what was going on about him or otherwise securing his body by any defensive amour. His behaviour so sank him in Magnus of Norway's opinion that he afterwards despised him and even put upon him the most menial offices, as serving his table since he would not fight, which made him take the first opportunity to escape. This he effected in the night time and came to the Scottish court where he stayed some time. Thence he went to England where he remained with an English Bishop, a voluntary exile till the death of Magnus Barefoot.

Simon of Dunelm and the Chronicle of Man give the history of this battle, though with different circumstances both as to the occasion and consequences of it. It is certain Magnus did not use the conquered with all the moderation imaginable. Nay, he even exercised all the insolence towards them that might be expected from an ambitious and fortunate barbarian. Upon ambassadors coming from the King of Scotland to buy peace by giving up all right and title to the AEbudae in the plainest and most explicit terms, Magnus threw into the bargain the peninsula of Cantyre. The terms were that all should belong to Norway which a boat steering a direct course could leave on one side. However, Magnus on pretence that the isthmus stopped the direct navigation, likewise extorted this from the Scots, who were willing to make peace on the best conditions they could. The Chronicle of Man says he forced the people of Galloway to bring wood for his fortifications. Nay he even sent his shoes to Murcard, King of Ireland, with orders to carry them round his hall on his shoulders in presence of his messengers, and this on the anniversary of Christ's nativity, on pain of his displeasure.

After these isles were thus reduced, Magnus proposed to winter there but this was by no means agreeable to his army, who now all wished to visit their homes. To murmurs against the King's insatiable lust for conquest, succeeded desertion, to prevent which he was obliged to apply the sorry shift of setting sentinels round his whole army, to prevent even his greatest favourites escaping. In a short time however he saw the urgent necessity of returning home and, touching at the Orkneys on his way thither, he understood Paul and Erland, the captive Counts, were both dead.

The ancient Norwegian chronicle says he made his son, Sigurd, (who was now only nine years old and whom he had contracted to a daughter of Murcard, five years of age), King over his new conquests and recommended him to the tutorage of Haco and Erland, sometime after Earls of Orkney. Here likewise he gave Gunnhilda, the daughter of Earl Erland in marriage to Kol a son of his favourite Kali, to console him for his father's death and, as a portion, he bestowed on her an estate in Orkney and a farm in Papa.

Although Magnus was obliged to return to Norway at this time, he returned , in the ninth tear of his reign, to Ireland where, falling into an ambuscade through his temerity, he was slain A.D. 1108 and tenth of his reign, leaving three sons, Eystein, Sigurd and Olaus.

Here our author enters into a long chronological dispute about the time Magnus' expedition to the western isles happened, which Simon of Dunelm and the Monks' Chronicle place in the year 1098, whereas the foregoing relation says positively Magnus made peace with the ambassadors from Malcolm Canmore. Now Malcolm died A.D.1093 which could not have happened if Magnus had made no more expeditions than this of the year 98. But our author, from Odericus Vitalis, says he made at least two if not three voyages westward before the year 98, one of which in the fifth year of William Rufus or A.D. 1092 which is probably that in which he struck up a peace with Malcolm of Scotland. The consequence of which is that Donald Bane had not it in his power to make the shameful cession to the Kings of Norway so iniquitously laid to his charge by our Scottish historians.

To return from this digressive expedition about which we should not have been so particular had it not produced such a evolution in the affairs of Orkney, namely that of reducing them once more under the power of Norway and that in the strictest terms, by right of conquest. For it is certain Magnus considered it in this view when he made his son Siward (Sigurd) King over them, though his friendship with his relations, Haco and Erling would not allow him to leave them destitute. Add to this, that his conquest happened at a time when Thorfin by his behaviour showed he considered himself as almost independent of Norway and had left his sons in peaceable possession and of the same way of thinking.

1. The Cornavy were, according to Camden, the ancient inhabitants of Warwickshire, Worcestershire, Staffordshire, Shropshire and Cheshire. As these are all inland except the last, I have rendered it Cheshire.

Chapter 11

After the slaughter of Magnus Barefoot, his sons Eystein, Sigurd and Olave made an equal partition of the Kingdom among themselves. From them, in the first or second year of their reign, Haco, in consideration of his services, received the half of Orkney together with the title Earl. His cousin Magnus, likewise on hearing of the death of Magnus Barefoot, returned to Orkney. Upon his demanding the half of Orkney from Haco[1], he refused it and began to prepare to keep him out by force although, at length by mediation of friends, he promised to restore his inheritance if he could get it confirmed by the King of Norway. Magnus agreed to these terms and went immediately to Norway where he was received with great kindness by Eystein (Siward being then in the Holy Land) and had his desire granted, both as to the half of the Isles and the investiture and, upon his return home, was welcomed with much cordiality by Haco with whom he lived a long time in the most friendly terms imaginable. Their agreement, says Torfaeus, had a great effect upon their country, the arts of peace were cultivated, every thing abounded and happiness reigned through the islands. This prosperous era was of no long continuance, soon the demon of discord raised between the two Earls, by a set of designing men who effectively erased any sentiments of friendship Haco might have for his cousin, to which indeed his own disposition lent them a helping hand. Haco, envious of his cousin's popularity and the sanctity of his life, as also fired by the lust of power, gave great attention to the calumnies that were industriously spread against Magnus. Two of Haco's favourite courtiers were most active in traducing Magnus, Sigurd (whose brother Thorstein, a pious and good man, was one of Magnus' guards) and Sigvad. These two were continually employed in filling Haco's ears with complaints so the at length they effected an open breach between the cousins which was never stopped up and ended in the death of Magnus. Robert, the writer of Magnus' life, says about this time he went to England to solicit assistance against Haco, where he was nobly entertained a whole year by Henry the first and, at his departure, had a present of five ships to enable him to recover his part of Orkney and Caithness which had been violently seized by Haco in his absence. Yet however by the interposition of friends all animosities were varnished over, but new provocation soon put an end to this hollow pacification which, though it continued some years, never had been hearty, at least on Haco's side. Everything now seemed to have warlike appearance, the exasperated chiefs never came abroad without troops of armed men attending them. At a public meeting of the Gentlemen of the Mainland each brought his fleet well manned and armed and drew them up as for immediate action. Their relations and friends still had influence to keep them from blows, nay they even brought them to shake hands as a sign of the league which they likewise confirmed by a mutual oath. This coalition happened in the time of Lent and not long after Haco proposed a meeting with his cousin to confirm their late pacification and take away all causes of strife, with an equal number of attendants and there, before the Gentlemen of the Country, every cause was to be argued and taken away according to their judgement. After the celebration of Easter, both parties set out for the convention, Magnus most religiously observed every part of the paction in regard to the number of his ships and men but Haco minded neither.

This was the age of miracles, signs and wonders. Magnus met with one of the latter on his passage to Egilsha. In a fine day without a breath of wind and sea perfectly calm, a monstrous wave arising all of a sudden overwhelmed the Earl's bark and, for the time, buried it under water[2]. This was immediately looked on as a prodigy by the Earl's followers and their surprise was nothing lessened when Magnus told them it was a certain sign of his death which would soon happen by the treachery of Haco. His friends, who it would seem put great trust in Magnus' prophecy, advised him earnestly to shun the danger that threatened him and keep out of the power of a person of whose perfidious disposition he had so many proofs. Magnus refused this, told them he and all that belonged to him were in the power of an overruling Providence into whose hands he was determined to commit them at present and therefore would proceed.

Haco likewise prepared for the convention but in another manner than his cousin. He collected a number of ships and embarked a large body of troops on board, nor did he disguise the intention of these but plainly told his friends that war and not peace was in his mind, that indeed all the grudgings, animosities and broils between him and Magnus would be ended at the convention but not in the manner they expected. He gave broad hints two such planets could not shine in the same hemisphere and that Magnus' death was resolved on. These insinuations were received with great joy by Haco's two great counsellors and flatterers, Sigurd and Sigvad, and his other followers, who did all they could to keep up his resolution to destroy his cousin. Nobody stood out but one, Havard the son of Gunnar, a near relation and equally fond of both the Earls. Till this moment he had been ignorant of the horrid designs contriving against Magnus, which he in vain attempted to combat by sound advice and, finding the Earl obstinately bent on destroying his rival, he threw himself overboard and swam to the next island which happened to be an uninhabited holm.

Magnus arrived first in Egilsha wither he soon saw Haco following with eight vessels rigged out with all the appearance of war. This left him with no room to doubt of Haco's intentions. His companions, likewise assured that Haco would pay no regard to his oaths or promises, proposed to defend their master by force. Magnus however, out of a pious regard for his oath, strictly forbad them to run themselves into evident danger on his account, professing that he would submit to any event providence should think proper to lay on him, nay even death itself should be welcome if peace to the islands could be procured on no other terms. With this resolution he retired to the church where he heard mass and spent the night in fervent prayer. After his devotion were finished he remained on the island though he had an opportunity to get off, sensible that his end was now approaching.

In the morning Haco sent out his men to apprehend Magnus. These went first to the church but, not finding him there, sought him through the island where he had gone to take a walk with only three of his attendants. They found him in a retired corner whence, when he understood they were in search of him, he was coming to meet them. When he was thus apprehended, Haco, going up to him, found him prostrate on the earth at his devotions which he allowed him to finish, when Magnus calmly addressed him as follows:- "Thou hast grievously sinned cousin in thus violating thy oath in hearkening to the malicious insinuations of wicked men rather than thy own reason, don't however add to the measure of your crimes the murder of an innocent man, don't despise the faith you plighted, don't render yourself a monster of iniquity by flying in the face of everything sacred. I will offer three things to make you easy. Give me ships and other necessaries for the voyage and I will retire either to Rome or Jerusalem to expiate both our crimes and I shall bind myself by oath never to revisit the Orkneys. Or send me into Scotland with only two companions to lighten my solitude and do you take particular care that I have it not in my power to return. Or, if none of these conditions please you, I will make you a third offer, which I do out of regard for your eternal salvation than to preserve my own life, as God is my witness. Mutilate my limbs as you think proper and throw me into perpetual imprisonment, all these will be less criminal than taking away my life."

The first of these proposals was rejected by Haco as, perjured himself, he did not think any person could be bound by oath. The second he likewise rejected. Haco would have been pleased with the third but this was rejected by his chiefs who, abhorring the thoughts of cruelty, insisted that one of them should die and restore peace which could not be while there was a double government. As this was the case, Haco did not deliberate but ordered Magnus to be put to death observing that, now he had it in his power to reign alone, he should embrace it rather than give up both life and government together.

Magnus when he heard his sentence submitted without resistance or repining. He instantly fell to his knees and, with tears addressing his Creator in a pious and fervent prayer which, being finished, he cheerfully waited the stroke of the executioner. Haco ordered his standard bearer Ufeig to strike the fatal blow which he, with great wrath, refused. Litolf, the Earl's cook at length, by threats, was forced to perform the office of headsman but with great ill will. Magnus, seeing his backwardness and the grief he was in at being obliged to the cruel office, comforted by all means in his power, he desired him not to grieve for, though the action he was forced upon was execrable, yet he was not to be blamed. He told him his garments were his by ancient custom, which he immediately threw off and gave him and, having obtained leave, he once more recommended his spirit into the hands of his Maker, prayed for his enemies and murderers, professing that he heartily forgave them. After communicating and confessing, he addressed himself to the executioner desiring him to stand before his face and to be sure to strike the blow with all his force for (sayd he) Princes are not to be put to death like thieves. He desired him to recollect himself and not allow himself to despair as his prayers would be heard for him. Signing himself with the cross, he waited the blow which was given him full and he instantly expired. To the recital of this cruel transaction, Torfaeus adds, that the place where Magnus was killed, from a rough and mossy bare, became soon covered with a beautiful verdure as a testimony of the innocence and great sanctity of the martyred Earl, but he believes this was a trick of the Monks in whose hands the spot was and, that by their superior cultivation the wonder, if there was any, was performed.[3].

Thus Magnus fell on the 16th of April 1110, in the thirtieth year of his age, having been Earl of half of Orkney seven years from the death of Magnus Nupides, or Barefoot, King of Norway.

He is said to have been tall and fair, his voice strong and clear, his manners engaging, he was fortunate in war, of great wisdom, beloved by his countrymen and remarkable for his eloquence. His behaviour to good men was gentle but severe against the worthless. He was particularly severe in the punishment of thieves, abolished piracy which in early youth he had practiced, punished murderers and thieves without respect to rank or wealth. He was an upright judge, observant of the laws, munificent to his nobles, kind to the poor and most attentive in all acts of religious worship even to the mummeries then in use. He mortified his body by many severe acts of penance known only, says our author, to God and himself, one of which he relates, as we shall see, by keeping the veil of the original still on. "Abstentia tanta, et cu virginem, in Scotia summo loco notam, uxorem duceret, universum tamen decennium cum qua absaque cella corporis permertione, cohabitaverit, neque enim venerea labe se contaminari passus est; sed ut primum pruritum talem sentiebat, frigid aquae se immergens, divino auxilio implorato, illico hos motos sopivit."

Thora, the mother of Magnus, had some difficulty to procure his body for burial. At the time of the meeting at Egilsha she had invited both Earls to her house (she now was married to a gentleman called Sigurd who dwelt in Papa) to an entertainment. Haco notwithstanding the murder of her son came with all his attendants. She entertained him as if nothing had happened and, whilst she served him, observing him to become merry, could not help reflecting a little on his cruelty. She told him she expected another who was likewise invited but, as it happened otherwise, she hoped he had come to console her for the loss of her son. She adjured him by everything sacred to supply the loss of her son, as she would be to him a mother, and allow her to bury his remains. Haco was sometime silent, considering whether he should grant her request for, if Magnus was looked on in a criminal light, (and this was what he intended to take hold of to clear himself to the world) he could not be buried as a Christian in a church. At length, however, struck with her behaviour, he burst into tears and gave his mother liberty to bury him where she pleased. His body was therefore carried to the Mainland and buried in the Cathedral at Birsa, William the first then possessing the Episcopal chair.

It would be a pity to pass by the use the monks made of the reputed sanctity of Magnus and the many miracles said to be wrought at his shrine, were it for no other reason than to shew that the same spirit was found wherever Papistry prevailed and St. Magnus' tomb became, at length, as much frequented as St. Thomas a Becket's or any other of the most famous Saints in the Romish calendar.

The author Torfaeus follows and seems to have been a good believing Catholic, assures us that his tomb was surrounded with a bright radiance like the sunbeams, and from it proceeded a fragrant smell very sanative for rich invalids, and drew many from all quarters to perform their devotions there, to the great advantage of the place, for few came empty handed. The fame of the wonders performed at Magnus' tomb soon brought flocks of pilgrims from Shetland, Orkney and Caithness who, according to their own account, were all dismissed whole. This however was kept secret till the death of Haco, because the priests imagined he would not bear without envy the concourse of people that flocked to his cousin's tomb, which he imagined would some time or other produce a revolution unfavourable for his affairs in Orkney.

William, as we observed before, was then Bishop of Birsa and called by the Norwegian writers the first Bishop of Orkney, which is not improbable. William it seems was something slow in believing miracles said to be wrought for clearing the innocence of Magnus, till a multitude of evidence so convinced him of it that he became like Saul among the Prophets.

It is unknown when Magnus was canonised, but this must have happened soon after his death, as his relics were placed by Bishop William in a shrine with vast solemnity, which drew visitors innumerable to Birsa, who all contributed more or less to adorn or enrich it. Many likewise sent presents from afar who did not visit it.

The day of his inauguration is fixed on the 13th. December, but neither the year nor the Pope is mentioned. His sanctity procured him the honour of tutelary patron for Orkney, under which character the day of his martyrdom was held with a solemnity equal to the Sabbath through the Northern Isles and Norway and a service appointed for it.

The first miracle brought to prove the sanctity of Magnus seems to be the punishment of the contrivers of his death, most of whom came to shameful and untimely ends, which was looked upon as a just judgement for their crimes. Among the miracles wrought at his tomb we have the following:

Bergfin a blind Shetland man and his son Halfdane a leper, coming to Kirkwall[4] to Magnus' shrine with offerings, were both cured of their infirmities.

Amund, a Shetland leper, by touching the Saint was cured.

Sigurd, a madman from Shetland, was restored to his senses. This person was from a place called Dale.

Sigurd, another Shetland man, whose fingers were shrunk up, had them restored to their original tone, at the Shrine of St. Magnus.

Thorgiorn, Olave's son, who was possessed with an evil spirit was, by the intercession of St. Magnus, cured.

Thord Birgfin's servant in Shetland, refusing to give over work on the eve of the feast of St. Magnus, ran mad and was bound for six days but, upon Birgfin's vowing to pay half a mark of silver for the use of St. Magnus Church, his servant was instantly cured.

A Caithnessman and an Orkneyman had agreed to rob Magnus' shrine, but were sufficiently punished for their sacrilege. The Caithnessman was drowned on passing the Pictland Firth, the other was soon after bereaved of his wits and, even a vow of a pilgrimage to Rome, could not restore him, this only happened on his being brought to the temple of St. Magnus.

Amund who, by a hurt in his head, had been deprived of the faculty of speech, cast lots whether he should make a pilgrimage to Rome or give a donation to the temple of St. Magnus, The lot cast up in favour of St. Magnus and, upon Amund paying half a mark of silver, he was entirely cured.

Sigridis, the daughter of Sigurd of Sand in Shetland, blind from her infancy to womanhood, who was brought by her father to Magnus' Shrine with large presents for the use of the church, soon received her sight.

Another and a third of the same name from Shetland (the former of which had broken her thigh, the latter distracted because she could no longer give over work after three o'clock in the afternoon of St. Magnus' Eve). The first was cured of her broken thigh and the other, being persuaded either to vow an offering to the shrine of St. Magnus or to go on a pilgrimage to Rome, she preferred the former and was restored to her senses. However (says our author) she performed the pilgrimage likewise for her soul's health.

Rognhild and Ara, two women cripples from their infancy, were restored to the use of their limbs at the tomb of St. Magnus.

Sigurd, a beggar from Notasand, whose knees ere so contracted that he could not walk upright, by the intercession of St. Magnus was made whole.

The following particulars shews our Orkney Saint, on a pinch, could stretch his power even to matters that one would imagine scarce came under his province.

Two German shipmasters playing dice, the one stripped the other of all his ready cash so that he had never another stake save his ship, this he ventured against all he had already lost and, invoking St. Magnus, he recovered all the other had won of him.

Reflections have been so often made upon similar anecdotes of intercessory saints, that they would be held entirely unnecessary, only this we may venture that the donarium magnum and the dimidia marca argenti were as necessary at the shrine of St. Magnus as ever they were at the house of Lorretto.

The service for St. Magnus' day our author has preserved and is as follows:-

Oratio

Adesto Domini supplicationibus nostris et intercedente Beato Magno Martyre tuo, ab Nostium propoceatus incursu per Dominum etc.

Lectio 1

Magnus apud Orcades insulas oriundus fuit nobilissimus generi et alti sanguinis parentela Pater ejus insularum Comis et Dominus nominatissimus, Mater ejus de nobilioribus illius terrae duxipe fertur originem ingestu jocundus et hilaris et sermone amottlis ey affabilis in incepu modestus extitit et gravis et non appareret in o quod popet offendure intuentes.

Lectio 2

Sed quia mores formantur ex convictu com ad intelligililum aetatem perventiret inter taen funalem et feralem gentam constitutus inter protervus ad mores ferales, ad ritus ad fidem impior ad legem barbaros pronos ad mala illorum motibur per dies aliquor conformari, maximus praedo existere, rapinus et spolus vivere caedabus indulgere quod tamer mages pravorum instinctie prvocatus quam propria iniquitate pulsatus creditur actitasse.

Lectio 3

Sia omnipotens Deus cui proprium est misere et parcere electum scium a talibus voluit mercinonus suspendere et ostendere illi quanta oportial cum pali pro nomine ipsius et qui sanguinem innocentem multolies fuderai ipse quandoque victima Spiritus Sancti fieret ut proprium sanguines Christo libaret, unde contigit cum de many viclenti Regis et predatoris evadere et Chataniam adire, ubi honorifice susceptus est, et in Comition sublimaties qui postmodum glorioso martyrio coronatus victor migravit ad Dominum.

A.D. 1298 Part of the relics of St. Magnus were carried to Iceland and placed with great solemnity in the Cathedral there.

Magnus being now dead, Haco took possession of the whole Orkney Isles under the notion of a conquest, forcing those that inabited Magnus' half to take an oath of allegiance to himself. But even this did not satisfy him, he was continually vexing Magnus' friends with new exactions while he continued in Orkney.

Some years after the death of Magnus, Haco, probably struck with remorse on account of his crimes, undertook a pilgrimage first to Rome and thence to Jerusalem when, having washed himself in the river Jordan, he returned from the Holy Land laden with relics. On his return he began to turn over a new leaf, lived in peace and formed a system of laws for the government of the Isles well adapted to the nature of the people. He softened the severity of the old Orkney laws, many of which were heavy upon the people and relieved them from many heavy burdens laid on by his predecessors. By this method of acting he entirely reconciled the inhabitants, whose regard extended even to his posterity.

At this time lived at Dale in Caithness one Maddan, a man famous for his riches, whose descendants make a figure in what follows of the history of Orkney.

He had two sons, Magnus surnamed the Munificent, and Ottar, Earl of Thorsa, and three daughters Helga, Frakuark and Thorlief. Helga was Haco, Earl of Orkney's mistress and bore him Harold surnamed the Orator and two daughters, Ingibiorge, married to Olave Billing, King of the Western Isles, and Margaret.

Frakuark, the second of Mddan's daughters, married a Sutherland Gentleman, Liot surnamed Niding. She brought him two daughters, Steiny married to Thorliot of Rekowick, to whom she bore five sons, Aulver Rosta, Magnus, Orm, Maddan and Endride, also a daughter Audhildi. Loit's second daughter Gudrun had a son Thorbiorn Clerk by Thorfein Hauld Fiarandmun.

Haco had a second son by another mother, Paul who with Harald succeeded him.

It is hard to say the year of Haco's death which happened by a disease to the great grief of the Orkney people, as the latter end of his life had been a happy time for their country, having enjoyed peace and its consequences for several years, both at home and abroad.

1. The Writer of the life of Magnus says Haco, after his investiture by the King of Norway, returned home and slew the Norwegian deputies that had been set over Magnus' half of the Orkneys which he seized himself. (Torf. p.26), than which there is nothing more probable, Haco was capable of more than that.

2. I shall not call in question what the above prodigy, as it is called, might portend. I should rather disbelieve that there was anything wonderful for the Earl's ship to be heartily ducked in a calm in the Orkney sounds. The matter is neither more nor less than honest Magnus had fallen into a Roust which is well known to rage most severely in a calm and can wash the deck of a much larger vessel than Magnus can be supposed to have in the year 1110.

3. Here follows in the original a long chronological disquisition on the time of Magnus' death, Robert his biographer placing it in A.D. 1104. Whereas the annals of Norway place this event A.D. 1115. The author follows none of these eras but, from many circumstances which could give no entertainment, fixes it A.D.1110.

4. This must have been after the Cathedral of Kirkwall was built which happened many year after the death of St.Magnus, in the time of Rognvald, the fourth of the name, Earls of Orkney.

Chapter 12

After the death of Haco, his sons Harald and Paul succeeded him and by their difference of disposition soon set all Orkney in a flame. As they could not agree on the civil administration, an equal partition was made of the isles that each might distinguish his own. This bred factions among the Gentry, each attaching himself to one or the other and hence arose a perpetual discord and animosities which were never settled till the death of Harald and only then laid asleep for a while.

Having divided the Orkney Isles, Harald and Paul equally shared the civil power. But in this respect Harold soon became an overmatch for his brother by the accession of Caithness to his fortune, which was granted him by the King of Scotland. Harold did not confine himself to Orkney, he passed a good deal of his time in Caithness and other places of Scotland where he had many relations. Whilst he stayed in Sutherland a man called Sigurd Slimber who had been bred to the Church and which he had deserted out of pride, as below his rank, came to him. He was the reputed son of a Priest called Adalbric by Thora the daughter of Sax de Wick a Norwegian, on whom Magnus Barefoot afterwards begot Olave his successor in .the Kingdom. Thora did not stick to say that Sigurd was likewise the son of Magnus. Sigurd was mightily puffed up by his supposed relationship to the crown of Norway and began to behave as presumptive heir of the Kingdom. He had lived a long time in great honour with David the first of Scotland before he came to Harald, whom he accompanied into Orkney, as did his aunt Thorlief, likewise a widow, though afterwards married to Haco Pik the son of Sigurd of Westness, Earl Paul's great grandson. Thus accompanied, Harald set out for the Orkneys where their arrival soon awakened the seeds of sedition which Harold's absence had for some time chilled.

Among Paul's intimates and counsellors were Sigurd of Westness and Thorkel Somarlid or Foster, because he was brought up by Paul, a different person however, though agreeing in name, from the Thorkel the great friend of Thorfin mentioned before. Thorkel, as a relation of St. Magnus was greatly suspected by Harold to bear a grudge to the issue of the perpetrator of his death and for this reason to take pains to raise mutual animosities between the brothers, which he hoped in time would gather to such a head that they would revenge his quarrel the one by the death of the other.

These suspicions against Thorkel at length rose to such a pitch that Harold by the advice and assistance of Sigurd put him to death. Paul was greatly enraged at the slaughter of his friend and immediately flew to arms to revenge his death. Every appearance of civil broils now threatened Orkney, however the Gentlemen interposing by much persuasion both in private and public brought the matter to an issue without bloodshed, one preliminary article to which, insisted on by Paul, was that the murderers of his friend by brought to justice. This, with some trouble, was obtained from Harald and he accordingly banished Sigurd Slimber and others who were most obnoxious to his brother. It was agreed likewise that all suspicions, grudges and animosities for the future should be laid aside and as a sign of a total oblivion both should meet at a certain place to be fixed on and there should celebrate the festival of Yule. At the time appointed Harald made most magnificent preparations at his seat in Jorfiar to receive his brother. Though the feast was to be at the common expense of both, yet Harald as landlord took on the care of preparation. He therefore got together everything that was rare, as well as what might be called common, that nothing might be wanting to render this pacification feast as complete as possible. When he came to Jorfiar he found his mother Halga and his Aunt Frakaurk employed at their needles preparing rich garments which they ornamented with great art. Upon his asking for whom these fine clothes were intended, they answered for his brother Paul. Harald answered with some heat that they were more careful to prepare fine clothes for his brother than himself and seized the Garment they had just finished. As he had lately risen he was dressed in his nightgown and drawers, he therefore began to unfold the vestment as if to put it on which his mother observing, snatched it from him, desiring him at the same time not to envy his brother the wearing of this robe at least. He again forced it from her and immediately put it on, at which his Aunt fell into the utmost rage of grief and, tearing her hair, with many tears cautioned him against putting on that robe which, notwithstanding its beautiful appearance brought immediate death to the wearer. Harald imagined this only a fetch of the women and obstinately disregarded their cautions which however he had soon reason to repent for, no sooner had he put on the poisoned shirt or robe, than his whole body was affected with the most excruciating torments and, in a very short time amidst the lamentations of his friends, he breathed his last.

Paul who had happily escaped the effects of this dangerous present, immediately banished the Mother, Aunt and whole family and took possession of his brother's part of the isles with the universal approbation of the inhabitants.

Frakaurk, upon her banishment from Orkney, retired to Caithness and thence further into Scotland where she had several estates wither her sister, Helga, soon followed together with Earl Haco's daughter Margaret. Frakuark likewise brought up Erland the son of Harold the fair spoken, the late Earl, as also Eric Stagbrillir, the son of Thorliot of Rekawick, also Thorbiorn Clerk her great grandson, who all became men of note in time, and every one pretended a title to the Earldom of Orkney, but by what right is not said. It is certain by what we have seen of their geneology none of them could have any pretensions except Erland, the son of Harold, the last partner in the Earldom.

It will not be amiss to take some notice of Sigurd Slimber who was banished the Orkneys for the murder of Thorkel the Earl's father. Upon his banishment he returned to his friend King David of Scotland where he became famous for his courage and strength of which he gave many proofs while he remained in Scotland. From Scotland he went to the Holy Land, where he washed himself in the river Jordan, then a universal medicine for foul consciences. After much wandering he returned to Norway, where he claimed half of the Kingdom from Harald upon the plea of his being the son of Magnus Nudiped. Harald was very unwilling to part with half the kingdom, the more so as he was afraid Sigurd would not be contented without aiming at the whole. He therefore thought of a stratagem which he imagined would at once free him from his rivals importunity. This was to have him seized, tried and condemned for the murder of Thorkel the Foster. Sigurd had address enough to escape from his execution and afterwards proved a severe scourge upon Norway. At length, however, being taken, he was put to the most cruel tortures which he endured with the utmost constancy, in the midst of the most acute pain repeating the Psalms of David without hesitation. From his constancy, the strength of mind and mode of behaviour which removed from the common road, many (says our Author) were inclined to think his pretensions to the royal blood not entirely apocryphal.

Here our Author gives us a Catalogue of the better sort of families living in Orkney in the twelfth Century, mostly sprung from or otherwise related to the Earls.

Sigurd of Westness in Rousa, of whom mention has been made already, had two sons Haco Pik and Bryniolf.

Havard, the son of Gunnar, had four sons Haco, Klo, Thorstein and Dufnial, greatly beloved by the Earl.

Erland of Tanskaruness, had four sons the names of whom are not metioned.

Olave, a valiant man and of great account with Earl Paul, inhabited Garsey. His wife Aslief was a woman nobly descended and of an heroic spirit, by her he had three sons, Valthiof, Gun and Swain and a daughter Ingigerde, all of them carefully instructed in every branch of learning or art then in fashion. We shall see what these were in course.

Sigurd, called the Earl's kinsman because he had married St. Magnus' mother Thora, lived in Papa. He held a high place in the Earl's favour, both on account of his accomplishments as well as his relationship. He had a son named Haco Karl.

In Ronaldsha lived a respectable Lady called Rona, whose son Thostein was famous in his day.

Kugi, famous for his wisdom and riches, lived at Gefisness in Westra. Helgi lived in the same island.

Thorkel Flet, a man of exceeding bad character, with his two sons Thorstein and Haflia equally wicked and detested by everybody, lived likewise in Westra.

In Swona, an island of the Pictland firth, lived Grim who, though a poor indigent man, was the father of two bold and active sons Asbiorn and Margad.

Dagfin lived in Fara.

At Fluguness in the Mainland lived Thorstein who had two sons, Bliam and Thorstein surnamed Krokauga or Crookeye, both men of great valour.

Jatvor, the daughter of Earl Erland, possessed the Castle of Knarrasteid (now Scapa) with her son Bergo, but neither of them beloved by the people.

In the Upland of Hoy lived Ion Wing; in Breck of Stronsa, Rigard, both of them in mean circumstances, although they were related to Olave of Garsey.

Grimkel lived at Glettuness. Where this Glettuness lies our author says not, but it is probably Gretness near Kirkwall.

It was necessary to mention these people and their relations to one another, also where they lived, that the reader might not be at a loss about them when he sees them appear in the course of the history.

We now come to Kali, the son of Kol, whose father Kali had married Gunhilda, the sister of St. Magnus, and, as he left no descendants, the right to half the Earldom of Orkney as in his sister's children although Haco had seized on it and his posterity had possessed it ever since. It will be necessary to begin a little higher with the history of Kali than his succession to the Earldom, as it lets us into the method of breeding the noble youth of the times, their exercises and method of passing their time till they came to manhood. In a word it is a system of Northern education.

Kol, the son of Gunnhilda, Magnus' sister, was a man of great wisdom and prudence, excelling in these most of his contemporaries. Being possessed of an estate in Norway he gave himself no trouble about the Earldom of Orkney, whence it happened that the posterity of Haco possessed the isles without any trouble from him.

His son Kali, a stout well made young man of the middle size, was adorned with all the learning of the age. His genius was excellent, which he took great care to improve.

In Olaus Wormius he says what follows of himself and what he had been taught to perform and which, with some exercises spoken of by Snorre Sturleson, composed the circle of Nrwegian learning.

> "Tast em ek aurr at ofla
> Ithrottir kan ek niu
> Tyni et tradla runum
> Fid er mer bok ok smider
> Skrida kan ek a skidum
> Skyt ek ok rae sua syter
> Huort veggia kan ek huggin
> Harpokatt ok brog thaetta."

Which is thus translated by Olaus: "Oblectamanta meni novem sunt, Scachicus ludus, Runarum ligatum, librorum lectio, fabrilium cultura, nives soleis calco ligneis areu quorvis supere et remis, fidibus canto et poesi."

Olaus Worm: Lit Run 22.

"I am dextrous at playing chess, in engraving the Runick characters, which I can likewise read, I am an expert smith, can skate nimbly, I excell at the bow and in handling an oar, I can likewise blow the horn and compose odes. These nine exercises are my continual delight."

Wrestling, riding, swimmimg, throwing the dart, climbing steep rocks, nay Olave Tryggeson boasted that he could walk without the boat on the oars while the men were rowing. That he could play with three darts at once, tossing them up in the air and would always keep two up and one down in his hand. These were the arts the northerns prided themselves in and in which Kali excelled.

He was brought up from his infancy in the house of his kinsman Solmund, a man of great influence in Norway. At the age of fifteen he entered upon trade in the prosecution of which he sometimes carried the produce of Norway even to England, in company with others of the same stamp. In one of his voyages thither he happened to be at a public fair in a town called Grimsby where, among a vast multitude of strangers from Norway, the AEbudae, Orkney Islands he fell in with a man calling himself Gilchrist who, after a deal of conversation of the manners and customs and much enquiry anent the history of Norway, privately declared himself to be the son of Magnus Barefoot, that his name was Harold and his mother was yet alive in the western isles. He then enquired of Kali what reception he imagined he would meet if he came to Norway. Kali replied he had no doubt he would be welcomed by Sigurd provided he was let alone by himself and was not prejudiced by others. They then parted but not without assurances of remembrance and assistance if either of their affairs required it in future times. Gilchrsit or Harold departed and Kali reurned to his usual residence in Norway.

Kali afterwards going to a fair in Bergen where traders from all parts both of north and south Norway attended, as also a multitude of strangers, at a public tavern, fell in with a young nobleman called Ion Peterson but afterwards, from an accident, better known as Ion Foot. A similarity of tempers and conditions soon brought on an intimacy which by degrees was improved into a strict friendship which however was of no long continuance.

Public taverns were, then as now, the resort of all ranks, even Kings did not think it below their dignity to appear in these places.

Though, says our Author, it was not so convenient for Kings to frequent taverns yet to them it might even be useful. Here the youths were allowed to converse with freedom on all subjects and with all ranks. In these places they were entertaind with disquisitions on the various tracts through life and these confirmed by arguments founded on the experience of their elders. Restrained by the eye of their Kings, Nobles and other men of rank and wisdom, they were kept from drunkenness and its commitant vices, they, from them, learned to walk in the paths of honour and virtue.

After Kali had finished his business in Bergen he returned home for the winter. His summers he passed as his trading adventures called him. On one of these, being detained by contrary winds in the island of Dollsey, he understood there was in that island a vast cavern which tradition had rendered famous for its hidden treasures. Kali and the other merchants determined to attempt getting possession of these. For this end they provided themselves with torches and entering the cave went on till they came to a large lake which crossed the road and which they must pass before they could arrive at the mark. This proved an effectual obstacle to all the Merchants except Kali and one Havard, one of Solmond's servants. These two, tying themselves together with a pretty long rope ventured to swim the lake. Kali had carried a torch in his hand, with flint and steel to light it but, when they landed, they found this no easy matter, the cavern became so close it would scarce burn and so rugged they could scarce make way, besides they were beset with stinking damps that they could not breath so that, despairing of the treasure, they were forced to return after leaving a token of remembrance of their having been there.

Kali better preserved the remembrance of this whimsical but dangerous prank in a poem preserved by Bartholin: Antiquit: Dan: Lib 2 Ch.2.

Upon their return from the Cavern the wind sprung up fair and they sailed for Bergen. Here Kali went to his inn as usual and found his friend Ion Peterson in company with a gentleman named Bryniolf and Havard, Solmund's servant, who accompanied Kali, talking about the Norwegian Nobility, each giving those of his own province of Norway; Bryniolf particularly affirming there was not one in the southern provinces that could be compared to his master, Ion, of his age, either for descent or for accomplishments both of body and mind. Havard stood as stiffly for those of his own country and particularly Solmund his master whom he did not stick to say indifferent people preferred to Ion.. Disputes of this kind generally rouse, especially dependants, but never more than when these are heated with liquor. This was the present case, Havard at length after much ill language on both sides, knocked his antagonist down, so that he immediately swooned. Havard instantly slipped off to Kali, who was in bed while the quarrel happened. Kali ordered him to take a companion and go straight to an acquaintance of his, a Clergyman, who would entertain him till the storm blew over. Havard took one of his attendants and, being obliged to row all night, they were so fatigued that, landing at a place called Graeningiasound, they thought proper to take some rest.

Bryniolf soon recovered of his faint, was carried to Ion his master, who was greatly enraged at the treatment his servant had met. Tracing out Havard's route, he ordered a boat manned with ten hands to be sent in pursuit of him. These, with Bryniolf their leader, came up with Havard where he and his companion lay asleep. They were known to be the runaways and were immediately slain.

Upon their return to Bergen the slaughter was soon spread abroad and Ion thought proper to offer Kali the legal compensation for the loss of his companion, at least what he could demand, for it must be observed that this did not prejudge the King nor the relations of the deceased, the one for the loss of his subject, the other for their friend.

Kali accepted this as saving his honour but, without coming to terms of reconciliation, went home and informed his father what had happened. The old gentleman chided his son for entering into any terms of reconciliation without consulting Solmund whose vassal Havard was. He told his son it was not in his power to settle the composition for Havard's death; that he was too rash in entering into measures for the vassal of another. The son acknowledged he had been too hasty but added that as no terms had been specified and no money received the matter stood much as it was, nor was Solmund's honour hurt by what he had done. Kol would not admit this, but insisted that no preliminaries should have been entered into between them. Solmund was sent for that his sentiments of the matter might be known. Kol proposed a pacific scheme to send messengers to demand satisfaction. Solmund and Halvard, Havard's next of kin, were for revenge by retaliation upon Ion and his friends. However they were at last brought over to Kol's sentiments, as he promised to have the matter settled and use his influence to procure satisfaction for all parties. When the messengers came to Ion he denied to make any compensation for the death of Havard whose rude behaviour, he alleged, had deserved the punishment he had met with.

Solmund declared he expected no other return from Ion and asked Kol what was now necessary to be done. Kol told Halvard that he must revenge his brother's death by the method he would point out, which was indeed a dangerous one but none else occurred. Halvard professing himself willing to undergo any peril so he could revenge his brother's slaughter, Kol desired him to go as secretly as he could to Sognia where Ion lived, where he would find a poor man that had long groaned under Ion's oppression. He desired Halvard to give him six marks of silver in his name and he would instruct him how he might be revenged on Bryniolf or any other of Ion's dependants he might think a sufficient compensation for his brother. When the matter is over, he says, desire him to sell his farm and come to me for protection.

Halvard did as he was ordered and the issue was that Bryniolf was sent for to this man's house where he was slain by Halvard. This, coming to Ion's ears, he gave strict orders to pursue the murderer but in vain, Halvard lay hid in the poor man's stable till he found means to escape to his friends.

Somund and Kol hugged themselves upon thus returning Ion like for like, however the matter was not finished there. Ion was greatly vexed at this foil and, about Christmas, got together thirty of his frends with whom he told his uncle Olave he intended to revenge on Solmund, Bryniolf's death. Olave dissuaded him from the attempt but without effect and, when he saw him resolute, gave him thirty more armed attendants. With these he proceeded to attack Solmund, taking his route through the mountains that he might catch him unawares. Kol however was informed of this by means of the man who had protected Halvard and, hastening to Solmund, they made preparations as quickly as they could to withstand this sudden surprise. It was thought the best method to go out to meet their adversaries which would shew them they knew of their coming and were prepared. Both parties met at a wood and an engagement was the consequence. Kol and Solmund were superior in numbers being amongst their friends and easily vanquished the handful commanded by Ion, who expcted no such reception. Ion himself was wounded in the foot of which he languished a long time and halted ever after. He however escaped into a wood near the field of battle with the very few that survived his defeat. From the circumstances of his wound his countrymen affixed on him the nickname of John Foot by which appelation he was distinguished till his death.

The matter did not rest there. Next summer Ion or his dependants slew two of Kol's friends, Cunar and Aslac, in a word the feuds ran so high between these irrated chiefs that Sigurd, King of Norway, was forced to take the matter under his cognisance. He accordingly ordered both parties to be summoned before him at Tunsberg where both appeared with their friends and dependants. At length, after some hesitation, both sides agreed to submit their differences to the King's arbitration. The issue of the matter came to this, that everything past should be forgotten and, that there might be no new cause of dispute, the King gave Ingindi, Kol's daughter, in marriage to Ion in order to confirm the new pacification. Both parties seemed pretty well pleased with this determination, the more so as blood had been repaid with blood on both sides. Add to this that each party by the treaty acquired a powerful ally who would be ready to help one another either at home or abroad.

The only reflection that can be made on the above is that though Harold Harfagre might have reduced the petty princes of Norway under one head yet this was not so effectually done as to hinder them carrying on their mutual quarrels without applying to government. Nay when the King struck in it seems only as an arbitrator who wished to see their differences terminated, not as an absolute monarch who could impose silence on their wrangling.

Sigurd, as a sign of his being well pleased with the reconciliation, invested Kali with the title of Earl and gave him, as a vassal of Norway, the half of Orkney which had been in the possession of his uncle St. Magnus. He likewise gave him the name of Rognvald, from Rognvald the son of Brus, whom his mother Gunhilda used to call the most accomplished of the Earls of Orkney and this he hoped would be a lucky prognostic of his future fortune. Thus, from the bitterest enemies, these two noble families by the King's management became the firmest friends.

The Spring after this reconcilaition proved fatal to Sigurd who died in the fortieth year of his age and twenty-eighth of his reign and was succeeded by his son Magnus who was present at his death.

Sometime before the King's death, Gilchrist or Harold had made his appearance in Norway together with his mother where he informed of the relationship in which he stood towards him and, in consequence of this, underwent a trial by ordeal, two bishops leading him barefoot on nine red hot plowshares. Notwithstanding his being thus proved the son of Magnus Barefoot, his brother forced him to take an oath of abjuration by which he cut himself off from all right or title to reign and this he had done even before he would admit him to probation. He however was not contented with this but made all his subjects take an oath of allegiance to Magnus.

Harald, as soon as he heard of his brother's death, setting nothing by his oath which he considered as extorted and of no avail, convened his friends and among the rest Rognvald the new Earl of Orkney and his father Kol by whose help chiefly he got through the affair of probation. These with other men of note resorted to Harald and by these he was adjudged to have right to half the kingdom and the oath by which he abjured that right set aside. Upon the news of this, great numbers flocked in to him, some of which he formed into a court, the rest into an army. Harold at length began to become formidable to his nephew yet the latter, being possessed of the royal treasury, had thus the sinews of war in his power and by these means still had the balance on his side. A truce was agreed upon for a week, in which time each debated his plea and at length the matter came to this, that each should have half the kingdom but that the treasure, the table furniture, gold and silver, the jewels, precious stones, valuable vassels, the whole fleet with their furniture, should be entirely the property of Magnus without participation.

This pacification lasted three years with much suspicion on both sides, Magnus hated Harald's friends but especially Rognvald, Earl of Orkney, and his father Kol and in consequence of their attachment to his uncle, he recalled the feu of Orkney with the title of Earl which Rognvald had now enjoyed for some years.

It is hard for a fierce and warlike nation to dissemble, no wonder that this state of mutual fear and distrust soon broke out into an open quarrel. This happened in the fourth summer after the death of Sigurd when both parties met at a place called Fyrislief in the province of Ranarika (now Bahuys) and a battle ensued. Christrod, Harald's uterine brother, Earl Rognvald, Ingimar Thiostolf and Soemund were the leaders of Harald's army which however was worsted by superior numbers with the loss of Christod and Ingimar. Harald fled to his ships and afterwards to Eric Eymund, King of Danemark, his sworn brother by whom he was well received and from him had the province of Halland for his present maintenance. He after gave him likewise eight ships which Thorkiolf soon after furnished and manned with the money arising from the sale of his own lands, in order for an immediate attempt on Norway. This they made in autumn of the same year and coming to Kornvog near Bergen they stayed there till the festival was over with a large well furnished fleet. After the celebration of Christmas they entered the town where they found Magnus deserted by everybody. Him they seized and brought on board the King's ship where Harald ordered him to be castrated, his eyes put out and one of his feet to be cut off. Harald, upon this, took possession of the whole kingdom of Norway and, as a testimony of the obligation he was under to Rognvald Kolson he confirmed the grant of the Orkneys which, with the title of Earl, had been conferred on him by his brother Sigurd, This happened in the spring of the year 1105.

Upon the confirmation taking place, Kol thought proper to send messengers to make a friendly demand upon Paul of the half of the Orkney islands and, in consequence of his compliance, to make offer of his friendship and alliance in the strongest terms. But in case of refusal he ordered his ambassadors immediately to proceed to Scotland and endeavour to engage Frakaurk and Aulver Rosta to his interest, promising them half of the Orkneys if they would join him against Paul.

The ambassadors faithfully delivered their commission to which Paul replied that he had been long aware of their underhand attempts to deprive him of his right, in order to bring in a remote branch of the family but as he despised their crafty manoeuvres so he was determined to defend his patrimony by every method and to the utmost of his power.

Upon this answer the ambassadors according to their instructions passed the Pightland Firth and, coming to Frakaurk, explained their message. Here they were favourably received and had as good an answer as they could have wished. Frakaurk after trumpeting forth her own importance as being sprung from a noble family and connected with others of the first rank, particularly with the Earl of Atjokl (to whom she had married Margaret, Haco's daughter) then the first of the Scottish nobility as being cousin to David the reigning prince, declared that Kol had acted most prudently in soliciting her assistance in reducing the Orkneys. She told him in fine that she was greatly pleased with the alliance of such wise and prudent men as Kol and Rognvald and had no doubt of success. She desired them to let Kol know her forwardness, that she would employ the winter in collecting men and other warlike preparations, amongst her friends in Scotland and the AEbudae and together with Aulver Rosta would meet him in Orkney where they would join forces against Paul about midsummer.

Kol and Rognvald were greatly heartened by the success of their embassy and instantly set about preparing for the expedition and, summer following, Rognvald, with a small but valiant body of men, set out for the islands in five or six ships having engaged Soemund and Ion Foot to go with him. Arriving at Shetland at the time appointed he sent out scouts to look for Frakaurk who brought him no intelligence of her, as the winds that had brought him from Norway detained her in the AEbudae,however he was kindly entertained by the Shetlanders who received his ships into port at Alasound and brought refreshments tohis men on their landing.

Frakaurk was not idle but was somewhat unlucky in her preparations for, though she got together a number of men and eleven ships, yet these were unfit for war by reason of their being flat sides and not sufficiently manned. Aulver Rosta commanded these who was to reap the fruits of the enterprise if it succeeded and Frakaurk and her friends accompanied him. About midsummer the fleet according to agreement sailed for Orkney to join Rognvald.

Earl Paul happened to be in Rousa feasting with his friend Sigurd of Westness, when news was brought to him of Rognvald's being in Shetland and Frakaurk's preparations in the AEbudae. He therefore consulted with Kugi of Westra, Thorkel . Flet and other prudent friends what was best to be done in this dangerous conjuncture. Some advised to make peace with one party so as to be able to deal with the other; others that he shold retire to Caithness and there solicit help from his friends, in a word they entirely disagreed in their sentiments, nor did the Earl himself approve of either method of proceeding. He justly imagined it would look mean in him fearfully to solicit that which he had formerly denied, when offered in terms so advantageous to himself. He thought it likewise disgraceful for a chief to fly before he had struck a blow. Paul therefore proposed that such a fleet as could be got together on such short warning should be convened on the ensuing night, with which they would fight Rognvald before he could join his allies from the western isles. All approved this advice and set about performing the Earl's orders with great alacrity so that by sun risng in the morning they had a small fleet in Rousa. Of these Eyvind Melbrigdin brought up one ship, Olave Rolfson of Gairsey another, Thorkel Flet appeared with a fourth as did Sigurd and the Earl with a ship each, being all they were at that time possessed of. When they came to the rendezvous it was concerted that they should next day sail for Shetland in search of Rognvald. Before they sailed the Earl was reinforced with a large body of men which flocked on board from all corners. Early in the morning news was brought that a fleet was seen streering northwards through the Pictland Firth and directing their course for the isles. This fleet which consisted of ten or twelve ships was soon known to be Frakaurk's and the Earl immediately determined to engage it and, for this purpose, gave orders for his fleet to weigh and meet the enemy notwithstanding the delays that were industriously thrown in the way of Olave and Sigurd who wished to have more men and which were continually flocking in before the engagement. By this time the enemy's fleet was advanced to a place our author calls Umla, almost opposite them, when the Earl gave orders to prepare for the engagement and the ships to be grappled together that he might hinder the enemy's galleys from breaking the line.

A few moments before the engagement Erland of Tankerness and his sons came and offered his service but by this time the Earl's fleet was completely manned. Paul therefore ordered on board a large quantity of stones and other missiles to annoy the enemy from the hand and their slings or crossbows. Such preparations as these were scarce finished when Aulver Rosta advancing, attacked the Earl with the utmost fury. Aulver's ships were less than the Earl's but they were more numerous though, notwihstanding the odds both of men and ships, their littleness proved a vast disadvantage in the battle, for Olave of Gairsey in a large ship attacked those of the enemy that were next him and soon defeated three of their small galleys. Aulver, in the Admiral ship distinguished by her bulk, singled out the Earl with whom he fought so stoutly that he drove all the combatants from the forepart, even to the last and, following this blow and the panic he saw among his opposites, with encouraging shouts to his men to follow he boldly leaped on board the Earl's ship which was instantly full of the enemy. Paul's second Swein, from his strength surnamed Briosteip or Toughbreast, was a man who passed his time between the Earl's hall and the pursuit of piratical adventures, possessed of vast strength and bulk of body, dark and ill-looked and so much addicted to heathenish superstition that he used to lie all night amongst the graves and expect responses from the dead. This person, who was a valiant soldier, sustained Aulver's first attack and gave breathing time to the rest, when the Earl, no sooner seeing his ship in possession of the enemy, than, jumping forward, he reanimated his men to renew the attack. Aulver by a lucky stroke of his spear drove the Earl's shield to some distance on the deck, which was like to breed great confusion had not Swein Briostreip snatched up a large stone with which he struck Aulver Rosta such a blow on the breast as tumbled him overboard. He was with great difficulty recovered from the waves but without any sign of life and put on board his own ship. The misfortune of the commander always affects the combatants. Aulver's men no sooner saw what had happened than they cut the grapplings and began to fly. It was in vain for Aulver, who had now recovered the shock, to attempt putting a stop to their flight, terror had now got such a hold of them, that it stopped their ears and lent them wings. The Earl followed them round the east side of the Mainland and S. Ronaldsha as far as the Pictland Firth but, seeing he could not come up with them, he gave over the pursuit and returned to his station in Rousa.

Here he found five of Aulver's ships deserted of their men, which he manned and added to his fleet which was reinforced with two more large vessels proper for war and a number of men, that he thought himself a match for Rognvald and resolved to seek him out in Shetland. Coming unawares thither he surprised Rognvald's fleet and killing the few that were on board he seized every ship that belonged to the fleet. Rognvald getting notice of his loss convened the inhabitants and came down to the shore thinking to provoke Paul t o fight it out on firm land but the latter who had no great confidence in the Shetlanders refused to land, only desired Rognvald to get more ships that they might end their dispute at sea but, as this could not be done in Shetland, Paul contented hiself with having made himself master of his opponent's fleet and returned to Orkney.

Chapter 13

Rognvald, so shamefully deprived of his fleet, continued in Shetland till Autumn when he embarked his men in several merchant ships and sent them at several times to Norway. Arriving there himself amid the jibes and jeers of his countrymen he enquired at his father, how he bore the loss and failure of his mission? The old man prudently answered that though he had come of with some disgrace yet his voyage had not been without some advantages as he had fixed the Shetlanders in his interest. It was therefore agreed between them that Kol should command the next attempt upon Orkney which they determined to make the following spring and, for this purpose, Rognvald petitioned the King of Norway for a new armament with which they determined to finish their point or perish in the prosecution of it.

Upon Earl Paul's return to Orkney after his so happy achievements, he took every precaution to secure himself in his government of the isles. One prudent and necessary step was to have such a communication through the different islands as might give sudden warning of the approach of an enemy from Shetland or elsewhere. This he effected by erecting watch towers everywhere, in which were placed sentinels furnished with piles of wood which they were to set on fire on the approach of anything suspicious and this was to be a sign to the inhabitants to fly to their arms.

The first of these watch towers the ruins of which are yet to be seen, he placed in Fair Isle, as being next to Shetland; the second in North Ronaldsha committing the charge of it to Thorstein the son of Rogna. He palced a third in Sanda under the eye of his brother Magnus; another in Westra to the care of Krugi; a fifth in Rousa to that of Sigurd of Westness, and many others through the rest of the isles, so that none could approach Orkney without being discovered.He dispatched Olave the son of Hrolf of Gairsey into Caithness who fixed his seat at Duncansbay and governed that province as the Earl's lieutenant. In a word he left no probable means untried to defeat Rognvald's schemes or those of his ally Frakaurk.

Thus passed the aurumn and winter till Christmas when the Earl invited all his friends particularly those who had behaved so well in summer to a feast which was prepared at his castle of Iorfior. Among the rest of the guests Valthiof was invited. This gentlemn with ten others in their way to Iofior perished by shipwreck greatly lamented by everybody.

About this time an accident happened which abundantly shows the pertinaceous temper of the Northerns and their genius for revenge which never lost an opportunity for acting. Olave Rolfson of Gairsey, Paul's lieutenant in Caithness, we have seen fixed his quarters in Duncansbay which he had fortified and manned with a number of men such as chose to attend him for the winter. Amongst these were his sons Swein and Gun, as also Asbiorn and Margad the sons of Grime of Swana, brave men and sworn brothers of Swein. On the third day before the feast of Yule, Swein with his friends Asbiorn and Margad had gone afishing and Aslief, Olave's wife, with her other son Gun had accepted an invitation to the feast of the season from some of their neighbours, so that none was left in the castle of Duncansbay with Olave but a few attendants. Aulver Rosta, taking advantage of this circumstance and a stormy night, surrounded the castle with the same men that had attended him in his summer expedition, and burnt it to the ground together with Olave and six of his men. The rest they allowed to depart and carried off every moveable they could find or move. Swein, on his return from fishing, hearing of his father's fate instantly crossed the Pictland Firth and, arriving at Swana in the middle of the night at the habitation of Grime, was by him conducted to Scapa for which service he rewarded the old man with a gold ring from his finger and dismissed him. Arnkel who then lived at Scapa with his sons Hanef and Sigurd attended Swein to Iorfior where his kinsman Eybind the son of Melbrigd, introduced him to the Earl by whom he was most kindly received and invited to remain with him. Paul expressed the highest sorrow for the loss of his father, nor was this any wonder as he had found him always staunch in his interets, his hearty friend on all occasions. He therefore thought it incumbent on him to repay the son by honourable treatment the debt he owed the father. After consoling him on his father's death Swein attended the Earl to the Chapel to evening service.

The Earl's magnificent seat of Iorfiar stood on the hill opposite to Urridafiord (now Bay of Forth) in which lay Damsaholm, fortified with a castle the Governor of which was Blain the son of Thorstein of Hidurness.

Iorfiar consisted of a large Hall for the entertainment of strangers. Near the east corner on the south side was the door of entry, before which stood a grand temple to which there was an entry from the hall by a covered passage. On the left of the entrance was the Cellar, seperated from the hall by a partition of stone in which was deposited many and mighty vessels filled with ale the beloved beverage of the northerns. Off the hall were doors leading to lesser chambers for different purposes.

At the conclusion of the evening service the Earl and his guests returned to the Hall where great care was taken to set every person according to his rank or the place he held in the Earl's favour. Swein the son of Asleif (for it seems this person was denominated from his mother) sat at the Earl's right hand and Swein Briostreip on his left and next him his kinsman Ion. The rest were marshalled in their proper order by the master of the ceremonies. After supper and the removal of the table came the death of Valthiof as before related but, though the Earl had sufficient cause to mourn the double calamity which had befallen Olave's family he gave orders that none should mention it particularly to Swein during the feast. After supper the evening concluded with a drinking bout as usual and at length all went to bed except Swein Brostreip who passed his night according to his custom among the tombs. At midnight all rose to prayers and next day being Christmas, after the same, dinner was served up in the Hall, where Eyvind the son of Melbrigd, as master of ceremonies, regulated the disposition of the feast and, for that reason, did not sit down to table. As every one drank in his turn Swein emptied his cup immediately after the Earl but, upon its being offered to Swein Briostreip, he complained that Eyvind had filled more largely to him than his namesake and had likewise taken the cup from him before it was empty, both it would seem crimes against the northern laws of drinking. This however was only a pretence to renew in the person of the son an old grudge Swein Briostreip formerly had with Olave of Gairsey. After they had drank sufficiently they returned to the church[1], and thence to the feast[2], where after meat the ceremony was oberved first to the Gods and then to the Heroes[3], so famous among the Gothic nations. After this was over Swein Briostreip who still suspected his namesake of unfair drinking, had a mind to change cups (horns) with Swein Asleifson which Eyvind observing filled a still larger horn to the latter which he presented to Briostreip. Briostreip enraged at his treatment muttered, yet so as to be heard by the Earl and a few of those that were near him, his intention of a severe revenge. When the Earl went to vespers Swein Asleifson went with him but Briostreip remained behind in the hall. Eyvind, who seems not to have had much regard for the latter, took Swein Asleifson aside and, informing him of what he had threatened, advised him to be beforehand with him. He likewise gave him an axe and desired him to watch for his adversaries coming at the partition which divided the Hall from the entrance to the Church and, if his companion Ion went before him, to give the blow on the face, if behind, on the back of the head. The Earl by this time was in church, quite ignorant of what was passing, wither likewise Swein followed, preceded by his friend John till they came to the door in which there was but little light as the night was cloudy, when Swein Asleifson struck Briostreip a motal blow with his axe which however did not bring him to the ground.Staggering a little he percieved his kinsman Ion, from whom he imagined he had received the blow and, not knowing him in the twilight, drew his sword and cleft him to the shoulders, when instantly both fell. Such generally was the issue of these entertainments among a haughty, passionate and fierce people but especially if their passions were roused by any ancient feud heightened by new affronts they seldom if ever parted without bloodshed of which the above is a remarkable instance.

Eyvind upon the perpetration of the murder ran hastily to Swein whom he hurried into the next chamber and let him escape through the window, where Eyvind's son stood ready with a saddled horse on which Swein fled to Urridafiord and, passing to Damsey, was received into the castle of Blain the Keeper and next day proceeded to Egilsha to Bishop William whom he found celebrating Mass. When Mass was over Swein informed him of the misfortunes of his family and the slaughter of Swein Briostreip which he committed and begged his assistance to screen him from the relations of the deceased and the Earl. The honest bishop instead of blaming Swein for the murder thanked God that Briostreip was out of the way, seeing he had given great scandal by his heathenish practices, as mentioned above, he not only gave him shelter while he continued in Orkney, which was till the festival was over, but also sent him off to Firey, one of the AEbudae, where he lived in great honour with Holbod son of Hundi through the winter.

No sooner was the murder known, than all was in an uproar at Iorfiar. The Earl left the church immediately and found Swein deprived of his senses though not dead, which happened however a few hours after. As the murderer was unknown, Paul ordered everyone to resume their seats when that of Swein Asleifson stood empty He therefore was justly suspected of the slaughter as on enquiry it was found he had fled. Eyvind coming forward excused Swein of the slaughter of Ion and, from the circumstance of the sword and which none but Briostreip carried to Church, showed that he must have slain his friend. The Earl seemed to be satisfied at this particular and declared that in strict justice there was no room for revenge in the recent case as there was some provocation given but that he should poorly vindicate his honour if he did not take notice of it seeing the slaughter was committed in the face of his authority and even in contempt of his dignity. Every person imagined that Swein had fled to Papa to Haco Charles, St. Magnus' brother but as he was not heard of through the whole winter, Paul banished him from the islands and confiscated his estate; not so much, says our Author, for the slaughter, although it was perpetrated on a holiday and even within the Earl's house, as for the affront against his honour and the outrage against the laws of civility.

Paul now began to bethink himself of Rognvald and to prepare for the visit he had all the reason in the world to think he would pay him in the spring. He began therefore to re-engage his friends by large presents to defend the islands from the invader. Among other instances of profusion, he presented Thorkel Flet with the farm in Stronsa which had been the property of Valthior, Swein's brother, and now, by his death, descended to him, on condition of his discovering Swein's lurking place. Thorkel readily told him: "It was an old proverb that princes had long ears" and that he was surprised it had not come to the Earl's knowledge that William the Bishop had conveyed Swein to the western Islands, to Holbod son of Hundi, who had afforded him protection for the winter. The Earl fell into a rage against the Bishop on hearing this and asked Thorkel how he thought he should punish him. Thorkel replied it would not be so proper at present to take any notice of what had passed as Rognvald's proposed expedition made it necessary for him to have all the friends he could in the Isles. Paul agreed with him thus far that he would pass it over till more peaceable times and, in the mean time, passed to N. Ronaldsha where he was feasted by Rogna, a lady famed for prudence, and her son Thorstein whose estate lay in Papa. Here he was oblged by contrary winds to remain three days and among other discourses, Briostreip's story coming on the carpet, Rogna told him though Swein was a valiant man and active in war yet his loss of him would not much be felt, as his manner always procured more enemies to the Earls of Orkney than friends. She added that the present exigency required that he should make friends and by no means fall out with the Bishop nor Swein Asleifson's friends who were both able and might be encouraged by soft means to engage in his quarrel with great heartiness. She advised him to be reconciled to the Bishop, to recall Swein and restore his patrimony which, by this means, would secure him for as trusty a friend as ever his father had been. She pointed out the example of other princes who ever took this method to reconcile even their greatest enemies. Paul was far from relishing this voluntary advice, in the greatest fury he told Rogna, "he always supposed her a woman of prudence but such council to the Earl of Orkney showed the contrary, however as she had no concern in the quarrel he was determined her advice should not weigh with him, nor should she usurp an authhority which she had no title to. At this rate" adds he "I must buy a peace from Swein Asleifson and be ever after his slave." After much blustering, Paul went away for Westray and, as the spring advanced, gave strict orders for the beacons to be erected in the Fair Isle, N. Ronaldsha and the neighbouring isles, to be ready to give the alarm in case of an invasion. He committed the charge of the Fair Isle beacon to Dagfin the son of Laudver or Lewis and that of N. Ronaldsha to Thorstein the son of Rogna, two person whom he could trust in case Rognvald shoud renew his attempts from Shetland.

Earl Rognvald passed the winter in Norway and stretched every nerve to engage a fleet and army against spring, in which he was tolerably successful as his father likewise took an active part. In the month of Gio, which comprehended the half of February and as much of March, Kol sent two merchant ships to England to buy arms and warlike implements, Soemund went with a third into Danemark for the same purpose, so that about Paschtide all was expected to be in readiness for sailing. Kol and Rognvald as leaders of the expedition had each his ship of war, Soemund commanded a third, they were attended by a fourth as victualler. Before they sailed for Orkney they touched at Bergen to bid farewell to King Harold, who presented Rognvald with a fine ship ready for battle. Besides these Ion Foot commanded a fifth warship and Aslec of Herey a sixth, also another storeship commanded by a grand son of Thorer of Steige, in all six great warships, three lesser barks and three of the ships called in Norway Byrding, for transporting their provisions and other necessaries. The fleet rendezvoused at the Herey islands and, while they waited for a fair wind they had intelligence by a ship from the westward what mighty preparations Paul was making against them and the confidence he had in being able to defend the isles against them, she likewise informed of his force and everything else necessary for them to know. This was very acceptable to Rognvald who instantly called all his men on deck where he informed them of Paul's preparations against them and with what obstinacy the Orkney people were determined to keep him out not only of his birthright but what had been confirmed to him by two Kings. He begged his men therefore to fight valiantly nor did he forget to inform them of his resolution never to return to his native country without success. All approved of his resolution and promised to stand by him to the last. Kol, in order to strengthen them in this way of thinking and throw what odium he could on the treachery of the Orkneymen towards the posterity of St. Magnus, harangued his son to the following purpose.

"It is evident to every person that outrages have been committed by the Orkneymen against the different branches of our family, which even time cannot put an end to. Not content with the injuries committed on our forefathers they extend the same to their posterity, not content with ousting us of our possessions, they now conspire to defend these against us by force of arms. You, therefore," adds he to his son, "to whom of right of the Orkneys belong, shall choose your Uncle Magnus for your patron in this expedition to whom the original title appertains and, in case of success, thou shalt vow a most magnificent temple of stone to his honour and endow it in such a manner as Kirkwall, where it shall be built, may become more opulant and his Relics with the Episcopal chair may be more conveniently placed in this new erection." This was a speech excellently well adapted for the times, no wonder when all approved it, Rognvald made the vow he was required and performed every other preliminary after which, the wind blowing fair, they sailed for Shetland where they were joyfully received by their friends there, who gave them much intelligence concerning the state of affairs in Orkney. While they stayed in Shetland Kol consulted every means to deceive the keepers of the Beacons in Fair Isle or N. Ronaldsha. Unius whose cunning he knew on another occasuion was his advisor on this, between them a plan was laid down that had the desired effect and was soon after put in execution.

Kol in puruance of his plan sent out some small vessels towards the Orkneys which he conducted in person as he had let no body else into the secret. As soon as they came in sight off the Fair Isle, Kol ordered all the sails to be hoisted half mast high and the course to be altered but, as they approached nearer, the sails were to be elevated by degrees to the masthead on purpose that those who saw them might take them for larger vessels and set fire to the beacons which would at least produce an uproar in Orkney upon their finding themselves deceived. Everything happened as they expected, Dagfin no sooner saw the fleet approaching from this suspected quarter but he kindled his beacon and, after his example, Thorstein in N. Ronaldsha and all the rest through the different isles, so that in a short time the alarm became general and all the inhabitants that bore arms flocked in to the Earl.

Kol had now gained his point, for he no sooner saw the beacons on fire than he ordered his small fleet to put about for Shetland, till they saw the issue of their stratagem. Unius in the mean time to see how things went took a fishing boat and Shetland men for rowers with which he made the best of his way for the Fair Isle, calling himself a Norwayman who had been married in Shetland and obliged to fly with these his three sons after being robbed and otherways maltreated by Rognvald and his pirates. In a word this lamentable story gained so upon Dagfin and the islanders that they took him under their protection.

Dagfin upon his firing the beacon immediately went off to find the Earl, where he found all the Gentlemen before him. The Earl enquired earnestly about the fleet which had caused the alarm which everybody supposed to be Earl Rognvald's but were surprised they did not appear; however they determined to wait three days to see what would happen. As no fleet appeared in this period the people began to murmur at the rashness of Thorstein who, upon the sight of a few fishing boats, had caused all this disturbance in the isles to the great loss of the inhabitants who were by their folly dragged from domestic and other business. Thostein justly threw the blame on Dagfin and argued that he could not be answerable to see the Fair Isle beacon on fire without communicating the alarm to the rest of the isles. To this Dagfin returned an answer which flung Thorstein in such a rage that he struck him a deadly blow with a battle axe which felled him to the earth. The whole assembly was soon in an uproar and ran to their arms, some siding with Lewis, Dagfin's father, and others with Thorstein.

This broil happened near Kirkwall and cost the Earl much pain to quell which however he accomplished with the help of Kugi before the parties went entirely by the ears together and this by representing the disgrace of private quarrel while their country was in danger from a foreign army. In a word Kugi applied to what he knew would settle them sooner than any argument, namely shame, and the event answered his expectation, they were soon hushed and all differences were referred to the Earl who soon broke up the assembly and sent everyone to his own home, upon a declaration that the Beacons were not treacherously but rashly kindled.The charge of the Fair Isle beacon was committed to one Eric to whom Uni offered his services and, after a short trial, was entrusted to the beacon, especially when he could be spared from catching and drying fish at which he was very dextrous. When Uni stood sentinel by hmself at the beacon he used to pour water on the wood so that it might not be lighted on a sudden which, together with his own management, was afterwards of great service to Rognvald. Rognvald put off his grand attempt upon Orkney till the Neaptide should calm the seas and an Eastwind should spring up to carry him from Shetland to Westra whence the passage was easy to the Mainland. This was successfully executed and the whole fleet put into Westra at a place alled Hofn without alarming the islands for, as soon as Eric saw the fleet from the Fair Isle, he put off to assist Paul leaving word with Uni to set the beacons afire but, as this person had another design on hand, he immediately, with his pretended sons, left the Island. Nor could the messengers Eric had sent light the wood, so effectually had Uni drowned it that, said our author, it was fitter to extinguish fire than be burnt by it. This was soon brought to Eric's ears who late perceived his folly in trusting a stranger in a matter of such consequence. Too late likewise he was obliged to inform Paul of the reason why the alarm was not spread through the Orkneys.

The inhabitants of Westra now saw Rognvald landed among them with a force they were not able to resist nor could they hope for any assistance quickly from Earl Paul. They therefore met and consulted how to behave in this sudden and unexpectd conjuncture. Kugi and Helgi who lived in Hofn were the only men of weight on the island who generally led the rest. They, seeing nothing better for it that they could neither fight nor flee, advised the poorer sort to submit to Rognvald and swear allegiance to him. The next Lord's day Rognvald attended divine service at the village church where his attendants the Norwegians were greatly surprised at the appearance of sixteen unarmed men with shaven crowns, concerning whom, as they had never seen any such in their country, they asked the Earl who, in a poem still extant, described their office and habit to his admiring countrymen. Next day messengers were sent out to collect the inhabitants in order to their submission and to take an oath of allegiance to their new master. Not long after however the Earl's people found out that the Westramen were not to be trusted and that thy were already hatching treason in several midnight meetings, of which they soon informed him. This information he received in the nighttime and when he got up he found many of the islanders had been whipped by his men and Kugi, as the author of the plot, flung in chains. Upon his protesting his innocence and adducing witnesses to prove it Rognvald, in an exptempore poem, cautioned him against treachery, forgave all that was past and renewed to them all his friendship.

Rognvald's sudden arrival in Orkney occasioned a great change in affairs. Paul soon found, notwithstanding the great pains he had taken to make friends, the Orkneymen were not to be trusted for already many of them had revolted to his rival. He therefore called a council of his friends in the Mainland, to deliberate what was to be done in this pressing exigency. Here, as it usually happens, many different projects were proposed and urged for restoring peace to the isles. Some proposed an equal partition and each to enjoy his own share independent of his rival, others, and these the richer party, imagined that it would be more expedient to buy Rognvald's right, to which they even offered Paul their pecunial assistance. Another party advised to risk the event of a battle which had been so lucky for their party before. What the Earl's sentiments were we do not find, however this was certain that Rognvald was soon informed of the issue of their meeting by one of the members he had bribed and who faithfully reported all that had passed. Upon the relation, turning to a Poet he made a poem on the subject, still extant, and soon sent messengers to William the Bishop to beg him that he would become a mediator between him and Paul. The Bishop returned a favourable answer and gained so far that he effected a truce for a fortnight, for consultation, the troops in the mean time to be cantoned in the different islands, a half to be alloted to each party. Rognvald had his headquarters in the Mainland and Paul in Rousa.

Much about this time Ion Wing or Vang of the Uplands of Hoy and Richard of Brek in Stronsa, relations of Swein Asliefson, set fire to Valthiof's (Swein's brother's) house which had been presented to

Thorkel Flet by Paul, and burnt him in it together with nine of his domestics in revenge for the treatment Swein had met with from Paul in confiscating and giving his estate. When they had thus satisfied their revenge they betook themselves to Rognvald and offered their service to him if he would take them under his protection, if not they would make up their peace with Paul as well as they could. Rognvald, considering that he had need of every twig he could lay hold of in Orkney to support his claim, granted their desire and took them under his wing. Haflid, Thorkel Flet's son, who it seems was in a wavering state what part to take, as soon as he heard of his father's death and the reception his murderers had met with from Rognvald, immediately withdrew to Paul by whom he was received with a most hearty welcome.

Paul's interest began now visibly to decline in Orkney, which made many powerful men in the Islands join with Rognvald who now found he had got such a footing that he determined to give his Norwegians leave to go home and, upon their offering to stay a little longer till all things were settled, Rognvald thanked them and told them "that he was sure, if God and St. Magnus had destined him to be Earl of Orkney, they would not fail to stir up friends to enable him to possess himself of it" and, with these words, he, in a friendly manner dismissed them.

We must now return to Swein Asliefson who made some noise about this time. In the beginning of the spring, Swein went to Scotland to visit his friends where he sojourned some time with Maddad, Earl of Atjocle (possibly Athole) who had married Earl Haco's daughter, Margaret. While here he had many and secret consultations anent the fate of the islands with the Earl and, hearing the Islanders were divided into parties, some favouring Paul and others Rognvald, he thought this would be a favourable opportunity to revisit his native country. On his way thither he stopped at Thursa in Caithness where, by means of Liotolf, a gentleman of his acquaintance, he demanded satisfaction of Count Ottar, Frakaurk's brother, for the slaughter of his father which was committed as we have seen above by order of his sister.

Here it must be noted that by the Laws of Norway then in use in Orkney, as also by those of Danemark, it was competent for the injured party to demand satisfaction from any of the relations of those that had injured him, which they were to pay in proportion to the degree they stood to the person who was guilty and, upon their refusing to make this partial satisfaction, they were to be held equally guilty. Swein, having received that part of the compensation that was incumbent on Ottar to pay and having given his promise to endeavour the restoration of Erland, the son of Harold the Fair Spoken, to his paternal inheritance, as soon as any opening presented for this purpose, became friends with Ottar and, in return, had a place in his friendship. Here he exchanged his ship and, going on board a bark with thirty seamen, he passed the Pightland Firth and, coasting the west side of Mainland, he entered Elfinsound in his way to Rousa. One corner of the island stretches far into the sea and the shore below the bank is rugged, broken and hollowed out into deep pits inhabited by multitudes of otters. While Swein was passing the Sound he observed on this promontory a number of men whom he would willingly have spoken with, to have enquired the news of the isles but was afraid the number of men might fright them away as the ship approached, which he directed to the quarter where he observd them. He therefore ordered twenty of his followers to hide themselves as he himself did, while the other ten should row slowly to the land. Those that were on the island, taking them for merchants, desired to know the lading of their ship and ordered them to proceed to Westness to Earl Paul who had been all that night with Sigurd at a feast. In the morning he took the diversion of otter hunting accompanied by twenty men, at the foresaid promontory, with a design to return to dinner. When Swein's seamen landed they had a good deal of talk with the hunters, at length they asked where Earl Paul was and, upon being answered "under the headland", Swein immediately ordered the ship to a place out of sight and his men to turn themselves and, setting upon the Earl's followers, soon killed nineteen of them and carried Paul, much against his will, on board their own ships. This bold enterprise was achieved with the loss of six men on Swein's side, who was no sooner possessed of his prey than he directed his course back the same way he came, by the west side of the Mainland and, running through between Hoy and Graemsay and then by the eastern wells of Swanna, they arrived at Eckialdzback (a place so called by our Author) and, leaving twenty men to guard the ship, they set out by land for Atjoile, carrying Paul prisoner to Maddad and his wife Margaret. Here he was received with feigned kindness by Earl Maddad and Paul's sister Margaret, who pretended to treat him with extraordinary humanity and honour. To divert his chagrin they introduced all kinds of hilarity and mirthful diversions, as feasting and anything that might elevate his spirits that were sadly depressed by this sudden change of fortune. This however was all a farce, Paul was as much a prisoner as if he had been worse treated and was every night locked in when he retired, with Swein a sort of sentry over him, by a bolt on the outside of his chamber door. Paul soon gave up all hope of a restoration to his former fortune, nay he was in some doubt of his life, the specimen he had of his sister's behaviour made him easily guess what he had to expect from her humanity and, upon her proposing one day to send Swein back to Orkney to demand of Rognvald one half of the islands in favour of Paul or of her son Harold, an infant of three years old, Paul, who saw her drift, after a heartfelt speech on his present condition, gave up all right and title he had to the Orkneys in favour of Harold, only asking as much money as as might maintain him in a monastery from which it was their business to prevent his escape. Addressing himelf to Swein, he desired him to return to the Orkneys and give out that he was deprived of his eyes and otherwise mutilated, as the only means he had of securing what he had resigned, against the indignation of his friends who would not fail to stir in his behalf if they were assured of his safety. It is certain Swein went immediately for Orkney and, according to some, told the story Paul had dictated but, according to other accounts, this was nothing more than the truth and that Margaret, with Swein's help, did really put out the Earl's eyes and throw him in prison but, which ever of these accounts may be true, it is certain Paul never returned to Orkney nor ever was publicly heard of in Scotland.

Margaret, in which ever light this story is viewed, acted most cruelly towards her brother, whose right to half the Earldom could not be disputed, though his father took a cruel method to possess himself of the other half. Paul seems to have considered the calamities that befell him as a judgement on him for the murder of St. Magnus by his father. In a word there seems to have been a particular providence in making one of the family thus the avenger of the crimes of the other. Ambition was the motive to the murder of St. Magnus and the same contributed to the deposition of Paul Hacoson. Paul was a man much beloved by the islanders, moderate in his appetites, peaceable in his disposition, open and liberal, so beneficent to his friends that he grudged no expense to gratify them, ineloquent to a great degree, spoke little in private and in public was obliged to use the tongue of his friends.

Return we now to Rousa where Sigurd, after some time waiting for the Earl, sent messengers to the sporting ground to look for him.

These on their return related that they had found there a number of men slain and, among the rest, the Earl. Sigurd without delay went to the ground himself where he found the Earl's twenty men slain that he knew and six that were strangers to him but no appearance of the Earl. Upon this disaster he sent messengers to Egilsha to acquaint the bishop of what had happened who, quickly passing to Rousa, found Sigurd full of the notion that this slaughter had happened through the contrivance of Rognvald. This however the bishop would not agree to, he told Sigurd that Rognvald would not have proceeded against his relation in such a cowardly manner and that time would discover another author of this cruel slaughter. Soon after they were told that one Borgar, who lived in Geitaberg, had observed a bark come from the westward, enter the sound, and soon sail the same way back, this started a notion that the Earl had been trepanned by Frakaurk or Aulver Rosta.

1. This was at nine in the forenoon the time for dinner in that age, as that of supper was five in the afternoon.

2. They had but two meals a day and in some houses but one. vid. Hen.Hist. Gr. B. Vol.3, p.588.

3. This custom was common after Christianity was introduced only instead of Thor and Odin they usually substituted Christ and the Apostles. vid. Mallet, North Ant. Vol.1, p.311.

Chapter 14

Paul's friends, now deprived of heir leader, were at a loss to know what part to take. In a public convention most of them were inclined to join with Rognvald and take an oath of allegiance to him, while some, and among them Sigurd and his sons Haco Pike and Bryniolf, refused to any side till they were informed whether Earl Paul was alive or dead. Many others follwed their example and proposed a truce till a certain day on which , if Paul did not appear, they would do homage to Rognvald and to this he, lest his refusal should irritate the friendly chiefs, at last agreed. Before the appointed day there were many consultations among the leaders and at each of them someone or other deserted to Rognvald. At one of these nine armed men, coming from Scapa, entered the forum, one of whom was soon known to be Swein Asleifson. Everyone was eager to kow what news he had brought as he had landed at Scapa and had come in such a hurry but Swein had some reason for baulking the general curiosity at least for the present. Ordering then his old and firm friend the Bishop to be called, he privately told him everything concerning the slaughter in Rousa and the kidnapping of Paul and begged his advice how to behave so as to weather the storm that threatened. The Bishop honestly told him that at present he could not flatter him with being able to reconcile the minds of the people which however, notwithstanding the odiousness of the fact, in consideration of their past friendship, he would attempt. He therefore ordered him to wait where he was till he had laid open the cause to the Earl and the people and saw how they were affected. Entering again to the congress he demanded their attention to what he had to say and began with explaining the reason of Swein's banishment, dwelling much on the injury he had received from Paul, inbeing forced to fly his country for the slaughter of a wicked wretch who deserved to have been made a public example for his crimes. He demanded likewise that the public faith should be pledged for the safety of Swein's person. This was promised on Rognvald's part, for three days, and in the meantime recommended them to the Bishop's care for, he adds, if I can read your countenance there is something more interesting yet concealed between you and Swein. The Bishop confessed there was and, what nearly concerned him, that Swein earnestly wished to join his side. Rognvald, after some scruple, told the Bishop he would first talk with him apart and, withdrawing with the Bishop and his father Kol, Swein informed him of every particular concerning the fate of Paul. Rognvald was afraid if this story was recited in the public convention of the people it might occasion disturbance which he rather chose to avoid. He therefore determined to dismiss the multitude before Swein told the history of what had happened and which he was afraid would touch them too nearly. This was executed in the morning and, after the departure of the mob, Swein, after engaging for his safety, pointedly informed the assembly of everything that had befallen Earl Paul, even to the story of his mutilation. Sigurd of Westness, Paul's firm friend, was greatly grieved at Swein's story which cut off all the hopes he had till now entertained of the Earl's return. He had often declared that he would bring him back from whatever corner he was concealed but now this was all over and Rognvald was without any objection recognised Earl of Orkney.

He now found leisure for what he had long planned and proceeded to lay the f foundations of a church in honour of St. Magnus which was more advanced in the same year than in the two or three years afterwards. Kol drew the plan and provided the materials for the building, as he also laid out the work but, as it cost a great deal of time and expense, the funds alloted for the purpose began to fail and put the Earl to his shifts to raise more money. here likewise his father Kol helped him out by advising him to relax the old law which since Turf Einar's time entitled the Earl to succeed to every estate that fell, until the next heir redeemed it and which he considered a burden on the inhabitants. Rognvald took his father's advice and, upon publishing his intentions to allow all to buy up his right for a sum of money and relieve their posterity from the bondage it had created, everyone who had possessions affected by it flocked in eagerly to take the benefit of the Earl's offer and every ploughland, or as much as could be laboured with a single plough, fetched a mark through all the isles. By these means Rognvald raised money enough money to finish the church in the neatest and most magnificent manner.

From the above circumstances we may guess at the nature of the right, which seems to have been given up by Sigurd the Fat to the inhabitants of Orkney

Two years after Rognvald had got possession of Orkney he celebrated the festival of Christmas at his seat of Knarrastad (Scapa). While he was thus employed with his friends, they observed a vessel steering towards them from the Pightland Firth, which the beauty of the weather invited the Earl and his companions (among them one Rolf) out to see her put into the bay. She had no sooner put in than fifteen or sixteen men landed. Before them walked a man clad in a blue gown and bonnet, the lower part of his chin clean shaven, while the hair on his upper lip was unshaved and hung loosely down. When everyone wondered at the strangeness of this person's dress, Rolf informed them that it was Ion, Bishop of Atjocle in Scotland, which, when the Earl heard, he immediately went to meet him, paid him all the respect due to a man of his character, placed him in the highest seat and even waited at table as a cupbearer. In the morning of the day following the Bishop celebrated mass and afterwards went to Egilsha to visit Bishop William with whom he stayed a few days. When he thought proper to unfold the business on which he came, both Bishops attended by a splendid retinue, waited on the Earl and, in presence of Swein Asliefson, Ion delivered his message which was from Earl Maddad and his wife Margaret, daughter of Haco Paul, Earl of Orkney. The subject of the embassy was to demand from Earl Rognvald a cession of half the isles, which Paul had possessed, in favour of their son Harald, for so it had been agreed on by them and Swein. Hence it was clear that Swein was at the bottom of the misfortune that happened to Paul, thereto enticed when he made the first visit to Margaret and the Earl of Atjocle. To make the requisition more palatable it was proposed that Harold should be sent over for his education to Orkney and that the whole power should be in Rognvald's hands even when Harald grew up. These were the terms the Bishop and Swein offered Rognvald and he seems to have agreed to them for, in a meeting between him and Maddad sometime afterwards in Caithness, this treaty was solemnly ratified by oath and Harald was brought over to Orkney. Thorbiorn Klerk, as the young Earl's governor, accompanied him, a bold valiant and active man, excellent at managing any kind of business but proud and overbearing, not at all scrupulous in regard to justice. He had married Ingiride, Swein's sister, and spent his time between Orkney and Scotland, in both which places we shall hear of him afterwards.

Swein, upon his making up matters with the Earl, took possession of his father's lands as also those that had been possessed by Valthiof by the jus primogeniturae, which obtained all over the Norwegian territories, of retainers, in the manner of life guards, whom he largely maintained by plunder, as neither was he a strict observer of the laws with regard to meum and tuum, though he was prudent, cautious and possessed of great foresight. None could be possibly more didligent in pursuit of any pirating project than Swein or Thorbiorn Klerk and none followed the trade more. It was on occasions of this kind that they conceived a friendship for one another which, from a similarity of disposition was of no long duration. Swein's natural genius could not be long kept under, the first instance, after his settlement, of his restlessness was his asking a fleet and men to revenge on Frakuark and Aulver Rosta, his father's death, paying no regard to the partial compensation he had received from Count Ottar of Thursa. Upon this requisition the Earl, who was less revengeful in his disposition, replied that there was little to be dreaded from a worn out old woman as Frakuark now was. This answer was far from pleasing to Swein, he told him he did not expect to be denied in such a small matter, since he had gone to such lengths for him, meaning what he had done against Paul which this gentleman had done to serve his own revenge and even without the knowledge or approbation of Rognvald, but had now the art to hold forth for his advantage to strive with a man of Swein's disposition, he therefore asked him what force would be sufficient and was answered two well furnished ships. These being granted he set out with a fair wind for Scotland and, landing at a town in Scotland called by our author Dufeyra, he passed though Murray to Athole. His old friend Maddad received him kindly and furnished him with guides who were well acquainted with the byways and through the mountains, which Swein rather chose than the ordinary paths through the cultivated spots and villages, the latter he avoided for fear of spreading the alarm and so be disappointed of his prey. He arrived at Helmsdale in Sutherland before anybody suspected his coming for though Frakuark had some inkling of the expedition and had placed sentinels on all the customary roads for fear of a surprise, yet she had neglected the desert, as imagining none would attempt that way nor had she any notion that Maddad who had married Margaret, Frakuark's daughter, whom she herself had brought up, would set on her mortal enemy against her.

Swein was first observed by Aulver Rosta in the hollow of a hill behind Frakuark's house, who went out to meet him with eighty men, when there happened a smart but short engagement in which Aulver was worsted and forced to fly over the water to Helmsdale with great slaughter of men, nor could he gain Frakuark's house, as Swein's men had got between him and it, thence he was driven to the mountains and afterwards took himself to the western isles, where he was never more heard of. Swein instantly flew to Frakuark's house which he plundered of everyhing valuable. he set it on fire and reduced it, together with Frakuark and all the men in it, to ashes. Thus fell Frakuark who certainly deserved punishment for her sorceries and villainous and revengeful intrigues, yet this ought to have been inflicted in another manner and not with such instances of cruelty which nothing but the practice of the times could excuse.

Swein's plan for the summer was not yet concluded, the murder of Frakuark only whetted his genius and was at first an excellent pretence for obtaining ships from the Earl to enable him to exert his talents. No sooner had he finished his revenge on Frakuark than he fell upon the neighbourhood which he plundered and, carrying the spoils to his ship, he spent the whole summer and autumn in piratical inroads on the coast of Scotland and, returning to Orkney, he was most graciously received by Earl Rognvald by whom he seems to have been made governor of Caithness, as he went thither to winter in Duncansbay, Sweinhad no long time for idleness, soon he had a new opportunity of indulging his ruling passion. An Englishman called from the Western isles at Duncansbay with a message from his friend Holbodi imploring his assistance against one Haulde from Cornavia who had plundered him and carried off all his goods. Swein thought his honour engaged to defend his friend, he therefore went to Count Rognvald and begged proper assistance to revenge the cause of a man who had in his distressful circumstances behaved in such a friendly manner to him. The Earl, after some caution, gave him two galleys sufficiently manned with which he proceeded to the AEbudae, but did not overtaake Holbodi till he reached the isle of Man. Holbodi was greatly elevated at his friend's arrival with the thoughts of revenge, as Haulde had done a great deal of mischief by wasting the country and slaughtering the people both in Man and the AEbudae. Amongst the rest he had slain a man of the first rank called Andrew, whose wife Ingiride, a rich widow, Holbodi advised Swein to marry, nor was she against it, if he would engage to revenge the slaughter of her husband. Swein and Holbodi with five ships sailed for Bretland where they wasted far and wide. One day entering a village where the inhabitants, being too weak to resist them, fled, they burnt it after plundering it and the same day, before breakfast,they had six villas on fire, as we undertsand from Eric an Iceland poet who was present. After this wanton cruelty they went on board and spent the whole summer in such like adventures, spreading terror wherevere they came. After an unsuccessful attempt upon Lundey, a town into which Haulde had shut himself up in autumn, they returned to the Isle of Man. In winter Swein, having married Ingeride, proposed another expedition against the Cornavians, in which he solicited Holbodi to join him. But he, pretending a multitiplicity of other pursuits, excused hiself. This however was only mere pretence, the real cause was, Haulde had made good use of the winter in pacifying his enemy and, by means of well applied presents, had bought a peace of him, which their mutual interest rendered desirable. Swein however set out without him, his force consisting of only three ships with which he performed several of his usual pranks. He was something unlucky in the beginning of his cruise meeting with nothing worth taking but at length, by the plunder of a merchant ship and the gleanings of some inroads on the coast of Ireland, he returned in Aurumn to the AEbudae with plenty of spoils. Not long after his return home, he was informed of Holbodi's treachery which at first he could not credit, notwithstanding the Earl Rognvald's caution anent the inconstancy of the Western Islanders, nor was he satisfied till next spring when, his watchmen calling him up one night, informed him that they observed a body of men approaching the house in a hostile manner. This roused Swein but did not terrify him, he immediatey called his men to arms by the sound of the horn and, as they lodged at no great distance, they were soon collected. He soon put his enemies to flight and killed many but Holbodi, their leader, fled and got to Lindey to his new friend Haulde, where they fortified themselves against all attacks. Swein returning home kept better guard for the future, as he saw he could not trust the islanders and soon after sold his lands in these parts for as large a price as he could and moved to the island of Lewis, enriched with the fruits of his summer's adventures.

While Swein Asliefson was thus employed in the Western Isles, Earl Rognvald had an invitation to an entertainment with one Hroald at Wick, whose son Swein, a stripling, served the table. While here Thorbiorn Klerk, coming from some other part of Scotland, declared that Valthiof, a Scottish Earl, had slain his father Thorstein Haulde Fiaransman.

Thorbiorn who was greatly in the Earl's good graces, so that he generally accompanied him wherever he went, while he was in Scotland, fell in with two of those persons who had been employed by Swein Asliefson in the murder of his grandmother Frakuark and her family and caused them to be slain. Swein took this greatly amiss, that the Earl should countenance one who was thus virtually his enemy that, instead of waiting upon the Earl as he usually did at the end of his summer's cruise, he went straight to his house in Gairsa. Rognvald surprised at this, enquired the reason at Thorbiorn Klerk who soon satisfied him that Swein was offended because he had slain some of the murderers of Frakuark. The Earl was sensible that their broils would be inconvenient for him, he therefore went to Gairsa and easily reconciled the contending parties, who continued their intimacy for a long time afterwards

About this time a trading ship touched at Orkney in which came a noble Icelander named Hall the son of Thorarin Breidmagi or Fatpaunch. This person visited Rogna and her son Thorstein in North Ronaldsha where, after some stay, he began to importune Thorsteain to recommend him to Rognvald as one of his satellites. This was done and he met with a refusal and, on his return to North Ronaldsha he composed a poem on the occasion in which he commemorated his being rejected as the Earl had already a sufficient number of valiant men. Some time after Rogna, who had some private business with the Earl, took occasion to appear before him in a red hood made of horse hair, on which the Earl composed an extemporary poem which is translated and preserved by Olau Wormius as follows:

Incipit hoec mulier occiput circumligare seque ornare ira cundia et futua equae cauda.

Rogna, pleased to see the Earl in such good humour, pled the cause of her friend Hall so effectully that Rognvald, though somewhat difficult at first, was at length prevailed upon to admit him into his hall. A similarity of studies soon produced an intimacy between Hall and the Earl, they were both exquisite poets and employed much of their time in collecting old poems or composing new ones. Among other works having a relation to Poetry may be numbered the *Clavis rhythmica* or Poetical Key, said by Wormius to be still extant. It seems to have been a kind of description of the different kinds of measure used in morthern poetry exemplified by several stanzas of each kind, our author says five, but on accunt of prolixity, the moderns had cut off three from each. This performance is still said to be extant in the Library at Upsal.

About this time Swein Asleifson, whose disposition never gave him rest, heard that his treacherous friend Holbodi had returned from Cornavia to the AEbudae. He determined to loose no time in punishing his treason. He therefore applied to Earl Rognvald for a sufficient force and received five ships with men and other necessaries proper for the expedition. Thorbiorn Klerk commanded one of the ships, Haflid the son of Thorkel Flet another, Dufnial the son of Havard Gunnar a third, Richard the son of Thorlief, Frakuark's sister, had a fourth and Swein himself commanded the fifth. When Holbodi heard of the force out against him he was struck with such a panic that he slyly fled from the AEbudae and never had the courage to return.

Swein however he had lost his enemy determined the expedition should not be made in vain, he therefore laid waste the islands with fire and sword, spreading rapine and destruction everywhere, carrying off everything that was valuable to his ships, in a word Swein behaved now as was usual with him, whatever the quarrel the consequence was always a plundering match. He had proposed to winter in the Western Isles but, as this was objected to by the rest, all proceeded for Duncansbay where, if they expected an equal partition of the booty, they soon found themselves mistaken. Swein claimed by far the largest share as captain in the enterprise, as having solicited singly the Earl's assisitance in it, as being alone the occasion of it. With these and suchlike arguments did Swein cover his avarice, to which he was answered by Thorbiorn Klerk that they had an equal right, as having undergone equal toil, shared the danger and had the same authority, that therefore all the commanders should be entitled to an equal share of the profit. At length they were obliged to put up with Swein's distribution as he was too powerful for them in Caithness to contend with, though this was complied with great reluctance, yet they had no other resource but a complaint to the Earl. Rognvald though not well pleased with Swein's behaviour, took some pains to hush the matter up, promising to make them amends and recommending to them to make no quarrel on that account as they well new Swein's pertinacity. This was promised and, after extoling the Earl's equity and generosity, Thorbiorn promised not to strive with Swein, though he frankly confessed he could not renew his former friendship towards him and would take some future occasion by way of retaliation to stick some disgrace upon him. This he did soon after by repudiating Swein's sister Ingeride whom he sent to Caithness. Swein received her kindly, though he affected to be greatly affronted by the disgrace put upon her, but this he laid up to another occasion.

Whilst Swein was absent on his Western Isles expedition, he deputed one Margad, the son of Grime, in his room at Duncansbay. Margad behaved himself so badly in his office that he soon merited the abhorence of the Caithnessmen. Some he fell out with slight, others for no causes, some he fined at his pleasure so that he was hated by all. Those who themselves abnoxious to his displeasure at length withdrew themselves to the protection of Hroald, between whom and Margad this bred an irreconcilable animosity. Margad had soon an occasion to go to Wick to transact some business, thither he was accompanied by twenty followers, by whose help he slew Hroald and several others and then betook him to his patron, as well as pattern, Swein. The latter, fearing the Earl's displeasure and at the same time willing to protect his friend, having got together as many men as he could, retired to the castle of Lanburgh (now Buccles Castle) and, having victualled it and provided everything necessary, he determined to stand a siege but, in the interim, was continually plundering the neighbourhoood of something or other valuable which he laid up in Lamburgh, all which set the inhabitants in a rage against him and made a speedy application to the Earl.

The Castle Swein had seized was excellently fortified by nature, situated on a sea rock, washed by the ocean; toward the land it had an impenetrable stone wall and all around to a great distance rugged rocks which bid defience to any assailant.

No sooner were these passages known to Rognvald and Swein, the son of Hroald, than the latter beseached the Earl to revenge his father's death and the injuries done to the Caithnessmen. He was joined by many of those that had suffered by Margad's oppression which, together with his own inclination, carried him over to Caithness accompanied by Thorbiorn Klerk, Haflid and Dufnial, all of them glad to take revenge on Swein for cheating them in the division of the plunder before mentioned. When he arrived at Duncansbay, he understood that Swein had seized the Castle of Lamaburgh and, going thither, he demanded Margad to be delivered up to punishment. Swein would not agree to this except the Earl would promise to pardon him but, as this was denied, Swein told him he would not deliver him up to Hroald's or any other of his enemies, though he himself wished greatly to be reconciled to the Earl. Thorbiorn turned this speech into derision and was answered in the same style by Swein who prophesied that the mighty benefits the Earl heaped upon him would not hinder him from making him the most ungrateful return for, says he, nobody will ever thrive in your company. Rognvald was at length obliged to put an end to their scolding and begird the Cstle with a siege. He however did not attempt to storm it as he knew it above his power, he rather seemed inclined to starve the besieged into a surrender which he was not long in effecting. As all supplies were cut off the beseiged were soon pinched with hunger and began to murmur which, Swein observing, called them together and, in a long harangue, set forth what a shameful thing it would be for them to be starved into surrender. He frankly owned his own folly in allowing himsef and them to be cooped up in a Castle and Rognvald's superior conduct in reducing them by a blockade rather than a storm. We, he adds, have done somethng in begging peace on condition of saving the life and limbs of Margad but it would be scandalous to give him up to the axe of the enemy but, adds he, I have found out a method to save him and you too; I am certain if he was sent off, all the rest would be safe on a surrender. All agreed to what he might propose and put it in execution accordingly. He, therefore, and Margad were let down over the precipice into the sea in the night time and, swimming along the bottom of the rocks, at length, after a most frightful navigation, gained the plain shore. They did not stay to make reflexion on their escapes but passed on foot through Sutherland into Murray and landed in a Scottish town our author calls Dufeyra. In their way they met with an Orkney boat with ten men on board, the chief of whom were Halvard and Thorkel, who conducted them along the shore of Scotland to the Isle of May on which was a Monastery, the Abbot's name of which was Balduin. Here they were detained by contrary winds for seven days and pretended they were ambassadors from Earl Rognvald of Orkney to the King of Scotland. This account however did not satisfy the suspicious Monks who, taking them for robbers, called assisitance from the continent to protect them. This behaviour of theirs so enraged Swein that he plundered the place and carried off a large booty to the bay, our author calls Myrkvafiord or the dark bay, and thence to Edinburgh, to David then King of Scotland, who received Swein with great kindness and gave him a hearty invitation to remain in his court. Swein frankly infomed the King of his reasons for leaving his own country, what had happened between him and Rognvald, nor did he conceal what had happened at the Monastery of May, which the King forgave and reimbursed the Monks according to their loss. Here Swein was honourably entertained for some time and the King desired him to send for his wife and children to Scotland, that he might remain there. This proposal Swein gratefully refused and rather begged him to entertain Margad and use his interest to make peace for himself with Earl Rognvald, professing he would submit to anything he should award against him. The King, after a hansome compliment to Rognvald, complied with Swein's petition and sent ambassadors with presents to Rognvald who easily obtained a pardon for Swein and, on his rerturn to Orkney, he was reinstated in his favour and had his patrimony restored. It is now time to return to Lamaburgh and what happened after Swein's escape. Soon after Swein and Margad were gone the besieged, with one consent, surrendered themselves to the Earl who, missing Swein and Margad and understanding by what sleight they had escaped, could not forebear admiring the boldness and dexterity of the action, which, he said, none but Swein could have executed. In the end he pardoned all those that had surrendered and, freely dismissing them. returned to the Orkneys, after sending Thorbiorn Klerk with a ship and forty mariners to pursue Swein Asliefson. This search however proved fruitless with regard to Swein but not so as to Thorbiorn's revenge for the death of his father. He understood Valthiof was not far off who had slain him and engaged his men by the promise of the plunder to be divided among them (not, says he, as Swein divides it, for you shall have it all) if they would stand by him in revenging his father's death, nor would he demand any part unless they inclined to present him with a share, as he professed that glory was to him more valuable than riches. His men were eaily persuaded by the last argument and, attacking Valthiof where he was engaged at an entertainment with his friends, they fired the house. The Earl ran hastily to the door and asked who they were that gave this check to his mirth. He soon knew Thorbiorn and offered him the compensation for his father's death which was refused and, seeing no method of escaping, he and those that were with him defended themselves bravely till the flames forced them to leave the house, whence thay came out half scorched to death and were easily despatched by the number of thirty. Thorbiorn's men got a large booty which he allowed them to keep and, returning to Orkney, was much commended by the Earl for what he had done.

Chapter 15

Much about this time a young man whose name was Kolbein Hruga built a castle of stone in Vigur (now Wyre) which he fortified in such a manner as to sustain such a siege as was laid in that age. This Kolbein was a man of great spirit, he married Herbiorg, the sister of Haco Biarn, descended from Earl Paul of Orkney's mother and by her had Kolbein surnamed Karl or Charles, Biarn a Poet and afterwards Bishop of Orkney, Suarlid and Aslac, with Frida a daughter, all of them much esteemed in their day and country.

Norway was at this time governed by Eistein Ingi and Sigurd Bronchus the sons of Harald Gilchrist. Ingi was advised by his nobles to invite Rognvald Earl of Orkney to his court as he was his father's old friend and they hoped by this treatment to form a connection between Ingi and the Earl, which might turn the scale in favour of their own King between whom and his brethren some sparks of discord had begun to appear. This invitation was given about the year 1140. Harold, Rognvald's colleague in the Earldom being then about 16 years old. Rognvald accepted the invitation and set out for Norway in the spring A.D. 1150, taking Harold with him who was fond to see Norway. They arrived safe at Bergen and were greatly caressed by the King with whom they stayed the greatest part of the summer and Rognvald took his opportunity to visit all his friends and relations. While the Earl continued in Orkney it happened that a certain Norwegian named Eindrid Iungi, sprung of noble parents and famous for his acquirements, returned from Constantinople from the Emperor Emanuel's court where he had sojourned for many years. This person gave such an account of the flourishing state of the Empire, the magnificence of the Emperor, the splendour of his court, his numerous armies, his inexhaustible treasures, the customs and manners of his people and many other particulars usually taken notice of by travellers, that he greatly delighted the King and his nobles but none more that Rognvald Earl of Orkney who was continually revolving in his mind what he had heard and never ceased asking questions at Eindrid, who at length persuaded him to make a journey thither and satisfy himself of the truth of what he had given him a faint idea. In this he was seconded by many of the courtiers, particularly by his relation Erling who promised to make one in the expedition, that he was at length obliged to promise he would go. They immediately set about making preparations for the business and Eindred who accompanied the Earl was unanimously chosen director of the scheme. Ion Pes the Earl's brother-in-law, Alsace Erland and Guttorm Maulur Koll of Holland were the ship masters. It was ordered that all their ships should be of the same bulk, not exceeding one another for fear of envy, only the Earl's ship was to be magnificently fitted out, the care of which was committed to Ion Pes. All things were now settled and the Earl was to return home in autumn to Orkney. At his departure the King made him a present of two small ships of war, most beautifully decorated, purposely built for sailing swiftly. The Earl called one of these Hialp and the other Fifa, tha latter from its velocity which he compared to the down of the herb whose name the ship bore, driving before the wind: The other the Helper.

The Earl left Norway on a Tuesday and sailed with a fair wind all that night, but next day it began to blow hard and the succeeding night which was pretty dark they found themselves engaged between a reef of rocks and the shore, amongst which they were so entangled that they must either perish or run their ships ashore and attempt to save their lives with the loss of everything valuable on board. As was natural they chose the latter and, running aground on a bold rocky shore, with some difficulty they got ashore but entirely lost their ships, merchandise and the rich presents they had received from their friends in Norway, of which only a few things were flung up by the rage of the sea. The Earl bore his loss as well as he could, the pleasure of having saved his life no doubt made this sit the lighter and he composed a very elegant poem on the occasion which however would be unintelligible to those who are not well versed in the northern languages of that era. It likewise requres a particular skill in the different kinds of northern poetry to relish any of these ancient compositions thoroughly, for which reason our author has entirely left out the Earl's poem describing the shipwreck.

They found, as daylight increased, they were wrecked on the coast of Shetland and, having gathered up what goods they could save, they went to enquire into what part they had fallen. They soon found out some of the inhabitants who were mightily rejoiced at the Earl's escape and assistd them in everything in their power. After some stay, autumn coming drove Rognvald home to Orkney for the winter, carrying with him two Shetlandic poets, Armod and Odd surnamed the little.

While the Earl was in Shetland he is said to have composed four poems still extant, some of them on trivial occasions. One was on an honest woman's reaching him a leather coat, another on a half chilled girl's warming herself, a third on a rich churl, Einar of Gulberwick, who refused to entertain twelve of his seamen unless the Earl himself would take up lodging with him.

At the Fesival of Christmas the Earl treated all his friends with great magnificence according to custom and gave them presents, among which was a spear ornamented with golden knobs given to Armod the Poet. On this occasion likewise they had a trial of skill in extempore composition, in which the Earl was challenger and the poets Armod and Odd the respondents, which they did with the utmost art and elegance and greatly to the atisfaction of their entertainer who was an excellent judge.

At this feast the Earl first publicly declared his resolution of visiting the Holy Land and other eastern countries and invited the Bishop who was a learned Clerk (which bye the bye was sometimes not the case in these days. Vid. Pitscottie's History of Scotland) bred at Paris, to be his interpreter. The Bishop easily agreed to this and, besides him the Earl carried with him Havard the son of Gunnar and Swein the son of Hroald and, of inferior rank, Thorgeir Skotokollus, Thorkel Krokaurga or Crook-eye, Grimkell of Flettuness and his son Biarn.

The time of the voyage now drew near and Rognvald with his people went over to Norway to see if the fleet was in readiness to transport them. Upon their arrival at Bergan they met with Erling, Ion Foot and Aslac who had waited for the Earl sometime, Guttorm soon followed. Rognvald found the ship he had ordered most magnificently fitted out under the inspection of Ion Foot who seems to have been as active as Eindrid was indolent. This ship must have been a piece of noble workmanship for the times, the head, stern, vane and many other parts of it were gilded, it was fit for war or pleasure and by far larger than the rest of the fleet.

Eindrid, after many excuses, now decalared he would be ready in a week, which new hinderance was very irksome, who began to mutter that the voyage might be performed without him, which last institution made him bestir himself and in a few days he was ready and desired the Earl to take the first opportunity for sailing. The wind coming fair they sailed from Bergen with an easy wind, but the admiral's ship which carried the Earl made but little way by reason of her bulk. To prevent the others outsailing the admiral, the commanders shortened sail till they came to the high sea, when a brisk gale sprung up and carried her along as swiftly as the rest, even with reefed sails.

Now, for the first time, they observed two vessels following the fleet with vast celerity, both of them larger and more splendidly decorated than the rest of the fleet. One of them was adorned with two heads of dragons gilded as were the stern and even parts of the sails and all of them that was above water painted most beautifully. These ships were soon known to belong to Eindrid and caused no small stir among those that had agreed to have none of their ships ornamented in this manner except the Earl's. Rognvald, after some pains, quelled these murmurs and this by observing that Eindrid's pride would make him wish to outshine them, that however they should be cautious in quarrelling with him as they were not yet certain whether he was to perform the voyage in company or not, that therefore they should keep carefully together and allow him to do as he pleased.

The Earl's advice always weighed much with those that heard it and, by observing his directions, they arrived safe in Orkney about the time of harvest, while Eindrid, who in scorn outsailed the fleet, made Shetland long before them and wrecked his elegant galley there, out of which he saved little or nothing of value. Though his fine ship was broke in Shetland, his proud heart (says our author) was not so much bent. He immediately sent orders to Norway for another which was to be fitted out in winter, which he himself passed in Shetland. The Earl wintered in Orkney with all that came from Norway in his fleet who were dispersed over the islands and were entertained partly at his, and partly at their own, expense and that of the country. The Norwegians soon fell out with the country people by their unfair dealings and their insolence towards the Orkney women, which cost the Earl a great deal of trouble from coming to an open rupture. One instance will be enough to show how the Norwegians treated the Orkney peasants. One Arni surnamed Spitulangue or spare, who served on board Erling's vessel, a courageous and robust but fierce and unreasonable kind of man, had bought some meal and flesh meat from a tenant belonging to Swein Asliefson which he refused to pay for. On a second demand, after a great deal of ill language, he struck him with a hammer and insultingly bid him complain to his bullying master Swein whom he thought so much of. The poor man did as he was bid and was heard with great seeming carelessness by his master. However in the spring when he went to gather in his yearly rents, which were paid in kind, he took occasion to touch at Hoy where Arni lived and, leaving his men behind to take care of his boat, he walked alone to where Arni was to be found armed only with a short battle axe. Swein entered the house where he found Arni with five others of his companions. After common salutations Swein civilly desired payment for his vassal's goods, the other told him it was time enough. Swein insisted for immediate payment, which would be laying an obligation on him. Arni at length denied that he would pay at all and would be no more trouble about the matter. Upon this Swein struck him such a blow as lodged his axe in his head up to the helve and, leaving it there, fled to his boat. Of the five that were with Arni, and all purused Swein, none overtook him but one who came up with him on the shore. Swein, turning about hastily, flung a handful of seaware in his face which blinded him in such a manner that while he was wiping his face and eyes, Swein got into his boat and went straight for his house in Gairsay and thence, on pretence of business, to Caithness. He afterwards sent messages to Earl Rognvald to pay the composition for Arni's death, to his relations. These Rognvald convened and payed them the established fine with which they were satisfied. Many other strifes he likewise compounded between the Norwegians and the Orkneymen paying the composition out of his own pocket.

Before the grand expedition, the Earl called a convention of all Orkney vassals where he solemnly informed them of his vow to visit the Holy Land to which he was soon to set out and that he was to leave his relation Harald to manage all matters in his room. He again and again recommended mutual love and caution in all emergencies between him and the people by whom imdeed he was greatly beloved for his prudence so that his tender age, being only nineteen, was no objection to his governing in the Earl's absence, though the time of his return was entirely uncertain.

Pretty late in the summer Rognvald left the Orkneys with a fleet of fifteen ships. He had waited the greatest part of the season for the arrival of Eindrid's vessel from Norway.

They touched first at Scotland and England before they made France where they halted. Arnod the poet dscribed every place, whether town, river, or country, as they passed. But this poetical journal seems to be deficient till they arrived at Narbonne, which does not seem to be the town of that name in Languedoc, as their after route manifestly proves. Indeed most of the names in Arnod's journal are now lost or so changed by time that they are no longer intelligible. The governor of this city was lately dead and had left his only daughter, a most beautiful lady now at woman's estate, the heiress of all his great wealth and title of Count. The young Countess who lived in great splendour, by the advice of her relations, invited Earl Rognvald and his retinue to an entertainment, which honour he accepted and, choosing out the likeliest of his train, according to custom, carried them with him. No pains or expence was spared to make the feast which was continued several days complete. On one of these days Ermingerde herself (so the Countess was called), attended by a large train of matrons and maidens, dressed in costly robes with golden ornament on her head, her hair dressed after the custom of noble ladies of that age, entered the hall where they were feasting with a golden cup in her hand and saluted the Earl, pouring wine in his cup, her maids at the same time playing a strain on their instruments, she presented it to the Earl. Rognvald, who was not deficient in the point of gallantry, received the cup and at the same time, taking the lady by the hand, placed her next him where he entertained her with sprightly conversation throughout the day and afterwards made a poem in her praise which he used to sing. Here he stayed for some time, passing his days in pleasure, honourably entertained by the inhabitants and especially by the lady's relations, who attempted to persuade him to remain among them, giving broad hints that she possibly might in time become his wife. Though this was very flattering to Rognvald, yet he would not give up his intended voyage, therefore told them on his rerurn he would conform to their inclinations. He took leave then of all his friends and, loosing from a place called Thraness (now unknown) he set sail for Galicia in Spain entertaining himself by the way in drinking healths and making verses in honour of his mistress Ermingerde in which he made the first couplet or stanza, Arnod the second and Odd the third.

Five days before Christmas they arrived in Galicia where they proposed to stay the festival. They were hard put to it for want of provisions and the oppression of a warlike, rich and at the same time avaricious man called Gudfreir. This person who lived in a well fortified castle was a scourge upon all the country round, whom he vexevd by various and intolerable oppressions, that at length the inhabitants applied to the Earl of Orkney to rid them of him, promising him the plunder of the Castle and also an open market for provisions till Lent for his pains. The Earl, after consultation, agreed to the terms and began to settle the mode of attacking the Castle. The method they agreed on was such as would never be thought of nor could be practised in our days. Everyone was to cut down a sufficient number of bundles of wood which were to be laid round the walls and set on fire, by which they proposed to split the walls and so make them fall in pieces. But the execution of the plan was deferred by the Bishop's prohibition till after the festival. This, at the time appointed, was performed with great courage and success notwithstanding the treachery of Eindrid who attempted to ruin the plan for his own advantage. Many of the besieged were slain and, when the ramparts fell into ruins, the Earl marched into the Castle preceeded by his son-in-law Sigmund, a brave young man who drove the besieged into the recesses of their fortifications. Eindrid (who seems to have had no goodwill towards the Earl) was beforehand with them with the plunder. His station in the assault had been the quarter to which the wind carried the smoke. This circumstance he had profitted himself of with a witness and had gone into the Castle and carried off the most precious of the plunder which he got off undiscovered. Those who were found alive in the Castle were allowed to surrender and dismissed safe but, though the booty they found was very great, they soon found that the more vluable moveables were secreted. The suspicion fell in the right place and, when Eindrid was sought for, it was soon known that he had taken the advantage of the stream of smoke to escape into a wood.

After this bold attempt on Gudfrier's Castle, the Earl departed from Galicia and went to that part of Spain which was in the possession of the Moors with whom they had several skirmishes and took a great deal of spoil. While they were in this part of Spain they were attacked with a dreadful tempest that threatened to put an end to the voyage at once, however they escaped by miracle and a fine light breeze carried them through the Straits of Gibralter into the Mediterranean where Eindrid withdrew himself from the fleet and went to Sicily. This behaviour of his fully confirmed the rest of his treachery in Galicia which many years afterwards was the cause of his destruction. His desertion did not discourage the rest who sailed along the coast of Barbary, called by the Norwegian author Serkland, as likewise in a poem the Earl composed on that occasion. From Barbary they proceeded to Sardinia, near where they met an adventure that called forth all their courage and resolution. In a dark foggy morning they saw what (as the day cleared) they took to be islands, two in number, of which one soon disappeared and, while they were wondering at this, the Earl informed them that what they took for islands were a sort of large ships used in these seas call Dromundes, that these two were sailing different ways, which caused the phenomenon they wondered at. They soon came to a resolution to attack the remaining vessel great as she was but were at a loss how, as her bulk frightened them. A council of war being called, Erling and the Bishop were requested to give their advice how this might be accomplished. The Bishop declared it would be matter of difficulty as her superior height, which was such as they could scarce reach with their battle axes, gave her a vast advantage over their small vessels, that the pitch, sulphur and other combustibles that would be flung on the assailants would take great effect from above and could not be warded off, that, for his part, he did not see any probability of success and therefore dissuaded the Earl from putting himself and all the rest in such imminent danger. Erling on the other hand, after paying proper attention to the Bishop's foresight, proposed that they should engage so close that the missiles flung from the other ship would fly over their vessels and he did not question that the superior swiftness of their ships would be of singular advantage in the engagement. The Earl approved greatly his counsel and gave orders for everything to be made ready for the attack, telling his people at the same time if they were Christian merchants they would let them go but, if Saracens, which was more probable, that Heaven would grant the victory to their joint endeavours to destroy the infidel; he made a vow likewise to distribute a fiftieth part of the booty among the poor. After these and other preparations more to the purpose, they plied their oars with great briskness and soon came up with the unwieldy vessels they had in chase and distributed themselves so that they surrounded her. The Earl and Erling fell on her stern, Ion Foot and Aslac on her bow and others on her sides and all so close that the fiery missiles flung at them passed over them into the sea. Indeed, those on board the great ship at first despised their feeble attack so much that in scorn they hung silk, purple and other valuable goods over her sides and pointed at them with shouts. The Bishop who had been most backward to engage was now most active. He, observing they made no impression by this method of close fighting, withdrew two of the ships to such a distance as to be out of reach of the enemy's weapons and put aboard these the most expert archers who galled the enemy with such a storm of arrows that in a short time they durst not so much as peep, much less defend themselves, or offend others. The Earl, upon this immediately ordered a hole to be cut in the great ship where it was least bound with iron, which was soon performed, and Erling at the same time, running his ship to the place where the anchor hung, his second, Audun, climbing up by the wood of the anchor, was succeeded by as many as could work there, soon enlarged the scuttel till it could easily allow them a passage. Erling and his men, having thus got entrance, poured in by the upper decks of the ship and the Earl, who soon followed by the lower, meeting together had a most fierce fight with the Moors and the Saracens which at length ended in vistory for the assailants but with much loss on their side, only Errling was desperately wounded in the neck under which he lingered a long time and, as his neck remained bent ever after, it procured him the nickname of Skacki or Crookneck.. The Earl, observing a man remarkable for his stature, valour and dress and guessing he might be the chief, ordered his men to take him prisoner but by no means to kill him. This was accordingly done by stratagem and he was conveyed on board the Bishop's ship to whom the Earl gave him in charge. Of the rest they spared not one and then proceeded to rummage the ship, in which they found vast riches of jewels and other rarities. After the battle the Earl composed two stanzas descriptive of the whole and concluded with the praises of his beloved Ermingerde whom he never forgot in the close of all his actions. When there was a dispute who first boarded the great ship, the Earl likewise, in verses proper for the occasion, gave that praise to Audun surnamed the Red, in which all the rest acquiesced, to every according to their merit he bestowed due praise. After they had stripped the Dromonde of everything valuable as they thought, they set in on fire, at which the prisoner expressed the most violent agitiation to which they soon, but too late, understood the meaning. No sooner had the flames seized the greater part of the ship, than a rivulet of melted metal gushed into the sea, whether gold or silver the Earl's people could not know but made them suspect what was really the case,that it was the prisoner's wealth which they had missed in their search.

After this exploit they steered for the coast of Africa on purpose to trade with the inhabitants. Here they offered their captive for sale in many towns but, as no one would buy him, they dismissed him. Next day he returned with a numerous attendance, declaring he was an African Prince and had sailed from the port they were now in with the large ship they had destroyed. He severely reprehended them for the loss of so much wealth, which was entirely owing to their rashness, told them he had it now in his power to take a severe revenge but would not as they had not only spared him but even dismissed him. However he cautioned them against falling in his way afterwards and, saluting them went away for Crete (now Candy) where they were attacked with a most violent tempest, as we learn from the verses of Armod made in the time of his watch. At length a fair wind sprung up and carried them to Ascalon (called by the Norwegians Akursburg) where they arrived the first day of Lent and entered the town with great solemnity and pomp, which Thorbiorn celebrated in a poem on the occasion. They met with a new desaster in Ascalon by a sort of plague which raged aboard the fleet and, among many others , swept off Thorbiorn the Poet.

From Ascalon they began their pilgrimage to the Holy Land and City and, having performed the necessary ablution in the river Jordan, the Earl and his relation Sigmund Aungule swam the river and made themselves pilgrim staves of twigs, on which occasion, as on most others, the Earl exerted his poetical genius. One of these, on a whimsical occasion, we shall select from our Author. After they had visited the Holy Land, on their way to Constantinople they put into a place called Imbolus (probably Imbros) where they stayed some time, indulging freely in the juice of the grape. It seems it was the custom of this place, because of the narrowness of the streets, for the citizens to call upon a stranger to give way, which frequently happened to the Norwegians. One night Erling, who was honestly drunk, did not or would not understand them but, when they came up, knowing the custom and probably having not much room to spare, jumped from the bridge into the mud where he stuck breast high to the utter spoiiing of his fine clothes. However those that challenged him had so much humanity as to pluck him out of the mire and give him a new coat which, coming to the Earl's ears afforded scope for a very witty poem with which he next day saluted Erling.

Here likewise Ion Foot, the Earl's staunch friend, was slain as he was going aboard with some others after a drinking bout and next day was found under the city wall and buried in one of the churches.

The Earl and his company made a splendid entrance into the City of Constantinople and were graciously received by the Emperor Emanuel who loaded them with presents and offered them high appointments if they would engage in his wars, which they declined.

Here they met with the traitor Eindrid who did them no good offices with the Emperor but this was overbalanced by the respect paid by the Varingi, said to be a race of Anglo-Danish exiles drove out by the Normans and composing the flower of the Imperial army. However this may be, Earl Rognvald remained the greatest part of the winter in Constantinople, hence he sailed round the Morea till they came to the famous city Dywhachium (called by the Norwegians Dyraksburg, now Durazza) on the Adriatic which, passing by Apulia, the Earl left his ships and the greatest part of his suite and, together with the Bishop and Erling, proceeded by land to Rome. From Rome they took the nearest route to Danemark and so to Norway, thus finishing with great honour this famous peregrination.

Chapter 16

Erling, by his brother's death, succeeded to his estate and afterwards, on the death of Ingi who was slain by his own faction, Erling's son Magnus, a pupil, was chosen to succeed him and he himself was created an Earl by Valdimar King of Danemark.

The treacherous Eindrid, some years after, returned to his native country where, concious of his crimes, he took care to shun Erling and, that he might act in character to the last, he joined Eystein's faction and, after his death, set up another against Erling's son and, after several exploits not necessary to be mentioned, he was put to a deserved death by order of Erling.

Rognvald, during his stay in Norway, heard of the distracted state of the Orkneys. Two factions reigned there, one in favour of his partner Harald and another in that of Erlend who was set up by Eystein, King of part of Norway. Detained for want of a ship to transport him to Orkney, he was at length obliged to take his passage in an Icelandic ship which landed him at Torfness in Scotland, thence he went to Orkney where he arrived about the festival of Yule.

Having now landed the Earl at his own home from his eastern expedition, it is but reasonable to recount what happened in Orkney in his absence.

The same year that Rognvald went abroad, Eystein, King of Norway, landed on N. Ronaldsha with a large and well manned fleet, where he understood that Earl Harald was in Caithness attended by eighty Satellites. Pleased with this he passed the Pightland Firth with three small vessels and, putting into Thurso, he first seized the Earl's vessel and next himself, all this before he knew anything of the King's being there, nor could he obtain his liberty till he paid a ransome of three, or according to others seven, marks of gold. He likewise obliged him to become his vassal and dismissed him.

From Orkney, Eystein went to Aberdeen, even then a famous market town, and, after plundering it, proceeded towards England where he is said to have fought three battles, at Hvitaboea (Whitbay), Scarpasker and Pilawick and also to have burned the Town of Langdon before he returned to Norway in Autumn.

These things happened in the reign of Stephen of England and David of Scotland, the latter of whom died the same year, being 1153.

This year likewise died Maddad, Earl Harald's father, and his mother Margaret, a woman of great beauty but of a shrewed and untoward disposition, came to Orkney.

Count Ottar of Thurso likewise about this period sumitted to the law of nature. Erlend, the son of Harald the Fairspoken (Oratos) Earl of Orkney, had remained with him while he lived, after his death he passed his time partly in Thursa and the AEbudae and partly in acts of piracy on the neighbouring inimical coasts. Erlend was a young man of fine accomplishments, brave, liberal and prudent, had a fine address and, on all occasions, open to friends and in consequence much beloved by his satellites and soldiers, of whom he always kept a large number about him to assist him in his summer expeditions.

Erland thought, in Rognvald's absence, it a good opportunity for him to claim his right in the Orkneys and Caithness. He therefore applied to Malcolm the Maiden for the half of Caithness on the same terms as his father held it from the King of Scotland. This he obtained together with the investiture as an Earl. Upon this he went home and, gathering his frinds he went next to Orkney and made a demand on Harald of what his father had possessed there which, notwithstanding the mediation of the Orkney Gentlemen to that purpose, was refused, as the latter depended so much on his strength that he imagined Erlend would not dare to take him by force. At length the matter came to this, that a year's truce should be signed between both parties and, if in that time Erlend went to Norway and obtained Rognvald's half from the King of Norway, that Harald would cede it. This was agreed to and Erlend, leaving Anokol his foster father to manage matters at home, went to Norway.

About this time a dryness began to appear between Earl Harald and Swein Asliefson. The occasion was this. The Earl had banished Gun Olafson, Swein's brother, because he had ravished his mother Margaret and had children by her. Swein took this very much amiss and sent his brother to the Island of Lewis to his friend Liotholf with whom he himself had stayed on an occasion formerly mentioned. Swein himself wintered in Caithness at Freswick, employed in overlooking his son Olave's affairs. This son was by a first wife Rognhilda, the daughter of Ingimunde who, living but a short time, he afterwards married Ingiride, Thorkel's daughter, by whom he had a son name Andrew.

Harald wintered in Wick while Erlend was absent in Norway and all his Orkney and Shetland rents were brought thither.

About the middle of the last week of Lent, Swein from Lamaburgh perceived a Bark crossing the Pightland Firth, which he understood was from Shetland. He immediately attacked and lightened it of the Earl's Shetland rents and set the mariners ashore. When this came to the Earl's ears he observed that riches ebbed and flowed alternately between him and Swein, he therefore without much ado distributed the seamen Swein had set ashore among the Caithness peasants till an opportunity could be got to send them home.

Swein after this exploit was sensible that Caithness would be too hot for him, he therefore set off for Orkney with a swift vessel and a merchant ship and, in his way to Scapa, met with and plundered Fugle, the son of his friend Liotholf, who was on his way from his father's house in Lewis to wait on Earl Harald, together with Sigurd Klauf the Earl's steward on the same errand, off whom he took twelve ounces of gold, equal to a mark and a half. After these pranks Swein went to Scotland, to King Malcolm whom he found at a place our Author calls Ardurne in Strathnaver. Malcolm gave him a handsome reception and, after a month's stay, dismissed him with the full right to all he pretended to in Caithness, in the same manner as he held it before his dispute with Earl Harald, a plain proof that Caithness was always a bone of contention between the Kings of Scotland and the Earls of Orkney.

On his return to Orkney, Swein was observed by Anakol who lived in Deerness, passing the Mull to the eastward. He sent therefore Gauti, who then lived in Skeggbiarnastad, to demand that he would satisfy Anakol's relation Fugle for the vessel he had deprived him of. Swein agreed to this and met with them at Sanda, where he made up the damage so much to Anakol's liking that he became his fast friend, promising to make up all matters with Count Erlend between whom and Swein there had long existed a normal hatred on account of the burning of Frakuark, the Earl's great-aunt. After this pacification Swein and Anakol went to Stronsa where lived Thorfin Bessin who had married Ingigerd, Swein's sister, after her divorce from Thorbiorn Klerk. While they stayed here Count Erlend arrived from Norway at Hofness. Thorfin and Anakol went out to meet him and, after congratulations, began to plead for Swein. Earl Erlend who had succeeded in all his plans at the court of Norway, did not easily agree to receive Swein as his friend. The truth is Swein had never been very friendly to his family, nor very scrupulous in keeping his engagements with it, of which he had given an example in deceiving Lord Ottar to whom he had promised his assistance in recovering his paternal inheritance, which he had not performed. The Earl at length was brought by the threats of Thorfin and Anakol rather than any cordial affection he bore him to receive Swein into the number of his adherents, for these two had threatened that they would leave him and rather follow Swein's fortunes unless he was reconciled to him. After this Erlend informed his friends that he had obtained Harald's half of the Orkneys from Eystein King of Norway, on which Swein proposed that they should immediately go and put him in possession before the report of this spread and gave Harald an opportunity of fortifying himself against them. This advice was approved of and, putting to sea, they came upon Harald unawares where he lay in Kiarckstad and struck him with such a panic that he immediately fled to the castle of Kirkwall. So great was the terror that seized some of Harald's attendants, that Arn the son of Rafn fled with his shield on his back, without knowing he carried it, which he only found out by its stopping him in his entrance into the castle.

Swein and Erlend quickly followed and, taking advantage of their panic, arrempted to storm the castle which, though it was stoutly defended, if night had not parted them after many rounds on both sides. Next day the friends of both parties endeavoured at a composition which after some difficulty from Erlend's party was at length agreed to on condition that Harald should give up all right and title to the Orkney Islands in favour of Erlend. This he swore to perform in presence of the Orkney genlemen present, after which Harald withdrew into Caithness and thence with a few Orkney attendants to his friends in Scotland.

Erland soon after called a meeting of the vassals at which most of them attended and there published the charter by which he had acquired a right to the Orkneys. Swein and his other friends strained every nerve to have his title recognised, which was at last agreed to, with a saving of Earl Rognvald. Though things were thus settled, Swein still suspected Harald would not give it over, so he therefore never failed to put the Earl on his guard against Harald and his Scottish friends. Things continued tolerably easy in Orkney from Michaelmas to about Christmas, when Swein, not forgetting to caution Erland against the cunning of his rival Harald, went home to Gairsay to celebrate the approaching festival.

On the eleventh day of the feast Swein, as he was drinking with his friends and domestics, from a certain sign declared that Harald was on his way to Orkney. When his friends began to stare at this and observe that it was improbable he would make such an attempt at that season and in such stormy weather, Swein acquiesced and said he would not send to Erlend on such a vague suspicion though he still feared it might be needful, nor was it long before his supicion was realised.

About the latter end of the festival Harald arrived in Orkeny with four ships and a hundred men and stopped two nights at Gairsey. Thence he sailed to Hafnarvog, a harbour in the Mainland, from which he proposed to go by land to the place where Erlend spent the festival and surprise him. In this however he found himself disappointed for Erlend, though he spent the day feasting, always slept on board his ship, as he had been advised by Swein. Harald, since he could not get at the Earl spent his wrath on two of his people that had stayed on shore. These he slew and, taking Arnfin, Anakol's brother, with some others, prisoner he, together with Thorbiorn Klerk, returned to Thursa but the two brothers Benedict and Biordn, Harald' satellites, went to Lamaburgh and carried with them Arnfin, Anankol's brother.

Erlend was a good deal startled at Harald's sudden appearance in Orkney. He sent immediate notice of what had happened to Swein Asliefson who hurried to his assistance with all speed and both, in expectation of another visit, remained on board their ships through the winter.

Upon a proposal to ransome Anakol's brother, for whom a demand was made of the ship taken at Kiarkstad when Harald fled to the castle of Kirkwall, Anakol dissuaded the Earl from complying with the terms, the truth being he had projected an easier way of relieving his brother. In consequence of this, on the Wednesday before Lent, Anankol chose out twenty of his trusty companions and, with Thorstein the son of Rogna, sailed for Caithness in the night-time. When day appeared they hid their bark in a deep and hollow cave near Freswick, as also concealed themselves in the caverns of the sea rocks, after placing logs on the rowers seats in a sleeping posture in order to deceive anybody that might discover the vessel. Some time after Ankol observed a small vessel put into the mouth of a river and two men approaching her, one of which was on horseback, the other on foot. Thinking this a proper prey, he divided his men in two bodies one of which he ordered towards the vessel, the other to the village which stood at a small distance. Eiric, one of those who had the custody of Arnfin, had just returned from some expedition and had gone to take a little rest but, hearing the noise of armed men, he started from his bed and, flying to the vessel, was seized by those that Arnakol had sent thither and carried prisoner to Orkney, whencehe returned in exchange for Arnfin.

Early in the spring Harald formed a design to revenge himself on Erling Iungi on his mother's account. This business however was made up by the interposition of friends, and Harald went to Norway.

Erlend, delivered from his apprehensions by Harald's absence, began to enjoy himself in peace and security but this was of no long continuance., as Swein's restless disposition soon engaged him in new pursuits. The latter proposed that they should make a summer's trip together, which was agreed to by the Earl and the scene of the expedition was laid on the east coast of Scotland. After several acts of piracy on the coast and in the bay called Breidsfiord, the adventurers proceeded to Berwick. In that town lived a merchant called Knut, surnamed the rich, from whom Swein seized a large merchat ship, on board which was Knut's wife, and carried her to Bleholm - probably Holy Island.

Her misfortune, coming to her husbands ears, he made large offers to the townsmen if they would assist him in retreiving his loss. Fourteen ships were immediately fitted out to pursue the ravishers who still lay at anchor under Bleholm. This mighty preparation would have done their business had not this been prevented by the vigilance and foresight of Swein Asliefson who, observing them from the island, gave the alarm and all made off to sea, directing their course to the Firth of Forth. On their arrival at the Island of May, Swein sent messages to the King of Scotland with the news of his having plundered Knut. On their entering the City of Edinburgh, they met a number of men and horses loaded with with silver designed to ransom Swein who, as the King was informed, had been made prisoner and, on their declaring how the matter stood, the King sent him a present of a shield and other valuable articles with which he, in company with the Earl, returned to Orkney. Harald had passed the whole summer in Norway, everything therefore was quiet in Orkney, till the arrival of Rognvald from his eastern pilgrimage.

Rognvald returned to Orkney about Christmas and, by his appearance, changed the face of affairs there. Erlend was uncertain what reception he might find with Rognvald and, to put this to the push, he took great pains to have a court called to feel the pulse of the

Earl and the vassals. This, after some pains, he effected and it was agreed that Orkney was to be equally divided between Rognvald and Erlend, who were to join forces against Harald or any other competitor. This coalition was confirmed by a mutual oath but was of no long continuance as we shall see.

As Rognvald had no fleet nor could expect any ships from Norway before summer, the winter was passed without anything remarkable. But, as spring came in, Erlend went to Shetland to guard that part of their dominions against the common enemy, if he should happen to make a descent there, as did Rognvald to Caithness where he knew Harald had a number of friends. This was a lucky disposition for Harald who landed late in the summer at Orkney with four ships out of seven he had brought from Norway, the other three, being driven to Shetland, fell into Erlend's hands who had waited there the greater part of the summer without hearing anything of Harald. When he arrived he soon heard of the dispositions that had been made against his interests, sensible at the same time he was not a match for both, he determined to win Rognvald over to his interest. For this purpose he went to Thursa where he heard Rognvald was in Sutherland at his daughter's marriage with Eiric Slagbreller. The news of his arrival at Thursa was no sooner carried to Berwick in Sutherland, where the Earl then was, but he hastened to Thursa with a large body of horsemen, where the utmost pains were taken to reconcile the two Earls by Eiric, Rognvald's son-in-law, who spared no arguments to effect it. He laid before Rognvald the absurdity of enemity to one who was his near relation, had been his colleague in the Earldom of Orkney and, above all, he laid open to him the mutual love that ought to subsist between a foster father and his nurslling, in which relationship he likewise stood to Harald, in short he urged him to make up the breach by all the arguments he could bring from either the divine or human laws, both which he argued would be lost by enemity between so near relations. He at length brought about a meeting in which both parties conversed in private and Harald had no reason to fear a reconciliation. Both Earls had come to the place appointed for the meeting attended by an equal number of guards, who remained without doors while they conferred. In the afternoon, when matters were almsot come to a conclusion, word was brought that Harald's men were approaching the castle under arms and instantly a clash of swords was heard which, though Harald denied his knowledge of or having any treacherous design, struck Rognvald with no little terror. The matter was, Thorbiorn Klerk had attacked Rognvald's satellites with a handful of of men and wounded a number of them, nor could they be parted till the townsmen struck in and seperated them by force. In the scuffle thirteen of Rognvald's satellites were slain and himself wounded in the face. No bad consquences happened from it, by the interposition of friends the ancient league was renewed between Rognvald and his foster and warrented with the usual solemnities. Soon after they went to Orkney.

To return to Erlend, who was entirely left out by both parties. While he and Swein remained on the watch in Shetland, word was brought them that Harald had touched at Orkney. Without delay they both put to sea in a large fleet in pursuit of him but were seperated for some time by a storm. Meeting again at Sanda they put in to Bardwick, where they soon nderstood the new alliance between Rognvald and Harald and, seeing a great number of men on North Ronaldsha, they began to doubt whether it would be safe to stand an attack. Erlend seemed willing to venture a battle and consulted his men on the subject. They referred the whole to Swein's determination, who advised Erlend to decline fighting as they were not able for both Earls. His advice was followed and they put to sea for Caithness the same night. He likewise gave out openly that they would winter in the AEbudae.

The evening before Michaelmas they passed the Pightland Firth and drove off the cattle and sheep from the lands of Caithness where they were detained some time by tempestuous weather and contrary winds. As soon as the storm abated so that the firth could be passed, Swein hired a man to go over to Orkney and spread the story of plunder of the Caithness cattle and that nothing was wanting but a fair wind to carry the Earl and him to the AEbudae.

This story soon came to Rognvald's ears who, well knowing Swein's cunning, called a meeting of his friends and earnestly entreated them to be on their guard, as at no time was a visit sooner to be expected from him than when he himself gave out he was going further. The event shewed the Earl's penetration for, in the beginning of winter, Erlend and Swein sailed from Thurso with a contrary wind directing their course for the west of Scotland, in a fleet of six large ships. This was no sooner known to the Earl who had spies on all their motions, than they ordered their fleet to be stationed in Scapa in order to have everything in readiness in case of a rude visit. As soon as Swein had got to the westward of Hoy opposite to the Staur rock, he pretendd he would not fatigue his men with rowing and ordered the sails to be set. This was done though it was thought dangerous and they sailed with a brisk gale to a place our author calls Vagaland in Orkney where they understood that the Earls with Eiric Slagbreller and a number of other gentle men were at Scapa on board the fleet which consisted of fourteen well manned ships and that Thorbiorn Klerk had gone to papa to visit a friend there. Swein was well pleased with this news and proposed to attack the Earls that very night, which was approved by Earl Erlend notwithstnding the sentiments of some others who were overruled.

The night, which was in November, happened to be sleety and dark and Earl Rognvald, trusting there would be no attack in such weather, chose out six men to attend him and went to his seat in Orfir. His road lay through Knarrastad (now Scapa) in which place lived an Iceland Poet called Botolf Bogla well known to the Earl. This person entreated the Earl to lodge with him that night with which he complied and went to bed, while his host watched. Swein and Erlend notwithstanding the badness of the night planned and made their attack on Harald who lay on board, so suddenly that he was only roused by the thunder of the charge. They fought stoutly on his side and particully on board his ship where all but five were killed and it was with great difficulty he escaped to land. On Harald's side there was a hundred slain, the chief of whom was Biarn, Erlend Iungi's brother, a man of great valour, besides many wounded and all routed, on Erlend's party few either killed or wounded. The whole fleet, in consqunce of this victory fell into Erlend's hands, with everything that pertained to it. Nor was this all, they soon found out where Rognvald lodged and went immediately in search of him as the most valuable part of the prey. The searchers found Botolf standing at his door, who returned their salutation and told them that the Earl had called there that night and, in answer to their further enquiry, pointed with his finger a road for them to follow him, expressing himself in verse said to be yet extant. They now thought they were sure of him and went off. Botolf, true to his trust, awaked the Earl and gave him the history of the hour and from what imminent danger he had just escaped. Rognvald needed no other hint to fly and he forthwith went to Orfir where he foud Harald before him and both fled to Caithness in fishing boats, as did some of their adherents after them.

After the surprise and defeat, the booty, which was great, came to be divided and Swein generously took care of all Rognvald's most precious moveables and sent them after him to Caithness.

A consultation was now held where to station the fleet, when Vagaland was proposed as the most convenient either for a view of the Firth and Caithness or Scapa Bay or a cruise if they had occasion, however Erlend carried it for Damsa Bay - now the Bay of Firth.

Here they spent their time as usual after an exploit in drinking all day in the Castle of Damsa and sleeping in their ships, for some part of the winter. About Christmas Swein had occasion to go eastward to Sandwick (probably Sandside in Deerness parish) to compose some differences between his friend and relation Sigride and one of her neighbours, leaving a strict caution to Erlend never to sleep out of his ship for fear of a retaliation in their own style. This sensible precaution Erlend forgot though the event showed the necessity of it.

Swein passed one night with his relation Sigride and another with a friend over a cup of ale, when word was brought that the Earl had slighted his advice with regard to the night watch and staying on board. Though this was so far from pleasing to him whose foresight never stood in need to be put in mind of duty, yet he sent Margad. the son of Grime and two others to beg of him to be more cautious for the future, for reasons his own reflection would suggest. His message was carefullly delivered but received with great contempt by the Earl's men who began to throw reflections on Swein, as sometimes so bold that no danger could fright him, at other times startled at every straw, but all agreed to stay ashore. The truth is theirs were similar to the disposition of the seamen of our times, who seldom rest if they are possessed of anything to spend and they had, it seems, something of their last booty unspent and all returned to their cups except twenty three that went on board with the Earl. Margad, Swein's messenger, lodged in the neighbourhood of the bay, whence he carried the news of the following night's adventure to his master.

Rognvald and Harald, who had fled to Caithness only for the time, determined with the first opportunity to return Erlend like for like. With this view they sailed from Caithness well accompanied and, coming to Orkney in the night time, attacked Erlend so unexpectedly that they were not so much as perceived by the land watch till they had boarded the Earl's ships.

Ulf and Orm had the watch on board and, on perceiving the enemies approach, the former attempted to awake the Earl. His last night's beer however lay so heavy in his head that, finding this impracticable, he took him up in his arms and put him in a boat where he was slain. Orm flung himself into the sea and swam ashore from the general slaughter, which continued against Harald's sentiments indeed, till Rognvald was certain of the death of Erlend.

Margad, Swein's messenger, heard the noise of the scuffle and, observing by the light of the moon what was going on, he concluded, upon seeing Erlend's men escaping ashore, that he was slain and sent messengers with the news of the disaster to Sandwick, retiring himself to Rindale.

Erland's body was found among the seaware and, being known by a remarkable spear which killed him, was buried in the Church.

All the people found alive were pardoned, among these three of Swein's domestic servants. Those that were ashore fled and, of these, Ion Wing and others went to St. Magnus' Church in Kirkwall but were soon forced to surrender by th Earls. Ion Wing had been formerly entertained by Haco Charles and had debauched his sister but was now forced to marry her and afterwards bacame an adherent to Earl Harald. This overturn in the affairs of Orkney happened A.D. 1115.

Chapter 17

Erland's death made a great alteration to Swein's influence. He retired to Rendale where he learned the whole of his party's disaster and afterwards to Rousa with what ships he still had preserved, where he billeted his men among the inhabitants till another opportunity to stir. For some time he and five of his companions were obliged to skulk among the hills, however he had still spies so planted that he understood what was going on in all parts of the country, as well as in the Earl's council. In twilight he always came privately to a farmhouse where he lay hid till morning. One evening, when it was pretty dark, he heard several men bragging of what they had performed in the affair at Damsa and, observing Thorfin and his relation Augmund with their relation Erlend, loudest, he sprung on them with a companion or two, killed Erlend and took Thorfin prisoner, whom he carried to Thingavoll (probably Tingwall) to his uncle Helgi.

This kind of life was put an end to by the lenity of Rognvald, who sent a message to Helgi to find out Swein and invite to spend the Christmas, which was now at hand, with him in Damsay, promising at the same time to make up his peace with Harald. Thither Swein went and was joyfully received by Rognvald, with whom he spent the remainder of the festival. A day was at length fixed for ending all strife between the Earl and Swein, which was far from an easy task, although Rognvald strained every nerve to bring it about, every one was against Swein openly blaming him for all the mischief that had happened. After much pains an oblivion was signed and Swein was fined in a mark of gold to each of the Earls and the half of his estate, besides a ship of war into the bargain. Swein was far from pleased to pay so dear for his release and plainly told them, if they granted him remission on easy terms, it would be the longer kept but, if the terms were hard, no longer than was convenient for him.

Rognvald remitted his part of Swein's fine with a declaration that he valued his friendship much more than money but Harald claimed his part most rigidly. At the proper season he went to Gairsey to carry off the corn and other redenda from his part of Swein's estate, which he complained heavily of to Rognvald, notwithstanding his late agreeing to pay the price Harald now claimed, and affirmed Harald had broken bargain.

He likewise threatened to go home to estimate the damage but was dissuaded by Rognvald who reminded him that though he was an active and valiant man yet he was no match for Harald, he therefore advised him to remain where he was and trust to Harald's generosity for future kindness. This most reasonable proposal did not please Swein, he got a boat and ten men, with these went in an evening to Gairsey where the Earl was, with the intention to burn his own house, so as Harald might perish in the conflagration. With great dificulty he was restrained from his purpose by Swein Blakar one of his principal men in this project, who prudently represented that they were not certain whether Harald was in the house or not and, if he was, that Swein's wife and daughter must suffer the same fate, as it was very improbable that they would be permited to depart. Upon this prudent advice his fury was a little abated and he made enquiry anent Harald at those who on his arrival had shut thenselves up in his house, by whom he understood that Harald was not there. Swein dismissed his servants safe on their surrendering up their arms and, after spilling all the drink, he took his wife and daughter and departed. He would fain have come to the knowledg where the Earl was hid and pressed his wife to inform him and, on her backwardness, desired her, if she had made any promise on concealment, only to point out the place with her finger. She however would not betray Harald as he was her relation and Swein, giving the servants their arms, went on board his ship and left the island. Harald who had gone to a neighbouring island a-hare hunting, no sooner understood what Swein had done, than he pronounced the paction broke on Swein's side and declared he would keep no terms with him and, observing him making off for the island of Hellirsey (probably Ellerholm) he instantly followd him thither.

In this island there is a remarkable cave which appears only at low water being quite shut up with the return of the tide and known only to few. To this Swein, as he knew he could not contend with the Earl, withdrew and reached it as the tide flowed in, laid up his vessel in the inner parts of it, concealed from all mankind. By the time the Earl arrived the flowing tide had closed up the cave that there was no appearance of any such in the island. Harald, after a strict search amd much wonder that a ship could come to the island and disappear in a moment since he was certain he had not passed it, continued the pursuit to the other islands, as he was sensible nothing was too hard for Swein's cunning.

Soon after the Earl's departure, the ebb tide allowed Swein to leave the cavern where he heard every word that had passed in the search. Leaving his vessel, he took a boat from the Monks and went to Sanda and, burning the boat, he betook himself to Voluness to a friend named Bard, whom he informed of his reasons for being kept secret till the Earl's wrath was blown over. Bard gave him a kindly reception and hid him in an inner chamber, parted from the rest of the house by a wall, and shut the door with a heap of stones.

The same evening Ion Wing, one of Harald's adherents, came to Bard's house with seven others and they were introduced to the fireside where a rousing fire and good company made the strangers so talkative that all the country affairs were talked of and news flew about like hail. Amongst other things, Ion introduced Swein's adventure and, with great bitterness reviled him as a treaty breaker and one who on no occasion could be trusted. He added what an iniquitous project it was for Swein first to make peace with the Earl and immediately after attempt to burn him, concluding that there would never be peace in the islands till he was out of the way. Bard and his family defended Swein and laid the blame of all on the Earl and, immediately after, Ion began to defame the memory of Earl Erlend calling him cruel, unjust and tyrannous and enemy to all freedom. Swein, who heard all that passed and whose patience was almost worn out by the reflections cast on himself, could hold no longer and, bursting open the door where he was hid, went out to secure the gate that none should escape him. However Ion was too nimble, at the first noise of the stones falling he snatched his shoes and, starting from the fire, fled in his waistcoat and breeches in spite of the cold and darkness of the night, which was such that, before he got to the next farm, his toes were frostbitten and senseless.

Swein, at Bard's instance, spared Ion's companions and next morning, borrowing Bard's boat, went further south to Bardswick where he sometimes lurked in the caves of the rocks and sometimes ventured out in the daytime to the villages to make merry with his friends, generally sleeping in a boat for fear of surprise.

As he was often obliged to shift his quarters, he next went to North Ronaldsha and, while he was there, Earl Rogmvald unluckily put in at the same place with a number of attendants. There was but little time for deliberation, Swein, as he saw no other method of escape, assaulted the Earl's followers with stones and thus kept them at bay but, others advancing, he hurried to the beach and run his boat into the water, without fear of pursuit as the Earl's galley was aground. Swein passed close by the Earl with his spear in his hand, who was covered with his sshield so that he did not attempt to strike him.

Rognvald, holding up his shield (the sign of peace), recalled Swein to confer with him and he returned. In the middle of ttheir discourse Earl Harald's Galley was observed coming from Caithness to Vagaland and Swein, who durst not face him, by Rognvald's advice, set out for Caithness. On their parting Swein sailed along the east side of Stronsa but had not proceeded far till he was observed by Harald and so hotly pursued that he was obliged to leave the coast and land on the island wither Harald soon followed. Swein's general character brought him off here for Harald, suspecting some trick, gave over the pursuit, however his friend Amund the son of Hnef, uncle of Swein's step-children, laboured so successfully that he renewed the former league between these stiff opponents and a little time after brought them together on the island, where they were detained by a tempest and, while it continued, used the same bed. From the island of Stronsa Swein went to Caithness and soon after heard from Orkney that Harald was far from being pleased at the renewal of the league which he reckoned highly dishonourable to him, the truth is he had no great reason to fear it would continue long, as Swein was no more pleased with it than himself.

Swein passed the festival of Easter with his friend Summarlid, at the end of which, on his return, meeting with Ion Wing's brothers Peter Bun and Blank, he took them both prisoners and plundered them and, after other afronts to their brother in their persons, left them and went to Lewis.

Ion Wing soon heard what had befallen his brothers but could not be informed whether they were alive or dead. In revenge he went to the Holy Island (probably Eynhallow) and carried of Swein's son Olave from Kolbein Hruga, with whom he had been some time for his education and brought him to Westra.

When this came to Earl Rognvald's ears he enquired Ion's reason for carrying off Olave and was answered, because Swein had his brothers prisoner and he was not certain but he had slain them. The Earl advised him instantly to carry back the lad, whatever had befallen the brothers, and restore him without hurt to Kolbein, otherwise he might depend on it he might bid farewell to the isles as he never would be abe to escape, or guard against, Swein's and Kolbein's revenge.

Swein returned from the AEbudae with sixty men, put into Rousa, where he took prisoner Haco Charles who had been in Harald's ship at the slaughter of Earl Erlend, nor would he give him his liberty till he ransomed himself at the extravagant price of three marks of gold. When he came to the Mainand he observed his fine ship (which he had, with other articles of the fine, been forced to give up to the Earls), stripped of a couple of planks which, Rognvald afterwards told him, had been done by his orders, as he would neither ransom it or except it as a present, for fear he should fall upon means to seize it and infest the Isles. Though he was far from pleased at the mutilation of this vessel, he was obliged to pass it over, as experience had taught him how vain it was to strive with the Earls. After passing a short time among the isles, he went to visit Earl Rognvald at Byrgisherad, by whom he was handsomely received and spent the greatest part of the spring with him. About Whitsunday Earl Harald returned from Shetland where he had been some time and Rognvald made interest with him to renew the so oft broken league with Swein. A day was set for that purpose in St. Magnus' Church, when all causes of strife were to be cleared up. Both Earls met at the time and place appointed and Rognvald brought Swein with him, himself armed with a battle axe as the badge of authority. The old paction was renewed and Rognvald present Harald with Swein's ship, giving him up everything else of his fine.

The next day Harald sent for Swein who had no great inclination to attend him but, by Rognvald's advice, went with six attendants. Swein found the Earl with Thorbiorn Klerk and a few others. After they had drank together, Thorbiorn Klerk went out, which Swein took for an ill omen and began to suspect the Earl of treachery. However he was soon relieved by Thorbiorn's return who brought a vest and purple mantle which he presented to Swein, though the real truth is these things could scarce be called a present, as they had been taken out of Swein's house in winter. The first opening towards a settled friendship however was embraced and Harald added what still pleased his new ally more, a return of his ship, half his estate and everything else he had formerly parted with. He also invited him to stay with him, that nothing might be wanting to render the limb strong which now began to heal. Swein returned to Earl Rognvald and told him what Harald had done for him and the Earl cautioned him seriously to live in peace with Harald and for the future deserve his goodwill.

Swein was now at peace with everybody at home and, in consequence, idle, which was far from pleasing to his restless disposition. He therefore projected an expedition to the Western Isles, in company with Thorbiorn Klerk and Eiric Slagbreller. These adventurers proceeded as far westward as the Scilly, whence they brought of a great deal of plunder and they returned to Orkney considering what they could thus reave from their neighbours as so much clear gain.

Ever since Harald's agreement with Swein the two Earls had lived together on the most friendly terms, only Rognvald, having the most experience presided. Thorbiourn Klerk was mostly with Harald as his cousellor, but Swein loved Earl Rognvald best. The former lived with Harald in the winter time, but Swein passed this time of inactivity in Gairsey with a numerous train of adherents who were maintained by him in winter from the fruits of his land and the returns of his summer expeditions and, in summer, assisted him in these exploits.

The concord which reigned between the Earls and their domestics was of no long continuance, being interrupted by Thorbiorn Klerk who, from a secret, became an avowed enemy of Earl Rognvald, from the following reason. Among Rognvald's chief satellites (Satellites purpurati) Thorarin Killenef held a high place in his favour. This person had fallen out with Thorkel, a great friend and companion of Thorbiorn Klerk, over a drinking match and, in the scuffle, Thorarin was wounded. His friend striking in, Thorkel was forced to fly to his friend Thorbiorn. The Earls, hearing the noise from the upper room where they sat, run down and parted the combatants but Thorbiorn would not submit to the decision of the matter to Earl Rognvald. When Thorarin recovered of his wound, meeting with Thorkel one day going to church, he slew him and immediately withdrew to the church as a sanctuary. Thorbiorn Klerk was not much troubled with religious fears and made no scruple to attack him there and would have slain him, even in a church, had he not been hindered by Rognvald, who arrived in the nick of time well attended and ordered him not to profane the church by murder, Thorbiorn replied the church was profaned by the man that had fled thither but at length, as he saw he could not complete his revenge, he went off to Caithness where he lived at great liberty, every day adding to the catalogue of his crimes. Not satisfied without his revenge for the death of Thorkel, he came privately over to Orkney with thirty men and landed at Scapa, walked on foot to Kirkwall with only four of his companions and, rushing into a house where Thorarin was, he instantly kiled him and as quickly escaped being favoured by the darkness of the night. This slaughter soon came to Rognvald's ears and, as there was no doubt of the perpetrator, Thorbiorn was banished. He went no futher than Caithness where he lurked with his brother-in-law Hosni whose son Stephen became his great friend and confident. After some stay he went to Malcolm, King of Scotland, by whom he was graciously received and continued with him for some time in great esteem.

While Torbiorn lived in Scotland there was a certain Scottish courtier named Odran Gilli, a man equally famous for his noble birth and fierce disposition. This Odran, to shun the King's displeasure for some slaughter he had committed, fled to Orkney, where he was employed by the Earls in overlooking their affairs in Caithness. In this office he continued but a short while, till he fell out with Helgi, a man much esteemed in Caithness and in great favour with Rognvald, and slew him. The Earl of Orkney's dominions were now too hot for Odran and he fled to the west of Scotland, where he was entertained by Summarlid, the Thane of Argyle.

Swein as usual was making ready for his summer's expedition and Rognvald gave him the hint to revenge Helgi's death on Odran, if he had an opportunity. A word was enough for Swein, who set out with five ships for the western isles where he understood that Summarlid was ready for an exploit of the same kind with seven ships of which Odran had the command of one and that he was gone to take in the soldiers necessary for the expedition. Swein made an attack on Summarlid before he was joined by Odran and, after a sharp conflict, slew him with the greatest part of his people. He then went in search of Odran and, finding him in Myrkvafiord, slew him with fifty of his men. A summer so luckily begun seemed a good omen and Swein was not backward to pursue his fortune to the utmost till the beginning of Autumn, when he returned home and was greatly caressed by Earl Rognvald for revenging his quarrel on Odran.

We come now to the last scene of Earl Rognvald's life in which Thorbiorn Klerk fulfilled Swein's prophecy.

It was the Earl's custom every year to spend part of the summer in deer hunting among the hills of Caithness. Here likewise Thorbiorn Klerk divided his time between the Scottish court and his friends, though in Caithness he seldom appeared in public, lurking in private with Hofn his brother-in-law, Liolf and Halvard or Hosculd, the son of Duff of Fors.

On Rognvald and Harald's arriving in Caithness it was whispered that Thorbiorn watched an opportunity to attack them with a large body of ruffians equally determined to kill him. This intelligence obliged them to be on their guard and get together a sufficient number of horse and foot soldiers to repel any sudden attack. One evening, after the day's diversion, returning to their quarters from the hill, Harald took notice that Rognvald sneezed louder than ordinary as he sat by the fireside, which was generally reckoned ominous among the northerns. Next morning, on their way to the hunting ground, the Earl foremost, Arolf and his relation Iomar with several others following, they fell in with Hosculd employed in carrying his corns into the barn. Hosculd, with a great deal of frankness, saluted Earl Rognvald and his companions and went on with them conversing on various trifles till they came to his house, which was situated in the rugged hollow of a hill, the road to it narrow and dangerous, fortified with a rampart all round. Here Thorbiorn was concealed in a back room, the door of which was filled up with stones and rubbish. He was drinking with his men but as soon as he heard Hosculd's voice, snatching up his arms, he threw down the stuff that concealed the door and stealing softly to where the Earl was, he struck him a dreadful blow about the chin, which stunned Rognvald and cut off Asolf's hand as he was attempting to ward off the stroke. Asolf cried out in a tone of reproach against Thorbiorn, for his ingratitude to the Earl, but nothing could save him. The first stroke stunned him so that his foot, in attempting to light from his horse, stuck in the stirrup and, in this posture, Stephen, Hosculd's son, struck him with a spear, which Thorbiorn repeated, at the same time he received a wound in the thigh from Iomar, the point of the spear running into his belly. Thorbiorn then ran off by the declivity of the hill and gained a neighbouring marsh. In his flight he was met by Earl Harald, who was advised by his friends to stop him, as they were not ignorant of his designs but he allowed him to pass as he was ignorant of what had happened, besides he was attached to Thorbiorn as well for his services as by blood. By the time Harald knew of the murder Thorbiorn had gained the firmer ground of the fen where a number of men from the house attempted to defend him. However, the Earl went round but could not pass the water which was deep, broad and full of stinking slime.

No other method was left to attack Thorbiorn but with missiles, which he could easily avoid and were soon spent.

Thorbiorn, when he saw the shower of darts begin to subside, called aloud to Harald to spare his life and he would make him his judge and surrender, at the same time taking care to put him in mind of his former services which had been great and, throwing in a dash of the advantage Rognvald's death would be to him, though he confessed it was a horrible crime to kill him.

By such insinuating language Thorbiorn gained the most of his hearers and even Harald himself seemed to be staggered with regard to punishing him, when Magnus, the son of Havard Gunnar, started up and, in a most elegant speech, shewed the Earl the danger of sparing Thorbiorn. He told him it would fix an immortal stigma on his name and memory, that all mankind would declare him the author and contriver of the Earl's death, which they would judge he had had a hand in hatching, that he would find it as much in vain to clear himself from the murder as the other would find it easy, even his pardoning the perpetrator would confirm his guilt on the minds of all thinking men. He concluded that, whether he was pleased or angry, he himself would dispatch the murderer if any other had the spirit to follow him. This speech turned the scale against Thorbiorn and Thorstein and Haco joined in their brother Magnus' sentiments and declared they would assist him in his revenging Rognvald's murder. Swein, the son of Hroald, likewise joined them and all left the Earl and went to look out for a proper place to get into the marsh. Thorbiorn, now perceiving the odds against him, began to despair of his life yet, to make one effort, he jumped the water, armed as he was in a coat of mail, where it was nine cubits broad. His companions, who followed as well as they could, advised him to fly to the woods or attack Magnus, but he would do neither, ordering all his people to shift for themselves he, with eight that stood by him, came to Harald and, falling on his knees, submitted to his sentence. Harald would not kill him in this posture but bid him begone and take care of himself to which he did not need to be told twice but went off along the river of Kalfadale. When the Earl observed Magnus following him he called to him to take care of himself as he could fight in his defence with everybody of his party that would take it into their heads to revenge Rognvald's murder.

Thorbiorn, upon this, went off to the shielings in the mountains with his companions, wither Magnus soon followed him and set fire to the cottage. Thorbiorn and his men defended themselves strenuously but at length were all slain. When they came to examine Thorbiorn's wounds they found his entrails hanging out of a wound in the belly that he had received from the hand of Iomar.

After Haralds departure from Fors, Magnus returned and carried off Rognvald's body to Thursa whence it was brought with great solemnity to Orkney and buried in a church dedicated to the Virgin Mary.

Thus fell, by the hand of an assassin, Rognvald Kali the most deserving of all the Orkney Earls, whose virtues, without the pretended miracles said to be wrought at his tomb, entitled him to a place among the Saints, even though his name had not been found in the papal Calendar. Rognvald was liberal, moderate, obliging and generous to his friends, an excellent poet and well skilled in other arts then in use, nor was his whole life disgraced by any bad action except in his behaviour to Earl Erlend. His death happened in the year 1158 and his canonization in 1192.

Chapter 18

Rognvald left but one daughter, Ingigerde, married, as was before related, to Eric Slagbreller by whom she had three sons Harald Iungi, Magnus Mangi and Rognvald and three daughters Ingibiorg, Elia and Rognhilde.

Harald, now that Rognvald was dead, took possession of the whole of the Earldom without any scruple even though Rognvald left three grandsons who certainly had a right to everything their grandfather possessed.

Harald was of a stately disposition, majestic appearance and great strength. By his wife Affreca he had two sons, Henry and Haco and as many daughters, Helen and Margaret. Haco the youngest was brought up from his infancy under Swein's wing who had given him the best education he was master of, that is to say, as soon as he was capable, he had instructed him with the utmost care in all the mysteries of piracy in which he had thoroughly initiated him in his summer expeditions where he always accompanied him, that Haco soon became as expert as his master. In a word, according to our Author, he left nothing undone that tended to complete his pupl's education of add to his honour.

We have already seen Swein Asliefson engaged in his piratical exploits, then accounted honourable, let us now view him at home in the character of a Farmer. He always passed the winter in his Hall in Gairsey, where he kept constantly eighty followers as his sole charge. But these were not idle. In the spring they were employed in tilling the ground and laying down the crops, in which Swein himself did not spare his own manual labour. After the seed time all went on board for a trip to the AEbudae or Ireland and returned before harvest to cut down and gather in the corns. The remainder of the Autumn months and the month of November were spent as the summer.

One of Swein's famous expeditions was undertaken in the spring with five large ships in which he was particularly unlucky among the western isles. The inhabitants were so used to his visits that at length they drove off the ground their cattle and hid their other valuable effects either in the earth or in caves when they expected him. He at this time proceeded as far as the Isle of Man without meeting anything worth taking and had no chance remaining but the coast of Ireland.

In his way thither, near Dublin, he met with two English ships on their voyage thither, loaded with scarlet cloth and other valuable commodities. These he took as they could not defend themselves against his large fleet and plundered them everything valuable. He now returned quite satisfied for this time and, parting the spoils at the AEbudae, set off for Orkney. As he drew near the islands a whim struck him to hoist the English clothes by way of sails and thus entered the harbour with great triumph, from this circumstance giving this trip the title of the purple or rather scarlet expedition.

On his return he made a most magnificent feast to which he invited the Earl and all his friends and, among the rarities got on the voyage, treated them with plenty wine and mead, liquors then in all probability not much known in Orkney. On this occasion, among other talk, Swein's summer expedition came on the carpet. Harald advised him to give over his trade of piracy in time and not drive his fortune to the utmost. He told him he had been very successful hitherto in enriching himself with the goods of other people but it was a maxim to give over while things were well, as it commonly happened that rovers perished in the prosecution of their piracies, unless they saved themselves by early retirement. Swein returned a laughing answer and, after some talk, concluded that he would confine his whole project to one more autumnal expedition, which he intended to render at least as glorious for him as that of the spring had been, and thus wind up his toil.

After such discourse as this Swein dismissed the Earl with much honour, and valuable presents, and soon after began to prepare his fleet which consisted of seven large ships. With these, accompanied with Haco, Harald's son, he set out for the AEbudae, the usual scene of his adventures. By this time the Islanders were grown too cunning for Swein and all he got there was trifling, he therefore went to Ireland where, attacking the city of Dublin, he was in the heart of it before the citizens were aware of such a troublesome guest. Besides a great deal of plunder, he got hold of the chief men of the city and forced them to redeem themselves and it by a large sum of money, besides receiving a garrison which he was to place in it. When they had sworn to perform these things he returned in the evening to his ships and next morning went to the city with a large body of men to receive the money and hostages, as also to place his garrison.

The Dubliners however, when they recovered from their first surprise, began to consider with indignation the disgrace it would be for them to comply with Swein's articles. In a council held that same night, they agreed on a stratagem to deliver the city from the tyranny of the Orkneymen and their ferocious chief. They cut large trenches within the gates and through the streets, where the enemy must pass, and covered them with straw, placed armed men in the houses adjacent to be ready to fall on them when thay were entangled in the snare.

Next day everything happened as they expected. Swein came up with his men and fell plum into the trap prepared for him where he was fiercely set upon by those in the ambush and all his men soon slain. He himself fell last and, with his last words, proclaimed himself St, Rognvald's Satellite to whose intersession he recommended himself and died.

Such was the fate of Swein Asliefson whose life gives us a true picture of the manners of the times in which he lived. He had the first character in his time and country when piracy was no disgrace and arms the exercise of their whole lives. If we judge Swein by modern rules we must agree with our Author who calls him a bold and fortunate robber, a crafty warrior and the author of all the misfortune that befell an indulgent and kind Lord, besides many other instances of wickedness, he concludes that his fall was more honourable than he deserved. The truth is, manners must be computed by the age in which they prevailed, as the scale of morality in regard to meum and tuum seems to have been subject to much fluctuation.

Those of Swein's people that remained on board carried the ships home to Orkney with the news of his death, on which his sons Olave and Andrew took possession of the estate and reduced their father's Hall to less dimensions. This Hall was the largest in Orkney as Swein always kept a train of brother pirates who shared with him all his public and private labours as before observed.

Andrew, Swein's son, married Frida, the daughter of Kolbein Hruga, Bishop Biarn's sister. Biarn succeeded Bishop William of whom mention has been made. He was famous for his noble birth and great liberality, for intimacy with Earl Harald and friendship to one Rafn, a noble islander, to whom, among other presents, he sent a seal ring weighing an ounce of gold on which as engraved a Raven circumscribed with Rafn's name.

Harald, upon the death of his wife Affreca (by whom he had two sons, Henry and Haco and two daughters, Helen and Margaret), married Huarflodi, the Earl of Moray's daughter, who bore him three(?) sons, David and Ion and three daughters Gunhilda, Herborg and Langlif.

At this time Magnus, the son of Erling Skacki, reigned in Norway. Thither went Harald, the grandson of St. Rognvald and son of Eiric Slagbrellir, with his brothers, in order to procure their grandfather's Earldom in Orkney. This he obtained with the investiture of Earl and returned to Orkney to prosecute his new right, accompanied with one Sigurd, surnamed Murtus, who afterwards fell with him. Harald, for distinction's sake called the "younger Earl", landed from Norway in Shetland, whence he went to Caithness to wait on William, King of Scotland, from whom that part of Caithness his grandfather had possessed was without difficulty obtained. Harald well knew, notwithstanding these grants of the Kings of Scotland and Norway, he must make way to the enjoyment of his right by force of arms and began to raise an army of Caithnessmen, as also sent a trusty friend to Orkney for information anent the state of affairs there. He had before sent to make a civil demand on Harald the Elder of his patrimony but was refused with threats. His spy, Lifolf, ferried the Pightland Firth and landed in S. Ronaldsha where he fell in with three men sent thither on the same errand by his competitor, Harald the Elder. Of these, Lifolf slew two and took the third prisoner whom he carried with him to Caithness. His information did not at all contribute to raise Harald's spirits or promise him an easy victory, on the contrary he represented the enemy's fleet and army to be such as they could never oppose with their little though valiant handful, for which reason he was advised to retire to Thursa where they might be assured of a supply of any number of men and be able at length to cope with their antagonist on equal terms. Sigurd Murtus returned a jeering answer on Harald's mighty fleet and army, he observed "They could never thrive who had left their courage behind them as Harald had in passing the Pightland Firth nor would it fare better with the rest on seeing Harald's little army".

After some more talk in which Lifolf once more advised to go to Thursa, they beheld Harald's fleet in view in the Pightllad Firth which soon changed their thoughts to treat of the manner they were to oppose him. On his landing they soon saw the superiority of Harald's numbers, which did not hinder them from preparing for battle, in which Harald the Younger's friend Lifolf and Sigurd commanded on each wing, most gorgeously dressed, as were the leaders of the opposite side. The onset was fierce on both sides, which continued to be disputed with the utmost pertinacity till Sigurd Murtus was slain and even his death would not have entirely dispirited young Harald's party had it not been succeeded by that of Lifolf who likewise fell fighting with the greatest bravery, after breaking through the enemy no less than three several times[1]. The two experienced leaders being slain the rest instantly fled. Harald, who seems to have been wounded in his flight, fell down dead in a peat moss, the spot being observed by a bright illumination that arose from the place where he lay in his gore, a phenomenon that was much improved on and procured young Harald the name of a saint among his contemporaries. His body was buried in Caithness[2] and the place where he fell was soon after sanctified and a church built on it.

Miracles were not wanting according to our Author to prove Harald's title to a place among the saints but, as these are omitted by our Author, it is impossible they can be recovered, were they worth it.

After this decisive battle, Harald the Elder reduced all Caithness and returned to Orkney in triumph, which was but shortlived, his subduing of Caithness soon procuring him a more formidable enemy.

William the Lion of Scotland no sooner heard of the conquest of Caithness by Harald and the death of the younger Harald on whom he had bestowed it than, in a great rage he threatened to take a severe revenge on the Earl of Orkney. For this purpose he sent messengers to Rognvald or Reginald, the son of Gudrod, King of the AEbudae, to engage him against Harald. This Reginald was a warrior from his youth, for three years, in imitation of the ancient heroes, "he never reposed under an immovable roof nor ever drank beer in peace by a fireside."

Reginald was very forward to undertake the business for William and raised an army of Islanders from Cantyre and even from Ireland, with which he soon conquered Caithness left defenceless by its new Lord. Reginald was not satisfied with the conquest but stayed till he settled the civil government, appointing three deputies over the province, Man the son of Olave, Rofn the chief judge and Lifolf Alli.

Harald meanwhile sat quietly at home, dissembling any knowledge of the King's designs but, as soon as Reginald was gone, he sent over a trusty messenger to Caithness with secret instructions to destroy either one or all of the Governors. This person, coming first to Rafn, was sternly interrogated anent his design in coming to Caithness and almost frightened into a confession but at length dismissed with a reprehension, He next went to Lifolf and him he slew, making his escape after the cruel deed, he returned to Orkney.

Soon after, Harald went over with a large army and landing at Thursa put the inhabitants into the utmost consternation as they now all expected the harshest treatment from the exasperated Earl. Bishop Ion, observing their fears, proposed to meet Harald first and try to pacify him, desiring the inhabitants to observe what treament he met with from the Earl, because they might depend on it they themselves would receive the same. Harald and his army were landed and coming to the town when the Bishop met them and was received by the Earl with a smiling countenance till he got him in his power, when he ordered his tongue to be cut out and his eyes pulled from their sockets (the monks, ever ready to take hold of any story fit for their purrpose, add that the Bishop, in the midst of his torture, invoked Saint Trollhaena and, when he was dismissed, coming to a declivity, he met with this Saint who restored him his tongue and his eyes). Not satisfied with mutilating the poor Bishop, Harald entered the town of Thursa and inflicted various punishments on the inhabitants according to the extent of their faults. Some he fined at his pleasure, others he punished in their persons and forced all without distinction to swear allegiance to him as their liege Lord, as also confiscated all that belonged to the Governors who had fled to the Court of Scotland and, to defend what thus he had made himself master of in Caithness, he sat down with all his men there.

The Caithness deputies when they came to King William informed him of all that had happened in their country and Harald's cruelty. The King received them kindly and promised to make up their losses, ordering them presents and a daily allowance while they continued in his court. In order to revenge himself on Harald, William raised a vast army which he rendezvoused in the valley which parts Caithness and Sutherland. Harald likewise was not idle but got together as many as he could though in no proportion to the Scots, our Author says seven thousand two hundred, but the Scottish army filled the valley where they were encamped. However this might be, King William seems not to have been much inclined to risk a battle for, on Harald's sending messengers with proposals toward an accomodation, he returned hard terms indeed but better than none at all. The terms were a fourth part of everything the Caithnessians possessed to be confiscated to the King's use, for every one of the inhabitants except those who had fled to the Scottish court. Upon a consultation held, they saw but an alternative either to submit to William's harsh terms or hazard a battle and, in case of losing, subject themselves to the effects of his rage. They agreed to the former but it would be impossible for us to credit that this fourth was of their estates as well as moveables, as the former could not, without being ransomed, be brought into the Exchequer, nor do we hear that it was thr fruits of these estates. Harald, on this agreement, received the right he formerly had to Caithness from the King of Scotland and afterwards held it in the same manner as before the quarrel with the young Earl.

While the matter was depending between the Earl and King William, Harald gave up his son Thorfin, as a hostage for the performance of articles, to William by whom, according to Norwegian authors, he was deprived of his sight.

The Scottish historians give us a different account of this matter. According to Boece (fol.277.20) Harald was Earl of Orkney and Thane of Caithness and, making some stir in the latter, obliged William in person to go thither in order to quell the disturbance. He soon got the better of the insurgents and brought them (except the chief) to condign punishment.. The leader fled to the western isles and so escaped for some time but, being afterwards caught and brought to the King, he ordered his eyes to be put out, himself and all his race to be castrated and the chief to be hanged.

Buchanan tells the same story with this variation, that he weakened Harald in several conflicts before he forced him to fly and, upon his afterwards getting hold of him, served him and his race as before related. He adds that the place where the execution was performed is called the Stoney Hill.

The Norwegians are entirely silent, which would not have been the case if such cruelties had been exercised on Earl Harald and on his children, especially as the writer Torfaeus copies seems to have been present at the whole transaction and takes no notice of the circumstances of castrating or putting to death either Harald or his sons, which is more remarkable as he is otherwise very particular in his relation.

To pass Torfaeus' conjectures in order to reconcile his author with Buchanan, I may venture one; Buchanan seems to have confounded this story which happened in the reign of Alexander II (1222) in which Boethius tells us Alexander punished the Caithnessians and their sons for burning Adam, Bishop of that country, in the manner above related and the place where these last suffered is still called the Stoney Hill.

Buchanan seems to have fallen into this error in the hurry of transcribing from Boece and Torfaeus, who seems not to have consullted the latter author on this place, when he wrote his conjectures, left them in the state we now see them but which we shall see afterwards cleared up. The annals of Norway place this fact A.D.1198, Buchanan A.D.1199, whereas the murder of Adam Bishop of Caithness did not happen till the eighth year of Alexander the Second's reign A.D.1222. Tradition agrees with neither.

We come now to a new revolution in the affairs of Orkney occasioned by the death of Magnus, the son of Erling, who was slain by his successor Swerir, the natural son of Sigurd Bronchus. When Sigurd and his children were slain by Erling Skacki, Swerir was likewise sought for but, in the hurry, his mother who had married a mechanic concealed him and made him pass for his son. His supposed uncle was the Bishop of the Faro Isles; Swerir was conveyed thither and received his education from him and at length became a Presbyter. Swerir stayed in the Faro Isles till he was twenty-four years of age, when he came to the knowledge of his true parentage. Departing from Faro he went to Norway where he was soon made King by the same party that had stood by his relation Eyestein, but he had much to do and many years disturbance before he fixed himself firmly on the throne. At length, after much slaughter, Swerir became master of the whole Kingdom A.D.1184. Using his fortune with great moderation he educated Sigurd, Erling Skacki's natural son, at court, as also suffered another Sigurd, the son of Magnus the late King, to be brought up with the Aunt Rognhilda who was married to one Hallkill. Both these were pretenders to the crown and afterwards occasioned Swerir much trouble for Hallkill, though he had accepted a place under Swerir, soon began by secret means to stickle for his nursling Sigurd. In the prosecution of this plan Olave, a relation of Harald Earl of Orkney and Sigurd Erlindson, joined him, notwithstanding the obligations the latter had with Swerir.

In autumn Sigurd left Norway and went to Shetland and thence to Orkney, where he met with a most gracious reception from Earl Harald A.D. 1192. The same summer Hallkell, on pretence of a piratical expedition, came to Orkney in order to raise men to support his nurseling's claim. Harald, in consideration of the friendship he had for his father, gave Sigurd a ship completely fitted out and also contrived at the raising of men throughout the Isles. Encouraged by this beginning, Sigurd took the title of King and, having raised a large army and procured a fleet, he returned to Norway to prosecute his plan there and, arriving suddenly, slew many of Swerir's party (which, out of contempt, they called Birkebeins - Woodenshoes) before his designs were so much as known. He now publicly assumed the title of King and named his faction that of the Insulobarbi and Auripedes (Giltshoes), becoming very formidable to the King his antagonist but, after a long struggle and many changes of fortune, Sigurd was at last slain in a great sea fight, where most of his Insulobarbi, his foster father Hallki ll and his friend Olave, Harald's relation, likewise fell and at once put an end to the faction.

After Swerir had set matters to rights in Norway, his anger began naturally to to point towards Orkney. Harald had taken an active part in the late stir, had furnished his rival with men and ships against him, therefore Swerir next directed is vengeance against him.

Harald soon heard of Sigurd's fate and began to dread the consequences to himself, as also to cast about how to ward off the blow. For this purpose he went to Norway carrying Bishop Biarn and all the Orkney Gentlemen with him, to deprecate the King's wrath by any means he could. On arriving at Bergen the matter was pled at great length before Swerir who appeared in great state, attended by his satellites and the nobility of the Kingdom. Harald's speech on the occasion is yet preserved in the manuscript of Flatey, in which, whether from his heart or not, the consequences shewed he condemns his allowing or coniving at rebellious practices, though to soften this he alleges he was not the author of the treason, he condemns his allowing piratical exercises though he observes none punishes these with greater severity, he laments his falling under the King's displeasure but that the fault was more, he hoped, from negligence than design. In fine, throwing himself at the King's feet he submitted himself to his will. Swerir, who was struck with his penitence, ordered him to rise and assured him his life and limbs should be safe but, in consideration of his and the Orkney people's folly, he confiscated the estates and goods of all those that were slain at Floruvog in the sea fight which had crushed the rebellion but allowd the nearest of kin to redeem them in three year time which, if they failed to do, they were to remain to the crown of Norway in perpetuity. He fined the Earl in the whole islands of Shetland and everything belonging to him there, which was ever after to belong to the King of Norway, as also the half of the Orkney fines which were to be rserved to the King. To collect these Swerir was to send over Questors who were to remit the reddenda arising from the confiscated lands to the Royal treasury. Of these collectors Arni Liora was to be appointed the chief and to reside in Orkney.

These terms, hard as they were, the Earl found it necessary to submit to and public deeds executed accordingly, which however the Earl intended should be no longer binding on him than he found convenient. As long as Swerir lived however Harald was obliged to behave cautiously as he had already felt his power but, so soon as heard of the King's death and that Norway was torn to pieces with new factions, he took possession of Shetland, killed Arni and reduced everything in Orkney to the same state they had been before Sigurd's rebellion.

This is among the last actions recorded of Earl Harald who did in peace in th 73rd. year of his age A.D.1206.

Harald was a prince equaly fit for the management of civil matters in peace or the hurry of war, he was prudent and discerning; was strong and active; his stature was large and his appearance but ordinary. He was one of the most powerful Earls of Orkney nor was he at all scrupulous in using extraordinary means to attain the summit of his ambition.

He was succeeded by his sons David and Ion - his eldest son, Henry, by his first wife having got his Earldom of Ross in Scotland - in what manner is not said.

About these times happened a quarrel between Bishop Biarn's nephew, Thorkel Kolbeinson, who had gone on a trading voyage to Iceland, and the famous Snorro Sturleson. The occasion was a difference arising about the price of some corn, in the course of which the Deacon of Borgarfiord was slain. Snorro, in order to avenge the death of his countryman, attacked the Orkneymen without effect, who soon after put to sea and, being forced back by contrary winds, were obliged to come to anchor in a place called Eyrarback, where they were well received and protected by the no less famous Soemund on Biarn's account, between whom and Soemund a strict friendship had long existed.

Soemud, the son of Ion (not the famous author of the more ancient Edda), was very powerful in Iceland and much respected for his noble descent, being the great-grandson of Magnus Barefoot, King of Norway. As he had no wife, he proposed to Harald a marriage with his daughter Langleif, to which the Earl agreed if he would come to

Orkney to perform the ceremony, but this Soemund refused and the affair came to nothing.

Though Swerir, King of Norway, as has been formerly related, with some difficulty reduced the faction called the Insulbarbi, another, no less dangerous, called Bagli, sprang up in the latter years of his life and gave him great uneasiness. The leader of these was one Ingi who pretended to be Sigurd Magnus' son, who was slain at Floruvog, and many of all stations flocked to his standard. Ingi struggled seven years but was at length slain by the peasants the same year that Swerir died. Another started up A.D. 1204 and heading the same faction for three years with the name of King, who was succeeded by one Philip who was more fortunate then the others, as Ingi, King of Norway, divided the Kingdom with him, to put an end to the faction. This had not the designed effect, the Bogli, on Philip's accepting the half of Norway, joined with the other faction, the Birkebeins, and both concurred in overrunning the Kingdom, the Orkney and Shetland Isles and the AEbudae, even the islandof Icolmkill which they spared not. Like other robbers they soon fell out and parted and, wherever they met afterwards, a battle ensued, in which they were at length reduced to a small number who returned to Norway and submitted to government.

After the death of Swerir and while Norway was thus confused, Harald and his successors in Orkney gave themselves little trouble as to their engagements with the crown of Norway and reclaimed Shetland, as also with-held the reddenda of Orkney many years. No sooner were the Earls David and John apprised that all disturbances were at an end and peace was restored to Norway, than they deputed Bishop Biarn to make up matters with Ingi. Biarn obtained thus far that the Earls should be at liberty to go without fear of their lives to plead their own cause in Norway. Of this permission they availed themselves and, as they could not excuse their behaviour, submitted themselves to the King's mercy, who fined them in a large sum of money, obliged them to give hostages and every security for their future loyatlty, to which he likewise bound them by oath. When all these preliminaries were settled, the King restored Orkney and Shetland according to the Norwegain chronicles - but our Author seems to have some doubts anent the latter as he never had seen any public deed restoring Shetland to the Orkney Earls and the writer he follows had said expressly before that Sheland was never restored from the time that Harald, the son of Maddad, lost it.

Not only the Orkneys but the AEbudae submitted to the sceptre of Norway. The petty princes of the isles, soon after the depredatory visit made them by the Norman pirates, went to Norway, made their submission in form and received their dominions in the isles a feu of Norway.

About the year 1215 David, Earl of half Orkney, died and, two years after, Sculi, who held the third of Norway, began, from ambitious views, to meditate a revolution and to solicit Earl John's assistance. For this purpose he wrote letters to Orkney sealed with the Royal Signet but the design miscarried.

What follows of the first and completest book of Torfaeus' Orcades is the story of Adam, Bishop of Caithness, taken from the annals of Norway and the manuscript of Flatey. The annals place this event A.D.1222, as does Buchanan, but the story is cleared up from the book of Flatey as follows. After the death of Ion, Bishop of Caithness, who had been mutilated by Harald, Adam - a foundling - succeeded him, was the cause of much mischief in the province by his rigour in exacting the titles which was however attributed to a monk his companion.

It was the custom in Caithness to pay tithes of cattle, for each cow a mark of butter and for every score twenty marks or a span; and so in proportion to the number they were possessed of. The rate it seems did not satisfy the Bishop and his avaricious companion, who first raised the rate from twenty cows to pay a span of butter to fifteen; From fifteen they imposed the same rate on twelve and, at last on ten, thus increasing the rate to double the original payments.

Such opression could not miss to irritate the sufferers and accordingly they complained to Earl Ion, then in Caithness, but he declined meddling in the affair from prudential reasons which obliged the Pope to proceed to justice in their own summary way. The Bishop dwelt in Halkirk and with him Rafn, the Fowd or judge of the country, as did the Earl Ion in a castle not far off, when the country people, convening on a neighbouring hill, demanded justice. Rafn, when he saw this, ardently urged the Bishop to remit something of his wonted rigour in collecting his tithes, as the people were becoming outrageous and everything was to be feared from their fury. Adam would not agree to his prudent advice, he desired the Fowd to fear nothing and insinuated that to give the people any part of their will would, in this case, be to part at once with his influence and independence for ever.

Ion the Earl was again solicited to become a mediator in the case but in vain, he absolutely declined any part in it, nay there are not wanting who say he rather spurred onthe multitude to revenge. When the country people saw they could not prevail with the Bishop to favour them, they rushed furiously down the hill and beset the house and were no sooner observed by Rafn than he once mors begged the Earl to think on some method for his own safety and agree to a composition.

The Bishop and Rafn were drinking together in an upper chamber, when the house wa surrounded and the Monk Serlo going out to pacify the people was instantly struck dead by a blow in the face. The Bishop soon understood the fate of his monk, nor did he seem to grieve at it but, observing by this specimen what danger himself was in, he sent Rafn to attempt an accomodation. The more sensible part of the assailants were well pleased to treat with the Bishop but, on his appearing to adjust the terms, some of the ruder and more ignorant, getting hold of him, hurried him in to a small neighbouring house and set fire to it and, before the friendly few could extinguish the flames which burnt with great rapidity, the Bishop was gone. His body was found, not burnt to ashes, according to our Scottish historians, and afterwards buried with great solemnity.

Alexander the second of Scotland, when he heard the treatment the Bishop of Caithness had met with, went thither in person to punish the perpetrators, of whom no less than eighty were executed, mutilated, confiscated or proscribed, the annals of Norway say eighty of the most active had their had their hands and feet cut off, of whom many died of their wounds. The Scottish historians tell the story something differently. According to them the Bishop was hurried into his own kitchen and burnt to ashes in the oven and his ashes scattered with the wind. Others say he was boiled to death. They likewise differ in the punishment, telling us all the males present were castrated which, and not the story of Bishop Ion, affords the tradition of the Stoney Hill.

Thus far the Icelandic author gives a pretty full and continuous history of the Earls of Orkney to the death of Harald Maddadson and succession ofhis sons David and Ion, what follows, in our author, is drawn from the histories of Denmark, Norway and the Chronicles of Iceland, to which we shall add what occurs inthe history of Scotland.

1. This battle according to Mr. Pope, Minister of Reay, was fought at Claredon near Thurso east.

2. The grave according to the same is yet known to be in a small chapel in the parks of Thurso east.

Chapter 19

This second part of our Author's work treats of the Orkney Bishops, as well as the Earls, but the former we shall throw into a separate section and now go on with the history of the Earls, as we find them from these annals. However from the death of Harald Maddadson A.D.1206 these do not seem to make such a figure in the history of the North except in a very few particulars, many reasons intervening, such as their history not being so much connected with that of Iceland; their soon after this period growing less in the eyes of the Kings of Norway; a change in the manners of the North after the introduction of Christianity which changed the method of recording events; a want of written records and the loss of those which have been written. To those and many other reasons we must attribute the mutilated state of the following periods of the history of the Orkney Islands. But to return to the annals.

A.D. 1225 Gilchrist and Ottar went to Norway wither Ion, Earl of Orkney, went also to make his peace with King Haco, with whom he left his son Harald as a hostage for his good behaviour, where he remained throughout the summer. The reason of this voyage, though not said, might be something anent Sculis' rebellion in Norway which had not been cleared up.

We find Earl Ion in Norway the year following in company with Simon, Bishop of the AEbudae and the Abbot of Ikolmkill, and the same year Harald his son was drowned.

A.D. 1228 The Earl of Orkney sends messengers into Norway with presents for the King and, in return, they receive a ship with all her tackle besides many other valuable gifts.

A.D, 1229 Allan of Galloway, at that time the most powerful subject in Scotland, who was wont to keep a large fleet in pay for exercising the trade of piracy on the coasts of Ireland and through the AEbudae, formed about this time a project to make hiself master of the Isle of Man and its dependencies but, in this, he miscarried by the bravery of Olave. In this business Reginald, Olave's brother, fell after two attempts to establish himself in that part of the isles possessed by Olave. His death, giving his brother some breathing time, he employed it in a visit to Norway in order to get himself confirmed in his government but, in the meanwhile, Haco had made Upsac, one of the Birkebein faction, the son of Owmund according to the Chronicle of Man (but of Dugal says Torfaeus), King of Osloa A.D. 1230, promising to fix him in the Kingdom the following summer. For this purpose, early in the spring, he furnished him with nine ships to which the Earl added three more with captains and men to navigate them. Just as they were about to sail, Olave arrived from Bergen complaining that he had been drove from his kingdom by Allan and, not content with this, he had determined to make war on Norway bragging that the Norwegian seas were as pervious to a Scot as the Scottish to a Norwegian. Olave, in his voyage, had touched at Orkney where he was presented with a large ship by Earl Ion.

Upsac, beseiging a castle in Bute, took it with the loss of three hundred men and, dying soon after himself, the Principality of the isles returned to Olave surnamed the Black.

In summer 1231 happened a quarrel between Earl Ion of Orkney and one Hanef, the King of Norway's collector there, the occasion of which was this. One of Upsac's Sea Captains named Aulver Illteit, a man of a cross and savage disposition as his name bears, had stayed in Orkney on the return of the fleet to Norway and lived with Hanef, as also Snokoll the son of Gun, sprung from Earl Rognvald. This Snokoll was disobliged at Earl Ion because he would not give up the islands belonging to Earl Rognvald and, of consequence, to his posterity and he, as the representative, with much entreaty claiming it, was refused. By much wrangling the matter was made worse and at length Snokoll, believing hiself unsafe, fled for protection to Hanef. In the following autumn Ion and Hanef went to Caithness at the same time and, putting up at different Inns at Thursa, word came to Hanef one evening, as he was drinking with his friends, to be on his guard because Ion had determined to attack him that very night and put him and all his friends to the sword. The Earl escaped into the cellar and hid himself among the casks whence he was brought by Snokoll and others and slain with many stabs. Several others likewise fell in this squabble of Ion's party and Hanef with his associates, immediately after the slaughter, went to Orkney and fortified the castle of Weir built by Kolbein Hruga in St. Rognvald's time (now called Cobberow) and carried into it arms and everything necessary in case of a siege.

It was soon invested by Ion's friends and endured a long siege. At length it was rendered on condition that both parties should live in peace through the winter and afterwards submit the whole matter to the judgement of their sovereign the King of Norway. Thither both parties went in summer and found the King in a mighty rage at this deed of Hanef's and the consequence was that many of the murderers were punished with death. Sigvald Skialg, the Earl's near relation, conducted the prosecution and Hanef with his brothers, Snokoll with some others were ordered to prison in the castle of Bergen. Aulver Illteit, Thorkell, Rafn and two others were executed on the island called Tauluholm. One Biorne was carried out to the place of execution, escaping into a church, got off. Thorkell surnamed the Black was led through the streets by Earl Skuli's lodgings who interceded for him in case his part in the crime had been small but, when Sigvald told him that he had wantonly and cruelly pierced the Earl's dead body, he allowed him to proceed.

After the execution of the murderers Sigvald, with all the Orkney gentlemen who had gone with him to attend the trial, went aboard their ships to sail homeward but all perished on their passage, where is not known, however the loss of so many of their chiefs proved such a heavy blow to Orkney as it did not recover for a long time.

Those of Ion's murderers that escaped death at length were received into favour by Haco but Hanef did not long survive his pardon.

A.D. 1233 is remarkable for the loss of a Jewish ship in Orkney, on what account she came thither is not said.

A.D.1239 died Magnus, Earl of Orkney, from whom the Orkney Act of State (to be noticed afterwards) says King Alexander of Scotland recovered the Shire of Sutherland.

The year following, Haco of Norway caused his son Haco to be invested with the ensigns of royalty in his own lifetime and ordered all ranks in the Kingdom of Norway and Orkney to take an oath of fealty to him.

About this time Alexander the Second of Scotland, a prince fond of arduous enterprises and desirous to extend the limits of his kingdom, began to form the design to recover the AEbudae and all the islands lying on the west side of Scotland that Magnus Barefoot had conquered from his ancestor Malcolm. For this purpose he sent over two Bishops to Norway to reclaim these but, to this demand, they met with a flat refusal. Haco told them he did not found his right on Magnus' conquest of the isles but that he and his ancestors had an hereditary right to them.

The Bishops, finding this mode of proceeding would not do, offered in the name of their master to redeem the isles with money and desired Haco to name his price but, to this, he replied that he had at present no urgent necessity for money nor would he on any terms disjoin these isles from his kingdom. With this answer the ambassadors were obliged to depart and, though these or the like offers were often renewed, they were as often rejected and the matter seems to have rested here until A.D. 1249.

A.D. 1246 died Iofreir, Bishop of Orkney.

A.D. 1248 is remarkable for the marriage of Cecilia, Haco's daughter, with Harald, King of Man. The marriage was celebrated with great magnificence at Bergen whence, Harald returning in a single ship to his own dominions with a splendid retine, was drowned with all on board in a place called Dynraust on the south side of Shetland, probably Sumburgh Roust.

A.D. 1249 Alexander in earnest set about recovering the AEbudae and, for this purpose, made vast preparations throughout Scotland, got together such a number of men that he boasted he would never sheath the sword till he had recovered all the islands the Norwegians had in possession round Scotland. He sent messengers to Ion, one of the Kings of the AEbudae, with great offers of a larger fortune in Scotland than he possessed in the isles if he would desert the Norwegian cause and deliver up the fort Kiarnaburgh and three other castles Haco had committed to his charge. Ion, however, in spite of his friends' advice and the large temptation, stuck to his integrity and retired to Lewis. Alexander, notwithstanding, invaded the isles but, while he lay with his fleet in Kialarsound, he had, says our author, a vision dissuading him from the prosecution of his design and threatening him if he persisted in it. Three men approached him while asleep, one of which was a person of great stature in prince's dress but had a stern and threatening look which he directed full on the King. The second was a young man very handsome and richly dressed. The third who was taller than the rest, as also fiercer, asked the King angrily whether he continued in his resolution to invade the isles. On Alexander answering in the affirmative the fierce phantom told him at his peril to give over his design and return home. This likewise his friends advised him to, but in vain. Alexander persisted in his resolution till he fell into a violent distemper of which he died. The

King's death, putting an entire stop to the project, his chiefs, returning home, placed his son Alexander on the throne of his fathers.

The Hebridians called the three phantoms the King saw in his sleep, St. Olave King of Norway, St. Magnus Earl of Orkney and St. Columba Abbot of Iona.

This year died Haufir or Hervey, Bishop of Orkney, and A.D. 1256 died Gibon the Earl, according to the act of state succeeded by Gibon or Gilbon the second, who enjoyed Caithness as well as Orkney, but of him Torfaeus makes no mention.

A.D.1263 Haco understood by letters from the reguli of the Isles that Kiarnach, son of the Earl of Ross, had most cruelly laid waste the AEbudae, that he had destroyed their towns and villages, burnt their churches and monasteries and that in the most barbarous manner he had slain all the inhabitants that came in his way without respect of either age or sex. By these he likewise was informed that the new King of Scotland had threatened that he would never desist till he had added the AEbudae to his empire.

Haco did not slight this information but that very summer fitted out a vast fleet, he sailed from Norway the 11th of July and arrived at Shetland on the 13th, where he stayed in the harbour of Breidyarsound (probably Lerwick harbour) near two weeks. Thence he went to Orkney and put in to the harbour of Elliarwick (now Ellwick in Shapinsha) near Kirkwall and, holding a council, proposed to send part of his fleet and forces to Breidafiord to plunder the coast of Scotland. This project was baffled by the backwardnss of his men who refused to proceed unless the King headed them. After some stay at Ellwick, he went to S. Ronaldsha and sent messengers to demand a tribute, under pain of fire and sword. Fear made the Caithnessians comply and accordingly they paid him his demand.

While Haco was in S. Ronaldsha there happened an eclipse of the sun in such a manner that nothing of his face but a small circle appeared.

Haco had sent Ion the son of Langlif to the AEbudae to see how matters stood there, who now returned and informed him of the revolt of Ion the Sodorian King to the Scots, which however the King did not believe.

From Orkney Haco directed his course to Lewis and afterwards by Rona to Sky. Here he was joined by Magnus, the King of Man, and others, as also by Dugal, King of some parts of the isles, who met him in a boat and piloted him fiirst tothe Sound of Mull and afterwaards to Kiarvarey and here he was reinforced by a fleet of ships belonging to the islands.

While he lay in Kiarvary he detached fifty ships tothe isthmus of Cantyre under the command of Magnus, King of Man, and several others. He also sent a squadron of fifteen to Bute caommaned by Erlend the Red and four or five others.

Whilst these were gone to make themselves masters of Cantyre and Bute, Ion, the revolted King, came to where Haco lay and pretended to excuse his fealty to Alexander as being obliged to give in consideration of a large province he held in Scotland and therefore begged Haco to dispose of the fief he held of him as he thought proper.

The squadrons Haco had sent to Cantyre and Bute had some trouble in reducing these parts but, upon his threatening to go thither in person Margad, one of the chiefs of Cantyre, surrendered it into the King's hands, who placed a garrison in it and gave the command to one Guttorm. The castle of Bute was delivered up and the whole island subdued, where a Scotish exile who claimed it as his patrimony afterwards did much mischief to his countrymen.

When Haco came to the Sudureys, ambassadors met him from Ireland promising him assistance in his expedition.

Directing his course to Arran after the reduction of all the AEbudae, ambassadors came to him from Alexander to treat of peace, who were well received and others sent from Haco to Alexander, viz. Gilbert, a Norwegian Bishop,and Henry, Bishop of Orkney, with several chiefs of the fleet, who were to act as plenipotentiaries to settle all differences. The Scottish Ambasadors insisted to have Bute, Arran and Cumbray restored to their own and on this condition their King was willing to wave his plea to the other isles. These terms were not accepted by Haco and the Scottish ambassadors were, after some delays, dismissed.

After this treaty was broke up re infecta, Haco moved to Cumbria and sent some Bishops and Lords to attempt a new accomodation but this, like the others, proved vain and, when they had sat some time the Scots, beginning to appear in great numbers about the place of meeting, bred a suspicion of treachery, the Norwegians fled with some precipitation to their ships and begged of their King to put an end to the truce, which he did and sent a message at the same time to Alexander to meet him, in order either to settle the terms of peace or determine their differences by the sword. This likewise seems to have been refused by Alexander, at least Haco's messenger brought back no explicit answer.

Haco, seeing plainly that he could do nothing with Alexander, immediately commencd hostilities by sending Magnus and Dugal with some Norwegian officers and a fleet of sixty ships to Skipafiord, where they landed and destroyed all the villages round Lokulofou, laid waste a whole tract of country which gave the title of Earl to a Scottish nobleman and carried off a vast deal of plunder to their ships. Allan, Dugal's brother, penetrated farther into the country and carried off among other things a great many oxen and did a great deal of other damage. A great deal of misfortune happening to the fleet in Skipafiord and elsewhere gave the Scots new life. A terrible tempest destroyed ten of this Squadron and, of the King's fleet, several were destroyed and all put in confusion. The storm rose to a great height, mixed with sleet and hail, which, driving the ships from their anchors, flung them foul of one another and particularly of the royal galley, that it was with the utmost difficulty it was saved. Five were left and Haco was obliged to escape from his galley in a boat .

The Scots, observing the confusion among their enemies who were busy among their ships in the shallows, flocked down to the shores and attacked them but they did not find the conquest so easy as they imagined, the Norwegians defended themselvs stoutly and a reinforcement, coming from the fleet, beat them to the higher ground. The day following Haco ordered everything to be got ready for landing to support his men who had stayed ashore all night but from this he was dissuaded and advised rather to send supplies from the ships.

One of his officers, Augmund Kroekidanz, with two hundred men, had taken possession of a little hill. Him the Scots attacked with slight skirmishings till their main army came up. All the Norwegians that were onshore did not amount to more than 200 men, who were soon attacked by the Scottish army consisting of 500 horse and a very large body of foot armed with bows, spears and stones.

The attack was fierce and the fight continued a long while notwithstanding the unequal number of Norwegians to every one of whom there were ten opponents. Little or no assistance could be given from the ships, only a few got ashore in the midst of the storm, which still continued, and sustained their countrymen till they drove the

Scots from the strand to the hill whence about evening they, by a bold push, dislodged them and the Norwegians with extreme difficulty recovered their ships.

Next day the King sent people ashore to collect the bodies of the slain, which he afterwards took care to have buried in holy ground. Among these were Haco Stein and Thorgils Gloppa, two fo the King's satellites; Karlshofud from Frandheim and Askell, both country gentlemen from Norway; with three others, Thorstein Bat, Ion Ballhofud and Hallvard Buniard.

After he had reimbarked his men and set fire to the stranded ships, Haco began, as the winter approached, to think of steering to the northward.

In his voyage he touched at Arran, the Mull of Canyre and Isla, at the last of which he stayed two days making a demand on the islanders of three hundred oxen or meal and cheese for any that inclined, in proportion to their share.

In his passage he dismissed Dugal, Magnus and the other islanders to their respective homes, thus having, in a single expedition, recovered all the territories Magnus Barefoot had ever been posessed of. Afterwards, touching at Rona and Sky, he sent some of his retinue to Orkney before him, wither he soon folowed and landed in S. Ronaldsha. Several of his ships he sent home to Norway in which went more of his men than he inclined but he himself was prevented by stormy weather and was forced to winter in the isles. In passing the Pightland Firth he lost one of his vessels which was swallowed up in the whirlpools, a second narrowly escaping.

Haco remained with his fleet of twenty ships and all his Lords except one, through the winter.

Thus did Haco finish this expedition which was glorious to himself and gainful to his crown. The Scottish historians, Boece and Buchanan, give a quite different account of the catastrophe of this summer's work as may be seen by consulting their books, but ,I should think, with little appearance of truth, as the consequences show that Haco's fleet and army were neither so much destroyed as they would make us believe for, if this had been the case, it is something odd that peace should be concluded with his successors and a bargain so very advantagous for Magnus made with him while his affairs in the isles were in such a ruined state. It is then little wonder that the writer of the Flatteyan Manuscript should be so severe on the Scottish historians and the Monks chronicle for saying that nothing was effected in this western expedition and for augmenting the number of slain to such a sum as sixteen or twenty-five thousand men.

After Haco had taken care to secure his fleet which mostly lay in Scapa Bay, he himself, landing at Scapa, proceeded to Kirkwall on horseback.

He billetted his Lords and their troops through the country which he divided for this purpose into Erislands and Marklands, each of the latter containing eight Eyrir or Ounces. On everyone of these Marklands so many chiefs and their retinue were placed at winter quarters and, after everything was settled, they everyone withdrew to the quarter alloted for him.

Haco seems to have been greatly worn out with the variety of toil, both of body and mind, he had undegone in this expedition and, no sooner was he on shore, than this began to appear. He was instantly seized with sickness which sometimes remitted so far as to allow him to walk a little about, once to the shrine of St. Magnus, and to bathe himself. Soon after, in the night following, it began to increase so that it was visible to all he was in danger. As long as he was able to bear it he made his people read Latin and Norwegian books, particularly the lives of the Saints and, when these were finished, the History of his country by Halfdane the Black. At length his malady increased so that he began in earnest to prepare for death and, after appointing legacies for his courtiers and servants, he wrote a letter to his son Magnus containing instructions anent the management of his most serious affairs.

He received the extreme unction from two Norway Bishops, Henry Bishop of Orkney and Thorlief an Abbot. Before unction he saluted the Bishops and his friends all round, being then scarcely able to speak. At length his speech failed and, in the night of the seventh day after the feast of St. Lucia, he expired amidst the sighs of his desponding friends, which were followed by the lamentations of all.

There were present at his death Bryniolf, Erling, Ion Drothing and Rognvald Orka with some of his domestic servants. These were forthwith despatched to call the Bishops and Clergy. The body was laid in state in an upper room of the Episcopal Palace, palmdressed in an elegant coffin fit for so great a King.

The Hall was superbly illuminated where the corpse lay and thither the Bishops, Clergy and superior order of Courtiers were admitted to see the body which still preserved a pleasant aspect, the ruddy colour still remaining in the cheeks as when alive.

After all the solemnities of lying in state etc. was over, the body was carried to St.Magnus' Church, where it was soon after put into a box and placed before St. Magnus' shrine where it was watched all winter by the nobility in rotation.

At the fast of Yule, the Bishop and Andrew Flytt, the King's treasurer, in obedience to Haco's dying orders, paid off all the legacies and other debts.

Haco before he died ordered his body to be carried to Bergen to be laid among the ashes of his ancestors. This was accordingly done in spring, when it was caried to Scapa, put on board the Admiral's galley and thence to Norway. Landing at Selivog in Norway, Haco's retinue sent messengers to King Magnus with the news of his father's death, who soon after met them accompanied by Bishop Peter of Bergen, when they conveyed the corpse to the town and, the day following, to Christ's Church wither a vast procession of all ranks followed.

This same year, 1263 A.D., Gilbert, Archdeacon of Shetland, was created Bishop of Hamar in Norway.

When Magnus had completed his father's funeral he began to look into the state of public affairs and particularly into the state of the Western Isles which had long been disputed and which his peaceable temper wished to see cleared up.

Chapter 20

At length a peace was concluded beteween Magnus and Alexander A.D. 1266, on these conditions, that Man, the AEbudae and all the isles except Orkney and Shetland, should be given up to the Scots, who on their part were to pay 4000 marks sterling in four years time after the treaty was signed, with one hundred marks sterling a year afterwards called the Annual of Norway. This was a saving to the church of Drontheim of her metropolitan jurisdiction over the See of Sodor and to the inhabitants of their heritages and privileges and an act of oblivion for all past transactions. I say all these things together shew us that this league was as honourable a one for the Norwegians and the inhabitants, as it could in the nature of things be supposed to be, and is a plain sign that things were not low with the Norwegians as our author would wish us to believe.

A.D. 1268 remarkable for the death of Dugal, petty King of the Isles, and a contract of privileges between Magnus, Earl of Orkney, and the King of Norway of the same name.

Next year Bishop Henry of Orkney died and was succeeded by Peter in whose time the Cathedral church of Stafanger was burnt to the ground and rebuilt by a contribution throughout the Kingdom and its dependencies.

A.D. 1274 Died Magnus Gibbonson, Earl of Orkney, and was succeeded by his son Magnus who was created Earl by Magnus of Norway at the feast of St. Olave A.D. 1276.

Magnus dying A.D. 1284, his brother Ion succeeded and married a daughter of King Eiric.

The same year likewise died Peter, Bishop of Orkney and after the See had been vacant near two years Dolgfin was created Bishop in his stead.

A.D. 1308 Haco, King of Norway abolished the title of Earl and Baron in his kingdom, with the exception of the King's sons and the Earl of Orkney.

A.D. 1310 One William was made Bishop of Orkney and, two year after, the treaty of Perth concerning the Western Isles was confirmed between Robert Bruce and his Council on the one side and Commissioners from Haco 5th. of Norway on the other. This meeting was held at Inverness and there it was agreed that whoever of the parties first broke the treaty should be laid open not only to the censure of the church but also to the payment of a fine of £10,000 sterling.

A.D, 1343 We find Argisel subscribing a deed in Norway but of him nor Eringislwise pretty exact makes no mention, so that the being of these two Earls must rest on the authenticity of these records.

According to the Act of the council or little Parliament of Orkney, Ion was succeeded by his son Magnus the fifth of that name, at whose death the male line of the ancient Orkney Earls failed. Magnus left only a daughter who was married to the Earl of Strathern in Scotland but there is no evidence of his immediate descendants. In consequence of this failure it appears, by a letter preserved in Torfaeus, that the King of Norway had taken possession of Orkney as his right by of the feudal system, until another heir appeared and received investiture. Such a claim was entered to the Earldom A.D. 1357 in favour of one Malis - in all probability the Grandson of Magnus by his daughter the Countess of Strathern. This claim was intimated to the inhabitants that they might not suffer the rents to be carried out of the country till Malis had obtained investiture.*

This Malis was twice married, first to a daughter of the Earl of Monteith by whom he had a daughter named Matilda afterwards married to Weland de Ord, By his second wife, daughter to the Earl of Ross, he had four daughters, the eldest of whom was married to William St. Clare, Baron of Roslin in Scotland. The second to Ginsel de Swetherick, the third to Gothred de Spirre and the youngest died unmarried.

Welend de Ord by his wife Matilda had a son named Alexander, which Alexander had the Earldom of Caithness and some part of the Orkneys conferred on him in right of his mother.

Alexander soon sold Caithness to Robert the first, King of Scotland, nor did he long enjoy the share he had of Orkney, as he died sometime after, childless. Even before his death A.D. 1369, Henry St. Clare, son of Willaim St. Clare by the eldest daughter of his second marriage, laid claim to the whole of the Earldom and obtained the investiture thereof from Haco the third, King of Norway, though, at the same time, it is clear that the descendants of the other two sisters of the marriage as well as Alexander de Ord, the descendant of the first daughter, had certain portions of Orkney alloted to them and that A.D. 1375 Alexander de Ord was made Governor of Orkney for one year, as the King of Norway's letters* fully testify.

A few years before this transaction (A.D. 1370) David, King of Scotland, published a proclamation forbidding all his subjects under the highest penalties to resort to Orkney unless to trade. The reason for this prohibition was Orkney had been for some time past so pestered by troops of Scottish rovers that it was become scarcely habitable to check their insults, therefore David published the above mandate. A.D.1379 Henry St. Clare, Baron of Roslin, made a voyage to Norway and obtained a full confirmation of his right to Orkney together with the investiture as Earl. And, as the ancient Earls had only done homage for the possession of their fief which, though it implied an obligation to all those services that are incidental to a feudal holding, yet it seems in this case this was not thought sufficient, as Henry was a stranger in the Kingdom of Norway and owed allegiance to another prince, the King of Scotland. Therefore, Henry St. Clare, Earl of Orkney and Lord Roslin, by a written obligation * dated at Marstrand the second of August of the above year, acknowledged himself to have taken an oath of allegiance and paid homage to Haco, King of Norway and Swedland and became thereby obliged:

1st. To be ready to serve the said King, his heirs and successors, with an hundred well armed men as often as he should be required, upon three months advertisement, provided that the King would maintain at his own charge from the time they should come to his presence

2nd. To defend the isles of Orkney and Shetland in case of their being attacked by any foreign power, not only with all the force that could be raised within these islands but also with the whole strength of his other friends and servants whose assistance he also promised to afford in case the King of Norway shall think fit to attack any foreign state or kingdom.

3rd. Not to build any castles or fortalices in the Isles without the King's consent.

4th. To protect all the inhabitants in their privileges and immunities, their laws and liberties.

5th. Not to sell or impignorate the Earldom or any part of it.

6th. To be subject to the Laws of Norway and to attend upon the person of the said King when required, either to give him council in general assemblies or assist him in his wars.

7th. To enter into no private compact with the Bishop of Orkney without consent of the King.

8th. To resign the said Earldom into the hands of the said King and his heirs in case the said Henry, Earl of Orkney, should die without heirs male of his own body; and that this issue though male should not enter to the pessession without the consent of the king.

9th. To pay to the said King at Tunisberg at the feast of Martinmas (then next) 1000 Nobles of Gold, English money.

And lastly. To prevail with his cousin Malis Spere and Alexander de Ord to give up all their pretensions to the said Earldom and Isles.

For implementing this obligation, William, Bishop of St. Andrews, and several other Scottish Nobility and Gentry became bound as cautioners. And it was agreed that hostages should remain in Norway as named in the obligation. All these particulars mark the species of holding by which Orkney was enjoyed by Earl Henry Sinclair.

There is likewise extant an obligation * by the same Henry dated at St. Andrews in which he binds himself neither to alienate nor pawn the Earldom of Orkney without the King of Norway's consent.

A.D.1383 was remarkable for the death of William, Bishop of Orkney, who was murdered but by whom or for what reason the Norwegian annals do not say.

In the year 1388 we find Henry St. Clare as Earl of Orkney, next to the Archbishop and before all the other bishops and senators of the Kingdom of Norway, subscribing to a Recognition of Eiric of Pomerania, whom they unanimously owned to be the true and lawful heir of the Crown and Kingdom of Norway.

Next year this Recognition was confirmed in a convention of the States, where Henry Earl of Orkney was present who afterwards, A.D. 1391, put his cousin Malis Spere to death with seven others in Shetland, his other companions escaping to Norway. What the reason of this murder was is not told, probably his attempting to interfere with Henry in the Earldom.

A.D. 1394 Henry, Bishop of Orkney, appeared in Norway amongst the other clergy of that Kingdom.

Henry St. Clare, first Earl of that name of Orkney, is said to have been first married to a daughter of the King of Denmark by whom he had no issue and afterwards to Jean, daughter of Walter Halyburton, Lord of Dirleton, by whom he had a son Henry who succeeded his father, who seems to have died soon after the murder of Malis Spere.

It is to be supposed that Henry the second was soon after put in possession of the Earldom of Orkney, as we find John St. Clare A.D.

1418 did homage to Eiric of Pomerania, probably in Henry's name as Commissioner for that effect.

A.D. 1405 Henry the 2nd. Earl of Orkney, as Admiral of Scotland, was sent to attend Prince James in France, was taken prisoner with him by the English and carried to London. He died A.D. 1420 leaving a son William who succeeded him in the Earldom of Orkney and is named A.D.1421 as one of the hostages proposed to be given for the ransom of King James.

It would appear that William had made no application to the King of Norway for a renewal of the investiture of Orkney since the death of his father, the possession therefore of that Earldom, according to the natural condition of the holding and the express stipulation of the grant in favour of King William's grandfather, reverted to the Superior, the King of Norway. Accordingly we find Eiric A.D. 1422 committed the Government of the Earldom to Thomas the Bishop not, according to the Bishop's account, in lieu of any debt or pledge but as feudal Governor of the Castle of Kirkwall and the whole country. In his letters to the King, he promises to govern the people with equity and according to the Laws, to maintain peace in the islands and to deliver up the castle of Kirkall and the County at the King's pleasure or to his lawful successors.

Next year the administration was committed to a Scottish Gentleman called David Meyner or Menzies of Weem, Bishop Thomas de Tholack and Walter Fraser being his cautioners. The nature of this grant may be seen from David's letter of acceptance*. Suffice it to say that he made very a bad use of his power and, on a complaont from the inhabitants consisting of no less that thirty-five articles of charge*, was turned out and, A.D. 1427, Bishop Thomas de Tholack was again reinstated in the Government of the Earldom as may be seen in his obligatory letter to the king.*

It is something singular nor is there any reason condescended on for William St. Clare's having so long delayed applying to the Crown of Norway after his father's death, for a renewal of the investiture he was entitled to, of the Earldom of Orkney. But it appears, that in the interim, his right thereto was not quite overlooked, it being one of the articles against David Menzies of Weem that he seized some rents to his own use that belonged to the Earl and had refused to append the public Seal to the proof the Earl had brought for instructing his propinquity and right to the succession of that Earldom. For a commission had been granted by Eiric, King of Norway, to the Bishop of Orkney and others of the Clergy, to inspect the archives and public records of the country in order to show the Earl's right and hereditary title to the Earldom. In answer to this the Bishop, Clergy and other representatives of the People of Orkney wrote the famous letter or Act of State preserved by Wallace and, from his book, copied into our Appendix in which they enumerate all the Earls of Orkney from Rognvald the first Norwegian Earl in Harald Harfagre's time down to William St. Clare A.D. 1403. Long afterwards in the year 1434 William obtained the investiture of Orkney on the same terms it had been granted to his Grandfather Henry*.

The most famous witnesses and Cautioners on this occasion Henry, Bishop of Aberdeen; Columba and Robert, two other Bishops; Archibald, Earl of Douglas; William, Earl of Angus and Geore, Earl of March; Sir William Corke or Gortucke and Sir Alexander Ramsey, Knight with John Sinclair and Andrew Keith, Esquires.

Several gentlemen were likewise sent as hostages to Norway and William promised to transmit copies of his obligatory letters properly attested to the chief clergy in Norway and Orkney, to be kept among their archives.

A.D. 1456 & 57. The not payment of the Annual of Norway, which indeed seems never to have been regularly paid, occasioned first a dryness and afterwards put on all the appearances of an open rupture but at length was settled by the mediation of Charles, King of Farnce, who on this occasion acted the part of Mediator between the contending powers of Scotland and Norway.

This dispute was renewed the years following, till at length it was finally taken away by a proposal Charles made of a match between James, afterwards the 3rd. of Scotland, and Margaret, only daughter of Christian, the 1st. of Denmark and Norway, which was concluded A.D. 1468 on the following terms. 1st. That the annual of Norway should be for ever remitted and discharged. 2nd. That King Christian should give 60,000 florins of the Rhine for his daughter's portion, whereof 10,000 should be paid before her departure from Denmark and the Islands of Orkney should be made over to the Crown of Scotland by way of pledge for security of the remainder with this express provision ,that they should return to Norway after complete payment of the whole sum. 3rd. That King James should, in case of his death before the said Margaret his spouse, leave her in possession of the palace of Linlithgow and the Castle of Down in Monteith, with all their appertenances and the third part of the ordinary revenues of the Crown to be enjoyed by her during her life, if she should choose to reside in Scotland. But, 4th. If she rather inclined to return to Denmark, that in lieu of the said Liferent, Place and Castle, she should accept of 120,000 Florins of the Rhine, from which sum the 50,000 due as the remainder of her portion being deducted and allowed, the Islands of Orkney should be re-annexed to the Crown of Norway as before. 5th. That in no case should she be allowed to marry with the King of England or with any subject within the jurisdiction of that Kingdom. Vide the Marriage.*

These articles were all agreed to but Christian, sometime after engaging in a war with the Swedes, found it inconvenient for him to pay the 10,000 florins when due, he therefore entreated that the Scots would be satisfied with the present payment of 2,000 and offered the Islands of Shetland to be held of the Crown of Scotland as those of Orkney, by way of pledge till the remaining 8,000 florins should be paid. This was agreed to at Copenhagen by the Scottish Commissioners upon the 10th. May 1469 and, in the month of July, the Princess arrived at Leith when her marriage was solemnized with magnificene and solemnity.

A.D. 1462 William, Bishop of Orkney, took an oath of allegiance to Christian the 1st. and his Queen Dorethea.*

A.D. 1463 Buchanan takes notice of a Robert, Earl of Orkney, probably the son of William Sinclair, perhaps entitled Earl in his father's lifetime. Possibly this may be the person of whom Torfaeus writes: A.D. 1467 William, Bishop of Orkney, was seized by the Earl's son and thrown in prison but afterwards set free by the mediation of Christian 1st. with the King of Scotland, whose subject the Earl's son was.

A.D. 1466 Christian wrote to the supreme Judge, ordering him to repair to Norway to confer with him about the best methods of collecting the Orkney tribute.

We have now seen above, the Norwegian account of the transaction by which King James the Third got possession of the Orkney and Shetland isles, it will therefore be necesary to take a short view of the Scottish account.

Boece's Continuator, after a particular account of the embassy, the bringing home of the Queen and her subsequent marriage, goes on to tell us that "to the north in the Deucaledonian Ocean lie the

Orkney isles near the Scottish shore, of which 28 are now inhabited and, beyond the Orkneys towards Norway, the Shetlands, eighteen in number which are inhabited and now belong to Scotland. In former ages there were great disputes about these isles between the Scots and Danes though they were possessed by the latter. At length they were given up by Christian, King of Danemark, on the occasion of a marriage between his daughter Margaret and King James of Scotland, aye and until he or his successors should pay the sum of 50,000 Florins of the Rhine yet unpaid of his daughter Margaret's portion. "For thus," says the writer, "I have seen it stipulated in the Marriage Contract between Margaret of Norway and James the 3rd. of Scotland, which was ruled with the Seal of each Kingdom A.D. 1468."

"But afterwards when Margaret brought forth her eldest son James, Prince of Scotland, her father, the King of Danemark, for joy of this event, renounced all claims for ever to the Orkney and Shetland isles and others which he had formerly pledged to Scotland on his daughter's marriage and, I have heard, that the instrument of resignation is yet preserved among the archives of the Kingdom of Scotland" *

On this improbable account Torfaeus justly animadverts that, if such a renunciation had taken place and the public documents concerning it had been able to be found, they certainly would have been long ago produced in answer to the repeated claims the Danes have made concerning these Isles.

Buchanan is quite uncertain as to the matter and says, "There are some who write they were given up as a dowry on the marriage with a saving of privileges and private property; others that they were pawned until the portion was paid but afterward, on the birth of a son, given up by the King of Danemark in perpetuity."

Chapter 21

It will now be necessary to examine a little more narrowly into what the Kings of Norway disposed of to the St. Clare family and what they afterwards had in their power to pledge to the Crown of Scotland.

By the marriage treaty James acquired a right from Norway "ad omnes et singularas terras nostras Insularum Orcadensium cum omnibus et singulis juribus serviciis ac justis suis pertinentiis nobis regali jure et praedecessoribus nostris Norvegiae Regibus spectantibus sui quovis modo spectare valentibus tenendas et habendas totas et integra terras nostras Orcadensium praedictarum una cum omnibus et singulis Custumis, proficuis, libertatibus, commoditatibus, ac allis justis pertinentiis quibus cunque tam nominatis tam innominatis ad praedictas terras spectantibus - donec et quousque per nos - praefato Jacobo - de summa quinquaginta millia florenorum Rainensium restantium de parte dotis - fuerit integralite satisfactum et persolutum cum effectu."

But the property of the Earldom had long ago been given away by Christian's predecessor, Haco, in favour of the St. Clare family, which none of the Norwegian Kings resumed but in case of the failure of an heir or when that heir failed to renew his investiture as in the case of William, now Earl. William had been afterwards invested and entered into the possession of the Earldom, therefore it seems clear Christian had no right to pledge anything but the Superiority and right of Investiture to the Earldom and the absolute property remained in the person of William, Earl of Orkney, which by the original obligation and his renewal of this, he could neither alienate nor pledge without the consent of his superior. Now, when by the marriage treaty the Kings of Norway had divested themselves of the Superiority of this Earldom and conveyed it to the King of Scotland, thus substituting him in their place during the not redemption, their consent was no longer necessary or essential to render any alienation valid, it was the consent of the King of Scotland now the Superior. Accordingly James, having by means of the marriage treaty acquired a right to the Superioity of the aforesaid Earldom, entered into a treaty and Transaction with William St. Clare the Earl in the year 1471 by which, in consideration of certain lands granted to him by the King, viz.the lands and Castle of Ravenscraig, the lands of Wilton and the lands of Carbery with a pension of 40 marks during his life, he made over to the King all the right and property he had to the Earldom of Orkney. This transaction is evident from the Act of Parliament 16th May 1471 preserved in the collection said to be Lord Haddington's.*

At no other time could the Earl of Orkney have legally transferred his right to the King of Scotland but an alienation of it to him, while he stood possessed of the Superiority, was unquestionably legal and valid in consequence, according to the principles of the feudal system by whch most part of Europe and these countries in particular were governed at that period.

In consequence of the Earl's thus transacting with the King there was passed an Act of Parliament dated 20th. February 1471 by which the Earldom of Orkney and the Lordship of Shetland is annexed to the Crown, not to be given away unless to one of the King's sons of lawful bed.*

The ignorance of this transaction between the King and the Earl of Okney attested above, has misled all our Antiquaries. Most of them mention the Orkneys falling to the Crown by forfeiture, whereas William St. Clare, Earl of Orkney, was not forfeited, even according to Abercrombie's account of the matter, till the year 1477 and it is evident from Pubic deeds that before that period he is only designed Earl of Caithness, a demonstration that he was then divested of Orkney.

Secondly, Abercrombie is in a mistake in saying that William St. Clare, Earl of Orkney and Caithness, was forfeited for maintainig the Castle of Crichton against the King, for William St. Clare was never possessed of Crichton. But Wiliam, Lord Crichton, was forfeited for defending the Castle against His Majesty in the year 1483, the process of forfeiture being extant in Lord Haddington's collections, whereby it appears that he was one of the Duke of Albany's party and forfeited along with him. Abercrombie's mistake in this matter has probably proceeded upon this erroneous supposition that the Earldom of Caithness, which belonged to the Crichtons, had been given to William St. Clare, Earl of Orkney, that the Castle of Crichton had been granted at the same time but this was not the case. Besides Abercrombie's account cannot be true for it appears that the Duke of Albany and his adherents were not forfeited, as before observed, till the year 1483, whereas William St. Clare died before the year 1481, as appears by a contract executed between his sons William St. Clare, th eldest son, with Henry his son on the one part and Sir Olave St. Clare on the other part, upon the 9th. of February of that year. This contract is mentioned by Abercrombie himself whereby Sir Oliver, the youngest son, resigns and gives over to the said William, the eldest son and heir of the deseased William St. Clare, Earl of Caithness, and Henry St. Clare,his eldest, the Lands of Cousland, Dysart and Ravenscraig and on the other hand the said William St. Clare and his son and apparent heir Henry make over in the same manner to Sir Oliver and his heirs all right, title and claim of right which they may have to the lands of Roslin, Pentland and Pentland Muir, Morton and Mortonhall etc.

After the aforesaid contract executed between King James and King Christian of Denmark and the above transaction between him and the Earl of Orkney and Caithness, the Kings of Scotland came to have the absolute and irredeemable right to the property of the Earldom of Orkney and to the superiority thereof during the not redemption, for upon redemption the King of Norway had no further claim but to the superiority only. Accordingly, by the above quoted act, the property was annexed to the Crown of Scotland.

Although the property of the Earldom of Orkney was sold by the St. Clare family, the King did not immediately thereupon enter into full possession. In these days it was usual and customary when any of the great Barons, for political reasons, was obliged to part with his property to the Crown, to make matters more easy he was allowed to retain the possession under a Tack, by which means he in some means preserved his influence over the men of the Country. Accordingly by an unprinted act of King James the 4th., A.D. 1489, the Lord St. Clare is appointed one of the Commissioners for collecting the King's rents in Orkney and Shetland and, it is more then probable, that such Collectors for the King in those days were not subjected to a very strict account. In the year 1501 likewise Lord St. Clare procured a Tack of the Earldom of Orkney for 19 years for payment of 650 merks Scots yearly rent.

A few years after the expiration of this lease, viz. in the year 1530, King James the 5th.was prevailed on, notwithstanding the above annexation, to grant these islands to his natural brother James, Earl of Moray, and heirs male of his body, in fee, with a clause of return to the Crown, under which it was possessed down to the year 1540. This step of the King's gave great offence to the Orkneymen and, on the Earl of Caithness and Lord Sinclair's coming over to take possession, they rose in arms and, on encountering the Earl at a place called Wasdale in Firth parish, drove him and his men along by Summerdale in Stenness, totally routed them, killed the Earl with 300 (according to Wallace) of his men and took Lord Sinclair, with the remainder, prisoners. To this day there are of the corpses of the slain found well preserved in the mosses through which the Caithness men were pursued, particularly two years ago one was found in digging peats with the clothes on and well preserved by the influence of the styptic waters.

The consequence of this rencounter was a visit of James the 5th. to Orkney where he composed all these broils, seized some of the ringleaders in the fray, placed garrisons in the Earl's and Bishop's castles but at last respited the chief, Edward Sinclair of Strome, with thirty of the most noted of his accomplices as may be seen from in a copy of the original parchment.*

A.D. 1540 these islands were once more annexed to the Crown by Act 84th. (part 6th.) of that year, in which state they continued till A.D. 1565, when Mary Queen of Scots granted these Islands to her natural brother Robert Stewart and his heirs male. This grant however seems to have been of short duration for James, Earl of Bothwell, was, in 1567, created Duke of Orkney but, his misfortunes and forfeiture following soon after, Lord Robert Stewart A.D. 1521 obtained a renewal of his former grant from King James the 6th,, together with the Titles and Honours of Earl of Orkney and a vast extent of power which, upon his coming to this remote corner, he made very bad use of.

Earl Robert, before his obtaining the grant of Orkney, had been provided to the Abbacy of Holyroodhouse but, upon his taking place, he made an exchange of that with Adam Bothwell for the Bishopric of Orkney and thus became sole Lord of the Islands.

On Robert's coming to settle in Orkney, he soon gave the inhabitants specimens of his disposition to oppression and extortion which afterwards, on a complaint of the inhabittants, brought him into disgrace and occasioned a recall of the Grant; James, pretending as it was made in his minority, to do so, in consequence of his general revocation in Parliament 1587, granted these islands anew to Sir John Maitland of Thirlstane, Chancellor and Sir Luddowick Ballenden, Lord Justice Clerk, jointly with the customs, tolls of ships, offices of

Sheriffship and Justiciary and all other particulars accruing from thence.

At length, upon a resignation of these Grantees, King James once more ratified the former grants in favour of his natural uncle Robert, Earl of Orkney, and, failing his heirs male, to the Duke of Lennox and his heirs, upon payment of 3000 merks of feu and 100 merks of augumentation.

To Robert, Earl of Orkney, succeeded his son Patrick, who trod in his father's steps and even out did him in his oppressive behaviour. On a charge consisting of many articles he was found guilty of high treason and beheaded at Edinburgh on the 6th. day of February 1614.

All who speak of Earl Patrick give him an excessive bad character, Spottswood says, "This Nobleman having undone his estate by riot and prodigality did seek by unlawful shifts to repair the same, making unjust acts in his courts and exacting penalties for the Breach thereof. If any man was tried to have concealed anything that might infer a pecuniary mulct and bring profit to the Earl, his lands and goods were declared confiscated. Or if any man did sue for Justice before any other judge than his Deputies upon whatsoever occasion, they should forfeit their movables and, which of all his Acts was the most inhumane, he ordained that if any man was tried to supply or give relief unto ships or any vessels distressed by tempest, the same shall be punished in his person and fined at the Earl's pleasure."

They tell a story of this Earl that, intending to have pluck at a man (Slater of Burness) who held a small estate on the Mainland, he went to him and demanded in a most authoritative manner "By what right he held his land". The man very probably understood his meaning and, on pretence of bringing his rights, disappeared but, in a little time, returning with a two-handed sword in both hands, told him "My Lord I am an Udal Man and this is my charter, by this I got my land and by this I defend it". The Earl it seems had no inclination to quarrel such a well constituted right and immediately retired.

The monument of the Stewart family yet to be seen in Orkney are the Palace of Birsa, the wings and front of which were built by Robert, Earl of Orkney, adding these to what remained of the St. Clare more ancient Castle there. The inscription above the gate, I am told, was carried off for its singularity by James, Earl of Morton. It runs thus:

Dominus Robertus Stuartus Filius Jacobi quinti Rex Scotorum hoc opus instruxit.

The motto assumed by Earl Robert yet to be seen on the Earl's seat in the Church of Kirkwall "Sic fuit est et erit", sufficiently shews without any further comment the temper of the man.

In building his castle at Birsa he assessed the whole country both in money, victuals and personal services which bore hard on the poor inhabitants and for which his memory is, by tradition, execrated even to this day.

Nor did his son Earl Patrick change his method in his building the Castle of Scalloway in Shetland, where he drove in the inhabitants like slaves, imposed a tax on every ox and sheep in the country which is yet continued under the name of Ox and Sheep-penny to be paid to this day.

The Palace of Kirkwall was likewise built by Earl Patrick and is by far the handomer structure than Scalloway.

After the death of Earl Patrick a grant of the revenues of Orkney was made to Sir James Stewart of Lillyth, afterwards Lord Ochiltree, in the quality of a Farmer General to whom succeded A.D. 1624 Sir George Hay of Kinfauns, another needy courtier, with the office of Heritable Steward over the islands.

A.D. 1643 Charles 1 made a grant of the Earldom of Orkney and the Lordship of Shetland with the pertinents, to William, Earl of Morton, redeemeable upon the payment of £30,000 Sterling which, being afterwards annuled by the general revocation of Charles the Second A.D, 1662, a new mortgage of the same kind was obtained by George, Viscount Grandison, in trust for the Earl of Morton, his use, as the involved situation of the then Earl William's affairs rendered it improper to make the grant directly to himself.

This last grant was likewise redeemable upon paying the original sum of £30,000 due by Government to the family of Morton.

It was about this time that Oliver's soldiers overran these isles, dispossessed the Earl of Morton and kept the isles under awe to the Government. While here, they erected a fort now called the Mount of Kirkwall, one of the guns is yet to be seen on the Air, having the Arms of the Commonwealth on it.

Whatever mischief these soldiers might have done here, they did in many particulars much good. To them we owe many improvements not known heretofore, particularly the use of Marle as measure which they introduced and which has partially taken place ever since.

A.D. 1669 A reduction of all the family of Morton's right to the Isles of Orkney and Shetland was brought at the instance of Sir John Nisbet of Dirleton, then His Majesty's Advocate, and in February of that year the Earl, Lord Dalkeith, Viscount Grandison and others were divested of that Earldom which was again strictly annexed to the Crown "to remain inseperably with the same in all time coming". By the same act the office of Sheriffship is supressed and the isles are erected into a Stewartry, with a saving of his privileges to the Bishop of Orkney.

From 1559 the Orkneys were let to a new race of farmers who leased them as they bid highest at the Exchequer. These leases continued only from three to five years and indeed these were too long, for these tax-gatherers seemed to be unanimous in plundering the poor vassals, so that from theAct of Annexation to when Dr. Wallace wrote, the Annual reddendum was sunk from near £3,500 to £1,800 Sterling.

In Queen Anne's reign, the Earl of Morton obtained a new grant of the Isles A.D. 1707, but this also subject to redemption upon the payment of £30,000 Sterling and A.D. 1743 James, Earl of Morton, obtained the Act of Parliament whereby the above mentioned faculty of redemption is discharged and, upon this, a charter was passed under the great Seal of the Earldom of Orkney and Lordship of Shetland, in favour of the above James, Earl of Morton, who A.D. 1766 sold these islands and all his interest there for the sum of £63,000 Sterling to Sir Laurence Dundas, Baronet of Kerse, in whose hands they now continue.

Index

Bane, Donald (see Donald Bane, King of Scotland) 114, 192, 201, 205, 315

Bard, friend of Swein Asliefson 281

Bartholinus 149

Beatrix, daughter of King Malcolm 2nd

Bede, Venerable 101

Belius, King of Norway 110

Bellus, see also Belius, King of Norway 96

Bellenden, Sir Luddowick 324

Belus, Pictish King in Orkney 96

Benedict 272

Bergfin, a Shetland man 213

Biarn, Bishop of Orkney 252, 291, 297, 298, 299

Biarn, son of Grimkell 259, 276

Biordn 272

Blain, 'King' of Dansay Castle 233, 235

Boece 197, 294-296, 300, 310, 319, 320

Boethius, see Boece also, 103, 108, 111, 296

Bothwell, Adam, Bishop of Orkney 324

Bothwell, James, Earl of 324

Borgar 245

Botolf Bulga, poet 276

Brian Bore, Irish King 143, 144, 146, 148, 154, 155, 162, 163, 201

Briostreip, see also Swein 230, 231, 234, 235, 236

Broder, pirate 144, 145, 148

Bruce, Robert the 313, 314

Brus, Earl of Orkney 165, 166, 169, 170, 173-176, 178, 185, 226

Brynolf, 220, 223, 224, 225, 246, 311

Buchanan, George, historian, 5, 10, 11, 13, 29, 36, 44, 46, 49, 55, 62, 78, 95, 97-102, 104, 111, 197, 220, 294-296, 300, 310, 319, 320

Budstikke 132

C

Caesar, Julius 101, 102

Camden, historian 206

Canmore, Malcolm 114, see also Malcolm Canmore, King of Scotland

Canute, King of England, see also Knut

Caractacus, Scottish Leader 97

Cecilia, sister of St. Magnus 199

Charles 1st, King of England 326

Charles 2nd, King of England 326

Charles the Simple, King of France 119

Charles, King of France 318

Charles, Scottish chieftain, see also Karl

Christian 1st, King of Denmark 318-320, 323

Christod, brother of King Harald 4th 227

Columba, Saint 307

Corke, Sir William 318

Cromwell, Oliver 326

Claudius, Roman Emperor 95, 107, 110

Crichton, William, Lord 322

Cunar, friend of Kol 226

D

Dagfin son of Laudver 237, 239, 240

Appendix

A CHRONOLOGICAL Sketch of the HISTORY of the ORKNEYS from the first accounts of their becoming a fief of the Kingdom of Norway

Anno 875

Rognvaldus Mariae comes* got the Investiture of the Orkneys and Zetland from Harald Haragre, King of Norway, who had conquered them and subdued the ancient to be held of him for homage and fealty. Rognvaldus, returning to Norway with Harald, resigned the Orkneys to his brother, Sigurdus, who obtained from Harald a renewal of the investiture. Sigurdus was succeeded by his son Guttermus who survived him but a year and died without issue. After his death Einar the youngest son of Rognvaldus got the Orkneys and Zetland. He was surnamed Turfei because he taught the inhabitants of Orkney to use dried earth and moss for firing.

893

Rognvaldus was killed by Haldanus and Gudrodus, two of Harald's sons. Einar, in revenge of his murder, put Haldanus to death.

Harald exacted sixty pounds of gold as the composition of his son's death and obliged the inhabitants of Orkney as well as Einar their Lord to make payment of it to him.

[On this occasion it is said by Torfaeus p.20 that the people of Orkney gave up the possession of the land to the Earl on condition that he would undertake for the payment of the whole sum. The event plainly shows that they were all his Vassals for we know that according to the ideas of the feudal law when it obtained in its greatest strictness, the rear or sub vassals were liable to the Supreme Lord for every fine or payment imposed upon the immediate Mesne Vassal and hence it easy to account for their giving up the possession of their lands because the sum imposed has probably

---

* Comes was a word of that age and denoted an office of dignity the exercise of which was connected to the use of the land. After Menevensis who wrote in the 9th century and uses it often. V. Spelmare, V.Comes.

been nearly equal, according to the rate of money at that time, to the full value of the Subaltern Rights.]

Einar was succeeded by his son Thorfinnus, to whom succeeded his son, Hlodverus or Ludevrius and to him Sigurdus, his son.

998

Olafus, King of Norway, claimed the sovereignty of Orkney and obliged Sugurdus to do him homage which had been for some years neglected and also obliged him and the inhabitants of Orkney to turn Christians. It is related of Sigurdus that he gave the Orkneses the the possession of the lands which had been given up to Einar, upon condition that they should accompany him in an expedition he made against Scotland. which is no obscure proof of the land being held by a military tenure.

[*Inde constat,* says Torfaeus, *non ibi magis quasalibi secuisse principibus Cives ad miletium extra patria fines 1/2rp libitu cogere. P. 27.* A reflection which could only be dictated by the Ideas of the feudal system. It was a principle of the feudal system that every man behoved to be a soldier within his own country but that the sovereign had no power to oblige him to fight out of it and this idea seems peculiar to a feudal government.]

1014

Sigurdus died leaving four sons. The right of primogeniture had not then taken place and the Islands of Orkney and Zetland were divided amongst the three eldest. Thorfinnus the youngest, the only son of Sigurdus by the daughter of Malcolm King of Scotland, had for his share the Earldom of Caithness which his father possessed in Scotland. Upon the death of Sumarled the eldest brother, Thorfinnus claimed a right in his succession in which at last by the moderation of Brusius, the third bother unwilling to engage in war, he prevailed. Einar, the second son, was killed by Thorkill a powerful man in Orkney. S dispute then arose with regard to the succession of his share, both brothers had recourse to the King of Norway and did homage to him for the lands they already held in Orkney. The King adjudged Einar's share to himself as the satisfaction or assythment for the death of his subject Eiwind whom Einar had slain, and made Brusius Governor of that portion of the Islands. The King also composed the differences that subsisted betwixt Thorkill and them on account of Einar's death. Einar's life was reckoned equal to that of three Barons and the same satisfaction paid for it. Upon th death of Brusius, Thorfinnus seized the whole Earldom of Orkney and Rognvaldus, the son of Brusius, was killed in attempting to take possession of his father's share.

1046

Thorfinnus was reconciled to the King of Norway and is said to have afterwards undertaken a journey to Rome to obtain remission of his sins.

1064

Thorfinnus died and his son Erbisus* succeeded. To Erbisus succeeded Erlandus and Paulus his sons.

*This name is not recorded elsewhere and Thorfin's sons are usually given as Erland and Paul – Ed.

1066

They attended Harald the Stout, King of Norway, in his expedition against England in which he lost his life at the Battle of Stamford Bridge.

1092

Magnus Barefoot, King of Norway, grandson of Harald reduced the Orkneys under his obedience and sent Paulus and Erlandus cpatives to Norway. He conquered also the Hebude and Mann and made his son Sigurdus King of the Western Isles

1103

Magnus killed in an expedition against Ireland.

1104

The isles of Orkney and Zetland returned to their former condition, the sons of Magnus restoring the possession of them to Haco, the son of Paulus, and Magnus, the son Erlandus.

1110

Magnus was slain by Haco. It is this Magnus who was afterwards canonized and became the Tutelar Saint of Orkney. About this time the Bishopric of Orkney was first erected. The sons of Haco were Harald and Paulus who both succeeded to Orkney but Caithness was conferred by the King of Scotland on Harald the eldest.

The right of primogeniture being then established in Scotland. Harald died leaving a son Erlandus who was brought up in Caithness.

1130

Rognvaldus, the nephew of St. Magnus by his sister, and Grandchild of Erlandus obtained from Sigurdus, King of Norway, the investiture of the half of Orkney in right of his uncle, the first instance of succession by the female line being admitted. He was at first repulsed by Paulus but, afterwards returning with a greater force, the possession of his share was yielded to him. Paulus made over his right to his sister's son Harald who was admitted by Rognvaldus to a share of the Orrkneys.

Rognvaldus in performance of a vow he had made to St. Magnus began to build a very large Cathedral at Kirkwall but not having money sufficient for so great an undertaking he sold to the Orknese the right of their reliefs for ever, upon condition that each plough of land should pay a merk.

1154

Rognvaldus made an expedition to the Holy Land. During his absence Erlandus, son of Harald, who was bred up in Caithness laid claim to the half of the Orkneys, as derived to him from his father, and obtained the investiture of it from Eystenus, King of Norway.

1156

Rognvaldus upon his return joined himself to Harald and attacked Erlandus who had got possession of a part of Orkney, defeated him in Battle and killed him.

1158

Rognvaldus was killed by Thorbiorn, a powerful man, in Caithness and left only a grandson by a daughter, called Harald. This Harald lay claim to the accession of his Grandfather and obtained the investiture of his share both of Orkney and Caithness from the Kings of Norway and Scotland. Harald the elder opposed his taking possession, vanquished and killed him. William, King of Scotland, then seized the possession of Caithness and made war upon Harald.

1188

A peace was made betwixt Harald and the King of Scotland by which the Earldom of Caithness was granted to him of new but a fourth part given to the King's use.

1192

Sigurdus, son of Magnus King of Norway, who was dethroned and killed by Swerir, fled to the Orkneys and by the assistance of Harald raised there a great army with which he returned to Norway and after having carried on a war against Swerir for some time was at last defeated and slain.

Harald to appease Swerir, incensed at the aid he had given to Sigurdus, was forced to make a voyage to Norway and to submit to his clemency, Swerir deprived him of Zetland and of the half of the Rent of the Earldom of Orkney. Swerir dying soon afterwards, Harald recovered all that had been taken from him, and killed those who had been appointed to collect for the king's use the half of the rents of Orkney.

1206

Harald died and was succeeded by his sons David and John.

1210

The Earls of Orkney were again obliged to submit to the conditions which had been imposed upon them by Swerir.

1215

David died and John was the sole heir.

1222

Adam, Bishop of Orkney, was burnt to death by the inhabitants incensed at his severity and oppression in the exaction of Tythes. Alexander, King of Scotland, revenged his death by inflicting the severest punishment on his murderers.

[This circumstance is a little singular, for there is no other part of the history that shows that the King of Scotland raised any dominion over Orkney at this time, the case must have been either that the Bishop's murderers were found in Caithness or that at this time the Earl of Orkney, being at variance with his sovereign the King of Norway, had put himself under the protection of Alexander which the next article renders most probable.]

1225

The Earl of Orkney made a voyage to Norway and made up the differences which subsisted betwixt the King and him.

1231

John, Earl of Orkney, was killed and was succeeded by his son Magnus.

1239

Magnus died succeeded by his son, Gilbert.

1256

Gilbert died succeeded by his son Magnus the second.

1263

Magnus attended Haco, King of Norway, in an expedition which he had made against the Western Isles and Scotland. Haco received a great overthrow at the battle of Largs and, returning to Orkney after his defeat, died at Kirkwall.

1266

Magnus, the son of Haco, who succeeded his father, concluded a peace with Alexander, King of Scotland, by which he yielded to him the Hebridae and Mann for the payment of 4000 merks silver and 100 merks yearly and it was agreed that Alexander's daughter, Margaret, should be married to Magnus' son.

1271

Magnus earl of Orkney died.

1276

Magnus, his third son, obtained the renewal of the investiture of Orkney. To this Magnus succeeded another Magnus who died without issue and a John, who upon his death, succeeded to the entire possession of Orkney and Caithness.

1300

John was married to the daughter of Eric, King of Norway.

1308

Haco, King of Norway, abolished the titles of Earls and Barons in his kingdom excepting those of the King's sons and the Earls of Orkney. John was succeeded by a Magnus, the fifth of that name.

1320

Magnus, Earl of Orkney and Caithness, is one of the nobles who subscribes the famous letter wrote by the Scotch Barons to the Pope. In this Earl the male line of the ancient Earls of Orkney failed and the succession was carried by his female descendants into Scotch families. When Magnus died is uncertain but we know that he left only a daughter who was married to the Earl of Strathern in Scotland. Torfaeus mentions an Earl of Orkney of the name of Argisel in 1343 and another of the name of Eringislus in the year 1357, of whose rights or descent we know nothing further, neither are they mentioned in the most authentic record which is extant with regard to the succession of this Earldom.

1357

It appears that the King of Norway had taken into his own hands the possession of the Earldom of Orkney (which by feudal law he was entitled as superior to do, until some heir of the last Earl had obtained from him the investiture) and therefore there is a claim made in the name of Malisius Conda called heir of the Earldom of Orkney by a Scotch nobleman designated Duncan filius Andriae and this claim is notified to the inhabitants of Orkney that they should not suffer the rents to be carried out of the country till he had obtained the investiture. It seems a very probable conjecture that this Malisius was the grandson of Magnus by his daughter the Countess of Strathern and we knew that Malius, Earl of Strathern, succeeded Magnus, earl of Orkney and Caithness, his Grandfather. The Earl of Strathern had only daughters of his first marriage with a daughter of the Earl of Monteith. He had one daughter Matilda married to a Scotch nobleman, Melandus de Ard. Of his second marriage to a daughter of the Earl of Ross he had four daughters, the eldest was married to William St. Clare, Lord of Roslin; the second to Ginsell de Swethrick; the third to Gothredius le Sperre; the fourth had no issue. [Besides these the Scotch historians mention a daughter who was Countess of Strathern and married the Earl of Warren in England]. Alexander de Ard, son of the eldest daughter, had the Earldom of Caithness and some part of the Earldom of Orkney. Caithness he sold to Robert the first of Scotland and his share of Orkney he did not long enjoy.

1369

Henry St.Clare, son of the eldest daughter of the second marriage, claimed the earldom of Orkney and obtained the investiture of it from Haco the 3rd.King of Norway. The right of the dependents by the other sisters was not overlooked for we find that Swethrick, husband of the second daughter of Magnus and Malisius Spere, son of the second daughter are said to have had cerain portions of Orkney, as well as Alexander de Ard.

Swethrick was dead before this claim but the other two Spere and Ard were alive and we find frequent mention of them. (What is the law of Norway with regard to the succession of a dignity when it devolved to daughters, is not easy to know. If it was similar to the old law of Scotland then St Clair had a good title to the dignity as in right of his mother the 2nd daughter, her elder sister having got the Earldom of Caithness for her share).

1375

Alexander de Ard was made Governor of Orkney for a year by the King of Norway.

1379

Henry St. Clare, Lord of Roslin, made a voyage to Norway and obtained the full confirmation of his rights. The ancient Earls of Orkney had only done homage for possession of their fief and performance of Homage of itself implied an obligation to all those services and duties which are incident to a feudal holding. St. Clare was a stranger in the Kingdom of Norway and owed allegiance to another prince, the King of Scotland. He therefore makes a written acknowledgement of his homage and fealty to the King of Norway and, in this deed, enumerates the several duties and services to which he is bound and obliges himself to the performance of each of them. In further security to the King of Norway he also gives hostages and some of the Bishops and Lords of Scotland join as sureties in his obligation.

The services which are enumerated in this obligation are the known and accustomed services incident to a proper military fee, attendance to the King in war or military service; attendance upon the King in peace when summoned *pro consilus impendendis;* that upon his death the lands shall remain in the King's hands and the heir be obliged to pdemand the renewal of his investiture from him (i.e. monentary and relief); that he shall answer in the King of Norway's courts and that he shall not alienate nor impignerate the land without the Kings consent and that, if he failed in any of the conditions, he should forfeit his right. All these conditions were the proper characteristics of a feudal holding at that time. It is worthy of notice here that St. Clare and the other Lords and even the Bishops of St. Andrews and Glasgow, who were his sureties, promise the performance of these conditions upon their honour only (*sub conservationis honoris nostri*) and not upon any religious oath. (This deed which is very well worth perusal is in Torfaeus p.174)

1388

Henry St. Clare, Earl of Orkney, signs a deed with the other great men of Norway acknowledging Eric of Pomerania for successor to the Kingdom.

1391

The Earl of Orkney put to death Malisius de Spere and seven others in Zetalnd. This Henry St. Clare was first married (it is said) to a daughter of the King of Denmark but by her had no issue, his second wife was Jean, daughter of Walter Haliburton, Lord Dirletoun, by whom he had Henry his heir. When he died does not appear but it must have been soon after this for we are told his mother survived him and had the possession of the Orkneys for some time.

1405

Henry the second Earl of Orkney was admiral of Scotland and being sent to attend the prince James (afterwards King James the 1st) to France, was with him taken prisoner and carried to London.

1411

The Earl of Orkney passed over into France along with the Earl of Douglas to assist the French against Henry the 5th of England.

1418

John St. Clare did homage to Eric of Pomerania, King of Norway. (This John St. Clare must have been a relation of the Earl's who did homage in his name. We find a John St. Clare about this time who fought in France and had a considerable command against the Duke of Bedford then Regent for henry the 6th.

1420

Henry, Earl of Orkney, died. He left, by the daughter and heiress of Douglas, Lord of Nithsdale, William his heir.

1421

In a treaty which was begun for the redemption of King James, William, Earl of Orkney, is named as one of the hostages that were proposed to be given for payment of the Ransom. Upon the death of the last Earl of Orkney the possession of the Earldom, according to the natural condition of the holding and also according to the express stipulation made with Henry 1st, Earl of Orkney, reverted to the superior, the King of Norway, until the next heir should demand and obtain a renewal of the investiture. According ly we find that –

1422

The King of Norway gave the government and administration of Orkney to Thomas, Bishop of Orkney.

1423

The Government of Orkney was granted in like manner to David Menzies of Weems who was afterwards removed upon the complaint of the inhabitants.

1427

The Government of Orkney was again given to the Bishop. The Earl of Orkney was, it seems, so much employed elsewhere that he had not yet found leisure to pass over to Norway to obtain an renewal of the investiture of Orkney. It is plain however that his rights all this while was not overlooked for it is one of the articles of Complaint against David Menzies that he had seized to his own use rents that belonged to the Earl and that he had refused the public seal to be appended to the testimonies which the Earl had obtained in proof of the right of succession.

1434

William St. Clare obtained the investiture of Orkney and the same conditions which were made for his grandfather, Henry 1st, are renewed with him. There is a very peculiar record by which William's rights is vouched. It is somewhat of the nature of a retour and proceeds from letters patent from the King of Norway to the clergy and people of Orkney directing them to produce all the evidence they had with regard to William St. Clare's right of succession to the Earldom of Orkney and to report and declare a distinct state of his righ and decent, to the King of Norway. In obedience to these letters, the Bishop, Chapter, Canons, Lawman, the peers and nobles and the people and community of Orkney Declare: 1st that there is a great defect of ancient writings, most of them perished, but that upon inspection of those that remained and by diligent enquiry, they find that William St Clare is the lineal and sole heir of the Earls of Orkney, all other descendents being dead and they declare the course of decent from the end of the 9th century. Amongst the papers to which they refer are particularly mentioned infeudations by the Earl of Orkney, another certain evidence of the feudal law having prevailed in Orkney. These infeudations have probably been Grants of lands to religious uses.

(A copy of this record is preserved in Wallace's description of Orkney. Lond. Edit. 1700, though there must be an error in the date as it is here marked 1403 for Henry, earl of Orkney, father of William died only in 1420, probably it should be 1430. Abercrombie V.2d. p.403 says that he himself had the manuscript of this record.)

1454

William, Earl of Orkney, was very powerful in Scotland, he had followed the King's party against his own nephew, the Earl of Douglas. He was this year made chancellor.

1457

The Earl of Orkney got a grant of the Earldom of Caithness which had been last possessed by Crichton in compensation of his claim to his mother's inheritance of the Lordship of Nithsdale which was probably given at this time to the Lord Maxwell who had married the only daughter of Crichton.

1468-9

A match was concluded betwixt Margaret of Denmark and King James the 3rd of Scotland. The Princess of Denmark's portion was 60,000 florins, 10,000 of which were immediately paid and in security of the remainder the King of Denmark and Norway (which long before that were united into one monarchy) assigned to the King of Scotland his rights of Sovereignty in the isles of Orkney and Zetland and all rights services etc appertaining to it redeemable always upon payment of the 50,000 florins.

1471

The King of Scotland having acquired the right to the sovereignty of the Earldom of Orkney made a transaction with the Earl of Orkney by which he in consideration of certain lands viz. The Castle of Ravenscraig, the lands of Wiltoun and the lands of Carberry, with a pension of 40 marks during his life, made over to the King the property of the Earldom of Orkney. This transaction is very memorable because we see here a clear foundation f the right which the King of Scotland had to the Earldom of Orkney at least to the property of it. The Earls of Orkney were restrained by his Grants from Alienating any part of the Earldom without the consent of the King of Norway, his superior. The King of Norway had by the treaty of marriage signed over his right of Superiority to the King of Scotland and substituted him in his place during the not payment of the 50,000 florins. During that period then the King of Scotland became superior to the Earl of Orkney and his consent, not that of the King of Norway, was essential to validate any alienation then made. At no other time could the Earl of Orkney have legally transferred his right to the King of Scotland but, an alienation of it to him while he had possessed of the right of Superiority was unquestionably lawful and a valid conveyance according to the principles of the feudal law by which most part of Europe and these countries in particular where then governed. The evidence of this transaction appears from an act of parliament 1471 preserved in Lord Harrington's Collection.

The ignorance of this fact has misled all our Antiquarians, most of them talk of the Orkneys falling to the king of forfeiture but William 1st St Clare who was Earl of Orkney was not forfeited, even by Abercromby's account till 1477 and he is designed before that in public deed, only Earl of Caithness plain proof that he was divested of Orkney. 2nd. There is no evidence of this forfeiture. Abercromby who relates it is obviously mistaken, for he says that William St Clare , Earl of Orkney and Caithness, was forfeited for maintaining his Castle of Crichton against the King. William, Earl of Orkney, never was possessed of Crichton but William, Lord Crichton, was forfeited for defending his Castle of Crichton in the year 1483 – the process of forfeiture is extant in Haddington's collections and shows that he was one of the Duke of Albany's party and forfeited amongst with him. Abercromby, who is very inaccurate, has probably imagined that the Earldom of Caithness, which belonged to the Crichtons, having been given to St. Clare, the Castle of Crichton also belonged to him but it is plain this was not so and therefore there is even not a probable proof of this forfeiture of William St Clare, Earl of Caithness. 3rdly Abercromby's account cannot be true for it appears that the Duke of Albany and his adherents were not forfeited until the year 1481 as appears by a contract betwixt his sons in that year.

After this deed the Kings of Scotland had an absolute and irredeemable right to the property of the Earldom and the only right which the King of Denmark could claim even after the redemption of it, was the right of Superiority. The earldom of Orkney was, by an act of parliament , annexed to the Crown not to be given away except to one of the King's sons of lawful bed. Though the right of the family of St. Clare to the Earldom of Orkney was thus sold to the King, yet we must not imagine that either they immediately quitted all connection with the Country or that the King entered directly into full possession of it. In those days it was not uncommon, when any great Lord was obliged to part with his property to the Crown that, to make the matter more easy to him, he was allowed to retain possession under a Tack by which means he, in some degree, preserved his influence over the men of the Country which was a material point and might thereby be more easily induced to sell. There is reason to think this might have been the case of Orkney for in

1489

The Lord St. Clare is named in an account for bringing in the king's rents as collector for Orkney and Zetland. We see that the other collectors named are the persons whose families had most interest in the respective districts and it more than probable these collectors were not understood to be liable to a very strict account as this was an act past in the minority of James the 4th while his government was yet unstable.

1501

Lord St. Clare obtained a tack of the Earldom of Orkney for nineteen years at the rent of 650 marks Scots. From this period the state of the rights of Orkney and Zetland and the various Grants under which they were conveyed are very distinctly set forth in an inventory belonging to Lord Morton. It is needless therefore to continue the deduction of them any further in a regular series, a few observations only naturally occur upon them.

Notwithstanding the act of Annexation in 1471, Orkney and Zetland never was in actual possession of the Crown for any considerable period of time. We have seen that they were granted in Tack to Lord St. Clare, whose family was the only proprietor of them, for a very moderate duty. A few years after the expiry of this Tack in 1530, they were granted by King James the 5th. To his natural brother James, earl of Moray, and the heirs male of his body in fee, with a clause of return to the Crown, under this grant Orkney was passed down to the year 1540 when. Upon failure of the heirs male of the first Earl of Murray, it reverted to the Crown and was again annexed by act of parliament 1540. It was again granted by Queen Mary in 1563 to her natural brother Robert Stewart in whose heirs it continued to the year 1640 that Patrick Stewart was forfeited. The grant to the Earl of Morton took place in the year 1643.

The claim of the Crown of Denmark to the Islands of Orkney and Zetland upon payment of the 50,000 florins has often been renewed and the decision of it has upon every occasion been averted. The Scotch Historians and Sir Thomas Craig have supposed that the right of redemption reserved by the Crown of Norway in the treaty of marriage with James the third was renounced either upon the birth of James the fourth or in a Treaty betwixt Christian the 3rd of Denmark and James the 4th but there is no authority to warrant any of these suppositions. It is also a common opinion that the right of redemption was given up in James the sixth Treaty of marriage with Ann of Denmark bu the Treaty itself shows that all this matter with regard to the rights of the Orkneys was then reserved entire to be the subject of a future treaty. But the right of the Crown of Scotland to the property of Orkney and Zetland stands upon a very firm foundation even in point of law though the length of the time during which it has been proposed by Scotland were not sufficient to defend it.

Christian King of Denmark and Norway in the year 1468 had only the Dominion and Superiority of Orkney and Zetland. The property undoubtedly belonged to William St. Clare, Earl of Orkney, who had received the investiture of it by right of succession to his ancestors the Earls of Orkney from Eric, King of Denmark, in1434. The King of Denmark could not transfer the dominion and Superiority to any person without the consent of his vassal. Neither could the Earl of Orkney alienate the property without the consent of his superior. The King of Denmark conveyed his all right in the most ample terms to James the 3rd in his daughter's contract of marriage. Redeemable indeed upon payment of 50,000 florins but, during the not redemption, the Kings of Scotland had all the power which were competent to the Kings of Denmark. There is no doubt that the Earl of Orkney consented to this and agreed to accept of the King of Scotland as his Superior in place of the King of Norway. The alienation then which was afterwards made by the Earl of Orkney to his Superior, for the time being the King of Scotland, was undoubtedly valid and according to the principles of the feudal law which would have given James the 3rd a good title to hold the property of Orkney though the redemption money had been paid the next day. In any case then the Kings of Denmark if they had paid the 50,000 florins could only have claimed those rights which belonged to Christian of Denmark at the time he pledged the Islands to James the 3rd and could not have quarreled or set aside the alienation of the property made by the Earl of Orkney.